The Moral Psychology of Hate

Moral Psychology of the Emotions

Series Editor: Mark Alfano, Associate Professor, Department of Philosophy, Macquarie University

How do our emotions influence our other mental states (perceptions, beliefs, motivations, intentions) and our behavior? How are they influenced by our other mental states, our environments, and our cultures? What is the moral value of a particular emotion in a particular context? This series explores the causes, consequences, and value of the emotions from an interdisciplinary perspective. Emotions are diverse, with components at various levels (biological, neural, psychological, social), so each book in this series is devoted to a distinct emotion. This focus allows the author and reader to delve into a specific mental state, rather than trying to sum up emotions en masse. Authors approach a particular emotion from their own disciplinary angle (e.g., conceptual analysis, feminist philosophy, critical race theory, phenomenology, social psychology, personality psychology, neuroscience) while connecting with other fields. In so doing, they build a mosaic for each emotion, evaluating both its nature and its moral properties.

Other Titles in this Series
The Moral Psychology of Forgiveness, edited by Kathryn J. Norlock
The Moral Psychology of Pride, edited by Adam J. Carter and Emma C. Gordon
The Moral Psychology of Sadness, edited by Anna Gotlib
The Moral Psychology of Anger, edited by Myisha Cherry and Owen Flanagan
The Moral Psychology of Contempt, edited by Michelle Mason
The Moral Psychology of Compassion, edited by Justin Caouette and Carolyn Price
The Moral Psychology of Disgust, edited by Nina Strohminger and Victor Kumar
The Moral Psychology of Gratitude, edited by Robert Roberts and Daniel Telech
The Moral Psychology of Admiration, edited by Alfred Archer and André Grahle
The Moral Psychology of Regret, edited by Anna Gotlib
The Moral Psychology of Hope, edited by Claudia Blöser and Titus Stahl
The Moral Psychology of Amusement, edited by Brian Robinson
The Moral Psychology of Boredom, edited by Andreas Elpidorou

The Moral Psychology of Hate

Edited by
Noell Birondo

ROWMAN & LITTLEFIELD
Lanham • Boulder • New York • London

Published by Rowman & Littlefield
An imprint of The Rowman & Littlefield Publishing Group, Inc.
4501 Forbes Boulevard, Suite 200, Lanham, Maryland 20706
www.rowman.com

86-90 Paul Street, London EC2A 4NE

Selection and editorial matter © Noell Birondo 2022. Copyright in individual chapters is held by the respective chapter authors.

All rights reserved. No part of this book may be reproduced in any form or by any electronic or mechanical means, including information storage and retrieval systems, without written permission from the publisher, except by a reviewer who may quote passages in a review.

British Library Cataloguing in Publication Information Available

Library of Congress Cataloging-in-Publication Data

Names: Birondo, Noell, editor.
Title: The moral psychology of hate / [edited by] Noell Birondo.
Description: Lanham : Rowman & Littlefield Publishers, [2021] | Series: Moral psychology of the emotions | Includes bibliographical references and index.
Identifiers: LCCN 2021046751 (print) | LCCN 2021046752 (ebook) | ISBN 9781538160855 (cloth) | ISBN 9781538164501 (paperback) | ISBN 9781538160862 (ebook)
Subjects: LCSH: Hate. | Emotions (Philosophy) | Ethics. | Psychology and philosophy.
Classification: LCC BF575.H3 M67 2021 (print) | LCC BF575.H3 (ebook) | DDC 152.4—dc23/eng/20211110
LC record available at https://lccn.loc.gov/2021046751
LC ebook record available at https://lccn.loc.gov/2021046752

For Catalina, Senna, and Mariano

with love

In 1517, Fray Bartolomé de Las Casas, feeling great pity for the Indians who grew worn and lean in the drudging infernos of the Antillean gold mines, proposed to Charles V that the Negroes be brought to the isles of the Caribbean, so that *they* might grow worn and lean in the drudging infernos of the Antillean gold mines.

—Jorge Luis Borges

Christ is the sign that the world is ripe for burning.

—Dietrich Bonhoeffer, critically characterizing Christian radicalism

Contents

Preface: The Road to Auschwitz Wasn't Paved with Indifference   xi
Rivka Weinberg

Acknowledgments   xvii

Introduction: Hate and Racial Ignorance   xxi
Noell Birondo

I: HISTORICAL PERSPECTIVES, EAST AND WEST

1. Hate and Happiness in Aristotle   3
   Jozef Müller

2. Hatred in Buddhist Thought and Practice   23
   Christopher W. Gowans

II: HATRED OF SELF AND OTHERS

3. The Snares of Self-Hatred   53
   Vida Yao

4. Misanthropy and the Hatred of Humanity   75
   Ian James Kidd

5. A Tradition Grounded in Hate: Racist Hatred and Anti-Immigrant Fervor   99
   Grant J. Silva

6. "Woman Hating" as Redescription   119
   Kate M. Phelan

| 7 | Why We Hate | 137 |

Agneta Fischer, Eran Halperin, Daphna Canetti, and Alba Jasini

III: HATE, ETHICS, AND RATIONALITY

| 8 | Good Hate | 165 |

Damian Cox and Michael P. Levine

| 9 | Hateful Actions and Rational Agency | 185 |

Mary Carman

| 10 | Trashing and Tribalism in the Gender Wars | 207 |

Holly Lawford-Smith

| 11 | Hatred as a Burdened Virtue | 235 |

Richard Paul Hamilton

Epilogue: An Imperial Passion — 251
Noell Birondo

Bibliography — 263

Index — 287

Notes on Contributors — 299

Preface

The Road to Auschwitz Wasn't Paved with Indifference[1]

Rivka Weinberg

We live in a time of increasing hate crimes and the rise of "extremist" ideologies. I am alive because my paternal grandfather's Spidey sense had him frantically looking for ways out of Germany in 1933. "When madmen are elected, it's time to leave the country," he said. Now I, and many others I'm sure, worry that a catastrophe is looming and wonder how we can guard against it. Schoolchildren are now taught: "Be an upstander, not a bystander!" History, we're told, shows that, as Edmund Burke supposedly said, "The only thing necessary for the triumph of evil is that good men do nothing." Or in the words of historian Ian Kershaw, "The road to Auschwitz was built by hate but paved with indifference." These aphorisms pithily conjure up images of wise men stroking their long white beards, but they're wrong.

HOW ATROCITIES HAPPEN

The road to Auschwitz was built by hate but it wasn't paved with indifference. It was paved with collaboration. Anti-Semitism was entrenched in Europe for centuries before the Holocaust, supplying the Nazis with many collaborators. During the Holocaust, the local population, the police and the army often helped the Nazis. Not always, of course. There were resisters (heroes) and bystanders (ordinary people). But one thing is clear: During the Holocaust, where the local population was more anti-Semitic, they tended toward greater collaboration, resulting in a markedly higher murder rate.

To kill people living within a population, you have to be told who and where they are. You don't just march into Poland or France from Germany and magically know who to round up and where they live. It's even more helpful when the local police do the rounding up for you (as some did in Lithuania, France, and Hungary). The correlation between local enthusiasm and the genocidal murder rate of the Holocaust is strong and stark, as Raul Hilberg and Hannah Arendt documented. In Bulgaria and Italy, where the culture wasn't as anti-Semitic, the local populations didn't cooperate with the murder of Jews; most Bulgarian and Italian Jews survived. Romania and Ukraine, on the other hand, had virulently anti-Semitic cultures and many Romanians and Ukrainians actively participated in murdering Jews. Few survived. Poland was also very anti-Semitic, and although there were Poles who sheltered Jews, many instead turned them in and looted their property. Some murdered Jews themselves. Very few Polish Jews survived.

The truth about how massive moral crimes occur is both unsettling and comforting. It's unsettling to accept how many people participated in appalling moral crimes but comforting to realize that we don't have to be heroes to avoid genocides. We just have to make sure not to help them along.

UPSTANDER VS. BYSTANDER REALITIES

Upstander ideology directs us to "stand up" to bullies and hate. Upstanding can be effective and inspiring, but it's dangerous. People who intervene to rescue victims or stop a crime often die in the attempt. It's hard to be a hero, to risk your safety and personal commitments in order to help a stranger. That's a big ask. And by asking people too much, we make being moral too hard—which, paradoxically, can make immorality too easy. "Clearly, being moral is too hard, I'm no hero! Forget it!" we can imagine people thinking.

The incorrect lesson upstander ideology draws from history ignores the fact that perpetrating vast crimes usually requires lots of help. Instead, it implicitly blames moral catastrophes on a failure of heroism. Yet, heroism is exceptional, saintly; that's not who most of us are, nor who most of us can be, so we're kind of off the hook. Most of us are ordinary people, neither cruel nor heroic. The fact is that when people can help others avert disaster at negligible cost to themselves, most do. That is, unless they're steeped in hate—in which case being a bystander is a step up from the role of perpetrator they've been primed for.

Bystanding is not the problem. What we need to guard against is hate and collaboration with hate. It's rare for people not motivated by hate to casually witness a serious crime and do nothing about it. (The notorious case of Kitty Genovese, the woman stabbed to death in 1964 in her apartment building vestibule, while supposedly dozens of people within earshot of her screams did nothing, is a case of false reporting.) Of course, we want to encourage resistance to injustice. That's an important part of being human, and when doing so doesn't entail outsized risks, we should do our part. But when helping others is perilous, to help nonetheless is heroic. It's great to be a hero—and encouraging greatness has its place—but it's also important to be realistic and give moral guidance to ordinary people. People of average moral fortitude, if history is our guide, should be educated against collaboration with hate and taught the reality of how widespread, repugnant and powerful that is. Heroism is aspirational, and worthy of admiration, but it is a pedagogical, moral, and historical error to spend our moral capital insisting on it.

When helping others is risky, the heroes who step forward don't do so because of effective "upstander" education. Research shows that heroic acts are usually done instinctively, without much thought at all. So to whatever extent we want to encourage heroism, moral upstanding training seems unlikely to help. Heroism is not morally obligatory, not teachable and not what we must demand of citizens in order to avoid catastrophic crimes against humanity. What we must emphasize is the cruelty and destructiveness of hate and the perils of collaborating with it.

THE LESSONS OF HISTORY

Some people unwittingly help atrocities occur by cooperating in an attempt to mitigate a monstrous situation. History demonstrates that this is nearly always a miscalculation. During the Holocaust, Jewish councils organized life in the ghetto and compiled lists of Jews for deportation, often thinking that they were helping Jews manage a nightmare. Ultimately, they helped the Nazis murder Jews by maintaining order and providing the Gestapo with the names of people to be deported and murdered. In his memoir, *Legislating the Holocaust*, Bernhard Lösener, a lawyer in the Third Reich's Ministry of the Interior, relays how he hurriedly traveled through the night to get to Nuremberg in time to write the Nuremberg race laws so that the rule of law would be preserved, and how he fought to have the race laws written to count as Jewish those with three Jewish grandparents rather than those with one drop of Jewish blood. He too made the mistake of participating in the atrocity in an attempt to minimize the damages caused by its perpetrators.

Lösener remains the lawyer who wrote the Nuremberg race laws, lending a veneer of legality to a crime. Maybe someone else would have ignored the rule of law or written more draconian laws if he hadn't, but maybe not. What we can decide is whether we will be a participant in terrible things done by terrible people. It never works to participate in the terrible thing in order to try to make it less bad. It's tempting, and can seem like the right thing to do: Lösener's race laws included fewer people than a one-drop rule would (though that had negligible effect). Adolf Eichmann reasoned similarly: "If this thing had to be done at all, it was better that it be done in good order." History shows that when you participate in an atrocity together with the perpetrators, in an attempt to make it somehow a little less horrible, in the end you're still participating in the atrocity—and it is no less horrible.

MORALITY AND MY MOTHER

Like so many other things about me, my perspective on bystanders horrifies my mother. She is appalled that I could think we aren't morally obligated to rescue each other, even at great personal sacrifice. To her, the obligation is obvious. "Do not stand idly by the blood of your neighbor!" she exclaims, channeling Leviticus. Heroic acts of upstanding have shaped my mother's life. She is alive because of someone's heroism, and she lost her job, prematurely ending a treasured career, because of her own. My mother was saved from the Holocaust by Chiune Sugihara, the Japanese consul who ignored orders and issued several thousand transit visas to Lithuanian Jews, allowing them to flee the advancing Gestapo. Many years later, when a colleague was unfairly fired, my mother organized senior employees to speak out against the injustice, even though she knew not only that she would be likely to lose her own job as a result but also that she was unlikely to get another job at her age. She did lose her job, and did not get another one. The loss profoundly affected the trajectory and quality of her life, but she still says she doesn't regret what she did and would do it again.

Listening to my mother, I feel somewhat ashamed. I think I feel the shame of the ordinary person in the face of those who are morally greater than us; my mother is a much better person than I am. But I doubt the average person can be as heroic. Luckily, that is not necessary to avert moral catastrophe.

THE TAKEAWAY

The belief that atrocities happen when people aren't educated against the evils of bystanding has become part of our culture and how we think we're learning from history. "Don't be a bystander!" we're exhorted. "Be an upstander!" we teach our children. But that's all a big mistake. All of it: It's false that doing nothing creates moral catastrophes; it's false that people are generally indifferent to the plight of others; it's false that we can educate people into heroism; and it's false that if we fail to transmit these lessons another Holocaust is around the corner.

Instead, the facts are more quotidian: Terrible things happen when people collaborate with terrible perpetrators; most people are generally helpful to the extent that their circumstances and temperament allow (unless they've been taught to hate); being a bystander is often morally permissible; being a hero is exceptional and instinctual (not taught); and what history teaches us is both easier and harder than the supposed dark dangers of bystanderdom. What history teaches us is: Don't perpetrate; don't collaborate. If you can be heroic, that is laudable. Those lessons are hard to learn, but effective and easy enough to follow to avert most vast moral crimes.

Next time the murderers come, it's understandable if it's too much to ask for us to risk our lives, our children, or even our jobs, to save others. Just don't welcome the murderers, don't help them organize the oppression or make it "less terrible" (that won't work anyway), and don't turn people in. That will usually be enough.

NOTE

1. This article first appeared in the *New York Times*, January 21, 2020, in anticipation of the 75th anniversary of the liberation of Auschwitz. It is reprinted here with permission.

Acknowledgments

This is very much a pandemic book. Its form and content are marked by the various global traumas experienced in the 18 or so months that made up the year 2020, including the worst pandemic in over a century and the highly volatile social and political situations across the globe, especially in my own country, the United States. I am therefore especially grateful to the contributors for their persistence and dogged professionalism in bringing these remarkable chapters into their present form. Thanks also to Rivka Weinberg, my one-time colleague at the Claremont Colleges in California, for her permission to reprint an article that first appeared in *The New York Times*. I am similarly grateful to Agneta Fischer, Eran Halperin, Daphna Canetti, and Alba Jasini for permission to reprint "Why We Hate," which first appeared in 2018 in *Emotion Review* 10 (4): 309–20. The line from Jorge Luis Borges is the first line of "The Cruel Redeemer Lazarus Morell," in his *Collected Fictions* (Harmondsworth: Penguin, 1999). The line from Dietrich Bonhoeffer is from page 85 of his posthumously published *Ethics*, edited by Eberhard Bethge (New York: MacMillan, 1955). The cover image is of Mount St. Helens, a semi-dormant volcano in the Pacific Northwest of the United States. I thank Edward Alfano for use of the photo.

Work on this volume began in earnest in the early months of 2020 at the Institute for Philosophical Research, National Autonomous University of Mexico. Thanks to Dr. Carlos Pereda for hosting my visit at the institute and for his hospitality in nearby Coyoacán. For their helpful suggestions early in the process or else in the final stretch, I thank Rachana Kamtekar, Samantha Vice, Mary Carman, Manuel Vargas, Kate Manne, José Jorge Mendoza, David Livingstone Smith, Steven Lukes, Amy Olberding, Dale E. Miller, and Keith Green. I owe a special debt to Mark Alfano, the editor of this series on the Moral Psychology of the Emotions, for his valuable support throughout this project. For institutional support in the final stages, I am grateful to Dr. Roberto Osegueda and Dr. Denis O'Hearn at the University of Texas at El Paso. Special thanks are due to Walker Peatross, currently a philosophy graduate student at UTEP, for his very helpful assistance with proofreading.

As this project wraps up, I have just transitioned from my previous institution in Wichita, Kansas, to a new home at the University of Texas at El Paso, so it seems especially appropriate for me to express my very deep gratitude to two invaluable former colleagues, David E. Soles and Deborah H. Soles, for their superb mentoring and unfailing support over the past eight years. Most of all, I thank Lillian Dickerson for her support and encouragement and her surprisingly good spirits during a global pandemic and a few years' worth of unblemished exposure to hate.

The Moral Psychology of Hate

Manzanar, California, 1942. U.S. War Relocation Authority camp, where evacuees of Japanese ancestry, including United States citizens, spent the duration of World War II. *Credit*: Photo by Dorothea Lange. U.S. National Archives and Records Administration. Restoration courtesy of Tim Chambers, Anchor Editions.

Introduction
Hate and Racial Ignorance
Noell Birondo

The Nazis were not wrong to cite American precedents. Enslavement of African-Americans was written into the U.S. Constitution. Thomas Jefferson spoke of the need to "eliminate" or "extirpate" Native Americans.[1]

1. Dietrich Bonhoeffer was executed in Flossenbürg concentration camp in Germany in 1945 for being an "upstander" in Rivka Weinberg's sense. He was an anti-Nazi conspirator, and he and some of his fellow Christians (he was a Lutheran pastor) were hanged in connection with a failed attempt to assassinate Adolph Hitler. Bonhoeffer's resistance to racist hatred stands in sharp contrast to what he calls "Christian radicalism," a total withdrawal from or an attempt to "improve" upon God's creation, something Bonhoeffer characterizes as "hatred" of the world. "When evil becomes powerful in the world," he wrote, "it infects the Christian, too, with the poison of radicalism" (Bonhoeffer 1955, 87). He presumably had Christian collaboration with Nazi genocide in mind. Today different examples might occur to us.

A much earlier churchman, the Dominican friar Bartolomé de Las Casas (*b.* 1484), bishop of Chiapas in what is today Mexico, was also an upstander in this sense. He denounced the European exploitation of the native peoples of the Americas, and he devoted his life's work to securing legal protections from the Spanish Crown against their brutal treatment. Regarding attempts to spread Christianity in light of the Spanish atrocities in the Americas, Las Casas asked how anyone could be expected to believe "such a proud, greedy, cruel, and rapacious nation" (Las Casas 1974, 221). Later in life Las Casas came to regret his own disastrous proposal—made in defense of the exploited native peoples of the Americas—to import African peoples instead. Las Casas was not indeed responsible for *initiating* the African slave trade, as it is sometimes wrongly thought, since that commodification of racial hatred had already been established. But being an upstander clearly has its costs. It can get one killed, for one thing. It can also contribute to greater injustice. Bonhoeffer and Las Casas were nevertheless right to be upstanders, and their opposition to injustice was in itself laudable (their mistakes were obviously not so). But as Weinberg rightly says—she is completely right about this—it will usually be enough if we can avoid collaborating with hate. What does such collaboration look like today?

The two cases remind us that collaboration with hate can sometimes only be avoided, at least if the case is particularly thorny, by standing up to hate. Remaining silent can itself be a form of complicity, a collaboration with what is evil—and a commitment to ignorance can be that as well, and cynical suppressions of history can too. These different actions can all be ways of collaborating with hate. Some would insist that we not speak today of transatlantic atrocities, or racialized aspects of North American wars, or the connection of such histories to enduring systemic injustice.[2] In fact it was Hitler himself who in 1928 wrote of his admiration for white U.S. settlers who had "gunned down the millions of redskins to a few hundred thousand" (Ross 2018, 66). Ugly facts about one's own country might indeed be difficult to acknowledge. But as I have argued elsewhere, any form of "patriotism" that is predicated on a willful ignorance of the history of one's own country, let alone propped up by the suppression of that history, cannot possibly be a virtue (Birondo 2020b). Willful historical ignorance is antithetical to any genuine form of patriotism. For that reason alone, the cynical suppression of history in our time, enthusiastically supported by flag-waving nationalists around the globe, actually amounts to a kind of "anti-patriotism." We might also highlight the fact that the suppression of history is often interwoven with a barely disguised racial hatred that is deeply antithetical to virtue. In this volume we introduce the moral psychology of hate in connection with these and other pressing issues in our time.

2. Contemporary discussions of hate in philosophy, psychology, and other nearby disciplines have of course been produced for many decades. But this book provides the first systematic introduction to the moral psychology of hate, compiling specially commissioned chapters by an international team of scholars with a wide range of disciplinary orientations. The chapters are philosophically rigorous and combine empirical and philosophical methods by engaging social psychology and other social sciences. My hope is that this volume will be especially valuable at this historical moment, given the recent

rise in hate crimes toward racial minority groups and immigrants across the globe, even in the world's liberal democracies; the rise in anti-Semitism and hateful attacks on people of Asian descent, even medical professionals during a global pandemic; and the fact that elected officials at the highest levels of government have credibly been accused of fanning the flames of hate for personal and political profit, even to the point of personally inciting insurrection. Such are the times we live in.

The overall aim is to present a systematic introduction to the moral psychology of hate. Its more specific aims are as follows. First, it aims to provide a comparison between the perspectives on hate found in Eastern and Western philosophical traditions given the pervasiveness of hatred across cultures. The first two chapters highlight specific ancient Greek and Buddhist conceptions of hate. Second, it aims to contrast self-hatred with other-directed hatred—even, at the limit, hatred of humanity. Third, it aims to explore the possibility, conditions, and limits of morally justifiable hatred and hateful behavior. The volume considers the relevance of hate with respect to issues such as racist and anti-immigrant fervor, misogyny, hatred within liberatory struggles, and hatred toward evildoers. The discussions have aimed to remain accessible to a wide range of potential readers, from advanced undergraduates and members of an educated public to faculty in philosophy and other disciplines concerned with the dynamics and the moral and political implications of this most powerful of human emotions.

With respect to structure and style, each of the 11 main chapters has an individualized references section at the end of the chapter. But I have also assembled a general bibliography at the end of the book. My hope is that this will satisfy the various demands of general readers and academic researchers. I have tried to minimize endnotes with in-text citations where feasible, in spite of some resulting clumsiness. My main thought was for making life easier on readers such as myself who like to follow the citations. As for racial group terms, I have left it to authors to decide on capitalization or not. Chapter 11 distinguishes between "black" South Africans and "colored" South Africans. These two separate local categories will be unfamiliar to many readers, but the latter phrase is not (to my understanding) in itself derogatory in any way, as it might be in the United States, for instance, if the phrase were used to refer to someone who is African American—unless it were in the full phrase "person of color," which is also not derogatory in any way. Such are the nuances of language.

3. Given the nature of these brief introductory remarks, which can hardly do justice to my very strong enthusiasm for these chapters, I should say that I hope never again to be finishing a book while transitioning from one

academic institution (one city, one house) to another. I try to make some amends by saying more about hate and racial ignorance, and much more about Las Casas and European imperialism, at the end of the book. But I also hope that these introductory remarks will not strike anyone as the final pages of MacIntyre's now-famous *After Virtue* struck Bernard Williams, who said in a 1981 review that the "brief and bewildering remarks" at the close of that book were "offered so desultorily as to suggest that, as he wrote them, MacIntyre was packing to depart" (Williams 2014, 186). I think that we are all now headed toward something new, beyond the aftershocks of 2020, for better or worse, and ready or not. If some interested later readers in a more distant and peaceful time happen to find their way to this book, to what I hope will still be a useful discussion of this most powerful but also bleakest of emotions, written in our age of unapologetic authoritarianism and racialized hatred, please think of us with forbearance.

—*El Paso, Texas, July 4, 2021.*

NOTES

1. Ross (2018, 71). Or consider further: "Hundreds of thousands of Americans died fighting Nazi Germany. Still, bigotry toward Jews persisted, even toward Holocaust survivors. General George Patton criticized do-gooders who 'believe that the Displaced person is a human being, which he is not, and this applies particularly to the Jews who are lower than animals'" (Ross 2018, 72).

2. For a superb discussion of Native American perseverance and "radical hope" in the face of cultural devastation, see Lear (2016). For a vigorous denunciation of European colonialism and the historical downplaying of atrocities committed against non-European peoples, see Césaire (1972 [1955]), especially his comments on Hitler and Europe. The notion that any individual might be "inherently" racist, sexist, or otherwise oppressive "by virtue of their race or sex" is simply daft. I have never heard any individual express that view, certainly not any of the authors in this book. It is the *noninherent voluntariness* of racist, sexist, and otherwise oppressive behavior that makes it so condemnable. For a careful discussion of ordinary and extraordinary virtue, see Stangl (2020).

I

HISTORICAL PERSPECTIVES, EAST AND WEST

Chapter 1

Hate and Happiness in Aristotle

Jozef Müller

1. INTRODUCTION

On Aristotle's view, it is a central feature of virtue of character that one enjoys (*chairein*) and hates (*misein*) just the things that one should (objectively) enjoy and hate.[1] For example, it is only when one loves (*stergein*) what is fine or noble (*to kalon*) and hates (*misein*) and is disgusted (*duscherainein*) by what is shameful (*to aischron*), that one becomes capable of being persuaded by argument (*logos*). Without this ability, one would not be able to derive any benefit from moral and political education (*didachē*) (*NE* 10.9, 1179b22–31). Accordingly, it is entirely essential to virtue, from both the intellectual and the motivational point of view, that one develops one's capacities for love and hate in just the right way.

There are two crucial, even if rarely emphasized, aspects of this view. First, virtue does not involve merely enjoying or liking the right sort of things and, correspondingly, finding other things (the wrong ones) disagreeable. There are many things that people find enjoyable or disagreeable (and so even to a high degree) without being particularly motivated to pursue or avoid them, much less to organize their lives around them. In contrast, virtue is supposed to weave certain concerns deep into the fabric of one's life, effectively leading one to organize one's whole life around those concerns. It is no coincidence that Aristotle uses verbs that signal not only that one should enjoy (*chairein*) the right sorts of things (i.e., the fine ones) but also that one should develop a loving affection (*stergein*) for them. The virtuous person is a lover of virtue (*philaretos*) and a lover of the fine (*philokalos*) (*NE* 1.8, 1099a11–2), one who is always eager and ready (*spoudazein*) to engage in virtuous and fine actions (*NE* 6.8, 1168b25 and 1169a7). That is why virtuous people aim at the fine (*to kalon*) in *all* their actions, rather than alternating among many different goals, as ordinary people (who sometimes aim at pleasure, sometimes at honor, sometimes at health, and so on) do (*NE* 1.4, 1095a22–28). They do not merely enjoy or judge the fine to be good or best—they truly love it and live for it.[2]

Second, of the two forces that mold our relationship to the world, Aristotle sees love rather than hate as the primary motivational drive of a good and virtuous life. Not love, of course, for a particular person (whether erotic or other kind) but love—an affectionate attachment—nevertheless. Aristotle thinks that any reasonable person (and so also a virtuous person) should choose some particular goal for the fine life (*EE* 1.2, 1214b6–14), a goal that one targets (or takes into account) in all of one's actions:

> Everyone capable of living according to their own decision should set [for themselves] some goal (*skopos*) for living finely (*kalōs*), whether it be honor or reputation or wealth or education, which they will look to in all their actions since not to have organized one's life in relation to some end (*telos*) is a mark of much foolishness. (*EE* 2.2, 1214b7–10)[3]

There are disputes concerning what Aristotle thinks this goal, which he says everybody agrees to call "happiness" (*eudaimonia*), is.[4] But it is a common assumption that it is something one desires in a positive way, something one loves and cares about. On Aristotle's view, a good life is one that is organized with reference to this goal and so a life in which one has oriented and committed one's whole being—both intellectually *and* affectionately—to its pursuit.

From this point of view, it is only understandable that scholarly discussions of habituation, varied as they are, have concentrated on the way in which one comes to enjoy or love something, in particular comes to love engaging in virtuous actions (or, at any rate, activities that constitute happiness), for themselves.[5] Insofar as the opposite attitude—that of hate—is concerned, they have simply assumed a parallel process—just as the learner is habituated to love certain things, she is also habituated to hate other things.[6] Despite their parallel development, however, it is love and not hate that takes the place of pride in the virtuous person's life. Hate seems to be a mere accompaniment of love, motivating not so much what one does but what one avoids doing.[7] But why should that be so? Why privilege love over hate? Why could not hate rather than love be the driving force of one's pursuit of "living finely"? After all, Aristotle thinks that the virtuous person will hate certain things and rightly so. In his world, there is a place for hate, just as there is a place for love: the virtuous person hates and is disgusted by shameful things. The way Aristotle puts it, one might well think that the virtuous person is not only personally eager and prepared to support virtuous things and engage in virtuous actions, but also eager and ready to prevent shameful ones. It is not only avoidance but also the removal of evils that Aristotle counts among the things that are good and to be pursued (*Rhet.* 1.10, 1366b23–25). And yet, Aristotle never suggests that one should center one's life around actively seeking and removing what one considers evil. In fact, the role of hate is rather subdued in his writings, even as he stresses that as one should love what is fine, one should also hate what is shameful.

But, one might well wonder, given Aristotle's claims, why hate should be so subdued. Why could it not play a more significant and active role? In fact, why could a good or virtuous life not be organized around something one hates (rather than loves) and aimed at the eradication of what one considers shameful and evil? Why could not hate, rather than love, be the primary motivational force of one's good life? This is the main question of this paper. It seems to me that the emphasis on the positive ethical character of Aristotle's conception of *eudaimonia* (happiness), and his (in the context of ancient Greek philosophy, uncharacteristic) acceptance of the positive role of emotions in a good life, might obscure the ways in which he thinks emotions also present an obstacle or even danger to such a life. My target in this paper is thus not the way in which hate can or does have bad or harmful consequences on others but, rather, the way in which hate—should it be allowed to flourish and motivate one's life—would influence one's own well-being and the ability to lead a good life. As I hope to show, there are good reasons why hate does not play a more active role in Aristotle's conception of a good life.

The idea of a life driven by hate is not entirely alien. We are all familiar with fictional characters whose lives are organized precisely in this way. Whether one thinks of Captain Ahab's hate for Moby Dick, Iago's hate for Othello, the Monster's hate for Dr. Frankenstein, Edmond Dantès's hate for Fernand Mondego, or Khan's hate for Captain Kirk, fiction is replete with examples of lives driven by hate. And it need not be a hate for a particular person: Tybalt's hate was aimed at all those associated with the Montagues, while Voldemort's hate for those of not pure blood aimed at eradication of not just them but of all that they created and stood for. But although the idea might not be alien, it is unpalatable. We generally do not regard hate as the kind of emotion that we should embrace. There is a very strong tendency to see hate in a negative way, if for no other reason than because of its association with groups that advocate hostility or even direct violence toward members of various social groups, whether based on religion, gender, ethnicity, race, sexual orientation, and so on (i.e., hate groups). Hence even if hate is not to be eschewed altogether, it is treated at best as a necessary accompaniment of love insofar as one is expected to hate things that directly threaten or actively harm those things or people that one loves.

And yet, even among the fictional characters mentioned previously, there are some whose hate seems justified and whose character is not evil (Edmond

Dantès), or whose moral status is unclear or subject to debate (Captain Ahab or Frankenstein's Monster). Accordingly, in imagining a life driven mainly by hate and organized around its object, I will not presuppose that hate is always unjustified or that its goal is morally wrong. In fact, I will be primarily interested in the virtuous agent who presumably hates the right things. The question can be posed, then, in the following way. If Aristotle thinks that in order to live a good life people should set for themselves some goal around which they organize their lives, why could that goal not be something to which one is driven by hate? For example, why could it not be a life which is focused on disabling, destroying, or otherwise removing from life something one considers (and passionately so) evil rather than a life in which one's focus is to promote and engage in something one loves? Or, in Aristotle's words, why could it not be a life in which one aims to destroy the shameful rather than to promote the fine? On the face of it, such a life seems a decent candidate for a good life. For example, it could be a life in which one would exercise virtues, such temperance, courage, and justice. It could also be a life which could offer a rather concrete goal and prospect of success (the eradication of whatever one deems evil). Why, then, should we avoid achieving *eudaimonia* in this hate-propelled way?

The case of hate I have in mind needs to be distinguished from cases in which "hate" signifies merely an expression of dissatisfaction over the state of something one likes. For example, Fred Rogers famously hated the television programs of his day so much that he exerted great effort to change them, creating *Mister Rogers' Neighborhood* to offer children a worthwhile alternative. Although it was hate and anger at television and what it was doing to children that initially propelled him to take action, Fred Rogers's life was not one centered on something he hated. He did not hate television and did not try to erase it from existence. Rather, he hated the way its true potential was squandered and made harmful instead of beneficial to children. The idea I have in mind is more akin to that of Senator Joseph McCarthy whose political life centered and aimed at the eradication of Communists and homosexuals from the public sphere. However, my primary concern will be the virtuous person who, unlike McCarthy, would presumably not aim at eradication of particular people (or even particular kinds of people) but, rather, at eradication of the various ways in which what she considers evil or shameful expresses itself—whether it be actions, customs, or institutions.

The plan of the paper is simple. In the next section, I will look at Aristotle's account of hate in the *Rhetoric* and, with some help from Plato, try to reconstruct the way in which hate develops not as a mere (necessary) accompaniment of love (i.e., as a derivative negative attitude toward things that would harm what one has come to love) but in its own right. In section III, I will apply the results of this inquiry to the questions raised in the introduction. As

I will argue, there are at least two reasons that disqualify hate from being the primary motivational drive of a good life, as Aristotle conceives of it. First, hate cannot maintain and can even undermine the right relationship between the rational and the nonrational part of the soul. Second, hate does not support acquisition of knowledge and in fact essentially involves or presupposes ignorance. In sum, although it might indeed be possible to organize one's life around something one hates, such life cannot be a good life.

2. THE NATURE OF HATE

Aristotle classifies hate as a feeling or emotion (*pathos*) (e.g., *NE* 2.5, 1105b21–23). Accordingly, his most extensive description of hate occurs in the discussion of emotions in *Rhetoric* Book 2. Since emotions exercise powerful influence over people's judgments, they are of particular importance for an orator and Aristotle aims to provide the mean that would enable him or her to command them in his or her audience. The possible limitations of this context for Aristotle's discussion of emotions have been extensively discussed in the scholarship. The debates have centered on two related controversies: (a) the extent to which Aristotle's discussion of emotions in the *Rhetoric* reflects his own theoretical (or scientific) views about their nature; and (b) the presence (or lack thereof) of a systematic, unified treatment or theory of emotions in the *Rhetoric*.[8] Fortunately, as our focus is on hate in particular, and especially on the ways it differs from love relative to the issue raised in the previous section, we can set (b) aside. Insofar as (a) is concerned, the worry might be that if Aristotle's discussion of emotions amounts to "a preliminary, purely dialectical investigation that clarifies [some of] the phenomena in question,"[9] it might not allow us to draw any firm conclusions about hate and its role in a good life. However, the debates concerning (a), focused as they are on scientific account of the nature of emotions, involve questions such as whether Aristotle thinks that emotions are or merely involve desires (and of what kind), whether they involve cognitive states (and of what kind), and so on. Our question, however, is about the way in which hate, should it become one's primary motivational force, could or would influence one's ability to lead a good life. From this point of view, it is precisely the *phenomena* of hate (i.e., the various ways in which it is experienced in life) that are of interest rather than the scientific account of its precise psychological nature.[10]

In the *Rhetoric*, Aristotle distinguishes three different ways in which a speech (*logos*) can affect persuasion: it can make the speaker's character appear good and trustworthy; it can stir emotions in the audience in such a way that they become favorably disposed to the speaker's cause, and it can persuade through argument by showing how something is or is not the case (*Rhet.* 1.2, 1356a1–4). It is in the second of these three ways that hate plays a prominent role since "we do not pass the same judgments when distressed or pleased, or when loving or hating" (*Rhet.* 1.2, 1356a14–16). From this point of view, it is perhaps surprising that Aristotle does not spend more time on hate—it is by far the most briefly discussed emotion and, along with his discussion of *philia* (love or friendly feeling) in the *Rhetoric*, presents special difficulties for those trying to fit them into the larger framework of his discussion.[11] Fortunately, for our purposes, we can set these worries aside and go directly to the passage in which he discusses hate:

> Concerning enmity (*ekhthra*) and hating (*misein*), it is clear that they are to be studied (*theorein*) from their opposites. Enmity may be produced by anger (*orgē*), spite (*epēreasmos*), or slander (*diabolē*). But whereas anger arises from things [done] against oneself, enmity also arises without things [done] against oneself since if we take someone to be a certain kind of person, we hate them. And anger is also always concerned with individuals, such as Callias or Socrates, but hate (*misos*) is also directed towards kinds (*pros ta genē*)—everyone hates a thief (*kleptēs*) or an informer (*sukophantēs*). Anger is also curable by time, but hate is incurable. Anger also seeks to inflict pain [to its object], whereas hate seeks harm or evil (*kakon*). An angry person wishes to perceive [their revenge] but for someone who hates this makes no difference.[12] Painful things are all perceptible, but the greatest evils, injustice (*adikia*) and folly (*aphrosunē*), are the least perceptible since the presence of vice (*kakia*) does not cause pain. And anger involves pain but hate does not. An angry person is pained, but one who hates is not. An angry person may also feel pity if many things happen [to those at who they are angry], but one who hates never does. For an angry person wishes that those they are angry at to suffer (*antipathein*), but one who hates [wishes] that they do not exist (*mē einai*). (*Rhet.* 2.4, 1382a1–14)

There are two preliminary questions that need to be dealt with before tackling the content of the passage. First, in the opening line Aristotle mentions not only hate but also enmity. Although the passage treats the two terms as equivalent, one might reasonably wonder whether there is an important distinction at play. Here, David Konstan's admirable analysis provides an answer:

> Aristotle seems clearly to treat *ekhthia* as the counterpart to *philia* just as *to misein* or hating answers to *to philein*. Hating is the simple emotion, whereas enmity represents the state of affairs that obtains when people regard each other with mutual hatred. (Konstan 2006, 194)

For our purposes, then, we can treat the notions as synonymous unless something Aristotle says clearly applies only to the case of mutual hate relationship (i.e., enmity).

Second, why does Aristotle not follow his own advice to study hate by contrasting it with what he regards as its opposite, namely love? Instead, as is obvious, he proceeds to contrast it with anger which he describes not as the opposite of hate but something that can give rise to it. It is difficult to explain, at least in any reliable way, why Aristotle does not do something. There is little question that, in the ancient rhetorical context, anger is one of the most important emotions and so for a number of reasons. To begin with, it is easy to provoke it in an audience. For Aristotle, anger is a basic emotional reaction[13] induced whenever something appears in some way threatening or diminishing something one cares about, including, of course, oneself. As he notes, in order to make one angry at someone, all one needs to do is to show (or make it look as if) that that someone in some way (whether directly or indirectly) obstructs or hinders one from achieving something one wants or that she or he merely does not assist one in achieving it (*Rhet.* 2.2, 1379a12-23). In fact, the bar can be set even lower since anger can be induced by a mere suggestion that someone dislikes or speaks badly about something one cares about (*Rhet.* 2.2, 1379a30–b2). As Aristotle further notes, anger is a quick and intense emotion that does not need to be developed and established over a lengthy period of time (*NE* 7.6, 1149a24–b3). This makes it particularly suitable for rhetorical contexts in which time and timing is of the essence. Finally, unlike many other emotions, anger does not require any preexisting emotional connection—positive or negative—to the person or people at which it becomes directed, even if such connection might be especially conducive to it.

As we shall see, there is a close but complex relationship between hate and anger which might lead one to confuse them (or their expressions). An orator who wants to persuade her audience about something by appealing to negative emotions would do well to be aware of the relevant differences. For example, one might try to persuade the Athenian assembly about taking a punitive but merely preventive action against Sparta (i.e., one that would not result and perhaps even prevent any further escalation). A person who is angry at Sparta might agree with the measure (regarding it as justified) but a person who hates could very well react differently. For example, they might think that the measure needs to be more severe since they do not really care about deterring Sparta from engaging in further hostilities but they do care about harming it. It might then be that the contrast between hate and love is more useful for scientific purposes, whereas the one with anger applies more directly to the rhetorical context. As Aristotle says, his advice or recommendation to contrast love with hate applies to those who wish to study hate theoretically (*theorein*) rather than, we might conjecture, those who wish to know about hate for the purposes of manipulating the emotion in order to effect persuasion.

These issues having been set aside, it is time to tackle the passage. Aristotle lists several features of hate and it will be useful to list them:

1. Enmity may be produced by anger, spite, or slander.
2. As opposed to anger, hate is directed not only toward individuals but also toward kinds of people—if we take someone to be a certain kind of person, we hate them.
3. As opposed to anger, hate is incurable by time.
4. As opposed to anger, which seeks to inflict pain, hate seeks to inflict harm or evil.
5. An angry person cares about perceiving the revenge and pain she inflicts, but one who hates does not care if she perceives the harm being inflicted.
6. An angry person is pained, but one who hates is not pained.
7. An angry person wishes that those they are angry at to suffer, but one who hates wishes that they do not exist.
8. An angry person can feel pity, but one who hates never does.

We can start by noting the tension between (1) and (2). In (1) we learn that hate does (or at least can) originate in anger.[14] Anger, as Aristotle portrays it in the *Rhetoric*, arises out of some action or speech of those that one thinks should treat one well but that one instead perceives as showing contempt (*Rhet.* 2.2, 1378a31-3). It is thus, as confirmed in (2), directed at particular people, namely those that one took to have shown the contempt. If hate, then, arises out of anger, it would be rather natural to take it to arise in relation to those who made one angry. In (2), however, we learn that all it takes to come to hate someone is that one takes them to be of a certain sort, for example, to be thieves, independently of whether or not, in relation to those particular people, we were at any point angry.

Although (1) and (2) are in tension, they are not necessarily contradictory. In particular, one might think that hate need not always arise from anger. For the moment, however, it will be useful to explore the way it might arise from it. When Aristotle outlines reasons for political change in tyrannies in the *Politics*, he tells us that people always hate tyrants (*Pol.* 5.10, 1312b20). He then goes on to contrast hate with anger insofar as angry people are more prone to (immediate) action than those who hate because, unlike hate, anger makes no use of reasoning (*logismos*). The reason is that anger involves pain which makes reasoning difficult, whereas hate does not (*Pol.* 5.10, 1312b32-33). Although this passage in the *Politics* largely echoes *Rhet.* 2.4 1382a1-14 translated earlier, it also gives us an example of an (inevitable) object of hate, namely, tyrants. In this connection, we learn two interesting details. First, anger *excludes* fear. As Aristotle says, "It is impossible to be both angry and afraid" (*Rhet.* 2.3, 1380a32). Second, hate involves or presupposes fear (*Pol.* 5.11, 1315b7–8). And, as we (luckily) learn in the pseudo-Aristotelian *Oeconomica*, people hate *and* fear tyrants—hate because they treat them wrong and with injustice (*Oecon.* 3.1) and fear because (presumably) they exercise (unlimited) control over their lives.

These passages suggest that anger can transform into hatred in cases in which one is not in a position to act on one's anger, that is, in cases in which one fears those who gave one the cause to be angry. Aristotle also gives us a clue as to why this might mean that one comes to hate not only the particular person that caused one the offense but anybody who falls under some relevant general description (what this is I will explain as I go on). As he tells us in the *Rhetoric*, anger can be partially or temporarily alleviated by being acted on in relation to someone else than the person one is angry with (*Rhet.* 2.3, 1380b5–10). Hence, if one cannot act on one's anger toward the person who caused it, and so relieve one's anger in the usual way (*NE* 4.5, 1126a20–3), one might find temporary relief by acting that way toward someone else who is, in some relevant respect, like the original offender. Presumably, the range of what counts as being "like" here is very broad and would largely depend on the way one has (subjectively) perceived the offense. Still, in general, if hate is (at least in some cases) transformed anger, this could explain why it can give rise to repeated bouts of angry actions toward people who themselves might not have given one any particular cause for being angry but who might have some, however vague or (objectively) random, commonality with the original offender. It is also of no small importance that one's actions toward those other people presuppose that one does not fear them or that one does not fear them to the extent that one would shrink from the desired (vengeful) action. Hence hate's tendency to motivate angry or harmful actions in relation to people who are (ostensibly) weaker (less powerful, more vulnerable, and so on). We thus have not only the possibility of anger transforming into hate but also the possibility of hate giving rise to outbursts of anger (or angry actions).[15]

Although the connection between anger and hate seems plausible, it is not this connection *per se* that I am interested in. Rather, it is the following two observations. First, although hate might involve (or appear to involve) a rational judgment or attitude (as Aristotle says, it is without pain and capable of using reasoning), it nevertheless involves a nonrational and painful affection of spirit (*thumos*),[16] whether in its origin (e.g., anger) or as its element or accompaniment (e.g., fear). Second, although hate's origins might be traced to a particular (negative) experience, it tends to involve generalization that transfers the negative attitude from a particular person or experience to a kind of people or things.

I start with the first point. As Aristotle tells us (point 7), hate involves a rational desire—a wish—of a particular kind, namely one that aims for its object to cease to exist (rather than merely to suffer). Why should hate involve this particular kind of wish? Although Aristotle highlights anger as a (possible) origin of hate, it is presumably not just any anger but a frustrated (or failed) one. On Aristotle's view, anger is due to spirit (*thumos*) rather than appetite (*epithumia*). A painful experience related to appetite (which is, in general, a desire for bodily pleasure) leads to avoidance of the source of the pain. If we find some food or activity painful, we avoid it. Spirit, on the other hand, tends to react with action. It aims to remove or otherwise neutralize the source of a perceived threat or harm whether to oneself or to others one cares about. Consequently, it calls for action as long as the threat or harm is perceived to exist. This is important because in the case of anger that leads to hate, the agent could *not* act in the way in which her spirit (in becoming angry) urged her to act. Hence, the perceived threat or harm was not (and could not be) removed. From the point of view of spirit, this is not a situation in relation to which one can simply move on (as one often can in the case of appetite since its particular desires, such as for something sweet, tend to be fleeting). If it is the task of spirit to preserve the sense of one's own safety, integrity, and self-esteem, then any situation that results from a failure in or inability to carry out that task continues to call for remedy.

It is here that the second observation becomes relevant since it is not just any kind of generalization that characterizes hate. Rather, it is a matter of forming the view that the source or cause of one's harm or hurt is of no or even negative value—it is something that one believes should *not* continue to exist. The transformation of anger into hate is a peculiar way in which one deals with the consequences of a frustrated spirited affection or desire. It involves negating the significance of one's failure or inability to act by *devaluing* the source or origin of the perceived harm or offense. If one becomes angry at people because, for example, one expects more or differently from them, in forming hate toward them one gives up on any such expectations—the (contemptible) way they acted becomes precisely the (only) way one could expect them to act. The generalization provides one with a ready-made explanation of the action and its consequences—they acted as they did because acting in that way belongs to (or is in) their bad nature (rather than, for example, because of mistake, ignorance, frustration, despair, and so on). It is this bad or negative feature of the world (one that should not exist) that is responsible for the harm one has incurred or continues incurring. The task then (dictated by hate rather than anger) becomes not to exact vengeance on the particular person that gave one the cause to be angry but, rather, to remove the negative feature, whatever and wherever it is, from the world. Even if one cannot act in relation to the original experience or event, one can still do so in relation to all other such things. If anger still leaves space for (and often in fact arises because of) an attachment to those that one is angry at (*Rhet.* 2.2, 1379b2ff), hate makes any such attachment irrational by rendering it objects worthless (or only worthy of destruction). Hate arises by turning one's own failure into the failure of the world.

This elaboration of Aristotle's remarks finds strong supporting evidence in Plato's description of the rise of *misologia* (hate of arguments) and misanthropy in the *Phaedo*. In the case of misanthropy, Plato emphasizes that it is not simply a matter of forming, after experiencing repeated disappointment, an unfavorable view of people. Rather, it is a failure (a lack of knowledge) on the part of the agent that both prepares the ground for the disappointment (e.g., by causing the agent to have unrealistic expectations) and later leads to concluding that the fault must lie with people as such rather than with the agent herself:

> Misanthropy comes when a man without knowledge or skill has placed great trust in someone and believes him to be altogether truthful, sound and trustworthy; then, a short time afterwards he finds him to be wicked and unreliable, and then this happens in another case; when one has frequently had that experience, especially with those whom one believed to be one's closest friends, then, in the end, after many such blows, one comes to hate all men and to believe that no one is sound in any way at all. (*Phaed.* 89d–e)[17]

Similarly, *misologia* arises when someone who lacks knowledge or skill in arguments experiences repeated disappointment or frustration in dealing with them and so, as a result, shifts the blame from oneself to the nature of arguments as such:

> It is as when one who lacks skill in arguments puts his trust in an argument as being true, then shortly afterwards believes it to be false—as sometimes it is and sometimes it is not—and so with another argument and then another. You know how those in particular who spend their time studying contradiction in the end believe themselves to have become very wise and that they alone have understood that there is no soundness or reliability in any object or in any argument, but that all that exists simply fluctuates up and down as if it were in the Euripus and does not remain in the same place for any time at all.
>
> What you say, I said, is certainly true.
>
> It would be pitiable, Phaedo, he said, when there is a true and reliable argument and one that can be understood, if a man who has dealt with such arguments as

appear at one time true, at another time untrue, should not blame himself or his own lack of skill but, because of his distress, in the end gladly shift the blame away from himself to the arguments, and spend the rest of his life hating and reviling reasonable discussion and so be deprived of truth and knowledge of reality.

(*Phaed.* 89d–90d)

These passages show that the process of generalization involved in the formation of hate is targeting precisely the feature in relation to which the agent was lacking and suffered loss. By forming a negative (hateful) view or relation to things that exhibit that feature (people, arguments, etc.), the agent not only devalues those things (wishing them not to exist) but also (at least seemingly) negates the significance of his or her own lack or loss. If there is no soundness and reliability found in either arguments or people, then it is not only the case that one's lack of success in dealing with them is not unsurprising and not one's fault but also that one's lack (or ignorance) that those failures revealed is not really a lack (or ignorance). There is, after all, nothing there (no knowledge) worth having.

The generalization involved in the formation of hate thus brings about a particular cognitive closure—once something is characterized by the bad or negative (i.e., hated) feature, it automatically becomes not only an object of one's hate but also something that is, in general, not worth knowing anything further about. For example, if one truly *hates* liars and discovers that someone is a liar, one could quickly conclude that that is all one needs (and wants) to know about that person. Their being a liar now explains whatever that person did, does, or might do since whatever other qualities they might have, they are all rendered insignificant by the fact that they are a liar.

If my argument has been along the right lines, Aristotle's conception of hate involves several crucial features: (a) frustrated nonrational (spirited) affection and desires; (b) negating the (perceived) value of the source of a (perceived) threat; (c) diminishing the (perceived) significance of any (original) failure to act on the agent's side to remove the threat; and (d) negating any (perceived) value of knowing about things or people that exhibit the feature that one came to blame for the perceived evil (or harm or threat). It is time to turn to the question raised in the beginning of the paper.

3. HATE AND HAPPINESS

On Aristotle's view, it is not possible to lead a good life unless one achieves a virtuous disposition of character. This disposition involves harmonizing the two parts of the soul that Aristotle recognizes—the rational part (or reason) and the nonrational part which houses nonrational desires (*NE* 1.13, 1102a28; *EE* 2.1, 1220a8–11)—in such a way that they become unified with respect to actions and feelings: they are supposed to "chime together" (*homophonei*) (*NE* 1.13, 1102b29–30). The idea is that the nonrational part, once properly habituated, comes to accept and obey reason's commands or prescriptions (*NE* 5.11, 1138b11). As Aristotle tells us, in the virtuous agent the nonrational part lives according to reason in the same way in which children live according to their fathers or tutors (*NE* 1.13, 1102b31–32; 3.12, 1119b12–1). The virtuous agent guides and directs her actions and desires by reason in a distinct way so that her whole soul aims at the right things (e.g., *NE* 3.5, 1114b26–28; 3.12, 1119b15–17; 3.7, 1115b11–12).

As I have argued elsewhere (Müller 2019), Aristotle thinks that the reason-ruled harmonization of the soul is possible because of the way in which a virtuous agent relates to her true inner self—she is a self-lover insofar as she is a lover of reason and its activities (*NE* 9.4, 1168b31–5). In this way, the virtuous person comes not only to guide her life (both in terms of actions and feelings) by reason but also to organize and direct it toward the kind of concerns that characterize excellent (exercises of) reason—whether in the theoretical sphere (i.e., truth and knowledge) or practical sphere (i.e., virtue and the fine)—rather than toward the kind of concerns that characterize her nonrational part, such as bodily pleasure (e.g., *NE* 3.8, 1117a6–9; 4.1, 1121a30-b10). It is this possibility of forming an attachment or loving affection for reason, knowledge, truth, and the fine, that allows the virtuous person to pursue the right "goal for living finely" in such a way that she can be said to live a life of *eudaimonia* ("happiness").

One problem with hate, should it come to be the primary drive of one's life, is that, unlike love, it makes reason act in the service of nonrational desires (in particular, spirit), rather than the other way round. If hate is formed in its own right or as a primary emotion (i.e., not merely as a derivative accompaniment of love), it involves a particular kind of generalization, one that directs one's negative attitudes or desires toward things that are (or can be) characterized by features that the agent has come to judge as bad- or worthless-making. The origin of this judgment, and so also of the wish that such things cease to exist, is however not found in the fact that those things are contrary to what is truly fine or noble (as it would be in an agent that is driven by love of the fine). Rather, it is found in the agent's frustrated or otherwise hindered nonrational desires, such as anger or fear. In developing hate, one transforms one's emotional distress or frustration into an ethical outlook. This outlook not only devalues the origin of the emotional frustration by making it bad or worthless in nature, but also makes the eradication of all things that are characterized by such nature a worthwhile achievement, one deserving of attachment. Although a person driven by hate thus might appear to be acting on the basis of rational or moral judgment or policy, her actions remain driven by the concerns of her nonrational part.

If this argument is along the right lines, then a person driven by hate—at least by hate formed in view of frustrated or hindered emotions—cannot have a virtuous character since hate relegates reason to a subordinate and (normatively) unnatural role, one that jeopardizes its function of issuing commands to the nonrational part. Hence, a virtuous person's life cannot be primarily driven by hate, independently of whether or not the objects of her hate correspond to the things that are truly evil or shameful. A more general conclusion can be reached by considering the fact that hate promotes detachment since it involves seeing and judging things that it is directed at as having no or negative value. A person who hates is, insofar as she hates, at best only attached to things that promote the eradication of the things she hates. But beyond that, hate does not involve seeing things as worthwhile of care, devotion, or admiration. Accordingly, someone who develops in such a way that hate (rather than love) becomes their primary motivational drive cannot hope to develop the right sort of relationship to oneself and, hence, cannot achieve the ideal, virtuous state of character. Her attachments, such as they are, would remain instrumental (i.e., directed toward things useful for satisfying her hate) and the overall orientation of her nonrational desires would remain anchored or oriented toward external things (the objects of her hate) rather than toward her true inner self (i.e., reason).

If hate cannot sustain virtue, it seems obvious that it cannot support a good life (*eudaimonia*). The analysis in section II offers at least two additional reasons for thinking so. First, if one's life is primarily driven by hate, it is not oriented toward an activity (of one's own) but, rather, toward the cessation of an activity (typically, someone else's). This means that, unlike love, hate aims at an end that is distinct from the activities that it gives rise to (*NE* 1.1, 1094a1–5). If love can keep one engaged in certain activities (those that one loves) for their own sake, hate can only aim at cessation of those things one hates. If *eudaimonia* is supposed to lie in some sort of (best) activity of the soul (i.e., in an activity that is an end in itself) in which one engages for its own sake, then it cannot be achieved by activities fueled by hate since they are not of the right sort (i.e., are not ends themselves). Moreover, although it might be that the goal (or product) of one's hate is valuable instrumentally (one could, after all, manage to remove a great evil from the world), once the goal is achieved, any further engagement in the kind of activities that led one to that goal is rendered pointless. Hence, should a person whose life is primarily driven by hate succeed, their success would render their further life bereft of a "goal for living finely" and, to that extent and from that point on, foolish (*EE* 2.2, 1214b7–10).[18]

The second point is this. As we have seen, a life primarily driven by hate is a life marked by (selective) cognitive closure toward things one hates. There is little controversy concerning Aristotle's views about the role of knowledge in a good life. Whether one adopts the inclusive or the dominant interpretation of *eudaimonia*, it is fairly clear that Aristotle thinks that a good life essentially includes, if not outright aims at, knowledge and understanding. It is a precondition for such a life that one becomes capable of appreciating the beauty of nature and finding not just any but the highest form of pleasure in understanding its workings and complexities (*PA* 1.5, 644b22–45a25). It is only then that one becomes capable of pursuing scientific knowledge, that is of seeking true explanations and causes of things. This concerns not only theoretical but also practical matters. As Aristotle often warns us, truth is in a way harder to determine in practical contexts since practical situations are, as a rule, too complex to be grasped and evaluated by and in view of universal rules or generalizations (esp., *NE* 1.3). It is, then, even more important in practical than in theoretical contexts that one becomes a lover of truth and of what is fine and beautiful. The pursuit of knowledge or understanding of human nature and behavior requires that one comes to see and marvel at beauty in things that exhibit an unusually high degree of luck and randomness (and so lack beauty) rather than of functional (teleological) organization and unity.

The problem is that hate promotes exactly the opposite attitude. It operates as if it already knew and determined, once and for all, what the nature of its objects is. Once it becomes attached to some feature as responsible for (or directly constituting) the harm or threat that one abhors, it makes it the primary or essential feature of all objects that exhibit it. It is because of *that* feature that those objects lose value and deserve to be eradicated. For a person who hates, once something can be categorized as belonging to the hated kind, there are no further questions to be asked or truths to be grasped. One problem is that what led one to pick the feature that turned things into objects of one's hate were (frustrated) nonrational desires (which could, of course, be accompanied by sophisticated rationalization),[19] rather than any reasoned inquiry. Hence, there is no guarantee that what one hates really is something that deserves to be hated. More importantly, from the point of view of the possibility of leading a good life, this means that one who hates becomes disinclined to see and understand the complexities of human behavior that Aristotle so often alludes to. Hate requires one to see human beings and their behavior as explicable by simple rules and generalizations (i.e., as either falling or not falling into the hated category) since it is only when they are perceived in such a way that they can be seen as only worthy of hate. Hence, in relation to those things one hates (and to the extent to which one hates), one becomes incapable of seeing any value, fineness, or beauty in the world and in human beings in particular.

4. CONCLUSION

Why, then should we avoid achieving *eudaimonia* in a hate-propelled way? As I have argued, for Aristotle there are (or could be) at least two reasons for doing so. First, it would undermine the right relationship between the rational and the nonrational part of the soul. If virtue involves establishing the right kind of internal ordering of one's soul, then this cannot be done if one's primary motivational drive is hate rather than love. Second, hate has negative cognitive effects insofar as it renders one essentially insensitive to the beauty of human nature and behavior and actively precludes one from acquiring knowledge and understanding. Accordingly, if a good life is a life that involves virtue and knowledge (and so full and ideal development of one's motivational and cognitive capacities), a life fueled by hate cannot but fall short of that ideal.

In conclusion, I would like to emphasize that it remains true that Aristotle recognizes that hate—understood as a general negative attitude toward evil—plays an important role in the virtuous life. The interesting fact is, however, that he does not recommend that this negative attitude be nurtured in its own right. Rather, virtuous hate is an attitude that one develops toward things that endanger what one has come to love and care about in the first place. In this chapter, I have tried to outline some reasons for his holding this view, reasons that do not appeal to the consequences (and possible harmful effects) of hate on others but, rather, to one's own well-being and the ability to lead a good life as Aristotle conceives of it.

NOTES

1. In the *Nicomachean Ethics* (*NE*) Aristotle says that the development of virtue of character proceeds through habituation in pleasure and pain (*NE* 2.1, 1104b3–8). As Gavin Lawrence describes it, "Habituation, in inculcating the human excellences, aims to bring us to enjoy and disenjoy the things we *should*, and this is a matter of coming to enjoy doing the fine and hating the base, *because* they are such" (Lawrence 2011, 262, emphasis original).

2. There is a famous Platonic precedent for the importance of love for both virtue and knowledge in Diotima's account of the ascent and redirection (or rather true development) of erotic love (*erōs*) from particular people to true objects of knowledge, and in particular the fine or the beautiful (*to kalon*) (*Symposium* 209e–212c). The person who comes to know (*gignoskein*) (211c) *to kalon* and so develops "true virtue" (212a) has, quite literally, reached the real goal of erotic love (210a).

3. Unless noted otherwise, the translations from Greek are mine.

4. There is no uncontroversial way to summarize the many different interpretations of Aristotle's conception of *eudaimonia*. The main divide is between inclusive

interpretations that view *eudaimonia* as a composite end that includes, at the very least, the exercise of practical virtues (of both character and intellect) and exclusive or dominant interpretations that see it as consisting or centering on a single activity of contemplation (*theōria*). For inclusive interpretations, see Irwin (1985), Cooper (1999), or Long (2011). For exclusive interpretations, see Kraut (1989), Kenny (1992), or Richardson Lear (2004).

5. To take but one example, Myles Burnyeat, in what is still probably the most widely recognized account of Aristotle's theory of habituation, concentrates entirely on the role of love (of the fine or noble) and pleasure, which he characterizes as "a disposition of the feelings comparable in intensity, though not of course in every other respect, to the passion of a man who is crazy about horses" and so on the way one comes to love and, consequently, enjoy things (Burnyeat 1980, 267).

6. This is true even as scholars differ in their interpretations of the role of pleasure and pain in habituation. Whereas some (perhaps most) have maintained that pleasure plays the primary motivational role in habituation to virtuous actions (Burnyeat 1980), others have seen pain as the central factor (Curzer 2002). In the former case, the learner is supposed to (somehow) progress from engaging in virtuous actions for the sake of external rewards (and so external pleasures) to finding the actions pleasant as such. In the latter case, the learner is guided by pain and punishment (and ensuing feelings of fear) to steer away from vicious actions and in that way come to realize the value of actions that are virtuous. On both views, however, the virtuous person develops love for the right sorts of things by the same process as she develops hate for the right sorts of things.

7. Aristotle often speaks of avoidance (*eulabeia*) or fleeing away (*pheugein*) from what is disgraceful or shameful (e.g., 1121b23–4; 1127b5) or from wickedness and evil (e.g., 1166b27).

8. For a brief overview of the controversy, see Dow (2015, 145–55). For a comprehensive discussion of Aristotle's treatment of emotions in the *Rhetoric*, see Rapp (2002, vol. 2, 543–83).

9. Cooper (1996, 239).

10. Aristotle makes a similar move in relation to the division of the soul into the rational and the nonrational part with which he operates in both the *Nicomachean Ethics* (*NE* 1.13, 1102a28) and the *Eudemian Ethics* (*EE* 2.1, 1220a8–11). As he tells us, it is a functional division which captures a distinction that is relevant for ethical and political purposes. In both works, he sets the precise scientific account of this distinction aside.

11. For an overview of the interpretative problems, see Cooper (1996, 243–44).

12. An alternative translation goes as follows: "An angry person wishes [that their revenge] is perceived [by those at whom the anger is directed] but for someone who hates this makes no difference."

13. It is famously available even to people who do not have more complex or nuanced emotions (such as psychopaths) or do not have them yet (i.e., children). For psychopathy, see Blair, Mitchell, and Blair (2005, 47–66).

14. Since spite and slander are, along with wanton aggression, among the causes of anger (*Rhet.* 2.2, 1378b14), I do not treat them separately here.

15. It is in this respect that anger and hate might be easily confused. They can both give rise to angry (vengeful) actions even as the motivational state behind them can be different.

16. Spirit is one of two nonrational kinds of desire that Aristotle recognizes, the other being appetite (*epithumia*). Whereas appetite is primarily concerned with bodily pleasures and pains (esp. those related to food, drink, and sex), spirit concerns matters that are broadly related to (one's) safety and well-being, self-esteem, and self-respect. For an overview, see Pearson (2012, 111–39).

17. The translations of the passage from the *Republic* are those of C. D. C. Reeve in Reeve (2004).

18. Of course, one could find a new object for one's hate and thus avoid the situation in which one is left without a goal or direction in one's life. But this leads to a dilemma of hate—either one succeeds and is left with a life that lacks any "goal for living finely," or one never reaches the goal and so never satisfies one's hate.

19. On the (possible) role of rationalization in Aristotle's account of vice see Barney (2020).

REFERENCES

Barney, Rachel. 2020. "Becoming Bad: Aristotle on Vice and Moral Habituation." *Oxford Studies in Ancient Philosophy* 57: 273–308.

Blair, James, Derek Mitchell, and Karina Blair. 2005. *The Psychopath: Emotion and the Brain*. Oxford: Blackwell.

Burnyeat, M. F. 1980. "Aristotle on Learning to be Good." In *Essays on Aristotle's Ethics*, edited by Amélie Oksenberg Rorty, 69–92. Berkeley: University of California Press.

Cooper, John M. 1996. "An Aristotelian Theory of the Emotions." In *Essays on Aristotle's Rhetoric*, edited by Amélie Oksenberg Rorty, 238–57. Berkeley: University of California Press.

Cooper, John M. 1999. "Contemplation and Happiness: A Reconsideration." In *Reason and Emotion: Essays on Ancient Moral Psychology and Ethical Theory*, 212–36. Princeton: Princeton University Press.

Curzer, Howard J. 2002. "Aristotle's Painful Path to Virtue." *Journal of the History of Philosophy* 40: 141–62.

Dow, Jamie. 2015. *Passions and Persuasion in Aristotle's Rhetoric*. Oxford: Oxford University Press.

Irwin, Terence. 1985. "Permanent Happiness: Aristotle and Solon." *Oxford Studies in Ancient Philosophy* 3: 89–124.

Kenny, Anthony. 1992. *Aristotle on the Perfect Life*. Oxford: Oxford University Press.

Konstan, D. 2007. *The Emotions of the Ancient Greeks*. Toronto: Toronto University Press.

Kraut, Richard. 1989. *Aristotle and the Human Good*. Princeton: Princeton University Press.

Lawrence, Gavin. 2011. "Acquiring Character: Becoming Grown-Up." In *Moral Psychology and Human Action in Aristotle*, edited by M. Pakaluk and G. Pearson, 233–83. Oxford: Oxford University Press.

Long, Anthony. 2011. "Aristotle on *Eudaimonia*, *Nous*, and Divinity." In *Aristotle's Nicomachean Ethics: A Critical Guide*, edited by Jon Miller, 92–114. Cambridge: Cambridge University Press.

Müller, Jozef. 2019. "Aristotle on Virtue of Character and the Authority of Reason." *Phronesis* 64: 10–56.

Pearson, Giles. 2012. *Aristotle on Desire*. Cambridge: Cambridge University Press.

Rapp, Christof. 2002. *Aristoteles: Rhetorik*. Translation and Commentary. 2 vols. Berlin: Akademie Verlag.

Reeve, C. D. C. 2004. *Plato: Republic*. Indianapolis: Hackett.

Richardson Lear, Gabriel. 2004. *Happy Lives and the Highest Good: An Essay on Aristotle's Nicomachean Ethics*. Princeton: Princeton University Press.

Chapter 2

Hatred in Buddhist Thought and Practice

Christopher W. Gowans

1. INTRODUCTION

The best way to understand the moral psychology of hatred in Buddhism is to recognize that Buddhist thought and practice is a self-cultivation philosophy.[1] That is, it supposes that there is something fundamentally problematic about human life, our existential starting point, and at the same time it maintains that we can overcome what is problematic and attain an ideal state of being. In addition, it offers us a set of therapeutic or spiritual exercises by which we move from the existential starting point to the ideal state of being, and it defends this analysis on the basis of an understanding of human nature. For Buddhism, our existential starting point is characterized as suffering and the ideal state of being is freedom from this, specifically a mental outlook that is tranquil and joyful, and a way of life that is morally virtuous. We achieve this ideal through a set of practices: the Eightfold Path in Theravāda Buddhism and the Six Perfections in Mahāyāna Buddhism. The heart of the understanding of human nature is that there is no self as we ordinarily understand it—what becomes in the Mahāyāna tradition the notion of emptiness, that all things are empty of an intrinsic or essential nature. However, it is also important that human beings have a capacity for achieving the ideal state of being, for attaining Buddhist enlightenment or awakening.

Traditional Buddhist teaching is adamant in regarding hatred as a thoroughly troublesome feature of human life. It is a source of suffering and an obstacle to overcoming suffering. For someone who has attained the ideal state of being, hatred is replaced with virtues such as loving-kindness and compassion. For this reason, much of Buddhist thought and practice focuses on eliminating hatred. However, hatred is often closely related to similar aversive states such as anger, and these aversions are often paired with forms of desire such as greed and lust that are considered equally problematic. In addition, both the aversions and the desires are thought to result from the delusion that we are selves or have an intrinsic nature. Hence, though opposition to hatred is central to the Buddhist analysis, this opposition must be understood in this broader context. From a Buddhist perspective, on account of our attachment to self, human beings are ordinarily afflicted with hatred, anger, greed, lust, and other psychological dispositions that generate suffering—but there are ways to overcome these afflictions.

It is widely observed that there are many different definitions of hatred in philosophy, psychology, and elsewhere.[2] Though the English word "hatred," as a translation of the Pāli term *dosa* and the Sanskrit term *dveṣa*, is quite common in Buddhist discourse, there is no standard Buddhist definition of hatred.[3] Traditional Buddhist texts contain many lists. For example, there are five hindrances (*nīvaraṇa*) of the mind that weaken wisdom: sensual desire, ill will, dullness, restlessness, and doubt.[4] However, these texts do not focus on developing conceptual analyses of key terms, such as necessary and sufficient conditions, as we find in some forms of contemporary philosophy. Their orientation is more practical than theoretical. Hence, they are more concerned to list factors relevant to striving for enlightenment and to observe the psychological connections among these factors with an aim to achieving enlightenment. Moreover, they sometimes employ terms with similar or synonymous meanings with little further analysis: for example, ill will (*vyāpāda*) in the list of hindrances is a synonym for hatred.

Nonetheless, as a point of departure, it is worth noting that there is a core class of cases of hatred referred to in many Buddhist texts: in these cases, hatred is a strong dislike of a person because the person is perceived as having wronged one, and this dislike is accompanied by the desire to harm the wrongdoer. Hatred in this sense is universally condemned in traditional Buddhist texts as a source of suffering and an obstacle to overcoming suffering. An enlightened person would be free of such hatred. In these texts, with these cases in mind, hatred is ordinarily described as an aversive mental state that is an affliction (*kilesa/kleśa*) that typically leads to unwholesome (*akusala/akuśala*) actions.[5] These afflictions and the unwholesome actions are sources of suffering, and are obstacles to overcoming suffering, and so they should be eliminated.

The opposition to hatred in traditional Buddhist teaching contrasts with the views of many Western traditions and outlooks, though not all.[6] One issue concerns the possibility of morally appropriate hatred. Though hatred is widely condemned, it is sometimes said that some instances of hatred are morally proper. For example, in the Hebrew Bible a king is praised because "you love righteousness and hate wickedness,"[7] and Aquinas says that we should hate the sins of a person, though not the person himself.[8] That we should hate what is evil or wrong, such as when a person's actions are unjust or oppressive, is not an uncommon belief. However, traditional Buddhist thought resists this: it ordinarily supposes that hatred is always problematic even in the face of oppression. However, there are some philosophers in the Western tradition whose broad condemnation of hatred is similar to Buddhism. For instance, the Stoics argue that we should be free of all forms of hatred and many other emotions.[9] Another issue pertains to the relationship between hatred and other psychological states. Hatred is sometimes clearly distinguished from other states that may appear similar to it. Aristotle, for example, stresses the differences between hatred and anger.[10] However, we will see that in Buddhism the similarities and psychological connections between hatred and anger are stressed to the extent that an important part of the condemnation of hatred in Buddhism is its condemnation of anger. On this point, once again the Stoics have a similar view.

Three kinds of challenge to understanding the Buddhist position on hatred deserve our consideration. First, there are philosophical objections to the Buddhist opposition to hatred and the arguments for this opposition. Second, there are psychological objections to the claim that we can overcome hatred and that the therapeutic exercises intended to enable us to overcome it are effective. Finally, there is a political objection that the hatred expressed by Buddhist nationalists in the past century puts into question the Buddhist position on hatred. Analysis of how Buddhists might respond to these objections will help us better understand the Buddhist position on hatred.

We will begin by examining the assessment of hatred in the teaching of the Buddha. We will then consider how this assessment was developed by the Theravāda Buddhist Buddhaghosa and the Mahāyāna Buddhist Śāntideva. These three accounts together will provide us with a representative picture of the understanding and evaluation of hatred in traditional Indian Buddhism. We will also see, more briefly, that this outlook is affirmed in a number of contemporary defenses of Buddhism. Finally, we will turn to the three challenges and examine the basis of them and possible responses to them.

2. THE BUDDHA: THREE UNWHOLESOME ROOTS

The Buddha lived in the Ganges River basin in Northeast India, probably during the fifth-century BCE. He wrote nothing, but a group of texts called the Pāli Canon purports to represent his oral teaching. The most prominent summary of this teaching is the Four Noble Truths, and the best way to ascertain his assessment of hatred is to see how these truths relate to it. In the background is a set of beliefs, what may be called the Liberation Paradigm, that was widely accepted in ancient Indian culture. According to this Paradigm, the life of each human being is one phase in an ongoing cycle of rebirths governed by karma. This means that each of us lives a series of lives extending unendingly into the past and, without liberation, forever into the future. The doctrine of karma is that the level of happiness or well-being in a person's life is largely determined by the morality of the actions of the person in the past (in the current and previous lives). However, whatever the level, every life in the cycle is problematic because it is permeated by suffering (*dukkha/duḥkha*). Fortunately, escape from the entire cycle of rebirth is possible through a set of practices that center on knowledge of the nature of the self. This liberated state is usually called *mokṣa* or nirvana.

The Buddha's Four Noble Truths purport to explain the nature, cause, cessation, and path to the cessation of suffering.[11] The First Noble Truth states that human lives are pervaded by suffering: though they may be better or worse in various ways, there is something fundamentally unsatisfactory about our lives. The Buddha associates suffering with aging, illness, and death as well as, more broadly, displeasure and unfulfilled desires. He also associates suffering with impermanence (*SN*, 4.1). Since everything changes, anything pleasurable or desirable we possess will eventually disappear, and anything displeasurable or undesirable we have so far avoided may yet reach us. However, we will see that it is not impermanence as such that results in suffering, but our attitude to that which is impermanent.

This is clear in the Second Noble Truth. This states that the cause of suffering is craving (*taṇhā/tṛṣṇā*), a term suggesting impulses that are intense, powerful, and insistent. In Buddhist thought, craving is often associated with desires such as greed and lust as well as aversions such as hatred and anger. From this perspective, hatred is an important source of suffering, but this is because it is a form of the broader phenomenon of craving. In addition, all forms of craving are said to result from the delusion that one is a self. In denying that there is a self, the Buddha means primarily that there is no self with identity through time that is distinct from other things. This is thought to follow from the impermanence of all things (which undermines identity) and what the Buddha calls dependent origination, that everything is causally dependent on other things (which undermines distinctness). The Buddha supposes the belief that one is a self gives rise to a possessive attitude, often called attachment or clinging, according to which we think happiness requires the permanent possession of what we believe is good and the permanent avoidance of what we believe is bad. This is what we crave. However, in a world in which everything is impermanent, such happiness is impossible. Our craving is constantly threatened by frustration, and this is why suffering permeates human life.

This analysis is summarized in the common Buddhist contention that the source of suffering is threefold: (a) desires such as greed (*lobha*) or lust (*rāga*), (b) hatred (*dosa/dveṣa*), and (c) delusion (*moha*)—what are sometimes called the three roots of "unwholesome" (*akuśala*) states or "imperfections" that defile the mind, and later in the tradition the "three poisons" (*triviṣa*).[12] For example, "greed is a root of the unwholesome; hate is a root of the unwholesome; delusion is a root of the unwholesome."[13] The importance of the three roots is illustrated in the well-known "Fire Sermon" in which the Buddha says that "all is burning." Specifically, each of the senses and the mind is "burning with the fire of lust, with the fire of hatred, with the fire of delusion" (see *SN*, 4.19). Fire is a metaphor for our troubled lives: just as a raging fire destroys all in its path so our driven, possessive impulses and delusions wreak havoc on our lives.[14] Once again, in the Buddha's teaching, hatred is problematic as an important part of this broader analysis.

The fire metaphor is also important for understanding the Third Noble Truth. It says that it is possible to achieve a cessation of suffering. This is brought about through the cessation of its causes—the belief that one is a self and the craving this generates. The cessation of suffering is called nirvana (*nibbāna* in Pāli). One meaning of the term nirvana is "blowing out," as in blowing out a candle. Since suffering is characterized as the fire of lust, hatred, and delusion, to end suffering is to extinguish this fire. The person who has attained nirvana is called an Arahant. We are told that, like the rest of us, an Arahant "still experiences what is agreeable and disagreeable, still feels pleasure and pain." What distinguishes him as an Arahant is "the destruction of lust, hatred, and delusion in him."[15] The possessive impulses and delusions have been extinguished. The Arahant is free of all forms of craving such as lust and hatred. This is described as a calm and blissful state, what we might depict as joyful tranquility. In addition, the Arahant also has perfected moral virtues such as compassion and loving-kindness.

The Fourth Noble Truth tells us that we can achieve nirvana by following the Eightfold Path, described as a "middle way" between a life of "sensual happiness" and one of "self-mortification" (*SN*, 5.421). Its eight steps are right view, right intention, right speech, right action, right livelihood, right effort, right mindfulness, and right concentration (for elaboration see *SN*, 5.8–10). In part, the path requires development of a philosophical understanding of the Buddha's teaching as just outlined (right view). Much of it involves developing our moral dispositions (right action, speech, and livelihood). The last three steps concern meditation. Right effort is an important preliminary to the mindfulness and concentration meditative practices at the end. It requires us to eliminate and prevent unwholesome states and to generate and maintain wholesome states. The roots of the unwholesome states are, as before, lust or greed, hatred, and delusion. The roots of the wholesome states are the negations of these, but they might be put in more positive terms as generosity, loving-kindness, and wisdom.

In short, hatred is an obstacle to enlightenment that needs to be overcome if we are to eliminate suffering. The Buddha sometimes puts this in emphatic terms. In an address to the *bhikkhus/bhikṣus* (his male monastic followers) he said, "Even if bandits were to sever you savagely limb by limb with a two-handled saw, he who gave rise to a mind of hate towards them would not be carrying out my teaching." The Buddha advised the *bhikkhus* to train so as to "abide compassionate for their welfare, with a mind of loving-kindness, without inner hate . . . without hostility and without ill will" (*MN*, 1.129). In the *Dhammapada*, a practice manual of the Buddha's sayings for his followers, we are told near the beginning, "Hatred is never appeased by hatred in this world; by non-hatred alone is hatred appeased. This is an eternal law" (Buddharakkhita 1996, 1.5).

The Buddha's outlook on hatred is affirmed in many contemporary explanations of his viewpoint. For example, Bhikkhu Bodhi, a prominent scholar and translator of Pāli Canon texts, says that for the Buddha "the three roots of evil—greed, hatred, and delusion—have terrible repercussions on a whole society, issuing in violence, the lust for power, and the unjust infliction of suffering" (Bodhi 2005, 23–4). In his commentary on the "Kālāma Sutta," in which the Buddha urges the Kālāmas to "know for yourselves," through your own experience, what is wholesome and unwholesome, Bodhi says,

> The Buddha's purpose is to lead the Kālāmas to see that, even when we suspend all concern with future lives, unwholesome mental states such as greed, hatred, and delusion . . . eventually redound to one's own harm and suffering right here and now. (Bodhi 2005, 85)

This is a key feature of the Buddha's analysis of the source of suffering in human life.

3. BUDDHAGHOSA: LOVING-KINDNESS

After the Buddha died, his followers continued to pursue and promote his ideas and practices for overcoming suffering. They also developed these in numerous directions. One important early tradition that has persisted to this day (in Sri Lanka and parts of Southeast Asia) is Theravāda Buddhism. The best-known classical commentator in the Theravāda tradition is Buddhaghosa, a Buddhist monk who lived in the fourth and fifth centuries CE in India and Sri Lanka. His long text, the *Visuddhimagga* (*Path of Perfection*), is a Buddhist manual for overcoming suffering by undoing "the tangle of craving."[16] As in the Buddha's teaching, his orientation is primarily practical. The *Visuddhimagga* is divided into three parts—virtue, concentration, and understanding—a traditional way of organizing the Eightfold Path.[17] In the course of his discussion, Buddhaghosa has much to say about hatred and how to overcome it—what Maria Heim calls his "phenomenology of hatred" (Gereboff et al. 2009, 192).

In many respects, Buddhaghosa follows the teaching of the Buddha closely. His aim was not to innovate, but to systematically develop Buddhist thought and practice as understood in the Theravāda tradition. He accepts the Four Noble Truths, including the Eightfold Path, and the philosophical basis of this in the no-self doctrine. For our purpose, an important instance of Buddhaghosa's adherence to the Buddha's teaching is that he regularly refers to and relies on the three unwholesome roots theme. For example, the "unprofitable" has "three kinds according to root, as (a) rooted in greed, (b) rooted in hatred, and (c) rooted in delusion" (*Vism.*, 14.89).[18] These three roots are depicted as defilements, and they are metaphorically described as stains and forms of dirt (see *Vism.*, 22.49, 22.61, and 12.63). Buddhaghosa also says that greed, hatred, and delusion are temperaments (see *Vism.*, 3.74). These temperaments have a karmic explanation: they "have their source in previous habits." For example, "one of hating temperament has formerly had plenty of stabbing and torturing and brutal work to do or has reappeared here after dying in one of the hells or the nāga (serpent) existences" (*Vism.*, 3.80).[19] In addition, the three temperaments each bring about other problematic states. For instance, "in one of hating temperament there is frequent occurrence of such states as anger, enmity, disparaging, domineering, envy, and avarice" (*Vism.*, 3.95). In addition, Buddhaghosa associates nirvana and the Arahant with the destruction of these three roots (see *Vism.*, 16.69).

In short, as for the Buddha, Buddhaghosa believes that hatred is thoroughly problematic: it is central to the analysis of the source of suffering, the difficulty of overcoming it, and what it would mean to overcome it. In addition to his descriptions in connection with the three roots, he depicts hatred in a number of pejorative ways. For example, hate "has the characteristic of savageness, like a provoked snake," and it spreads "like a drop of poison" or burns its own support "like a forest fire" (*Vism.*, 14.171). It may be accompanied by grief or resentment (see *Vism.*, 14.92), and it may make one ugly in a future life (see *Vism.*, 13.77). Buddhaghosa's most important discussion of hatred, however, is in connection with the meditations concerning the four divine abidings in the concentration section of the book.

The divine abidings (sometimes called immeasurable deliverances of mind) are moral virtues discussed in the Pāli Canon. Buddhaghosa's contribution is to explain extensive meditations for developing them. The four abidings are loving-kindness (*mettā/mairtī*), compassion (*karuṇā*), gladness (*muditā*), and equanimity (*upekkhā/upekṣā*). Loving-kindness is the concern to promote the happiness of all beings. Compassion is the concern to end the suffering of all beings. Gladness (sometimes translated as sympathetic joy) is taking joy in the happiness of others. Equanimity is regarding each being as equally important.

For our purpose, Buddhaghosa's account of the meditation on loving-kindness is the most important. After sitting in a secluded place, Buddhaghosa says, the meditator "should review the danger in hate and the advantage in patience" (*Vism.*, 9.1). This preliminary is important because, in order to develop loving-kindness, hate must be abandoned and patience developed. One danger in hate is that a person obsessed by hate may kill living beings, a violation of basic Buddhist teaching. The aim of the meditation itself is to develop one's concern for the happiness of all other persons. In the meditation, the meditator first directs concern for happiness to himself and then, in stages, directs it to a dear person, a neutral person, and finally a hostile person (in each case thinking, "may I be happy," "may he be happy," etc.). In this way, the barriers between these different categories of persons may be overcome, and happiness may be extended impartially to all. Buddhaghosa recognized that the last category, a hostile person, is especially important since such persons are those to whom we are most likely to feel ill will (described as the enemy of loving-kindness) and those for whom we are least likely to feel a concern for happiness. In such cases, anger and resentment are common reactions, and so Buddhaghosa discusses at length how to overcome these when confronted by persons who have directly harmed us. This is an example of the way in which hatred and other states such as anger are often linked in Buddhist teaching.

In the discussion of anger, Buddhaghosa cites passages from the Pāli Canon in which we are told not to be angry with those angry at us and not to hate even those who have severely harmed us. Various reasons are offered in support of this (see *Vism.*, 9.15–9.40). For example, acting from anger will lead us to perform actions that will affect us negatively on account of karma and they will preclude us from attaining enlightenment. This can be seen from the previous lives of the Buddha in which he responded to those who harmed him with patience rather than hatred and anger. Moreover, in the endless round of rebirths in the past, at some point or another virtually every being—and hence the being you may now be angry with—has been your mother or some other relative: surely we should not hate someone who has been our mother. In addition, in reference to the no-self teaching, since what we call the self is nothing more than the sum of its parts, there is no part of the person (such as a momentary physical or mental state) to which anger can properly be directed.[20] In this way, the meditator aims to eliminate hatred and anger so that it is possible to wish for the happiness even of persons who have harmed us. Heim says that this is "a striking cognitive therapy that may well radically alter the meditator's relationship with the 'enemy'" (2017, 179).

This and the other divine abiding meditations are moral habituation exercises in which we try to overcome problematic states such as hatred, cruelty, and envy, and to replace them with virtuous states such as loving-kindness, compassion, and the like. On account of our attachment to self and possessive orientation, we are deeply habituated to have these problematic states. We need to overcome them in order to overcome suffering, and when we have done this by achieving enlightenment, we will have fully attained the virtues.

Though the *Visuddhimagga* is a rather dense compendium of practices in the Theravāda tradition, it has received considerable attention in recent years from both Buddhist scholars and proponents of Buddhist practice addressing a broad audience. For example, B. Alan Wallace developed a contemporary guide to the four divine abidings meditations explained in Buddhaghosa's text. Wallace notes that "in the Buddha's experience the number one adversary to loving-kindness is hatred" (Wallace 2010, 91).[21] Hence, he says, for Buddhaghosa "the goal is to be able to direct loving-kindness to a person towards whom we naturally feel hostility or hatred" (Wallace 2010, 98). This is why loving-kindness for a hostile person comes at the end of Buddhaghosa's meditative sequence. It is the most difficult case, especially when the person has committed an unjust or oppressive action, and special efforts are needed to wish that such a person be happy. We will now see that there are similar perspectives in other Buddhist traditions as well.

4. ŚĀNTIDEVA: FORBEARANCE

Mahāyāna Buddhism emerged in India around the beginning of the Common Era and subsequently spread to much of Asia. It is the dominant form of Buddhism in the world today. Though grounded in the Buddha's teaching, Mahāyāna Buddhism has several distinctive features that distinguish it from Theravāda Buddhism. One is the philosophy of emptiness: for Mahāyāna Buddhism, everything is empty of "own being" (*svabhāva*), that is, empty of an intrinsic or essential nature. This idea is rooted in the no-self teaching, but it is broader by referring to everything and more radical by implying that, in ultimate reality, there are no real distinctions between things. A second distinctive feature is its practical ideal: in Mahāyāna Buddhism, we are encouraged to pursue enlightenment, not simply in order to overcome our own suffering, but so that all sentient beings may be free of suffering. Hence, the ideal figure is a Bodhisattva, a being committed to staying in the cycle of rebirth helping others until they have all overcome suffering. We become a Bodhisattva by pursuing the Six Perfections (*pāramitās*): generosity, morality, patience, vigor, meditation, and wisdom. In many respects, these are a reworking of the Eightfold Path in light of the distinctive features of Mahāyāna

Buddhism.[22] For example, wisdom is the realization of emptiness, something that is thought to bring about the universal compassion of the Bodhisattva.

Śāntideva was one of the most important Indian Mahāyāna philosophers to develop an ethical outlook. He was a monk who lived in India in the seventh and eighth centuries CE and taught at Nālandā, the premier university in India at the time. He is best known for his book, *The Bodhicaryāvatāra* (*The Guide to Bodhisattva Practice*), one of the most important texts in the Mahāyāna tradition.[23] It is especially influential in Tibetan Buddhism and is held in high esteem by the current Dalai Lama. Śāntideva's *Guide* may be read as a manual for developing and sustaining the "Awakening Mind" (*bodhicitta*), a commitment to end the suffering of all beings, something necessary to pursue the Bodhisattva path. The central chapters of the text are structured around cultivation of the Six Perfections.

For our purpose, the most important Perfection is forbearance (*kṣānti*), sometimes translated as patience or tolerance, the focus of chapter 6. Forbearance is the ability to confront adversity, especially situations in which other persons have harmed us, without succumbing to hatred or anger (terms that Śāntideva uses more or less interchangeably).[24] The chapter begins by declaring that "there is no evil equal to hatred, and no spiritual practice equal to forbearance" (*BCA*, 6.2). There is no peace of mind, Śāntideva says, "while the dart of hatred is stuck in the heart," and "there is no sense in which someone prone to anger is well off" (*BCA*, 6.3 and 6.5). He gives several reasons for overcoming hatred and anger. For example, in terms of the karma system, they will result in a painful rebirth (see *BCA*, 6.74). By contrast, forbearance will result in "serenity, freedom from disease, joy, and long life, the happiness of an emperor, prosperity" (*BCA*, 6.134). In addition, the harm we suffer now at the hands of others may be explained by the karma system: this is the result of our own harmful actions in the past (see *BCA*, 6.42, 6.45–6 and 6.68). Hence, hatred of the person who is the proximate cause of our suffering is unwarranted.

In addition, Śāntideva argues that hatred and anger are incompatible with the Bodhisattva commitment to help all sentient beings overcome suffering since these afflictions lead us to harm those who have harmed us. "If I did retaliate [against those who harm me]," he says, "they would not be protected and I would fail in my practice" (*BCA*, 6.51; cf. 6.80). In fact, Śāntideva says, we should be grateful for those who have harmed us because they have given us the opportunity to develop the Perfection of forbearance: "Since he helps me on the path to Awakening, I should long for an enemy like a treasure" (*BCA*, 6.107). An enemy, he says, should be worshiped "as the True Dharma" (*BCA*, 6.111).

The most important philosophical argument against hatred and anger appeals to the Buddhist doctrine of dependent origination. As Śāntideva says, "All arise through the power of conditioning forces" (*BCA*, 6.25). The key idea in this argument is suggested by this passage: "As I do not become angry with great sources of suffering such as jaundice, then why be angry with animate creatures? They too are provoked by conditions."[25] Śāntideva appears to be arguing that both animate and inanimate sources of suffering are alike in being conditioned, and so, since we are not angry when the source is inanimate, we should not be angry when the source is animate. It might be claimed that there is nonetheless an important difference between suffering brought about by a disease such as jaundice and suffering brought about by the intentional actions of another person. We ordinarily think that anger, or even hatred, might be an appropriate response to the intentional actions of a person, if they were meant to harm us, though we would not think this would be a proper response to forces of nature that cause a disease that harms us. However, Śāntideva apparently thinks that our response should be the same on the ground that the salient fact is that both are conditioned. "When people harm one's teachers, relatives, and others dear to us, one should . . . regard it as arising on the basis of conditioning factors and refrain from anger towards them" (*BCA*, 6.65; cf. 6.33).

Śāntideva's reflection on the Perfection of forbearance, and his argument against hatred and anger, have deep Buddhist roots and for that reason might be thought to have limited appeal to persons without Buddhist commitments. However, some contemporary figures have argued that Śāntideva's teaching has broader appeal. For example, the Dalai Lama, in a commentary on this teaching, maintains that overcoming hatred and anger is necessary to develop the "compassion and love [that] are the foundation of all spiritual paths."[26] In response to the objection that oppression and injustice must be opposed, and that anger if not hatred are needed to oppose them, the Dalai Lama argues that "one can, out of compassion for the perpetrator of the crime and without generating hatred or anger, actually take a strong stand and take strong countermeasures."[27] He refers to this stance as the basis for the Tibetan response to the Chinese occupation of Tibet.

5. THE CHALLENGE FROM PHILOSOPHY

Buddhism has a distinctive and powerful perspective on hatred. However, it may also be challenged from several points of view. Assessing these challenges will help us better understand the position. From the standpoint of philosophy, perhaps its most central claim is that there is no self. The Buddha and his followers gave arguments in support of this claim (and later on behalf of emptiness). For example, he said that human beings consist of five "aggregates" (*khandhas/skandhas*): material form, sensations, perceptions, volitions, and consciousness. He proposed that, if we examine each of these, we will recognize that there is no basis for thinking that there is a self that has identity through time and is distinct from other things. For instance, all we observe are particular perceptions that are constantly changing and are dependent on other things. These arguments are controversial, and it is beyond the scope of this chapter to examine them.[28] In any case, the Buddha did not think intellectual considerations were sufficient for enlightenment: he said this is "unattainable by mere reasoning" (*MN*, 1.167). As we will see, moral dispositions and meditative awareness are important as well.

The Buddha's understanding of the person may be put in more positive terms: what we call a self is nothing more than an ensemble of constantly changing and causally connected physical and mental processes—namely, the aggregates—that are dependent on other things. It might be wondered why realizing this process view would enable us to overcome suffering. The central contention is that, though an enlightened person would still feel pleasure and pain, he or she would not encounter these with a possessive orientation: specifically, he or she would not feel greed and lust for sources of pleasure nor hatred and anger with regard to sources of pain. Part of the point seems to be that realizing that one is not a self with identity through time, but simply an ongoing sequence of physical and mental processes, would mitigate regrets focused on the past and anxieties looking toward the future. This would bring about greater tranquility. Another part is that the realization that we are not selves that are truly distinct from one another, but we are causally interconnected, could help transform tendencies toward hatred and anger directed to other persons into virtues such as loving-kindness and compassion.

The specific discussions pertaining to hatred and anger in Buddhaghosa and Śāntideva have different functions, but they are partly arguments for why we should eliminate hatred and anger. Some of these arguments appeal to common consequentialist points: hatred and anger have harmful effects on ourselves and others. For example, if I am in a rage out of hatred of another person, this disrupts my own well-being and it may lead me to harm other persons in ways that are unjustified. Such analyses are similar to arguments we find elsewhere, for example, in the Stoic Seneca.[29] They are familiar and plausible considerations, at least up to a point. Many people see in such arguments reasons at least to restrain hatred and anger, though perhaps not to eliminate them altogether.

Other arguments for eliminating hatred and anger depend on distinctive Buddhist perspectives such as karma and rebirth and, in the Mahāyāna outlooks, the commitment of the Bodhisattva. Without acceptance of the framework of karma and rebirth, some Buddhist arguments have no plausibility: for example, claims that the injustice I suffer in this life results from wrongful acts I committed in previous lives, or that those I am tempted to hate in this life might well have been my mother in a previous life. In fact, it might be objected to the first of these that this is an unwarranted "blame the victim" point of view. However, if we accept the framework of karma and rebirth, it may be a plausible albeit unverifiable claim (as is the argument that the hated person may have been one's mother). In any case, the Buddhist outlook is not that we should condone oppressors, but that we should strive to change them from the standpoint of loving-kindness and compassion. This is clear in the Dalai Lama's stance toward China. The Bodhisattva is committed to ending the suffering of all persons, including oppressors, though from a Buddhist standpoint ending that person's suffering would mean that he or she is no longer an oppressor. The attitude toward oppressors is not vindictive. Rather, it is meliorative. Śāntideva says, "I am medicine for the sick. May I be both the doctor and their nurse, until their sickness does not recur" (*BCA*, 3.7). This applies to all persons: "Even if people are extremely malignant, all that is skillful should be done for them."[30]

A central consideration in support of this outlook may be found in the arguments against hatred and anger based on the Buddhist no-self teaching. As we have seen, both Buddhaghosa and Śāntideva argue that recognition that there is no self undermines the rationale for these aversive responses. For Buddhaghosa, since the person is simply an ensemble of aggregates, there is no agent who is the appropriate object of these attitudes. For Śāntideva, since each aspect of the person is conditioned by other things, these attitudes do not make sense. Hatred and anger presuppose that there is an agent who deliberates, chooses, and acts. However, on the Buddhist view, there is no such agent: there is just an ensemble of constantly changing, conditioned mental and physical processes.

Various objections may be raised against arguments of this kind. One is based on the analysis of P. F. Strawson (1974) that what he calls "participant reactive attitudes" such as resentment and anger, and also gratitude and love, are "natural human reactions" that are deeply embedded in human life. For Strawson, it is a basic feature of ordinary human relationships that we regard one another as morally responsible agents. The reactive attitudes are expressions of this stance. Though we might withhold them on special occasions, when particular persons lack agency, we could not simply abandon them as a whole, thinking that no one is an agent. Yet this seems to be what Buddhaghosa and Śāntideva are proposing.

One Buddhist response to this objection is to argue that it is both possible and appropriate to do what Strawson denies we can do. On this view, Buddhism advocates that we should fundamentally transform human relationships: instead of regarding other human beings as morally responsible agents we should regard them as beings who suffer and require our help. From this perspective, the medical analogy may be an apt depiction of the

Buddhist perspective. The "objective attitude" that Strawson thought was appropriate only in special cases in which a person should be regarded as an object of treatment, and not suited for the reactive attitudes, is the way in which we should regard persons in all cases.[31]

However, another objection to the Buddhist position suggests that this may not be the full story: Buddhist texts do not consistently regard the no-self teaching as undermining our attitudes toward responsibility. In some cases, both Buddhaghosa and Śāntideva appear to speak of personal responsibility in terms closely related to the language of the reactive attitudes. For example, Buddhaghosa says, in speaking of karma, "You are the owner of your deeds, heir of your deed" (*Vism.* 9.23), suggesting that I am responsible for the consequences of what I have done, and Śāntideva says we should honor enemies for giving us the opportunity to develop forbearance, implying perhaps that the enemy deserves this honor for what he or she has done (see *BCA*, 6.109–110). Hence, Buddhaghosa and Śāntideva do not uniformly take Strawson's objective attitude toward persons.

A Buddhist response to this inconsistency objection is that Buddhaghosa's and Śāntideva's texts are plausibly read as self-cultivation manuals that provide a set of practices for achieving the fundamental Buddhist goal of overcoming suffering in oneself and others. Hence, in some respects at least, they should not be assessed in terms of their consistency in deducing conclusions from the Buddhist premise of no-self or emptiness. Rather, they should be judged in terms of the efficacy of their practices in achieving the goal. Some practices may appeal to the Buddhist no-self teaching, but others may appeal to ordinary attitudes that presuppose that there are selves.[32] Since hatred and anger are sources of suffering and obstacles to attaining enlightenment, whatever practices are effective in eliminating hatred and anger are justified as therapeutic exercises. These practices need not employ a consistent set of premises (Bommarito 2011).

In any case, the central Buddhist contention is that hatred and anger are ill-advised responses to adversity even in—in fact, especially in—cases in which someone harms us without provocation.[33] Rather than trying to "get back at the person" or "making the person pay," Buddhism typically claims, we should try to help the person overcome suffering. The overriding commitment to end suffering brings to light the fact that, in traditional Buddhist thought, the dominant moral vocabulary is that of generosity, compassion, and loving-kindness rather than that of justice, rights, and retribution.[34] It might be objected that we cannot do without the concepts of justice and rights—and perhaps retribution as well. However, the Buddhist contention is that, whatever we may say about these concepts, the Buddhist virtues are more important. This orientation is reflected in many discussions by contemporary Buddhists. In a world in which there is great emphasis on justice and human rights, the importance of these is often affirmed, and yet there is an effort to shift the moral presuppositions of the discussion.

For example, the Dalai Lama has granted that "it is natural and just for nations, peoples and individuals to demand respect for their rights and freedoms" (1998b, 105). However, what he has stressed the most is the importance of universal responsibility:

> Each of us must learn to work not just for one self, one's own family or one's nation, but for the benefit of all humankind. Universal responsibility is the key to human survival. It is the best foundation for world peace. (1998a, xx)

The Dalai Lama's emphasis on universal responsibility may be seen as rooted in the Buddhist values of compassion and loving-kindness. Again, the Buddhist monk Thich Nhat Hanh has granted that it is important to "take a clear stand against oppression and injustice" (2005, 99). However, he has also urged the importance of transforming "the energy of anger" into "the eyes of compassion."[35] This is evident in his signature theme of interbeing: "I am, therefore you are. You are, therefore I am. That is the meaning of the word 'interbeing.' We interare" (2005, 88). This is an expression of the central Buddhist idea that human beings are not truly distinct, but are dependent on one another. Nhat Hanh vividly expressed the implications of this idea in a stanza of a poem entitled "Please Call Me by My True Names":

> I am the twelve-year-old girl,
> refugee on a small boat,
> who throws herself into the ocean
> after being raped by a sea pirate.
> And I am the pirate,
> my heart not yet capable
> of seeing and loving.[36]

The concept of interbeing encourages us to identify with oppressors as well as their victims, and it teaches us to transform the hatred and anger we may feel toward oppressors into compassion for all persons, victims, and oppressors alike.

6. THE CHALLENGE FROM PSYCHOLOGY

Much of the Buddhist teaching on hatred and anger concerns psychology—what afflicts human beings and how to overcome this. This is another perspective from which this teaching may be evaluated. A central claim is that suffering is a pervasive feature of human life. It might be objected that this is not true, that most human beings are satisfied with their life.[37] However, the Buddha did not think we are always miserable: the doctrine of karma implies that people are more or less happy. The problem is that, thinking that we are selves, we relate to the world in a possessive way: we want to attach ourselves to what we judge to be pleasant or good, and we likewise want to detach ourselves from what we judge to be painful or bad—in both cases, not just for a short time, but in a permanent way. The difficulty is that the world is constantly changing and much that happens is beyond our control. Hence, we either fail to satisfy our desires and aversions, and so are frustrated or, when we succeed, we worry that success will not last for long. Hence, a measure of dissatisfaction is always with us.

However, it might be argued that, contrary to the Buddhist claim, desires and aversions are inevitable features of human life, and they are not always problematic (see Irvine 2006, part 2). The Buddhist response is that the possessive orientation is always problematic—in the language of the Fire Sermon, we are burning with the fire of lust, hatred, and delusion—and it is this that is not inevitable. The Arahant and Bodhisattva overcome the possessive orientation: he or she lives a life of joyful tranquility animated by virtues such as loving-kindness and compassion. These virtues may involve a form of desire and aversion, namely the wish that all people be happy and not suffer, but this is not the craving, clinging, and attachment that accompany the possessive orientation.

In some formulations, the Buddhist ideal is expressed in extraordinarily strong terms, as when it is suggested that we identify with pirates who rape, refrain from hating bandits who mutilate, and honor those who harm us for providing us with the opportunity to develop forbearance. Though these statements might be understood in different ways (perhaps more as mythic exemplars than as sources of literal advice), there is no question that the Buddhist ideal is quite demanding by most standards. In view of this, it might be objected that human beings are not capable of such a life because, by nature, we are inevitably driven by possessive aversions and desires.

The Buddhist response to this objection is twofold. On the one hand, it grants that it is very difficult to reach the ideal state: ordinarily we are deeply habituated to perceive, feel, desire, think, choose, and act in ways that are shaped by the three poisons of greed, hatred, and delusion. We find it natural to live in this way and find it difficult to change. On the other hand, Buddhism maintains that it is possible to reach the ideal by pursuing a wide range of Buddhist practices such as those described in the Eightfold Path and the Six Perfections. These practices are therapeutic or spiritual exercises that are supposed to enable us to overcome the three poisons and attain enlightenment and so overcome suffering. Of course, on account of rebirth we have innumerable lives to do this. There is tremendous diversity in these practices. Nonetheless, at risk of some simplification, we can examine the practices in the traditions we have discussed together according to the standard three categories of wisdom, morality, and concentration (meditation).

As a preliminary, it should be noted that context is very important. In the traditional Buddhist accounts, it is ordinarily assumed that the practices are undertaken by a community of committed followers in a Buddhist monastery under the guidance of a master. This might suggest a rather ascetic regime, but the Buddha and Buddhaghosa described the Eightfold Path as a "middle way" between a life of "sensual happiness" and one of "self-mortification" (see *SN*, 5.421 and *Vism.*, 1.9–11). Though many discussions presuppose an audience of male monastics, the Buddha said that lay persons as well as women, both monastic and lay, could attain enlightenment (see Gowans 2003, chap. 14). In addition, the Buddhist exercises have a variety of functions. In part, they enable us to understand its philosophical outlook. In order to do this, we need to develop the appropriate cognitive abilities and ensure that they function properly by purifying the mind of various distorting factors. Most important, the purpose of many exercises is re-habituation: for example, replacing dispositions to greed and hatred with virtues such as generosity and compassion.

All forms of Buddhism emphasize the fundamental importance of wisdom (*paññā/prajñā*). This is centrally understanding that there are no selves or, in the Mahāyāna traditions, that all things are empty of an inherent nature. In part, this understanding requires intellectual inquiry: as we have seen, there are philosophical arguments in support of these positions.[38] However, much more than rational understanding is required to attain enlightenment. In Buddhism, awareness of no-self and emptiness through the meditative disciplines is also important, and often more important than intellectual understanding. It is commonly claimed that through these disciplines we come to directly experience everything as empty of selves and inherent natures rather than merely accepting these ideas as propositional truths. It is often suggested that wisdom is the culmination of the Buddhist path, however, it is sometimes stated that there is a reciprocal relationship between the different aspects. For example, morality helps us attain wisdom, but wisdom also promotes morality.

The Buddhist practices pertaining to morality are twofold. First, practitioners are to abstain from lying, killing, stealing, and sexual misconduct. In addition, the Eightfold Path includes a provision to earn our livelihood in a way that is consistent with these abstentions. Violations of these abstentions are thought to create psychological obstacles to understanding the Buddha's teaching (e.g., by encouraging belief in one's self and its overriding importance). Second, followers are encouraged to develop a set of moral virtues.

As we have seen, these include loving-kindness, compassion, gladness, and equanimity. In Mahāyāna Buddhism, the compassion of the Bodhisattva is emphasized, and the Six Perfections include generosity and forbearance. Development of these virtues requires habituation exercises in which followers train themselves to promote the happiness of others and to reduce their suffering.

Finally, a prominent feature of Buddhist training is a set of meditative disciplines. As a preliminary, in view of the difficulty of the path, we are told that practitioners need to strive to eliminate obstacles such as greed, hatred, laziness, and discouragement as well as to develop positive sources of motivational energy such as determination and persistence (called right effort in the Eightfold Path and vigor in the Six Perfections). According to Śāntideva, the "desire for what is good must be created" (BCA, 7.46). The meditative practices are sustained and enhanced by this orientation.

Two forms of meditation were first presented as the final steps of the Eightfold Path, and in various ways these are found in many later Buddhist traditions. For these practices, it is often assumed that, ideally, the meditator is seated in the lotus position in a secluded and quiet location. Right mindfulness is an array of contemplations of features of body, feeling, and mind as well as aspects of Buddhist teaching. The first of these includes the "mindfulness of breathing," frequently considered a foundation of other Buddhist meditative practices. Right concentration is a series of four progressively purified mental states (*jhānas/dhyānas*) culminating in "neither-pain-nor-pleasure and purity of mindfulness due to equanimity" (MN, 3.252). These two meditative practices are commonly related in this way: right concentration is seen as a form of serenity meditation (*samatha-bhāvanā*) that brings tranquility and purity to the mind, and with this as a foundation, right mindfulness is a kind of insight meditation (*vipassanā-bhāvanā*) that provides direct knowledge of Buddhist teaching.

It is often supposed that realizing experientially through meditation that there is no self enables a person to live in a selfless way that makes it possible to overcome hatred and other aversive states. According to Georges Dreyfus,

> When the meditator realizes selflessness, she loses her self-centered attitude and attachment to herself. This in turn leads to the abandonment of negative emotions such as attachment, hatred, and pride, which are all based on ignorance, that is, a self-grasping attitude. (Dreyfus 1995, 45; cf. Garfield 2017)

Hence, meditation is a crucial aspect of Buddhist moral development. In addition to serenity and insight forms of meditation, there are many other kinds of meditation in Buddhist traditions. As we have already seen in the divine abiding meditations, some of these directly develop a moral outlook.

Other examples of this approach are two meditative practices put forward by Śāntideva. The first, called "the equality of oneself and others," draws on aspects of the no-self teaching to encourage followers to be concerned with the suffering of others as much as with themselves (BCA, 8.90ff). On account of dependent origination, we are thought to be connected with one another and so to have reason to be concerned about one another. For Śāntideva,

> just as the body, with its many parts from division into hands and other limbs, should be protected as a single entity, so too should this entire world which is divided, but undivided in its nature to suffer and be happy. (BCA, 8.91)

On account of impermanence, since "the continuum of consciousness" is not real just "like an army" (in each case, there is nothing more than the parts), suffering has no owner and so should be eliminated wherever it is found. In the second meditation, practitioners are urged to practice "exchange of self and other," meaning they should generate compassion by imaginatively exchanging their own happiness for the suffering of others (BCA, 8.120ff).

In short, for Buddhism, it is possible to overcome aversive states such as hatred and anger, but only through an extensive array of practices involving wisdom, morality, and meditation over a long period of time. It is natural to wonder, however, whether these practices are actually effective in eliminating or reducing these aversive states. It might be argued that the fact that these Buddhist practices have endured for many centuries tells us that they must be effective. Yet traditions endure for all sorts of reasons (e.g., because people in power use them to sustain their position), and so longevity by itself does not carry much evidential weight.

In recent years, there has been considerable empirical study of some forms of Buddhist meditation by psychologists and others in related fields such as neuroscience. For example, there is now substantial evidence that meditation techniques that develop nonjudgmental mental attention (often called mindfulness meditation in psychological discussions) can enhance life-satisfaction and reduce stress and anxiety.[39] However, it is another question whether some form of Buddhist or Buddhist-inspired meditation could reduce our propensity for hate and anger and help develop loving-kindness and compassion. There have been some studies that suggest that compassion meditation rooted in Buddhist teaching does increase compassion.[40] However, most studies of this kind have limitations in terms of what they might teach us about the effects of traditional Buddhist practice: they commonly involve a small sample, instruction in some meditation practice without the context of overall Buddhist teaching, meditation practice during a relatively short interval, and a brief test of compassion shortly afterward. It is hard to know what such studies tell us about the effects of a lifelong Buddhist practice centered on wisdom, morality, and meditation as outlined earlier.

7. THE CHALLENGE FROM POLITICS

It might be argued that some political developments in the last century raise questions about the commitment of contemporary Buddhists to the traditional Buddhist approach to hatred. In some cases, this approach appears to be closely followed. For example, both Thich Nhat Hanh in his opposition to the American war in Vietnam and the Dalai Lama in his stance toward the occupation of Tibet by China have resisted hatred and violence as appropriate responses to oppression in a political context. However, there are also several prominent cases in which Buddhists have allied themselves with nationalist forces and sometimes supported violence against various political opponents in ways that might seem contrary to the Buddhist opposition to hatred and anger we have discussed so far. In some respects, nationalism may be a valuable form of group identity and it was often important in the opposition to colonialism. However, it is also obvious that nationalism can be a very destructive force. In this context, there is also a long and complex history in which Buddhists have interacted with political authorities and institutions in a variety of ways, for example, in some cases supporting them while in other cases being persecuted by them. Here it will suffice to note briefly three recent examples of Buddhist nationalism in the modern era (for background, see Harris 2012).

First, in *Zen at War*, Brian Daizen Victoria argued that many Zen Buddhists were eager supporters of Japanese militarism in the period from the Meiji Restoration in 1868 to the end of World War II in 1945. Though there are critiques of Victoria's work, his central claim is widely accepted. During this period, he showed, Zen Buddhists identified Buddhism with the Japanese nation in the person of the emperor and supported, on Zen grounds, Japan's expansionist wars against China and other countries. For example, the Zen soldier Sugimoto Gorō wrote that "the national polity of Japan and Buddhism are identical." Specifically, he said, "because of the non-existence of the self everything in the universe is a manifestation of the emperor," and he argued that the goal of Japan "should be the expansion of imperial power" (Victoria 2006, 122 and 117).[41] Though Buddhism is often thought to be committed to nonviolence, in this instance Buddhism and Japanese nationalism were united, and Buddhist justifications were offered for wars of aggression against other nations. On the face of it, this stance sharply contrasts with the Buddhist arguments against hatred and anger we have seen earlier.[42]

Second, in Sri Lanka during the 1983 to 2009 civil war between the majority Theravāda Buddhist Sinhalese population and the minority Hindu Tamil people, some Buddhist monks supported the government's suppression of the Tamil. Though others opposed this support, Buddhist involvement in politics has a long history in Sri Lanka. As Tessa Bartholomeusz has shown, in the *Mahavaṃsa*, a chronicle from the sixth-century CE written in Pāli, Sri Lanka is depicted as an "island of Dharma" that the Buddha declared to be a sacred Buddhist nation (Bartholomeusz 1999, 2002). In the modern era, this has been cited in support of the claim that Buddhism is an essential feature of the identity of Sri Lanka. Moreover, monks supporting the war appealed to the *Mahāvaṃsa* as offering a justification for the use of violence in defense of a Buddhist Sri Lanka. Bartholomeusz pointed out that in doing this they referred to versions of both the just cause and proportionality conditions of Western just war theories (Bartholomeusz 1999, 8–10).[43] Once again, in view of the rhetoric and violent actions of the government in the civil war, this outlook appears to be opposed to the Buddhist position we discussed earlier. Recall that the Buddha said that there should be no hostility or ill will even if wrongly attacked (*MN*, 1.129).

Finally, a similar phenomenon has developed in recent years in Myanmar (also known as Burma). The population of the country is predominantly Theravāda Buddhist, but many of these Buddhists see a significant threat to Buddhism in the minority Muslim population. In the past decade, this has led to the development of Buddhist nationalist movements such as 969, associated with the charismatic and virulent Buddhist monk U Wirathu and MaBaTha (Organization for the Protection of Race and Religion).[44] According to Matthew J. Walton and Susan Hayward, the originators of MaBaTha "see Burmese ethnic, racial, and national identity as bound up in Buddhism" (Walton and Hayward 2014, 14). Figures connected with these movements have employed charged anti-Muslim rhetoric, and some observers believe this has contributed to the Buddhist violence against Muslims. Though there are Burmese Buddhist critics of the nationalist movements, their supporters point to a long history of state defense of Buddhism in Myanmar (similar to Sri Lanka). From this perspective, the defense of Buddhism has been deemed preeminent despite the Buddhist values of loving-kindness and compassion.

Should these Buddhist nationalist movements modify our understanding of the Buddhist teaching on hatred? Or should these movements be criticized on account of that teaching? Part of the debate about Buddhist nationalism in Japan, Sri Lanka, and Myanmar concerns whether or not violence in defense of Buddhism could be justified. There is no simple answer to that question. However, even if it could in special cases, perhaps out of compassion for those who would benefit from the continuation of Buddhist teaching, the question would remain whether some form of hatred of groups perceived to threaten Buddhism could be warranted. The traditional teachings we have discussed suggest that it could not. From this perspective, the problem with aversive states such as hatred and anger is that they are forms of possessiveness or attachment that are sources of suffering and obstacles to enlightenment. Insofar as Buddhist nationalists encourage these aversions, they are problematic for this reason. All forms of possessiveness, including attachment to any group we may identify with—any collective self David Loy has aptly called a "wego"—are problematic (Loy 2009).

In the cases we have considered, religious identities have been blended together with national and political identities in ways that are common in the world and not altogether uncommon in Buddhist history.[45] From the standpoint of traditional Buddhist teaching, however, the pervasiveness of such identities and their capacity to generate destructive possessive attitudes is one sign of the depth of the problem human beings face. For this reason, the hatred that might be associated with Buddhist nationalist movements—and actions contrary to the values of loving-kindness and compassion it may promote—are not merely instances of hypocrisy, weakness, or misunderstanding. They are an indication of the substantial challenge to attaining enlightenment Buddhists may face (see Arnold and Turner 2018). Attachment to Buddhism itself has long been recognized as problematic, as much so as any form of attachment, and hence as an important issue for Buddhist self-cultivation philosophy.[46]

NOTES

1. For the idea of self-cultivation philosophy, see Gowans (2021).

2. See Royzman et al. (2005) and Sternberg and Sternberg (2008, chap. 2).

3. The languages of Indian Buddhism are Pāli and Sanskrit. Henceforth, when the spellings of key terms in these languages differ, the Pāli spelling is given first.

4. See Bodhi (2012) (hereafter *AN*), 3.63 (here and elsewhere standard systems of reference are employed).

5. Western discussions usually classify hatred as an emotion. However, emotion is not a category in traditional Buddhist discourse, though there is reference to many states that are considered emotions in these discussions (see Dreyfus 2001).

6. For a helpful comparative discussion of some different views, see Gereboff et al. (2009).

7. Ps. 45:7.

8. See Aquinas (1981, II-II 34).

9. See Cicero, *Tusculan Disputations*, 4.16 in Graver (2002). Cf. Graver (2007, 56). The Stoics did not think we should be free of all emotions: they believed the sage would have some "good emotions" (see 4.12–14). The Stoic outlook has had considerable influence in Western philosophy (see Sellars 2016).

10. Aristotle (1946, 1382a1–17). See also Jozef Müller, chapter 1 this volume.

11. See Bodhi 2000 (hereafter *SN*), 5.420–24.

12. Though greed and lust are obviously different, they tend to be referred to interchangeably in statements of the three roots of unwholesome states: they are prominent examples of driven, possessive desires. We will see that hatred is closely related to anger (*kohda/krodha*) in Buddhist thought.

13. Ñāṇamoli and Bodhi 1995 (hereafter *MN*), 1.47. In this context, the unwholesome is associated with moral faults such as killing, stealing, lying, and so on. Cf. *MN*, 1.91 and 1.489.

14. For the importance of fire in Buddhist thought, see Gombrich (2009, chap. 8).

15. Bodhi (2005, 366). The text is from the *Itivuttaka*. See also *SN*, 4.251 and *MN*, 1.75–122. The description is of an enlightened person who is still alive ("with residue remaining"). The Buddha had little to say about what happens to an *Arahant* after death except that there will be no more rebirths (for analysis of what he does say, see Gowans 2003, chap. 13).

16. Buddhaghosa 1999 (hereafter *Vism.*), 1.2. References are to chapter and section number.

17. Virtue (*sīla*) includes right speech, action, and livelihood; concentration (*samādhi*) includes right effort, mindfulness, and concentration; understanding (*paññā*) includes right view and intention.

18. See also *Vism.*, 4.87, 7.59, 12.63, 13.64, 22.11, 22.49, and 22.61.

19. Hells are possible stations in the cycle of rebirth.

20. A prominent Buddhist no-self argument is that, just as a chariot is only a collection of properly arranged parts, so a person is only a collection of properly arranged aggregates (see *Vism.*, 18.28).

21. Wallace relates the four divine abidings meditations in Buddhaghosa to a *samatha* (tranquility) meditation practice rooted in Tibetan Buddhism, an example of a syncretic approach common in contemporary Western approaches to Buddhism. For other discussions of Buddhaghosa on the divine abidings, see Aronson (1980), Heim (2017), and McRae (2018).

22. For an account of the Six Perfections, see Wright (2009).

23. See Śāntideva (1995) (hereafter *BCA*). References are to chapter and verse.

24. See Thupten Jinpa's Introduction to Dalai Lama (1997, xx). Cf. Thurman (2005, 30–1).

25. *BCA*, 6.22, using the translation in Dalai Lama (1997, 40).

26. Dalai Lama (1997, 1). For another contemporary defense of Śāntideva, see Thurman (2005).

27. Dalai Lama (1997, 10). In apparent deference to his understanding of English, the Dalai Lama allows that anger motivated by compassion may be good (see 7). However, the key Tibetan term, *zhe sdang*, corresponding to the Sanskrit *dveṣa*, which might be translated as hatred or anger, is always negative.

28. See *SN*, 3.66–8. For sympathetic analyses of the Buddhist no-self arguments, see Garfield (2015, chap. 4) and Siderits (2007, chap. 3). For critiques, see Ganeri (2012, chaps. 6–7).

29. See Seneca's "On Anger" in Seneca (2010).

30. *BCA*, 6.120. The medical analogy is very common in Buddhist discourse (see Gowans 2010, 2021).

31. Issues of responsibility, freedom, and determinism were not thematized in traditional Buddhist thought, though they have received considerable attention by philosophers in recent years (see Repetti 2017).

32. Though they understand it in somewhat different ways, Buddhists commonly distinguish ultimate truth, the way things really are (no-self, emptiness, etc.), and conventional truth, useful ways of speaking about the world (self, inherent nature, etc.). The distinction is often invoked to explain apparent inconsistencies.

33. In the case of anger, a partial exception is tantric practice (see Dalai Lama 1997, 7).

34. It might be thought that the doctrine of karma is a theory of cosmic justice or retribution according to which people get what they deserve. However, though in some contemporary presentations it may sound this way, this is not how it was traditionally understood. Rather, karma is an account of natural causal relationships: just as a plant flourishes with proper nutrition, water, light, and so on so a human being has a better life when performing morally wholesome actions. Hence, karma is explained with a biological metaphor: "Whatever sort of seed is sown, that is the sort of fruit one reaps; the doer of good reaps good; the doer of evil reaps evil" (*SN*, 1.227). It might be argued, however, that there is a sense in which karma meets the concerns of justice.

35. Hanh (2005, 95). For his approach to anger, see Hanh (2001).

36. Hanh (2005, 67). The context is a pirate's rape of a girl trying to escape Vietnam and her suicide afterward.

37. For example, some psychologists report that most people are happy (see Diener and Diener 1996).

38. Chan and Zen Buddhism might be regarded as exceptions in view of their anti-intellectual rhetoric. However, in my view, the relationship of Chan and Zen to philosophical reasoning is more complex than this rhetoric suggests.

39. See Keng et al. (2011). However, for cautions, see Van Dam et al. (2017).

40. For example, see Condon et al. (2013) and Weng et al. (2013). For analysis, see Gowans (2015, 204–6). For a helpful overview of approaches to studying the effects compassion meditation based on Buddhism, see Lavelle (2017).

41. Sugimoto was killed in combat in China. Victoria (2006) shows that his book was promoted by the prominent Zen master Yamazaki Ekijū.

42. Victoria argues that Buddhism is committed to nonviolence (see Victoria 2010). However, Buddhist positions on war and violence are more complex than this (for an overview, see Gowans 2015, chap. 13).

43. Though not killing is a standard Buddhist moral precept, there are some texts that suggest that killing is sometimes justified. However, there is no developed tradition of just war theory in Buddhism. Bartholomeusz claims that the *Mahāvaṃsa* nonetheless appeals to some common conditions of this theory.

44. 969 is a Buddhist numerological symbol for the "triple gems" of the Buddha, Dharma, and Sangha. In July 2013, U Wirathu was featured on the cover of *Time* magazine with the headline "The Face of Buddhist Terror."

45. On the blending of religious and national identities, see Corrigan (2008).

46. In the simile of the raft, we are told that the Buddha's teaching "is similar to a raft, being for the purpose of crossing over, not for the purpose of grasping" (*MN*, 1.135 and 1.261).

REFERENCES

Aquinas, Thomas. 1981. *Summa Theologica*. Translated by the Fathers of the English Dominican Province. Westminster, MD: Christian Classics.
Aristotle. 1946. *Rhetorica*. Translated by W. Rhys Roberts. In *The Works of Aristotle*, edited by W. D. Ross, vol. 11. Oxford: Clarendon Press.
Arnold, Dan and Alicia Turner. 2018. "Why Are We Surprised When Buddhists Are Violent?" *New York Times*, March 5, 2018. https://www.nytimes.com/2018/03/05/opinion/buddhists-violence-tolerance.html. Accessed March 7, 2021.
Aronson, Harvey B. 1980. *Love and Sympathy in Theravāda Buddhism*. Delhi: Motilal Banarsidass.
Bartholomeusz, Tessa. 1999. "In Defense of Dharma: Just-War Ideology in Buddhist Sri Lanka." *Journal of Buddhist Ethics* 6: 1–16.
Bartholomeusz, Tessa J. 2002. *In Defense of Dharma: Just-War Ideology in Buddhist Sri Lanka*. London: Routledge.
Bodhi, Bhikkhu, trans. 2000. *The Connected Discourses of the Buddha: A New Translation of the Saṃyutta Nikāya*. 2 vols. Boston: Wisdom Publications.
Bodhi, Bhikkhu, ed. 2005. *In the Buddha's Words: An Anthology of Discourses from the Pāli Canon*. Boston: Wisdom Publications.
Bodhi, Bhikkhu, trans. 2012. *The Numerical Discourses of the Buddha: A Translation of the Aṅguttara Nikāya*. Boston: Wisdom Publications.
Bommarito, Nicolas. 2011. "Bile and Bodhisattvas: Śāntideva on Justified Anger." *Journal of Buddhist Ethics* 18: 356–81.
Buddharakkhita, Acharya, trans. 1996. *The Dhammapada: The Buddha's Path of Wisdom*. 2nd ed. Kandy, Sri Lanka: Buddhist Publication Society.
Condon, Paul et al. 2013. "Meditation Increases Compassionate Responses to Suffering." *Psychological Science* 24: 2125–7.
Corrigan, John. 2008. "Religious Hatred." In *The Oxford Handbook of Religion and Emotion*, edited by John Corrigan, 333–45. New York: Oxford University Press.
Dalai Lama XIV. 1997. *Healing Anger: The Power of Patience from a Buddhist Perspective*. Ithaca: Snow Lion Publications.
Dalai Lama XIV. 1998a. "Human Rights and Universal Responsibility." In *Buddhism and Human Rights*, edited by Damien Keown, Charles S. Prebish, and Wayne R. Husted, xvii–xxi. Richmond Surry: Curzon.
Dalai Lama XIV. 1998b. "Humanity's Concern for Human Rights." In *Reflections on the Universal Declaration of Human Rights: A Fiftieth Anniversary Anthology*, edited by Barend van der Heijden and Bahia Tahzib-Lie, 101–6. The Hague: Martinus Nijhoff Publishers.
Diener, Ed and Carol Diener. 1996. "Most People are Happy." *Psychological Science* 7(3): 181–5.

Dreyfus, Georges. 1995. "Meditation as Ethical Activity." *Journal of Buddhist Ethics* 2: 28–54.

Dreyfus, George. 2001. "Is Compassion an Emotion: A Cross-Cultural Exploration." In *Visions of Compassion: Western Scientists and Tibetan Buddhists Examine Human Nature*, edited by Richard J. Davidson and Anne Harrington, 31–45. New York: Oxford University Press.

Ganeri, Jonardon. 2012. *The Self: Naturalism, Consciousness, and the First-Person Stance*. Oxford: Oxford University Press.

Garfield, Jay L. 2015. *Engaging Buddhism: Why It Matters to Philosophy*. Oxford: Oxford University Press.

Garfield, Jay L. 2017. "Mindfulness and Ethics: *Attention, Virtue, and Perfection*." In *A Mirror is for Reflection: Understanding Buddhist Ethics*, edited by Jake H. Davis, 203–22. New York: Oxford University Press.

Gereboff, Joel, Keith Green, Diana Fritz Cates, and Maria Heim. 2009. "The Nature of the Beast: Hatred in Cross-Traditional Religious and Philosophical Perspective." *Journal of the Society of Christian Ethics* 29(2): 175–205.

Gombrich, Richard. 2009. *What the Buddha Thought*. London: Equinox Publishing.

Gowans, Christopher W. 2003. *Philosophy of the Buddha*. London: Routledge.

Gowans, Christopher W. 2010. "Medical Analogies in Buddhist and Hellenistic Thought: Tranquility and Anger." In *Philosophy as Therapeia*, Royal Institute of Philosophy Supplement 66, edited by Clare Carlisle and Jonardon Ganeri, 11–33. Cambridge: Cambridge University Press.

Gowans, Christopher W. 2021. *Self-Cultivation Philosophies in Ancient India, Greece and China*. New York: Oxford University Press.

Graver, Margaret. 2002. *Cicero on the Emotions: Tusculan Disputations 3 and 4*. Translated and with Commentary by Margaret Graver. Chicago: University of Chicago Press.

Graver, Margaret R. 2007. *Stoicism and Emotion*. Chicago: University of Chicago Press.

Hanh, Thich Nhat. 2001. *Anger: Wisdom for Cooling the Flames*. New York: Riverhead Books.

Hanh, Thich Nhat. 2005. *Being Peace*. Berkeley: Parallax Press.

Harris, Ian. 2012. "Buddhism, Politics and Nationalism." In *Buddhism in the Modern World*, edited by David L. McMahan, 177–94. London: Routledge.

Heim, Maria. 2017. "Buddhaghosa on the Phenomenology of Love and Compassion." In *The Oxford Handbook of Indian Philosophy*, edited by Jonardon Ganeri, 171–89. New York: Oxford University Press.

Irvine, William B. 2006. *On Desire: Why We Want What We Want*. New York: Oxford University Press.

Keng, Shian-Ling, Moria J. Smoski, and Clive J. Robins. 2011. "Effects of Mindfulness on Psychological Health: A Review of Empirical Studies." *Clinical Psychology Review* 31(6): 1041–56.

Lavelle, Brooke D. 2017. "Compassion in Context: Tracing the Buddhist Roots of Secular, Compassion-Based Contemplative Programs." In *The Oxford Handbook of Compassion Science*, edited by Emma M. Seppälä et. al., 17–25. New York: Oxford University Press.

Loy, David. 2009. "The Suffering System." *Lion's Roar*, July 1, 2009. https://www.lionsroar.com/the-suffering-system/ Accessed Dec. 10, 2020.

McRae, Emily. 2018. "The Psychology of Moral Judgment and Perception in Indo-Tibetan Buddhist Ethics." In *The Oxford Handbook of Buddhist Ethics*, edited by Daniel Cozort and James Mark Shields, 335–58. Oxford: Oxford University Press.

Ñāṇamoli, Bhikkhu and Bhikkhu Bodhi, trans. and eds. 1995. *The Middle Length Discourses of the Buddha: A New Translation of the Majjhima Nikāya*. Boston: Wisdom Publications.

Repetti, Rick, ed. 2017. *Buddhist Perspectives on Free Will: Agentless Agency?* London: Routledge.

Royzman, Edward B., Clark McCauley, and Paul Rozin. 2005. "From Plato to Putnam: Four Ways to Think about Hate." In *The Psychology of Hate*, edited by Robert J. Sternberg, 3–35. Washington, DC: American Psychological Association.

Śāntideva. 1995. *Śāntideva: The Bodhicaryāvatāra*. Translated by Kate Crosby and Andrew Skilton. Oxford: Oxford University Press.

Sellars, John, ed. 2016. *The Routledge Handbook of the Stoic Tradition*. London: Routledge.

Seneca. 2010. *Anger, Mercy, Revenge*. Translated by Robert A. Kaster and Martha C. Nussbaum. Chicago: University of Chicago Press.

Siderits, Mark. 2007. *Buddhism as Philosophy: An Introduction*. Indianapolis: Hackett Publishing Company.

Sternberg, Robert J. and Karin Sternberg. 2008. *The Nature of Hate*. Cambridge: Cambridge University Press.

Strawson, P. F. 1974. "Freedom and Resentment." In *Freedom and Resentment*, 1–25. London: Methuen.

Thurman, Robert A. F. 2005. *Anger: The Seven Deadly Sins*. New York: Oxford University Press.

Van Dam, Nicholas T., et al. 2017. "Mind the Hype: A Critical Evaluation and Prescriptive Agenda for Research on Mindfulness and Meditation." *Perspectives on Psychological Science* 13(1): 36–61.

Victoria, Brian Daizen. 2006. *Zen at War*. 2nd ed. Lanham, MD: Rowman & Littlefield.

Victoria, Brian Daizen. 2010. "A Buddhological Critique of 'Soldier-Zen' in Wartime Japan." In *Buddhist Warfare*, edited by Michael K. Jerryson and Mark Juergensmeyer, 105–30. Oxford: Oxford University Press.

Wallace, B. Alan. 2010. *The Four Immeasurable: Practices to Open the Heart*. 3rd ed. Ithaca, NY: Snow Lion Publications.

Walton, Matthew J. and Susan Hayward. 2014. *Contrasting Buddhist Narratives: Democratization, Nationalism, and Communal Violence in Myanmar*. Honolulu: East-West Center.

Weng, Helen Y. et al. 2013. "Compassion Training Alters Altruism and Neural Responses to Suffering." *Psychological Science* 24: 1171–80.

Wright, Dale S. 2009. *The Six Perfections: Buddhism and the Cultivation of Character*. New York: Oxford University Press.

II

HATRED OF SELF AND OTHERS

Chapter 3

The Snares of Self-Hatred

Vida Yao

1. INTRODUCTION

In imagining self-hatred, we see a person turned in on herself. Her suffering seems driven by two seemingly antagonistic, but nonetheless complementary forces. From one angle we see a repeated pattern of self-directed hostility. From another we see, curiously, a *receptivity* to that hostility. Unimpeded, these movements together form a cyclical and dynamic progression difficult to resolve or subdue. As with certain other self-reflexive emotions, such as guilt and shame, our understanding of self-hatred may be aided by views of the mind which posit an internalized other whose perspective on oneself embodies and focuses a set of concerns and values, and whose perspective one is in some sense vulnerable to. To feel guilt for some transgression is not solely to feel the anger that one would feel toward another's trespasses, now directed back onto oneself as an object of that anger; it is at the same time to react to that anger—perhaps, for example, to accept it as deserved, or to welcome the lashing of one's bad conscience. To feel shame before oneself is not just to see oneself in some compromising way, it is to feel compromised by one's own gaze.

Likewise, the person who hates herself does not feel the hatred that she might have for another, simply taking herself as object of that attitude. She is not merely the seat of an internalized hostile voice and perspective that she may, for example, react to with indifference. She does not only tell herself that she is "worthless" but will typically *feel* herself so in response. And her suffering may not just result from pain she is inclined to *inflict*, but suffering that, in some sense, she is inclined *to suffer*. But how is this so? How, in self-hatred, does one become not only subject to, but *vulnerable* and even *receptive* to one's own hostility?

2. AUTHORITY AND VULNERABILITY

Begin with an account of self-hatred that has been inherited at least by our culture, if not by contemporary philosophers and psychologists, and which finds its sources in Freud. That self-hatred can impede one's hopes for happiness is obvious. What is less obvious, according to Freud, is that it is the price we pay for developing a superego, and thereby a moral conscience, at all. On this picture, the self-hating man is relentlessly cruel and abusive to himself, seeks out forms of self-punishment and self-sabotage, castigates himself for actions he has not in fact performed, and may even, as a "pale criminal," act in ways that affirm the persecutory stance of his own psyche (Freud 1916). This is because he is, though unaware of it, wracked by feelings of *guilt*—guilt which is, in part, a response to motives and impulses that he may be able to conceal from others, but which upon developing a superego, he cannot conceal from himself.

But Freud also sought to explain why one's hostility toward oneself will tend to be disproportionate, or seemingly wholly indifferent to whether or not one has in fact done, intended, or even merely entertained the thought of doing something that would warrant feelings of guilt. This is because, he suggests, the superego does not only serve as a seat of moral conscience, "keeping a watch over the actions and intentions of the ego and judging them . . . exercising a censorship" (Freud 1989, 136). It also redirects the energy of a set of hostile, aggressive, and destructive impulses, part of our shared natural endowment. One's mind must find release of this aggressive energy *somewhere*, and so, this explanation goes, one's superego redirects it back onto oneself, channeling this aggression through pangs of bad conscience.[1] Thus, we arrive at a proposal that promises to explain not only how and why self-hatred arises, but why it may be so ubiquitous, and why it can be so persistent, as well.

But suppose we take the seeming sources of self-hatred as genuine. What people seem to hate themselves for, again, does not seem limited to those things that would give rise to the feeling of guilt. This will often include nonmoral characteristics of one's *self*, including much that one could not be, in any sound sense, morally responsible for. Of course, one might insist that guilt is pernicious in just this way: it captures and holds in distortive construal a wide range of things that one would not, if only one were perhaps more clearheaded or well-disposed, feel guilty about. Survivor's guilt, and the guilt commonly experienced by victims of sexual assault, for example, may testify to this. But we might also consider that self-hatred, after all, may take different forms—and that at least one form would itself be distorted by thinking of it as a manifestation of guilt, even confusedly or pathologically experienced. We might also consider that while it may be a condition we become liable to upon becoming socialized, the social conditions that give rise to it and influence its content are more contingent than Freud allows. It is not just the constraints of society, at all, but the particular and concrete arrangements of a particular and concrete social reality that will influence and inform the manifestations of self-hatred that arise within it.

To illustrate the kind of self-hatred I have in mind, consider James Baldwin's 1964 novel, *Another Country*.[2] At the center of this novel is the unraveling and eventual self-destruction of Rufus Scott—a young Black man living in New York in the late 1950s. Once self-assured and full of life, we are introduced to a man who is a ghost of his former self. It is a lingering mystery to Rufus and his friends and family what has happened. While it is suggested, after his death, that Rufus was wracked with *guilt*—guilt felt in response to his brutal and violent treatment of his lover, Leona, a white woman from Georgia—this explanation, offered by a character who admits that he never cared much for Rufus, anyway, strikes one as both unimaginative and incomplete. There seems to have been some other force at work here, some other explanation for Rufus's self-hatred: one which explains his subsequent mistreatment of Leona and his subsequent guilt.

There are two other aspects of Rufus's self-hatred worth pausing on. The first is the quality of Rufus's suffering. In response to his own hostility he feels diminished, hopeless, and alone. He experiences a kind of psychic pain and anguish that he comes to believe will only be alleviated should he no longer exist at all. The second aspect is that Rufus's self-hatred seems to perpetuate itself, and persist, in spite of his love of Leona, as well as of his close friend, Vivaldo. It is repeatedly stressed that he loves them both, and they love him. But their reassurances are drowned out by his own self-loathing: the hostility he feels toward himself is too persistent, or powerful, to be lessened or diminished by their love. Their attempts to express their love for him only seem to *exacerbate* his hostility—both toward himself and toward them.

These two features of Rufus's suffering inform my focus and investigation here. But again, my central question, roughly stated, is how self-hatred manifests not only in hostility toward oneself, but in a certain kind of vulnerability to that hostility: how someone becomes, as Rufus becomes, susceptible to one's own venom. Because it isn't obvious that these two components of self-hatred could be understood as operating independently of one another, I will frame this investigation in light of another question that has arisen from contemporary philosophical engagement with Freud's views—a question that gives rise to what I will refer to as *the problem of authority*. The problem of authority arises given a Kantian approach to Freudian psychology and given a Kantian ambition of explaining how the superego, as the purported seat of moral conscience. The problem is how to plausibly explain how the superego gains *authority* over the ego. Beginning with this question will, I hope, serve as a way of seeing why the question I pose about self-hatred is an open one, to begin with.

The contemporary philosophers puzzled by the problem of authority have remarked on several striking parallels between Kant's view of moral motivation and Freud's discussion of the superego.[3] And Freud himself suggests that the superego *just is* the Kantian "moral law within us." For Kantian moral psychology, this is of significance because Freud's account of the superego seems to be a promising, and perhaps naturalized, account of the Kantian conception of moral conscience, and a Kantian conception of guilt. The superego bears the strictness and disciplinary qualities of this ideal. As a part of a more general moral-psychological view, Freud's proposal also seems to capture the idea that to violate a moral law one acts in *disobedience* to some governing authority within oneself, and typically because of some motive of self-gratification. And, importantly, in developing a superego, a person becomes disposed to subject himself to feelings of bad conscience which arise independently of concerns about having his transgressions witnessed or punished by *actual* others—a necessary condition for possessing a recognizably moral conscience, at all.

But the problem of authority arises once we see that mere *internalization* of an aggressive figure cannot adequately account for the disposition to feel *guilt* should we understand this emotion as also, necessarily, a response to a perceived violation of one's moral obligations, rather than as a kind of anxiety one feels in response to being *punished* for that violation. In a canonical piece of analytic-philosophical engagement with Freudian psychology, David H. Jones (1966) argues that Freud does not adequately distinguish between refraining from violating a moral duty because one fears the hostility of one's superego and refraining because one fears an external threat from an actual other. Thus, Jones concludes, Freud's views cannot accommodate genuine moral motivation nor a proper conception of guilt.

The problem, David Velleman argues, is that Freud does not give a plausible account of how the ego *views* the superego so that it is seen as a source of morally *authoritative* demands and punishments, rather than as a source of demands the subject might simply take a dismissive or defiant attitude toward, and threats he simply fears, "despite issuing from a part of himself" (Velleman 1999, 544, n. 35). We must account for how the ego, as Velleman puts it, "buys into" the superego's demands (1999, 563). According to Velleman's reconstruction of Freud, the ego "buys into" the superego's demands when it views the superego not just as an *internalized* source of demands and threats, but also as an *ideal figure* that it both loves and strives to emulate. But fear of the loss of the love of an internalized figure is, just like the fear of that figure's anger, not yet to grant that figure moral *authority*.[4] So, furthermore, Velleman attributes to the ego a capacity for normative judgment, exercised when the subject reflects on what ideals she ought to have. While her ego-ideal is originally shaped around her parental figures, as she develops and matures as an autonomous moral agent she must determine for herself what the content of this ideal should really be, thereby coming to act under laws, or according to demands or ideals, that she has given to herself.

My concern here is not with whether the problem of authority is successfully met by Velleman's proposal—or indeed, even whether it should be.[5] One might think, after all, that our moral emotions lie somewhere in between the crudest fears of being caught, punished, or exiled, and a response felt in violation of a law that one has given to oneself. Nonetheless, considering the form of the problem provides a path forward in considering what I can now label, in contrast to the problem of authority, *the problem of vulnerability*. First, as with the problem of authority, the problem of vulnerability arises in the course of attempting to understand a particular emotion—in this case, self-hatred—that, because of its self-reflexive nature, may be illuminated through the positing of an internalized other whose hostile perspective on oneself characterizes and partly constitutes the emotion in question. Second, as I'll argue, the problem of vulnerability also arises once we see that the mere *internalization* of some hostile figure is not sufficient to account for self-hatred, given that one is also in some sense *vulnerable* to that figure's hostile perspective. So third, the solution will involve positing a way in which the ego views, or relates to, the internalized other, so that the subject experiences that hostility in a way that will account for the vulnerability one experiences in self-hatred. And in particular, the solution I will offer—like Velleman's proposed solution to the problem of authority—will involve the ego viewing and experiencing the internalized other as an object of a certain kind of interpersonal *love*.

In order to see why mere internalization of a hostile figure is not sufficient to account for self-hatred, we must also see what kind of vulnerability we are attempting to account for. One might propose that if we can account for the vulnerability and receptivity to one's own hostility that one experiences in guilt, we will, *a fortiori*, be able to account for these features of self-hatred—assuming, as Freud suggests, that self-hatred just is a manifestation of guilt. But as I've suggested, this proposal seems incomplete. Again, most notably, self-hatred can stem not from a concern about what one has done or is inclined to do, but rather, in response to qualities or traits that one believes oneself to possess. And while one might hate oneself for traits one believes best explain why one has acted (or is disposed to act) in morally wrong ways, feeling what Jean Hampton (1990) calls "moral hatred" for oneself, it is just as familiar that one can hate oneself because of one's looks, one's lack of talent, or membership in a class or group of people—and not because one implicitly believes that one has a duty or obligation not to possess these qualities, or that one is morally responsible for having such qualities in the first place. The sources of self-hatred are wide in kind, particular to the person, and not reducible to considerations of what one perceives oneself obligated to eliminate or alter. In these respects, the sources of self-hatred resemble the sources of shame.

A further distinction between the vulnerability one experiences in guilt and the vulnerability that one experiences in self-hatred can be drawn if we were also to assume that in order to feel guilt of the kind that motivates the problem of authority, one must have acted in violation of a law that one has established for oneself autonomously. But self-hatred is often notably, and for some, maddeningly, heteronomous. Imagine, for example, a woman who has spent her life understanding and rejecting traditionally feminine norms of behavior and appearance for good reasons, but who nonetheless begins to hate herself for her thinning hair and sagging skin.[6]

In coming to hate oneself, then, one does not need to have granted any kind of *authority* to one's internalized other. However, one nonetheless views that other as possessing what I will call *epistemic*, *definitional*, and *evaluative* credibility about one's self. Imagine, for example, a man who has come to hate himself for his lack of ambition. First, in hating himself, he accepts the descriptive aspect of this self-assessment. Second, he does not simply hate his lack of ambition, understood as just one of his traits among others. He hates *himself* for his lack of ambition. And so, he accepts too, that this quality *defines* him: that his lack of ambition is of *central* significance to who he is. Hatred of oneself mirrors hatred of others in this respect: it tends to both globalize certain traits as defining the hated person and presents those traits as essential to the hated person's identity (see, for example, Fischer et al. 2018). And third, along with accepting this defining assessment of himself, he does not just view his lack of ambition as something he can accept dispassionately, with equanimity, or good humor: he is *wounded*, his emotional response is evidence that his being an unambitious person has a certain kind of evaluative significance for him.

But what kind of "evaluative significance" is this? One might suggest that it stems from the general vulnerability that we experience in light of the perceptions and judgments of other human beings—a respect in which we are not vulnerable to, for example, natural disasters or disease, even when such things frustrate our ends or ravage our bodies. As discussed by P. F. Strawson (1973), in being wronged by another, what we object to is not solely, or sometimes centrally, the material injury or harm that their action has brought about: we object to what that action suggests about how we are being *viewed* by the wrongdoer, and what we believe, or fear, it suggests about ourselves—hence our emotional reaction of resentment when we can presume that they, given what they have done, regard us without due respect or good will. As Jeffrie Murphy has put this point,

Most of us tend to care about what others (at least *some* others, some significant group whose good opinion we value) think about us—how much they think we matter. Our self-respect is *social* in at least this sense, and it is simply part of the human condition that we are weak and vulnerable in these ways. (Murphy and Hampton 1990, 25, emphasis in original)

But the weakness and vulnerability one experiences in self-hatred is in one respect narrower, and in another respect broader, than the kind that Strawson identifies and that Murphy and others have elaborated on. First, we are not in fact vulnerable to the views of *any hostile* human being. There are actual human beings who may be hostile toward us, who are full of ill will and who view us in negative ways, and who may express their hostility in cruel and aggressive manners—but to whom we may react with dispassionate reciprocated hostility, management, or even indifference. Consider, for example, Bernard Williams's discussion of Ajax's shame and suicide after his delusional slaughter of a flock of sheep:

[Ajax] could not go on living. . . . It was in virtue of the relations between what he expected of the world and what the world expects of a man who expects that of it. "The world" there is represented in him by an internalized other, and it is *not merely any other*; he would be as unimpressed by the contempt of some people as he would be led by the reassurances of others. (1993, 84–5, my emphasis)

Given that we are not emotionally vulnerable to the hostility of *any* other human perspective on ourselves, mere *internalization* of a hostile perspective is not enough to secure the kind of vulnerability to ourselves we experience in self-hatred. I might react to this internalized perspective just as I react to actual others whose views I am, as Williams puts it, "unimpressed" by. And we can spell out this lack of vulnerability along the lines I described earlier: I might not grant this voice epistemic credibility, disbelieving or easily dismissing what it says—for example, that I am a terrible singer, that I am overly cynical, or that I am too eager to please—as simply inaccurate. Or I might feel hatred for these qualities, but experience this in a localized, rather than globalized manner—hating some aspect of myself, without hating *myself* in light of that aspect, because I do not accept that it is something which defines who I am. Or I may even accept that I possess a certain trait or quality *and* that it defines me, but not experience this as having the kind of evaluative significance that seems necessary to experience both sides of self-hatred: it may not matter, in the relevant kind of way, for me to feel wounded or diminished, even though I see that it is true that I have this quality or trait, and that it defines me.

Second, while Strawson tends to emphasize attitudes that we can reasonably expect or demand from one another—a modicum of good will and respect, for example—our hopes for how some people view us will not be limited to what we can reasonably *demand* from them. Just as we can be wounded, hurt, and diminished by how certain others see us without presupposing that we can reasonably demand of them to see us any differently, the self-hating person's emotional vulnerability to his own hostility is not one that presupposes such a demand that he be seen by himself in certain ways rather than others. And when others fail to see us in ways that we may hope for or need, but which we do not think can be reasonably demanded, we may not feel *resentment* toward his own hostile perspective, but again, feelings of diminishment and anguish. (Though, for a plausible argument that resentment is in fact a form of anger that understands itself as unjustified, see Carlsson 2018.) A person who is able to convince himself that he doesn't *deserve* this hostility, and is thereby able to emotionally bolster himself against his own criticisms and protest their credibility, is already shoring up a *lack* of vulnerability one may need to mitigate one's self-loathing.[7]

Here then, is a restatement of the puzzle of vulnerability. In self-hatred, how does one view one's internalized other, so that one experiences this figure as having epistemic, definitional, and evaluative credibility, where that evaluative credibility is evinced by a person's suffering from feelings of diminishment and anguish in response to that other's hostility? When one "buys into" the hostile perspective that one has on oneself, one is not experiencing that perspective as simply the perspective of "any other," as Williams points out. So *how is* one experiencing it?

As I suggested, the answer to the problem of vulnerability I will propose stems from one more similarity it shares with the problem of authority. Their answers, I propose, both rely on another basic attitude to explain how the emotion under investigation develops: our *love* for others. On Freud's picture of the emergence of guilt, it is our love of our parents (understood in its most rudimentary form as a love for them given their responsiveness to our physiological needs), paired with our hostility toward them, that results in the emotional ambivalence that must be resolved through the development of the superego and thereby the disposition to feel guilt. For Velleman's Freud, the superego gains its authority over the ego partly through the love that one has for one's parental figures, which explains why they become the ego's first ego-*ideals*: a form of love that also develops from a recognition of their ability to respond to one's physiological neediness, but which, Velleman argues, is fundamentally responsive to their humanity, in the Kantian sense.[8] Following this lead, my answer to the problem of vulnerability will begin by first considering how and in what respects we are vulnerable, in general, to our loved ones. And upon isolating a particular *kind* of vulnerability to our loved ones that I will discuss here—one that arises from a kind of neediness for them not reducible to our physiological neediness nor reducible to our needs for respect—we will be able to see *why* we are vulnerable to ourselves in self-hatred, as well as why we are vulnerable in the specific ways that I have described.

3. LOVE AND THE RELATIONAL SELF

Interpersonal love renders us emotionally vulnerable to others, as well as susceptible to certain forms of hostility and pain. As Harry Frankfurt (1999) has argued, to love another is to will her well-being for her sake, and to experience her well-being as an extension of one's own; thus, one is liable to suffer when she suffers. As Martha Nussbaum (2001) emphasizes, to love another *human being* is to love a finite, vulnerable, and fundamentally *mortal* creature. Grief, then, we might think, is a necessary development of that love. As Monique Wonderly (2017) has recently discussed, developing the psychological views of John Bowlby, certain forms of love manifest themselves in *attachments* to our loved ones, and thus, we are left feeling less competent and confident in our agency when we are separated from them. And, of course, we tend to empathize, sympathize, and even sometimes emotionally identify with our loved ones; thus, their joys will be our joys, but so too, their pain and suffering will be ours as well.

Here I want to isolate one more way in which we are vulnerable to our loved ones. Begin with an observation by Herbert Morris. In a discussion of the various forms of suffering one may experience in feeling guilty, Morris discusses a case in which one wrongs not just a person who is a member of one's moral community, but who is also a person one loves. Alongside the pain of guilt, and the pains of empathy, sympathy, emotional identification, and separation, Morris describes a distinctive kind of pain that one may feel in recognition that one is responsible for the dissolution of a *union* that one was once party to. As he writes,

> To be cut off from what we love is intensely painful, and the pain involved in guilt resembles this. But there is more involved, for I have suggested that in union, best exemplified in love, *there is an intensely satisfying feeling of wholeness or completeness*. . . . In cutting oneself off from others one comes to see oneself as being cut off, not whole, *as if one had destroyed what one loved and thus also destroyed a part of oneself.* (Morris 1971, 426, my emphasis)

What explains this "intensely satisfying feeling of wholeness or completeness" in union? Why, in losing the union or the relationship necessary to sustain it, might one feel as though one has also "destroyed a part of oneself"?

These experiences can be captured and explained should we take seriously the idea that not only does our self-respect depend on the attitudes of at least some others, but (as philosophers who have argued that the self is essentially *relational* have discussed) our *identities*, too, are so vulnerable. The attitudes of our *loved ones*, in particular, play a central role in the formation and maintenance of our identities. Developmentally, it is within the context of intimate relationships that one receives the kind of interaction that will form one's most basic sense of self: one *learns* that one is an agent, and that one has needs that need to be met, and so on, through being recognized and responded to as an agent with such needs by one's early caregivers.[9] And it is also within intimate relationships that we continue to discover, develop, and maintain who we are: one's self-conceptions become richer, and more developed, in tandem with and in response to the conceptions that others have of oneself. One both becomes and discovers what kind of sister one is, for example, in relation to one's siblings, and as one discovers their conceptions of what kind of sister one is (see Lindemann 2014). Moreover, the kind of first-personal authority that we sometimes have in *defining* our self-conception (i.e., the qualities that we take to be central or essential to who we are) is one that we sometimes share; in particular, we share it with our intimates.[10] And—importantly for my argument here—it is within certain loving intimate relationships that one can sometimes experience the kind of attention that can discover, reveal, and partly constitute one's identity and personality. This attention, when provided by a loved one, will ideally partly crystallize and constitute our identities in ways that are consistent with both the truth about who we are, and our flourishing, more generally. As Amélie Rorty writes (writing pseudonymously, as Leila Tov-Ruach) of this relationship between love and attention,

> When the lover's attentions are active in forming and crystallizing the beloved's personality, the lover is also careful to attend to the real structure of that personality, not foisting or projecting an identity that, by becoming constitutive, will so conflict with the rest of the beloved's character that the person cannot flourish. (Tov-Ruach 1980, 468)

Because of the roles that our loved ones play in discovering, forming, and maintaining our identities, we can come to experience their perspectives on who we are as possessing the epistemic, definitional, and evaluative credibility I described earlier. Most straightforwardly, we may acknowledge that our loved ones know us best. They tend to be the people we experience as sometimes having definitional authority over ourselves—an authority that is typically reserved for us alone. They may attend to us in ways that can both reveal and crystallize our identities, leaving us with the immensely satisfying feeling of being "truly oneself" with and in the eyes of a loved one. And because we may not only love them but also long for their reciprocated love, we also care what they think about us, and how they view us; we can, along with having our identities partly constituted by how they see us, feel diminished and injured by their perceptions of us in ways that the perceptions and attitudes of others may not matter to us at all, let alone partly constitute us. And importantly, we may not want our loved ones to view us in solely positive ways, or with good will or respect. This is because, more fundamentally, we may want or need them to view us as beings who are *loveable* by them— "mattering" to them in just this relatively narrow sense.

Return now to Morris's reflections on the pain of wronging a loved one, and thereby losing or threatening one's union, or relationship with her. As Rorty writes, within such a relationship, it may become the case that "the person regards certain traits as centrally defining his personality and believes that he could not retain those traits outside of the particular attentional relation" (Tov-Ruach 1980, 468). Thus, this pain is not mere pain, but a response to the perceived loss of *wholeness* or *completeness* of one's identity. And it may not be *simply painful*, but also involve the disorientation, anxiety, and disassociation that results from one's losing a sense of who one is. That we are vulnerable to one another in this way is why acknowledging the perceptions and interpretations that others may have of us can come with an anxiety that may bear similarities to the anxiety felt in acknowledging our own biological deaths: we are not merely hurt, disappointed, or angry when others see us in certain ways, or when they do not attend to us at all. We may feel as though we are losing a centrally defining part of, and so sometimes entirely, ourselves.

4. FROM LOVE TO REMORSE, REMORSE TO SELF-HATRED

Given this particular kind of vulnerability to our loved ones, we can now return to the question of how our love of others may render us vulnerable to self-hatred in the ways I've described, and which I've suggested aren't best captured by thinking of the self-hating person as suffering from a guilty conscience. First, consider that love renders us susceptible to not only guilt, but *remorse*, which we become disposed to feel simply given our love of another, and given the possibility of being responsible for the damage or loss of the relationship that one shares with her. Unlike guilt, remorse need not be prompted by thoughts that one has violated a duty or obligation. Nor does it necessitate that one perceives oneself as *morally* responsible for what has happened. But importantly, as with guilt, remorse will presuppose *some* form of responsibility, and so, will implicate oneself, and thereby give rise to, and sustain, hostility redirected onto oneself as the party responsible for this damage, or loss.

The different sources of guilt and remorse account for differences in their phenomenology. On a Kantian conception of guilt, one feels both anger and anxiety, as a species of *fear*, at having violated an authoritative moral law. In feeling the worthy object of the anger of another, one may feel the pain of having taken something one has no right to, or of occupying a status that one does not deserve—one that that it would be justifiable for another to knock one down from. One may see in oneself a kind of self-conceit that calls for humbling, perhaps through the pain of deserved hard treatment.

Remorse, in contrast, is best understood as a form of *sorrow*, rather than as a form of fear. In remorse, one's attention may be focused more directly on the loved object that has been lost: in the cases relevant here, the beloved, her love, or one's relationship with her. If the union with her has been lost in a way where she has also suffered, one may keep returning to images of her, and her pain: as John Deigh (1996) suggests, a paradigmatic example of someone suffering from remorse is Vronsky, after the suicide of Anna Karenina. We see a man tormented not by the thought that he has violated a moral duty or obligation, but rather, by images of the person he loved, and whose suffering and ultimate death he perceives himself responsible, though not *morally* responsible, for. And given the role of our loved ones in maintaining our identities, one is again susceptible not just to the pains of separation from them (as well as the other forms of suffering mentioned above), but to the disorientation and disassociation of no longer being *oneself*.

To these extents, remorse is similar to another form of sorrow: grief. But unlike grief for a loved object that has been merely lost, remorse is felt when one perceives oneself as responsible for this loss. In remorse, the basic hostile responses that one would feel toward anyone who threatens or brings about the destruction of an object of one's love, one's relationship with the loved one, or the possibility of her love, can be redirected onto oneself as the responsible party (again, understanding "responsibility" here more broadly than "moral responsibility"). For example, consider the hostility and aggression that one might feel toward an actual other in jealousy. One perceives and feels that a rival has come to threaten an existing relationship of loving, mutual attention with a loved one, and feels hostile in response to the rival, even if she has not *done* anything to encourage the attention of one's beloved other than just being, for example, her lovely and charming self. One may nonetheless view the rival as *responsible* for threatening that relationship, even though one holds no (insane) moral expectation that she not be as lovely or charming as she is.

Consider now when it is oneself who is the responsible party. And consider too, when the reason why one can no longer sustain a union with the beloved, and her attention, has nothing to do with what one has *done*, but with what one is *like*. *Whatever* qualities one perceives as explaining why the beloved's attention has been lost or threatened can become the basis of one's hostility toward oneself: nonmoral aspects of one's character, one's physicality or style, background, race, or class-membership may become implicated in the explanation of the loss of this union, and so become the focus of one's hostility toward oneself. This is one reason why self-hatred can find its sources in such idiosyncratic aspects of the self, and why one can experience it as resulting from concerns that are only indirectly one's own. I may come to hate my lack of physical grace only once I imagine that it is why I can no longer capture my beloved's loving attention—just as I might hate a rival's beauty for being what I imagine does capture it, instead. And this hostility is liable to intensify into hatred precisely in cases where what is threatened or lost is not only the relationship one has with a loved one, but also, one's *own identity* insofar as that relationship was identity-conferring. Given that the threat posed by another, or oneself, is experienced as a threat to *who one* is, one's hostile feelings may intensify to the point where they may, as they do with the hatred of others, culminate in a desire to destroy or eliminate the hated object.

Characteristics of remorse, when it develops into self-hatred, can also explain the self-hating person's willingness to accept and absorb hostility—whether that is her own hostility, or the hostility of the loved one, and so why self-hatred is liable to self-perpetuation. First, one's own suffering can take on a particular symbolic meaning in the context of the dissolution of a loving union, when one still has hope that the union might be restored. As Morris writes,

> The satisfaction that one obtains in self-inflicted or accepted pain here comes from the very conduct as painful, for it is this that evidences . . . how much it means for one to restore. . . . Indeed, part of what it means to love another, as well as oneself, is not only pain felt when the loved object is hurt, but pain one is prepared to face for the loved one. Therefore, in a genuine restorative response there may be a satisfaction derived from restoring, a satisfaction derived from giving something to one for whom one cares, and a satisfaction derived from experiencing pain, for this makes apparent how deeply hurt one has been by the damage and how deeply committed one is to the relationship. (Morris 1971, 431)

While the pain that of may come to symbolize how much one cares for one's *moral* relations to be restored with others, one's will- ingness to pay back one's debts, or an acceptance of humility, Morris here distinguishes from these the pain that one is willing to undergo as proof of one's *love*.[11]

Second, another explanation becomes available in cases where one has lost hope that love will be returned or the relationship will be restored. In remorse felt because I have lost or can no longer maintain the beloved's *loving* attention, I may be motivated to retain *just* her attention, or what it has left in its wake. I may be willing to accept my (perhaps entirely) imagined (and perhaps exaggerated) perception that she has of me. At least, then, I will be able to retain *some* existence in her eyes, and thereby retain whatever aspect of my identity depended upon her, and her attention. Thus, *pace* Strawson, what we want from others cannot be limited to, or centered around, a desire that they have good will for us; *pace* Murphy, one may not solely, or most fundamentally, care for the "good opinion" or respect of another. When it comes to one's loved ones, what one may sometimes want is simply their *attention*, given how it may anchor and stabilize one's identity—even if that identity is one that they cannot also admire, respect, or love.

But importantly, self-hatred need not arise in the context of a failed relation to an *actual* other. Just as we don't need to be viewed by an *actual* other in a compromising way to feel shame, nor have our moral transgressions witnessed by an actual other in order to feel *guilt*, so we don't need to compromise a union with an *actual* other in order to feel self-hatred. Thus, we must return to questions about the various ways in which we relate to the *internalized* other. And in doing so, we can also begin to see—as we see with the self-hatred of Rufus Scott—how this other may come to drown out the voices of actual loved others who may actually love us.

To begin, consider Williams's remarks on the role of the internalized other in the experience of shame. He argues that we should not understand this other as reducible to an actual, identifiable other, nor are they identical to just my own voice and perspective. According to Williams, she embodies and focuses a real set of values and concerns that I am vulnerable to. I am vulnerable to her perspective of me given that I also respect her and hope for her respect. This provides us with the resources, he argues, to show how genuinely ethical motivation can emerge from sources that may initially seem too *immaturely* heteronomous to be ethical in nature, driving us, mistakenly, toward the Kantian picture of the autonomous moral agent instead. As he puts this point,

> It is a mistake . . . to suppose that there are only two options, that the other in ethical thought must be an identifiable individual or a representative of the neighbours, on the one hand, or else be nothing at all except an echo chamber for my solitary moral voice. . . . The internalized other is indeed abstracted and generalized and idealized, but he is potentially somebody rather than nobody, and somebody other than me. He can provide the focus of real social expectations, of how I shall live if I act in one way rather than another, of how my

actions and reactions will alter my relations in the world about me. (Williams 1993, 84)

Consider, next, that it is not (or not just) that I respect this internalized other and hope only for her reciprocated respect; nor do I aspire (or just aspire) to become like her. Another way in which I may relate to her is that she is an internalized figure of the kind of love that I have described, and whose reciprocated *love* I seek.[12] What she provides is not solely a focus of real social expectations and concerns, understood as a set of ethical or moral values. Rather, she also provides a focus of real expectations and concerns that determine whether or not a person is *lovable* by a hypothetical someone (an idealized, generalized someone) whose love I would seek. She is not, as Williams puts it, an identifiable actual other, but nor is she just *me*. *My* standards of the lovability of others will inform who this idealized and generalized person is, but it is *her* standards, or what I imagine them to be, that I am vulnerable to—not because I have in any way endorsed them, but simply because I hope for her love. But just as with ethical standards, both my own standards and the standards that the internalized other embodies and focuses will largely be informed by the culture and society that I am raised in, and I need not grant these standards any kind of *authority* in order to be emotionally vulnerable to them.

Again, one may want from this figure both identity-conferring attention *and* love, and in happy cases, these do not greatly diverge from one another. But now imagine a less happy case. I realize that I am some way that compromises not just the internalized other's respect or admiration of me, but her *love* of me. I will feel the particular wound, the particular *kind* of unworthiness, hopelessness, sorrow, and disorientation that one feels in not just being unloved by a *particular* and *actual* loved person, but as unlovable by anyone whose love I would care or need to have reciprocated. And my self-directed hostility will fixate on whatever it is I believe renders me unlovable to her: the idiosyncrasies of these qualities will depend on whatever standards of lovability have been embodied and focused by my internalized other.

To illustrate these points, consider how Pecola Breedlove in Toni Morrison's *The Bluest Eye* comes to hate herself for her darkness, which in the eyes of actual others marks her as "ugly." Given that the existing social standards of both the identity and lovability of girls and women heavily emphasize their physical appearance, she experiences her "ugliness" as both central to her identity, and as explaining why she is *unlovable*. She fixates on what she believes will make her beautiful, and thereby lovable, by those whose love she seeks: "the blue eyes of a white girl." And this is not just the love of *actual* others—she also sees herself as unlovable in the eyes of an idealized, generalized, and abstracted other, who, given that she is a child, is represented by her as an imaginary friend whose love and attention she longs for (Morrison, 203–4, emphasis in original):

> But suppose my eyes aren't blue enough?
> *Blue enough for what?*
> Blue enough for . . . I don't know. Blue enough for something. Blue enough . . . for you!
> *I'm not going to play with you anymore.*
> Oh. Don't leave me.
> *Yes. I am.*
> Why? Are you mad at me?
> *Yes.*
> Because my eyes aren't blue enough? Because I don't have the bluest eyes?
> *No. Because you're acting silly.*
> Don't go. Don't leave me. Will you come back if I get them?
> *Get what?*
> The bluest eyes. Will you come back then?

In my hopes to nonetheless achieve some sense that I am lovable by this internalized other, I may focus my energies on attempting to *become* so—sometimes with self-defeating and devastating results given that these standards will encompass much that a person simply cannot change about themselves, because they are often conceptually inconsistent or otherwise practically impossible to meet, or because they conflict with what would make for a good human life.[13] One will be drawing from, after all, the imperfect materials of the social world that one is in, including the content of the fantasies of that world.

But we may also imagine someone who has lost hope. I simply cannot become the kind of person who—in the eyes of my internalized other—is loveable. Perhaps all I can do is inspire her contempt, or disgust. I may nonetheless strive for her identity-conferring attention, given that it holds the promise of maintaining a sense of my identity both in relation to her and in her eyes. Given this need, I may become willing to bear and absorb the *unlovable* self-conception that I imagine she has of me: again, at least *someone* contemptible, or disgusting to her, rather than no one, at least in relation to her, at all. My self-directed hostility will fixate on whatever it is I believe renders me unlovable: aspects of my identity that I imagine have cost me her love, but which may hold the promise, at least, of her attention.

Of course, given that this identity is also one that one also hates—it is what one believes has rendered one unlovable, after all—this particular manifestation of self-hatred is liable to become unbearable: adherence to one's identity will not entail an adherence to life. Return, finally, to the self-hatred of Rufus Scott. Among other aspects of himself, Rufus's Blackness has become a source of his self-hatred. And it was his *love* for Leona which introduced in him a new kind of vulnerability that he had not, until then, experienced. In imagining how he is seen, now, as the Black lover of a white woman (abstracted and idealized), his identity as a Black man gains a new kind of evaluative significance: it has rendered him, in her eyes, and thereby in his eyes, unlovable. Spelled out with the resources that have been brought to bear, we can now see that his self-hatred persists partly because he cannot escape the eyes of this imagined, idealized and abstracted, internalized other whose love he longs for, but who he imagines cannot really love him, given his Blackness.[14] The gestures and expressions of the actual Leona who insists that she *does* love him, whatever they are intended to be, are now interpreted by Rufus through a lens: one partly constructed by his imagined identity in the eyes of this internalized other. It is not *love* that he then experiences her as expressing, but instead, a mix of condescension and sexual fetish:

> "She loves the colored folks so much . . . sometimes I just can't stand it. You know all that chick knows about me? The only thing she knows?" He put his hand on his sex, brutally, as though he would tear it out, and seemed pleased to see Vivaldo wince.[15]

Rufus is trapped by this self-conception, by his need to be both loved and seen by this internalized other in particular, and by his conviction that the person he is being seen *as* from that perspective cannot also be one that is loved by her. Neither, however, is he able to continue living as the unlovable object of his own hatred. Tortured, Rufus walks onto the George Washington Bridge:

> He stood at the center of the bridge and it was freezing cold. He raised his eyes to heaven. He thought, You bastard, you motherfucking bastard. Ain't I your baby, too? He began to cry. Something in Rufus which could not break shook him like a rag doll and splashed salt water all over his face and filled his throat and his nostrils with anguish. He knew the pain would never stop. He could never go down into the city again. He dropped his head as though someone had struck him and looked down at the water. It was cold and the water would be cold.

> He was black and the water was black.[16]

NOTES

1. As Freud writes, "Conscience arises through the suppression of an aggressive impulse, and . . . it is subsequently reinforced by suppressions of the same kind" (Freud 1989, 92). John Deigh (1996) argues that Freud's account of the emergence of

the superego in *Civilization and Its Discontents* is an alternative to his earlier account, according to which the superego develops as the resolution of the Oedipal complex. My aims in this paper are not exegetical, and I will largely assume Deigh's reading of Freud here. In *Mourning and Melancholia* (1915), Freud characterizes the self-hatred that is experienced by the "melancholic," which is also constituted by a person's redirection of hostility toward the lost loved object onto oneself, It's not obvious why the accusing role once that object has been internalized, and is also expressed as moral castigation of the self. The self-hatred I will explore here differs from this form, as well, for reasons similar to the ones I will focus on here.

2. I use this example to fix our attention. There are many different forms of what we could rightly call "self-hatred," perhaps understood most abstractly as some kind of persistent negative stance taken toward oneself, given some view that one has of oneself. It is not an ambition of mine to suggest that the kind of self-hatred under investigation here is the one true kind, or the only kind: just one genuine kind with ethical and political significance. I also proceed on the assumption that certain writers and artists, including Baldwin, successfully describe genuine human experiences which give rise to certain philosophical questions, and that Freud, as well as other psychoanalytic thinkers, are, as Richard Moran puts it, adding to the forms of understanding of our minds and others at the level of "folk psychology": "the hopes and fears, pains and experiences we relate to each other in daily life, and not states or processes defined either neurologically or computationally" (Moran 2001, 7). There are no doubt neurological explanations for aspects of hatred, as Berit Brogaard has recently explored, for example, the tendency for hatred to become all-consuming "correlates with an increase in norepinephrine and dopamine signaling in the brain's prefrontal cortex" which is the same thing that happens after "a big hit of methamphetamine or cocaine" (Brogaard 2020, 38). But this is not the level of explanation I am offering here.

3. Velleman (1999); Deigh (1996, 1999); Scheffler (1992); Longuenesse (2012).

4. John Deigh (1996) makes a similar point in criticizing John Rawls's account of how the sentiment of justice develops from love.

5. It is precisely the peculiarity of moral authority explicated along Kantian lines as either fully intelligible or necessary to recognizably moral life that Williams criticizes in *Shame and Necessity* (1993) and elsewhere.

6. Brogaard also discusses how certain psychic divisions are necessary to explain certain self-reflexive attitudes, such as self-blame. On her view, our conscience "plays the role of the cynical unfeeling judge, and the part of us that feels bad plays the role of the accused," and "the division of labor is one between reason and passion" (Brogaard 2020, 226). It's not obvious why, on Brogaard's view, the accusing role is identified with "reason" here, though perhaps an example that she discusses later may help. She considers the self-hatred of women who (rationally) *endorse* certain misogynistic standards about women, and who then hate themselves when they fail to live up to those standards. But my point is that no such endorsement is necessary—a woman can hate herself while rejecting these standards.

7. For discussion of how protest against how one is being seen by another, grounded in a demand or expectation to be seen differently, can defend against emotional vulnerability, see George Yancy's (2006) discussion of anger.

8. "What the child experiences in being loved by his parents, and what he responds to in loving them, is their capacity to anticipate and provide for his needs, often at the expense of their own interests. And this capacity of the parents is nothing other than their practical reason, or practical good sense, by which their immediate self-gratification is subordinated to rational requirements" (Velleman 1999, 556).

9. For discussion of the "intersubjective self," its reliance on relationships of mutual recognition with others, and its development out of the relationship between infant and mother, see Jessica Benjamin (1988).

10. For related discussion, see Elizabeth Spelman (1978). Spelman argues that there is a "maximal" sense of treating a person "as a person" that involves treating them in a way that takes into consideration their conception of themselves, as a necessary (but not indefeasible) constituent of their identity. She concludes that we should only expect a more minimal sense of treating a person "as a person" from non-intimates, given that our self-conceptions are aspects of ourselves that render us vulnerable, and which we are thereby inclined to keep private. I am suggesting that our intimates will be the ones most credibly suited to both take into consideration what we think about ourselves, as well as when and how we may be mistaken about this. Their credibility, along with their constitutive powers over our identities, is partly why we may become motivated to mask ourselves *especially* from our loved ones.

11. Another explanation, consistent with those that I offer is that a person, in fearing the perceived, likely hostility of an actual other, or an internalized other, will become motivated to *preemptively* experience that hostility, perhaps in the hopes of controlling how and when that hostility will be meted out. As Sandra Lee Bartky (1990, 89) observes (about certain rituals of self-induced shame), "An ordeal is often easier to endure if we can choose its time and place." Thank you to Francey Russell for raising this point.

12. Marking the significance of this distinction between a hope for respect and a hope for love, Wesley Yang remarks of being Asian in the United States that "it was always the most salient of all facts, the one most readily on display, the thing that was unspeakable precisely because it need never be spoken: that as the bearer of an Asian face in America, you paid some incremental penalty, never absolute, but always omnipresent, that meant that you were by default unlovable and unloved; that you were presumptively a nobody, a mute and servile figure, distinguishable above all by your total incapacity to threaten anyone; *that you were many laudable things that the world might respect and reward*, but that you were fundamentally powerless to affect anyone in a way that would make you either loved or feared" (Yang 2018, 9–10, my emphasis).

13. It may be a common experience that there will be no actual consistent standard here, or the standards will directly conflict with one another, or be impossible to achieve for other reasons. This will compound the difficulty one has in achieving a

sense that one is *wholly* lovable, as the internalized figure will love only in irreconcilable and impossible ways. Pecola is able to resolve this tension only through a delusional break from reality, in which she comes to believe that her eyes are in fact blue.

14. Of the general need for recognition, George Yancy writes,

> While I recognize the historical power of the white gaze, a perspective that carries the weight of white racist history and everyday encounters of spoken and unspoken anti-Black racism, I do not seek white recognition, that is, the [racist] white woman's recognition. Though I would prefer that she does not see me through the distorting Black imago, I am not dependent upon her recognition. For me to seek white recognition as a stimulus to a healthy sense of self-understanding is a form of pathology. (Yancy 2008, 847–8)

The possibilities, routes, and repercussions of weaning oneself off certain forms of recognition are beyond the scope of this paper, though a clear and obvious benefit would be to escape from the self-hatred it, or particular forms of it (such as the recognition embedded in interpersonal love), can feed.

15. Baldwin (1992, 114, original ellipsis); the subsequent passage is 1992, 144.

16. My thanks to Kate Nolfi, George Sher, Francey Russell, Steven Klein, Ulrika Carlsson, Jonathan Gingerich, and Ram Neta. I am especially grateful to Robert Smithson, Samuel Reis- Dennis, and Oded Na'aman for discussion and comments on earlier versions of this chapter. Special thanks are owed to Noell Birondo, for his encouragement, comments, and editorial acuity. I am also grateful for discussions at The University of British Columbia, The Institute of Philosophy of the University of London, Boston University, Claremont McKenna College, as well as to participants and discussants at the 2021 Pacific Division Meeting of the American Philosophical Association, especially to Melissa Yates, for her delivered comments.

REFERENCES

Baier, Annette. 1985. *Postures of the Mind: Essays on Mind and Morals*. Minneapolis: University of Minnesota Press.

Baldwin, James. 1992. *Another Country*. New York: Vintage.

Bartky, Sandra Lee. 1990. "Shame and Gender." In *Femininity and Domination: Studies in the Phenomenology of Oppression*, 83–98. New York: Routledge.

Benjamin, Jessica. 1988. *The Bonds of Love: Psychoanalysis, Feminism, and the Problem of Domination*. New York: Pantheon Books.

Brogaard, Berit. 2020. *Hatred: Understanding Our Most Dangerous Emotion*. New York: Oxford University Press.

Carlsson, Ulrika. 2018. "Tragedy and Resentment." *Mind* 127 (508): 1169–91.

Deigh, John. 1966. *The Sources of Moral Agency*. Cambridge: Cambridge University Press.

———. 1999. "All Kinds of Guilt." *Law and Philosophy* 18 (4): 313–25.

Fischer, Agneta, Eran Halperin, Daphna Canetti, and Alba Jasini. 2018. "Why We Hate." *Emotion Review* 10 (4): 309–20. Reprinted in this volume, chap. 7.

Frankfurt, Harry. 1999. "Autonomy, Necessity, and Love." In *Necessity, Volition, and Love*, 129–41. Cambridge: Cambridge University Press.
Freud, Sigmund. 1915. "Mourning and Melancholia." *The Standard Edition of the Complete Psychological Works of Sigmund Freud*, Vol. 14 (1914–1916), translated by James Strachey in collaboration with Anna Freud, first published 1957. London: Hogarth Press.
———. 1916. "Some Character-Types Met with in Psycho-Analytic Work." In *The Standard Edition of the Complete Psychological Works of Sigmund Freud*, Vol. 14 (1914–1916), translated by James Strachey in collaboration with Anna Freud, first published 1957. London: Hogarth Press.
———. 1989. *Civilization and Its Discontents*. Translated by James Strachey, W. W. Norton & Company.
Jones, David H. 1966. "Freud's Theory of Moral Conscience." *Philosophy* 41 (155): 34–57.
Lindemann, Hilde. 2014. *Holding and Letting Go: The Social Practice of Personal Identities*. New York: Oxford University Press.
Longuenesse, Béatrice. 2012. "Kant's 'I' in 'I ought to' and Freud's Superego." *Proceedings of the Aristotelian Society*, Supplementary Volume (86): 19–39.
Moran, Richard. 2001. *Authority and Estrangement: An Essay on Self-Knowledge*. Princeton: Princeton University Press.
Morris, Herbert. 1971. "Guilt and Suffering." *Philosophy East and West* 21 (4): 419–34.
Morrison, Toni. 1970. *The Bluest Eye*. London: Penguin.
Murphy, Jeffrie, and Jean Hampton. 1988. *Forgiveness and Mercy*. Cambridge: Cambridge University Press.
Nussbaum, Martha C. 2001. *Upheavals of Thought*. Cambridge: Cambridge University Press.
Scheffler, Samuel. 1992. *Human Morality*. New York: Oxford University Press.
Spelman, Elizabeth V. 1978. "On Treating Persons as Persons." *Ethics* 88 (2): 150–61.
Strawson, P. F. 1974. "Freedom and Resentment." In *Freedom and Resentment*, 1–25. London: Methuen.
Tov-Ruach, Leila [Amélie Oksenberg Rorty]. 1980. "Jealousy, Attention and Loss." In *Explaining Emotions*, edited by Amélie Oksenberg Rorty, 465–88. Berkeley: University of California Press.
Velleman, David. 1999. "A Rational Superego." *The Philosophical Review* 108 (4): 529–58.
Williams, Bernard. 1993. *Shame and Necessity*. Berkeley: University of California Press.
Wonderly, Monique. 2017. "Love and Attachment." *American Philosophical Quarterly* 54 (3): 235–50.
Yancy, George. 2008. "Elevators, Social Spaces and Racism: A Philosophical Analysis." *Philosophy and Social Criticism* 34 (8): 843–76.
Yang, Wesley. 2018. *The Souls of Yellow Folk*. W. W. Norton & Company.

Chapter 4

Misanthropy and the Hatred of Humanity

Ian James Kidd

1. INTRODUCTION

Hatred is often discussed in terms of *doctrines of hatred*, those expressing and endorsing attitudes or feelings of hatred against specific groups. Typical examples include misogyny, racism, anti-Semitism, and other invidious "phobias." Such doctrines have shared features: they target specific social, ethnic, or religious groups, for instance, and their wrongness is generally articulated in terms of discrimination, fairness, and other moral concepts central to modern liberal ethical and political theory. More obviously, those doctrines of hate are also clearly atrocious and indefensible.

Given these features, one could conclude *all* doctrines of hate would be ruled out of consideration as philosophically serious doctrines. In this chapter, I want to argue this is too quick because there may be some doctrines of hatred, albeit of broader scope, which can be regarded as worthy of serious philosophical consideration. Specifically, some doctrines of *misanthropy* might be promising candidate doctrines of hate with the requisite wider scope—namely, directed at humanity or human existence, rather than specific groups of humans. After all, "hatred of humankind" is a standard definition of that term, which is usually taken to involve attitudes of hate, contempt, and scornful condemnation directed at humanity at large. But, as we will see, this is not the only reasonable definition of "misanthropy."

Many literary misanthropes conform to this characterization. Consider Alceste, the title character of Molière's 1666 play, *Le misanthrope*, here in conversation with his friend—if that's the right term—Philinte:

PHILINTE: You say you loathe us all, without exception, and
There's not a single human being you can stand?
Can't you imagine any situation where—

ALCESTE: No. My disgust is general. I hate all men—
Hate some of them because they are an evil crew,
And others for condoning what the villains do,
Instead of treating them with loathing and contempt,
As they deserve

(Act I, Scene I, lines 115–22)

Alceste expresses his hateful scorn for "all men," which arises from a morally charged disgust at their commission or condonation of systematic acts of wickedness. Moreover, the hatred is universal and uncompromising: everyone appears to him as either "villain" or morally complicit coward. Obviously, Alceste excludes himself, since no one could accuse *him* of any cowardice, given the ardent, public, performative character of his misanthropy. Indeed, by the end of the play, the personal cost to him of enacting a misanthropic vision of life is made clear.

Actually, an often-overlooked feature of Molière's play is that its dramatis personae includes *two* misanthropes. The obvious one is Alceste, vocal and vociferous in his hate and contempt for his peers, and clearly the central character. The other misanthrope is the cool, quiescent Philinte—he, too, agrees that "all humanity is a disgrace," plagued with "vile corruption" and inveterate "wickedness" (Act V, Scene I, lines 1547–50). What distinguishes Alceste and Philinte are their distinct ways of enacting their misanthropy. Philinte's quiescence lets him combine moral disdain for others with limited but satisfying forms of sociality, while Alceste's fractious discontent causes him nothing but frustration, scorn, and, eventually, self-exile. If there are different ways to be a misanthrope, then hate might not be inevitable.

In this chapter, I argue we should resist claims about hate as an essential component of misanthropy. Instead, the truer picture is that there are a variety of misanthropic stances, only some of which are fairly characterizable in terms of hatred.

2. MISANTHROPY, HATRED, AND VIOLENCE

The claim that there can be many ways to be a misanthrope creates a clear role for moral philosophy: to provide guidance for those either developing misanthropic convictions or working out the proper ways to express them. Regrettably, there is little work on misanthropy by philosophers. A rare exception is the first chapter of Judith Shklar's book, *Ordinary Vices*. She distinguishes several kinds of misanthrope, including the "calm misanthrope," who sees us as inveterately awful, but nonetheless develops styles of guarded accommodation, such as Philinte or Michel de Montaigne. By contrast, a "violent misanthrope" is angry, hateful, and violent, like Alceste or Shakespeare's Timon of Athens. Shklar argues this is the "most extreme," "most dramatic" form of misanthropy—one which, left unchecked, mutates until it "envelops all mankind and even oneself" (Shklar 1984, 193, 194). This is what became the "dictionary definition" of misanthropy.

When not a merely inchoate attitude of derision, hateful misanthropy, as I will call it, tends to arise from profound frustration about the moral condition and conduct of human beings. This analysis of misanthropy owes to Socrates, who argues in *Phaedo* (89d3–e2) that it arises from consistently disappointed trust in the truthfulness and reliability of others. But Socrates adds that the misanthrope errs, by failing to recognize that "extremely good and bad people are both very few and [that] the majority lie in between" (*Phaedo* 89e7–90a2; see Jacquette 2014). This is a mistake because a misanthrope's condemnation is directed not at individuals, but at humanity or human existence as it has come to be.[1] Shklar affirms this by noting the global character of philosophical misanthropy, as when she dramatically declares that "most moral psychology of any worth is a scream of disgust" (Shklar 1984, 193).

Shklar focuses on the extreme forms of hateful misanthropy and three aspects of her analysis stand out when thinking about the connections between hate and misanthropy. To start with, we must clarify the *target of the hatred*. At its broadest, this can be human vices and failings tout court, although usually misanthropes are motivated by specific vices, those judged most reprehensible. Shklar notes that Shakespeare's Timon began his movement to misanthropy with "a hatred of vice; to be exact, of one vice—cruelty," the worst of them all (Shklar 1984, 217). Other misanthropes may focus on specific clusters of vices as manifested in certain broad areas of collective human life, like our systematically atrocious treatment of animals (see Cooper 2018; Kidd 2020a).

Second, specify the *scope of hatred*. A misanthrope could hate all humanity as an "evil crew," or be more circumspect, like Timon, who "hate[d] only his contemporaries and his own immediate world" (Shklar 1984, 194). Some misanthropy is historically situated, for good epistemic reasons. I may feel immense hatred for all humanity, even if my experience only reaches certain aspects of it. In other cases, the misanthrope may have a sense of the atrociousness of our *current* moral condition. Perhaps I think humans are awful compared to what they once were, perhaps in some prior state of moral excellence—as Christians might look back to our innocent state in the Garden of Eden, or as the classical Chinese looked back to our consummate moral performance during the dynasties of the ancient Sage Kings. Such retrospective misanthropes differ from the prospective misanthropes, who judge our current condition negatively in contrast to what we will or may become in some imagined or anticipated future, transformed state.[2]

The final feature of Shklar's analysis is the insistence on its epistemic value of hateful misanthropy. What the misanthrope says about humanity may not be cheerful or flattering, but that is no sign of its falsity. Shklar argues that misanthropy "often impels one to reveal much that would otherwise remain hidden," manifesting a "passionate honesty" (Shklar 1984, 194, 203). This alethic argument for misanthropy adds depth to what might otherwise seem a gloomy counsel of despair or a perverse exultation in our entrenched moral crapulence.

Shklar's account of hateful misanthropy is importantly different from the doctrines of hate central to modern moral discourse, such as misogyny. The title of her book, *Ordinary Vices*, makes clear her use of the framework of what we might call *vice ethics*. This is a style of character ethics which frontloads our vices and failings, rather than our excellences and virtues. Historically, character ethics has been reduced to virtue ethics, to the point of presenting virtue ethics as the sole dimension of the ethics of character. Indeed, neglect of misanthropy is surely of a piece with the wider neglect of philosophical reflection on our vices and failings, not to mention related concepts like corruption and wickedness (some honorable exceptions include Midgley 1984 and Taylor 2006).

Hateful misanthropy is problematic, argues Shklar, on three related counts. First, it is liable to mutate into "an unlimited hatred," quickly developing from some specific legitimate frustration with this or that person or group into an indiscriminate "diffuse contempt" (Shklar 1984, 217). Second, hateful misanthropy exacts severe emotional, psychological, or existential costs, corrupting our comportment toward other people and the wider social world. Shklar warns it tends to "make us miserable and friendless, reduce us to spiritual nausea, and deprive us of all pleasures except invective" (Shklar 1984, 192). It can reflect and reinforce a certain vicious pleasure—a sort of schadenfreude—where one experiences "a certain satisfaction in the unending spectacle of human depravity" (Shklar 1984, 212). The allure of a misanthropic vision of human life is very hard to articulate, but surely includes the morally murky pleasures some gain from provocation, perversity, and hate.

Shklar's final worry plays on the connections she sees between hate, misanthropy, and violence. Adoption of a hateful stance on humanity, if fueled rather than tempered, can "inspire and justify active violence against a detestable and corrupt humanity," even to the point of motivating large-scale "projects of violence" (Shklar 1984, 217). Hatred of the current forms of human existence is initially emotionally and morally self-destructive, then ultimately a source of acts of violence. Indeed, an irony of hateful misanthropy is that one comes to be what one hates. Bernard Williams warned that what starts as a morally sincere hatred of human failings mutates into a "desolating misanthropy which can itself be a source of cruelty," a dark stance on our moral condition which has the power to "destroy almost any virtue" (Williams 1985, 6). Hateful misanthropy puts one at risk of becoming an exemplar of the vices and failings which they hate, unless they maintain those calmer, cooler forms of misanthropy modeled for us by Montaigne and Philinte.

This potentially self-condemnatory tendency of hateful misanthropy exposes the error of Andrew Gibson's bold claim that misanthropy is an "impossible doctrine," since in practice it entails a "profound self-hatred." His argument is that the misanthropes, haters of humanity, are themselves a member of humanity, and therefore must hate themselves, too—something he claims "impossible," a "fundamental contradiction" (Gibson 2012, 2–3). Unfortunately, there is nothing "impossible" or "contradictory" about self-hatred. It's not only possible in principle, but common in practice. By denying this, Gibson occludes the self-condemnatory tendencies that are integral to the moral psychology of hateful misanthropy.

It is sensible and proper, of course, to worry about the bad effects of internalization of hateful misanthropy. Among other dangers, it can create or intensify one's vulnerability to the corrupting and self-destructive tendencies that worry Shklar, Williams, and others. It is also right to worry that misanthropy could feed social isolation, dispositions to violence, and other worrisome attitudes. But the movement from misanthropy to hate to violence focused on by Shklar and Williams is neither automatic nor guaranteed. Consider, first, the fact that, if misanthropy is an attitude toward something collective—humanity or human forms of life—then it does not distribute over individuals. Therefore, acts of violence directed against individuals would not be justified by a misanthropic vision. Jonathan Swift declared that, "principally, I hate and detest that animal called man, although I heartily love John, Peter, Thomas, and so forth," since "all my love is toward individuals" (1843, ii. 579). If so, there are no automatic grounds for translating a general condemnatory attitude toward humanity into a practical policy of violence aimed at individuals.

Second, misanthropy does not automatically connect to hate and violence because an individual misanthropy may have other commitments that act to block or moderate a drift into hateful, self-loathing misanthropy. Since Philinte did not share Alceste's fate, there was clearly something in place that helped ensure the cooler character of his misanthropy. Such moderating influences may include ethical and religious convictions—a sense of the dignity of the person, say, or an undimmable religious confidence in the moral rectifiability of humankind. Other causes may be more prosaic—Philinte's gentle misanthropy seems to be a product of hedonism and pragmatism: if people are awful, then try to avoid the worst of us, as much and as far as possible, and try to keep careful company with the rest. Presumably this is why Shklar speaks of degrees of more or less "dramatic," "extreme" misanthropy and distinguishes its cooler forms from those which are hotter and more hateful.

A third reason the connections between misanthropy, hate, and violence are more complex and contingent is that misanthropy is rarely, if ever, rooted in some single feeling or emotion, such as contempt or hatred. It has many sources—a whole dynamic assemblage of moods, feelings, emotions, experiences, reflections, structures of expectations and worries, background cultural and contextual sensibilities, and so on. Wittgenstein once said that "life can educate you into 'believing in God,'" that certain experiences, thoughts, and "sufferings of various sorts" can "force this concept" onto us (1998, 97). I think something like this is also true of misanthropy. It is not some set of propositions, coldly accepted, but a charged way of apprehending and responding to the particular ways that human existence has come to be. If so, we should adopt a pluralist and dynamic conception of misanthropy as a broad, negative appraisal of humankind that can be articulated and expressed through a variety of stances. Only some are fed and driven by hatred and related negative effects and liable to manifest in enthusiasm for "projects of violence." To develop this claim, we need a systematic account of misanthropy, for which we can turn to Immanuel Kant and Arthur Schopenhauer.

3. KANT AND SCHOPENHAUER

Kant noted a double connection between misanthropy and hatred: a misanthropic vision of human life can arise from an increasing hatred of our atrocious moral conduct, which in turn can inspire potent attitudes of hatred toward humanity and its ways of living. This denies or ignores the importance of *humanitas*—"the cultivation of *humanity* as such," "the first duty of man towards himself" (LE 27: 671)—which for Kant makes misanthropy "a hateful thing" (LE 27: 672).[3] This concern echoes throughout his remarks on misanthropy, scattered throughout his lectures on ethics and anthropology, as recorded by his students, and his writings on the theme of religion, especially *Religion within the Boundaries of Mere Reason*.

Kant's interest in misanthropy is part of a wider moral pessimism about humanity, the conviction that human beings are "not particularly loveable," owing to our propensities to self-love and an inextirpable "radical evil." Patrick Frierson is right that "Kant's view of the human species is not particularly happy," even if it "orients us to real moral threats and thereby makes both moral philosophy and moral reform more relevant to actual conditions of human life" (Frierson 2010, 55). He criticizes misanthropy, though, arguing that "what is worthy of respect is *not* perfect virtue, but the *capacity* for virtue," which even the worst of us possess (Frierson 2010, 53). Granted, "respect," here, has the specific sense of the respect appropriate to any rational being, endowed with moral capacities. Of course, one wants those capacities to be exercised and cultivated as well as possessed, which may be what Kant had in mind when he described the arduousness of the moral life as a "conversion," "the putting off of the old man and the putting on of the new" (R 6: 74). In a nice phrase, pursuit of the moral life means we must become "*other* people and not merely better people" (SF 7: 54, my emphasis). Such conversion and transformation is difficult, prolonged, and painful—a point exploited by the misanthrope as a confirmation of their claim that goodness and virtue are not possible for creatures constituted as we are. To escape our moral awfulness, we must become something very different. This is a pessimism also expressed in Kant's anthropological writings, such as his talk of the "crooked timber of mankind," of which, according to his famous line, nothing can be made straight.

An obvious influence for Kant's pessimistic misanthropy is Rousseau's vivid critique of the morally corrupting effects of the institutions and imperatives of "civilized" life, such as private property, which scaffold vices such as jealousy, greed, and our fundamental source of wickedness, amour propre. "Everything degenerates in the hands of man," as the Savoyard Vicar gloomily lamented in *Emile*, while "man's breath is deadly to his kind" (1969, 322, 277). Whatever the original moral constitution of "natural man," the complexity and artificiality of the contemporary forms of life constitutive of "civilized man" afford means and motives for vicious, wicked conduct on the large scale. As Ernst Cassirer argued, a legacy of Rousseau to Kant was a conviction that certain invidious forms of evil tend to arise uniquely within forms of "civilized" human life, especially vices of duplicity, falseness, and self-regard (Cassirer 1945).

Kant's conception of misanthropy is not systematically stated, but its general form is clear enough from the lectures on ethics and anthropology. Misanthropy involves a complex of feelings and judgments, inspired by prolonged experience of the abundant moral failings of human beings. In his lectures on ethics, Kant offers a two-stage account of misanthropy. First, one becomes aware of the "long, sad experience" of human vices and failings, such as "ingratitude, injustice," "disloyalty [and] misuse of integrity" (LE 27: 671–2ff). Elsewhere, the indicative charge-list of human failings is extended—"jealousy, mistrust, violence," and "propensity for enmity against those outside the family" (LA-Friedlander 25: 679) to the "long melancholy litany of charges against humankind" offered in *Religion within the Boundaries of Mere Reason*: these include the "secret falsity even in the most intimate friendships ... the remark that 'in the misfortunes of our best friends there is something that does not altogether displease us'" (R 6: 33, the latter remark quoting the Duc de La Rochefoucauld's *Maxims and Reflections*, I.99).

Such catalogues of human vices and failings do not, by themselves, though, establish a misanthropic verdict. Someone with a rosier vision of humanity can agree on the reality of our vices, but deny they are pervasive or characteristic of human life in the way which would then justify condemnation of *humankind*, rather than just particular individuals and groups. A sanguine moral optimist could insist our moral failings are genuine, but still only occasional, irregular blemishes on the otherwise attractive moral character of humanity.

Anticipating this objection, the second stage of Kant's account of misanthropy is the insistence that our failings must be *ubiquitous*, *entrenched*, and *pronounced* features of human life. Consistent with their condemnation of humanity, the misanthrope sees our vices and failings as deeply built into the structures of human life as it has come to be—not as localized, superficial, or recessive aspects that occasionally come into view. Indeed, a misanthrope will maintain that our vices and failings are so entrenched within the projects and projects of human life that they are distinctive and constitutive of human life as it has come to be (see Cooper 2018, ch.1). As Kant's observes, we do not need to look hard or look long to find examples of human vice: even cursory reflection on human life reveals "the multitude of woeful examples that the experience of human deeds parades before us" (R 6: 32-3). Across all the different departments of human life, "envy, tyranny, greed, and the malignant inclinations surround" us, openly displayed, often proudly and publicly (R 6: 93-94). Some vices are hidden or camouflaged, whether out of shame, guilt, or self-interest. Others, though, are openly displayed as objects of acclaim. One mark of a corrupted society is a culture of tolerance for blatant, unabashed displays of one's vices and failings—of naked self-interest, say, or brazen acts of duplicity.

Misanthropy emerges, from Kant's writings, as systematic, negative moral evaluation of humankind. Affectively charged awareness of our failings starts processes of reflection that, over time, reveals to us the facts of their ubiquity and entrenchment, something we may previously have ignored or denied. So far, though, none of this automatically connects misanthropy with hatred and other "hot" affects, such as contempt. After all, Kant mentions "woe," a "cold" affect related more to anguish and sadness (R 6: 32), which points to a style of mournful misanthropy modeled by Heraclitus, the "weeping philosopher." Moreover, many of the examples offered by Kant, such as disloyalty, can evoke a range of affective responses—bitterness and disappointment, say, rather than anger or hatred. If so, misanthropy needs more before it takes the form of a hatred of humankind.

The connection of misanthropy to hatred for humankind becomes stronger in writings by Schopenhauer, whose philosophy manifests "a decidedly negative attitude toward life," for which Frederick Beiser claims we have "no other word . . . than 'pessimism'" (2016, 46). But there is another word—*misanthropy*—which in the Schopenhauer scholarship is frequently conflated with pessimism (see, for instance, Dienstag 2009, 83 and C. Taylor 1992, 442). The relationship of the two concepts is explained by David E. Cooper:

> [The pessimist and the misanthrope agree on] negative assessment of the human condition, but their respective emphases are different. The pessimist's focus is on aspects of this condition—suffering, frustration, absurdity—that are destructive of the possibility of happiness. The misanthrope's concern, by contrast, is with human failings, ingredients of life for which humankind is answerable and rightly held to account. (Cooper 2018, 4–5)

Schopenhauer is a philosophical pessimist and a misanthrope, attuned to the negative existential and moral character of our existence. He argues an acute perception of humanity as "a den of thieves" creates "a melancholy mood." If that mood is stirred by new experiences and reflections, and so "persists, then misanthropy arises" (TFP 205).[4] Consistent with Kant, the misanthrope sees our failings as constitutive of our current forms of existence, but there are two novel components added by Schopenhauer. First, the range of kinds of human failings is considerably expanded—"vices, failings, weaknesses, foolishness, shortcomings, and imperfections of all sorts" (TFP 205). Although the moral vices, such as cruelty, may seem primary, there is a whole array of aesthetic, affective, epistemic, psychological, and interpersonal failings to which a misanthrope ought to be alert. Schopenhauer mentions "frequent and relentlessly evil gossip"; "outbreaks of anger"; deep-seated grudges and coils of resentment, "compressed as hate long-preserved through inner brooding"; and "inevitable collisions of egoism" (TFP 205).

A second novel feature of Schopenhauer's account of misanthropy is emphasis on what we can call *auxiliary aspects* of our vices and failings. These are specific aspects of our failings, attention to which amplifies and protects the critical condemnation issued by the misanthrope. Consider, for instance, our systematic tendencies to conceal or deny certain of our vices and failings—the ways, says Schopenhauer, that "prudence and patience . . . do not allow us to see how universal is [this] mutual ill-will" (TFP 204–205). Our perspective on our collective moral character is self-servingly distorting, in all sorts of ways. For instance, some vices are self-concealing, like arrogance, while awareness of others is suppressed for the sake of our daily business. Schopenhauer could have added that the very fact that occlusion of our failings is "prudent" attests to the awfulness of our condition—the truth about us is too awful to confront, as, perhaps, is the deeper truth of our world, the product of an inexorable cosmic will (see, for instance, WWR 4: §57).

A second auxiliary aspect of many of our vices is variations in their frequency, which Schopenhauer invokes when referring to "the boundless egoism of everyone, the malice of most, the cruelty of many" (TFP 200). Some of our failings are universal, while others are more characteristic of certain groups or individuals, perhaps those especially susceptible to certain temptations and corrupting conditions. By emphasizing the variegated patterns in our failings, Schopenhauer guards against a tendency to presuppose their relative rarity. Some may think that cruelty, for instance, is confined only to extreme people or conditions—psychopaths or moral monsters or those living under conditions of violence. Schopenhauer therefore directs our attention to more continuous patterns of subtler forms of human failing, alongside the more overt sorts exposed by Kant's emphasis on the "woeful examples" that "parade" before us.

Schopenhauer's exposure of active efforts by people to self-servingly ignore or occlude their vices and failings offers an argument for hateful misanthropy, although not one which to my knowledge is made explicit in his writings. Humanity is characterized by a whole tangled array of vices and failings that are "frequent," "relentless," and "universal"—so far, the same as Kant. Yet few people are trying to overcome these failings. Quite the contrary, those self-serving patterns of denial, concealment, and occlusion are constantly active, thereby propagating the awfulness of our condition. Writing in *Parerga and Paralipomena*, Schopenhauer remarks that a "genius" faces a painful choice—"of recognising truth but then of pleasing no one," or, instead, "teaching the false with encouragement and approbation" (PP 1: 135–36). Choosing the ardent affirmation of truth, on this view, incurs serious costs—one will be "secluded," "killed by silence"—but achieves a certain existential nobility. By tolerating our awfulness and turning away from the truth, we make ourselves legitimate objects of hate. It is not as if we are bad but trying to get better by ardently working to identify and overcome our failings—quite the opposite.

Kant and Schopenhauer offer a useful framework for conceptualizing misanthropy as a negative critical verdict of humanity or human existence, motivated by reflective awareness that it is suffused with a variety of failings that are ubiquitous, entrenched, and pronounced. Clearly, though, misanthropy thus construed can be expressed in many different ways, not all of which rely on hateful feelings or moods. Granted, there can be hateful misanthropes, enraged at their entrapment within a "den of thieves," of vicious people self-deceiving about their awfulness. But other, gentler possibilities are available. By considering some of them, a properly pluralistic sense of misanthropy comes into view.

4. ENEMIES AND FUGITIVES

Kant recognized that only some forms of misanthropy are built on hatred. He distinguishes two main forms of *misanthropic stances*, ways of living out an internalized misanthropic vision of human life, an integrated set of affective, evaluative, and practical components. A stance consists of a structure of emotions, moods, feelings coupled to cognitive components like appraisals, judgments, and patterns of argument and thinking. All these come together in styles of comportment, expressing those dynamically related affective and cognitive components. Hatred can drive violence, for instance, while colder affects, such as sadness or resignation, may lead to determined self-seclusion. We should therefore reject claims that misanthropy *inevitably* involves hatred and leads to violence: the variety of stances, differing according to their components, ensure only *some* point in the direction of hate, rage, and violence. When we reject that claim, and go looking, what we find are "so many variations that it is impossible to imagine a complete catalogue of misanthropic characters" (Shklar 1984, 194).

Kant's lectures on ethics describe two stances, the "enemy of mankind," also called the "positive misanthrope," and the "fugitive from mankind," or "negative misanthrope." The Enemy is characterized by enmity, a combination of dislike and ill will; their affective profile is dominated by hatred—not localized, like Timon's, but universal, aimed at the entirety of humankind (LE 26: 432). Kant describes them as having "the purpose and will to destroy the welfare of others," something he judges "hateful," since it involves "a declared disposition to do something harmful to the other" (LE 27: 672, 431). The Fugitive stance differs affectively and practically. The Fugitive misanthrope is "a recluse, who distances himself from all men"—he or she "apprehends harm from everyone," meaning they are governed by anxiety, fear, and uncertainty (LE 27: 672). In practice, a Fugitive may literally flee from society, retreating to some isolated place—an uninhabited island or lonely region—although usually their flight is primarily psychological and existential, a structured disengagement from the human world.

What distinguishes the Fugitive from the "virtuous solitary," described at the end of section 29 of the third *Critique*, is their stance of "principled solitude," or what Joseph Trullinger calls "a kind of salutary self-isolation," anchored in a "philanthropic spirit" (Trullinger 2015, 68). This spirit is lacking in the Fugitive misanthrope, who apprehends others with fear, lacking philanthropic trust in the goodness of others; they see humanity as inveterately vicious and with little serious prospect of reform. Arguably, the Fugitive's is a double fear—of the viciousness and failings of human beings, individually and collectively, and the corrupting effect of the social world, which act upon them, too. Crucially, though, there is no hatred or desire for violence, for the Fugitive, says Kant, "does not hate them [people], and wishes some of them well, but simply does not like them" (LE 27: 432).

The Enemy and Fugitive stances are obviously of special concern to Kant. It would be an interesting project to work out why, something that would take us deep into his religious and ethical views and his philosophical anthropology. Kant scholars disagree on his account of the sources of our propensities to wickedness and "radical evil." Frierson (2010) and Wilson (2014) favor social accounts, many owing to Rousseau, while Grenberg (2005) and Israelson (2019) explore the dominant influence of Christian theology. I set aside these exegetically complex issues: my immediate task is to indicate other types of misanthropic stance, alongside the hateful Enemy and the fearful Fugitive.

In *Critique of the Power of Judgement*, Kant actually endorses a form of misanthropy, albeit one lacking the enmity and fear he regards as hateful and contemptible, respectively. Although the stance is not named, it is affectively characterized by "sorrow," and "grounded in moral ideas," ultimately, perhaps, an enduring, if frustrated love of humanity (CPJ 5: 276). Its practical manifestations are close to those of the Fugitive, involving desires to pull away from the social world, even to the point of entertaining some romantic dreams of escaping to distant lands. Without giving a fuller sketch, Kant says this:

> Nevertheless there is a kind of misanthropy (very improperly so called) the predisposition to which is often found in the mind of many well-thinking people as they get older, which is certainly philanthropic enough as far as their benevolence is concerned, but is because of long, sad experience far removed from any pleasure in human beings. (CPJ 5: 276)

Inclusion of this third stance—one of sorrowful misanthropy, perhaps—is useful because it underscores the plurality of ways of enacting a misanthropic vision of the world. Kant, after all, was clearly congratulating the misanthrope on their perception of the dark sides of humanity. His worry is not epistemic in character, but ethical, for what he fears are those attitudes of hatefulness and fearfulness that are incompatible with a sense of *humanitas*—which is why, for him, there can be such a thing as a virtuous solitary, who retreats from humanity only to restore their moral energies prior to throwing themselves back into the fray of an often difficult, dispiriting world.

Still, the stances sketched out by Kant are not the whole story. Confronted with the unending "parade" of vices and failings constitutive of human life, one might respond with anger, bitterness, disappointment, frustration, or sadness. In turn, the practical responses are similarly diverse—acquiescence, determined reformism, pragmatic tolerance, localized mitigation, and so on. Consider, then, two other broad types of misanthropic stance. An Activist responds to our entrenched moral awfulness by attempting, however tentatively, efforts aimed at our rectification—political activism, religious preaching, moral teaching, or whatever. Seeing our awfulness, they endeavor to improve things through large-scale, ambitious projects. The scope and ambition of their reformative efforts depend on their wider commitments, of course, such as what trust they have in tradition, science and technology, social movements, Fate, or the gods. A Quietist misanthrope, by contrast, is chary about the prospects for success of any attempted enforced reconstruction of our moral condition. They fear such efforts tend either to fail or to backfire, exacerbating our problems, perhaps by giving new scope to such vices as egotism and hubris. Their quietist strategy is to accommodate, as best they can, to the entrenched failings of human society, perhaps by adopting unobtrusive ways of living that minimize their entanglement with the corruptions of the wider world—the sort of misanthropy seen in Montaigne or members of closed religious orders, perhaps. Confronted with our vastly entrenched failings, the Activist attempts amelioration, while the Quietist opts for accommodation.

Clearly there are complex psychological and contextual stories to tell about the ways that particular individuals come to accept specific misanthropic stances. I say "accept," since it isn't clear that those stances are *chosen* in any voluntary sense. Many misanthropes seem to feel irresistibly compelled to adopt certain stances as a consequence of their internalized vision of our condition. The misanthropic predicament may fundamentally concern how one lives out that vision of human existence, given the variety of possible stances and their costs. Rather than launch in those deep waters, I want to return to Kant's account of the Enemy and relate it to Shklar's and Williams's worries about hateful misanthropy encouraging "cruelty" and "projects of violence." Several questions arise. What sorts of features must a misanthropic stance incorporate to make it a real source of cruel, violent destructiveness? What kinds of experiences, actions, or reflections could lead one to adopt a stance toward human life characterized by a desire "to destroy the welfare of others"? Under what sorts of conditions could the Enemy stance become intelligible or compelling or even attractive? Does anyone actually subscribe to some form of the Enemy stance in practice?

In a sense, the last question is decisive. If there have never actually been "Enemies of mankind," outside of Kant's writings and imagination, then the others are moot. Gibson, after all, argued that hateful misanthropy is "impossible," even though his arguments for that may not be compelling. Certainly, some criticisms of the possibility of misanthropy miss the mark. It is possible to be misanthropic about humankind while still liking individual humans, some of whom could be judged to be morally exemplary.

Still, there are complicated questions about the lived experience of misanthropy posed by those skeptical of the possibility of misanthropy. In what follows, I consider a recent group of candidate hateful misanthropes. I want to show that there *are* hateful misanthropes, then explore some of the personal and social conditions that made that stance compelling. In the process, I describe a specific form of "eco-misanthropy," where a professed love of nature informs and inflects a profound hatred of humanity.

5. HUMANITY, NATURE, AND MISANTHROPY

Environmental ethics is a rare site of philosophical discussion of misanthropy. Sober reflection on our systematic exploitation and destruction of natural places and creatures encourages an acutely critical appraisal of humanity, often articulated in an explicit language of misanthropy, characterized in terms of hatred. The environmental ethicist, Jeremy Bendik-Keymer, defines misanthropy as "deliberately inhumane, hateful of people" (Bendik-Keymer 2006, 85), while Lisa Gerber describes it more broadly as "mistrust, hatred, and disgust of humankind" (Gerber 2002, 41). Similar sentiments can be found throughout academic and popular environmentalist discourse, where even gentle, avuncular nature broadcasters, like Sir David Attenborough, speak of humanity as a "plague."

Sincere concern for the natural world can inspire misanthropy, but so, too, can certain specific environmental ethical doctrines. Bendik-Keymer, for one, argues that deep ecology, in many of its forms, incorporates a significant strain of "conceptual misanthropy" (Bendik-Keymer 2006, 86). The core of deep ecology is "biospheric egalitarianism," which affirms the intrinsic value of all living things, independently of their instrumental value to human beings. If this conviction comes to dominate one's stance in the world, then a path is laid out to denunciations of a variety of instrumentalizing human practices and ambitions. An early instance of the misanthropic articulation of that tendency was Tom Regan's warning, during the 1980s, that at least some forms of "holistic," "biocentric" doctrines fuel "eco-fascist" tendencies (see Regan 1983, 362; cf. Salwén 2014). Some environmental activists really did propose "exterminat[ing] excess people" and declare that "massive human diebacks would be good" (cited in Callicott 1999, 70). Employing an epidemiological metaphor popular among eco-misanthropes, the landscape architect, Ian McHarg, gave a much-reprinted lecture, titled "Man: The Planetary Disease." Whatever their sincerity, such remarks were sufficiently frequent for J. Baird Callicott at one point to remark that the "extent of misanthropy in modern environmentalism may be taken to the degree to which it is biocentric" (Callicott 1980, 326)—a claim from which he later retreated, after embracing an expanded "communitarian" theory of value that weighed familial, civic, and biotic communities (e.g., Callicott 1998).

Certainly, the charges of misanthropy apply to certain forms of deep ecology, at least as they were developing at certain points in their history, even if the provocative language of "eco-fascism" or "eco-terrorism" was preferred. But it would be a mistake to suppose that they are confined to biocentric, holistic, and related environmental doctrines, even if they may be more liable to encourage them. It is useful to distinguish, albeit loosely, three broad ways that environmental doctrines could be described as misanthropic.

Consider, first, that environmental doctrines can encourage and affirm global moral condemnation of humankind or human civilization, typically by calling attention to the wrongful destruction and defacement of natural places and creatures. Such condemnation could be rooted in terms of different normative theories, and be ethical, aesthetic, or existential in character. Morally, the charge-list is familiar—the suffering and death of billions of animals; deforestation; carbon emissions; pollution of air, water, and soil; and other staples of green discourse. Aesthetically, there is profound dismay at the loss of natural beauties, whether due to the encroaching "landscapes" of modern industrial agriculture, disgust at landfills and trash piles, or the consequent vast, imposed ugliness that contrasts, for one environmental ethicist, with a deep-rooted human "longing for purity and cleanliness" (James 2014). Existentially, a misanthrope may resent the erosion of nature's meanings—a hollowing out of our experiences of forests, rivers, and landscapes that were once charged with meaning and significance, the loss of which is a source of profound alienation and disenchantment (James 2013). Such moral, aesthetic, and existential deficiencies are all mutually inflecting, even if the former dominate modern "green" discourses. The collective results are negative attitudes toward humankind, the source of the awfulness, ugliness, and emptiness caused by systematic destruction of nature.

Second, environmental doctrines can employ and endorse misanthropic attitudes and convictions, augmenting the condemnation of humanity with specific sorts of emotional and evaluative responses. Contrasts between humanity and animals or nature, for instance, often serve to underscore our distinctive moral deficiencies, often by exploiting dualisms between what is natural and what is human, artificial, or civilized. Within North American environmental ethics, this is clear in deployments of a wilderness ideal and the associated "cultural ideology of the idea of wilderness" (Cronon 1998). A misanthrope could use the wilderness literally, as an attractive natural place to escape the corrupting artificialities of a civilized world—like Kant's Fugitive or Rousseau's "solitary." But there are subtler misanthropic aspects of the wilderness ideal. One is the assumption that humans "taint" the wilderness, something Arne Naess noted among those deep ecologists who "talk as if they look upon humans as intruders in wonderful nature" (quoted in Bookchin and Foreman 1991, 32). Another is the assumption that humans can *only* relate to nature in harmful, destructive ways, an acute Cynicism fueling the distrust of humanity that is a characteristic of misanthropy (Gerber 2002, 53).

A third way for environmental doctrines to be misanthropic is to incorporate or endorse radical practical proposals, expressive of misanthropic attitudes or convictions. The typical examples from recent eco-misanthropes include dismantling the social and material infrastructure of modern human life, to dramatic proposals to dramatically reduce the human population to the point of human extinction, to those grotesque plans to bring about "massive human diebacks." Sometimes, the proposals are clear in their aims, if not their detail, as with Paul Taylor's argument that "the total final extermination of our species" would result in improvements for the earth's "community of life" (P. Taylor 1992, 108). In other cases, the details are blunter, such as a bumper sticker, seen in the United States, bearing the curt instruction, "Save the Planet, Kill Yourself" (quoted in Gerber 2002, 41).

An environmental doctrine can therefore be misanthropic due to its condemnations, attitudes, and practical implications, whether those are stated or left implicit. This means that there are many potential forms and degrees of eco-misanthropy. Gerber wisely advises us to judge environmental ethical doctrines as differentially receptive to misanthropy, "not to say that a particular ethic is linked to misanthropy, but rather that we need to be careful about how misanthropy creeps into our life" (Gerber 2002, 44). "Creeps," though, may be the wrong term. Some environmentalist doctrines may *actively* promote a more starkly misanthropic stance, perhaps encouraging those marked by contempt, hate, and violence. One can imagine a Fugitive eco-misanthrope who quietly lives "off the grid," minimizing their participation in the carbon-intensive rapacity of modern human life, enacting what the environmental historian, Roderick Nash, called the "garden vision" of our relation to nature (Nash 1982, 379–88; see, further, Kidd 2021).

When assessing the misanthropic character of an environmental doctrine, attention should turn to its whole complex of attitudes, starting points, and values and the question of whether they are liable to push it in the direction of hateful eco-misanthropy. We can see this more clearly with a case study.

6. "UNMAKING OF CIVILIZATION"

One group of hateful eco-misanthropes were certain members of the American radical environmental activism organization, Earth First! Founded in 1980 by the environmental activists Dave Foreman, Mike Roselle, Howie Wolke, Bart Koehler, and Ron Kezar, several of its members began to voice increasingly severe misanthropic attitudes and proposals into the mid-1980s. The organization attracted many leftists, anarchists, and counterculturalists and was very effective in developing and implementing new forms of activism—the now widely adopted practice of "tree-sitting," for instance, and the happily less widely adopted practice of "puke-ins" at shopping mall (an excellent study of the organization's history is Lee 1995).

Among their inspirations was the activist and anarchist, Edward Abbey, who was deeply esteemed by the founding members. A prolific author, his writings are filled with misanthropic pronouncements—"I'd rather kill a man than a snake" (Abbey 1988, 18)—often expressed in striking aphorisms: "The industrial way of life leads to the industrial way of death" (Abbey 1990, 100). Abbey introduced the term "monkey-wrenching," methods for disrupting the offending forms of human activity, from dam-building to deforestation. What drove his activism and writing was a powerful conviction that humanity, at least in modern industrialized forms, is "a scourge . . . a pestilence upon the Earth, a threat to all life" (quoted in Gerber 2002, 42).

During the mid-1980s, the Earth First! members began to interact with the emerging philosophical doctrines of "deep ecology," a family of environmental philosophies inspired by the Norwegian philosopher, Arne Naess (1973). Unlike "shallow" theories, focused on specific issues like pollution, the self-described "deep" ecologies called attention to the metaphysical visions responsible for our estrangement from nature. As a corrective measure, they also encouraged a sense of the intrinsic value of nature enjoyed by all living things—what they called "biospheric egalitarianism," which valued all living creatures. The deep ecologists thus also perceived humanity as increasingly dominated by anthropocentric vices, like greed and hubris. So entrenched were those vices that a sense of the intrinsic value of living creatures was increasingly difficult for many people to take seriously, let alone cultivate and take up into their lives. Unsurprisingly, the infusion of deep ecological themes began to intensify the misanthropic mood of Earth First!

At the organization's meetings, some members started to chant "Down with human beings!" and exaggerate their rhetoric of tearing down the engines of violence needed for the operation of the "industrial way of death." More moderate members protested that this performative "misanthropic antihumanism" was at real risk of mutating into a dogmatically "anti-scientific, anti-technology" stance (McIsaac, Foreman, Brookchin 1991, 60, 61). Most of the members, though, reasoned that if nature enjoys intrinsic value, then there could be no acceptance of its destruction by the ever-accelerating "industrial way of death." Moreover, given the vast scale of that "way," nor could one rely on small-scale "monkey-wrenching." At the most extreme was a proposal by one activist, Christopher Manes, for nothing less than the "unmaking of civilization," the subtitle of his book, *Green Rage* (Manes 1991). Amid such energizing calls for radical action to stop radical crises, the soberer voices were drowned out—like those urging gentler conceptions of deep ecology as "a recommendation about how humans should live," a striving to "identify with all life" (McLaughlin 1995, 262).

The most acute expressions of eco-misanthropy within Earth First! came with a trio of articles in the March and May 1987 issues of its eponymous journal, authored by Manes under the pseudonym "Miss Ann Thropy" (see Lee 1995, 101). Blandly titled "Technology and Mortality," "Overpopulation and Industrialism," and "Population and AIDS," they welcomed HIV/AIDS, mass nutritional crises in Africa, and the prospect of a global nuclear war and urged the dismantling of health care infrastructure, including for epidemic diseases. "Radical action" of this sort would reduce the human population and collapse its existing ways of life.

Here one sees extreme misanthropy, a realization of Kant's worries about "declared dispositions to harm others" and the "projects of violence" anticipated by Shklar. Manes was forthright and unapologetic, declaring that, if offered a cure for AIDS in exchange for the loss of technology, he would choose the latter (quoted in Lee 1995, 110). Although aware of the deeply controversial character of his proposals, he professed confidence that others in Earth First! shared his views. Presumably Manes was exaggerating, since he also added that moral rectitude does not matter in the urgent context of the global ecological crisis. "What matters," he declared, was "wilderness . . . not the prestige of spiritual beautification" (quoted in Lee 1995, 110).

Such active hateful eco-misanthropy immediately met with criticism from Earth First! members. Murray Bookchin described Manes and his followers as "barely disguised racists, survivalists," "outright social reactionaries," and champions of "a kind of crude eco-brutalism" (quoted in Levine, Bookchin, Foreman 1991, 11). The defense of nature should neither come at the cost of urging deliberate immiseration and death of human beings, nor be allowed to conceal morally invidious doctrines. By 1987, two factions had emerged, divided on the issue of misanthropy. The first group maintained that preservation of wilderness was the sole measure of action and they often brought with them apocalyptic visions. Abbey envisioned a "higher civilization" of scattered human groups, modest in number and lifestyle, pursuing the simple agrarian life and assembling annually in "the ruins of abandoned cities" for "festivals of moral, spiritual, artistic, and intellectual renewal" (quoted in

Lee 1995, 99). Since they judged humanity to be irredeemable, they urged a "return to the Neanderthal," although, in practice, this would only be possible for an ecological elite: those not possessed of the vital "wilderness gene" would not survive (quoted in Doherty 2005, 158). Sometimes, these apocalyptic eco-misanthropes appealed to a Protestant vision of this deep ecological elite as the "chosen people," uniquely possessed of the discipline, skill, and courage needed to survive the impending civilizational collapse and then create a new, perfect, ecologically sustainable world (quoted in Lee 1995, 83).

The second group urged a more positive, optimistic vision of humanity as capable of achieving a moral and practical balance between the needs of human culture and nature. The excesses of unfettered biocentrism were mitigated by moral and social concerns for humanity and a recognition, voiced by the environmental ethicist Warwick Fox, that "being opposed to human-centredness is logically distinct from being opposed to humans," a subtlety lost to the misanthropists (quoted in Curry 2006, 45; see Lee 1995, chap. 6). Further criticisms came from Judi Bari—feminist, anarchist, and Earth First! activist—who argued that the problem is not *humans*, but "the way certain humans live, that is destroying the earth," specifically "industrial-technocratic societies" (Bari 1991, 25). As Vandana Shiva puts it, "Blaming the entire human species for the crime of white, technocratic men . . . avoids any real analysis of who is responsible for the death of the planet" (quoted in Bari 1991, 25). Although this second group was not homogenous, the common themes were a combination of philanthropic sentiment, philosophical self-reflectiveness, and aversion to an exultant anticipation of the "unmaking of civilization." Luckily, by the early 1990s, the second group had won out (see the exchange between Foreman, Abbey, and Eugene Hargrove, in Keller 2010, chs. 40–44).

The case of Earth First! offers a rich case study in the formation of full-blown forms of hateful eco-misanthropy. Without aiming to be comprehensive, consider four features of the movement that pushed its condemnations of humanity in hateful, violent directions. First, the presence of negative affects among the original motivations for the movement. Abbey, for instance, said of *The Monkey Wrench Gang* that "my original motive was, I guess, anger. Trying to get some sort of revenge for the destruction I had witnessed in the American Southwest" (quoted in Trimble 1995, 28). Such initial motivations can shape the developmental trajectory of misanthropy by pointing it in the direction of stances of hatred, contempt, and loathing.

Second, the movement developed under the influence of a variety of "anti-humanist" attitudes and convictions. For Earth First!, these included, inter alia, the wilderness ideal, a postlapsarian vision of humans as irreparably corrupted, and identifications of nature with culturally resonant values—authenticity, genuineness, original purity, innocence, wholeness, and wholesomeness. If humans are false and corrupt, and nature authentic and pure, then a clear course is set to a misanthropic derogation of humanity and all its associated cultures and forms of life. The third and fourth components are enthusiasm for radicalism and the presence of other background doctrines of hate. The radicalism is reflected in the zeal for "monkey-wrenching" and infrastructural sabotage up to and including the engineered eradication of whole groups, such as targeted genocide and the "unmaking of civilization." The supporting doctrines of hate, evident in "Miss Ann Thropy's" articles, are racism and homophobia—recall that their targets were specifically sections of the African and gay populations, rather than humanity as such. It might be true that the radical eco-misanthropes wanted to direct violence at humanity at large, but their initial targets were specific, vulnerable groups.

I suggest that many environmental doctrines may contain latent tendencies that could be called "conceptual misanthropy," although if and how they are activated and expressed will depend on a wider structure of personal experiences and motivations interacting with social, historical, cultural, and ideological conditions. A misanthrope stance emerges from a complex and dynamic context. This introduces variations which will shape if and how it develops in more hateful, violent directions. In some cases, a misanthrope might have values that proscribe hatred—something like Kant's *humanitas*, say, or some religious teaching of love and compassion. Other misanthropes may operate the "garden vision" of our relations to nature, rather than a wilderness ideal which encourages hostility to human "artifice." Granted, environmental ethical doctrines shaped by such moderating influences lack the drama and provocative energy of a radical eco-misanthropy marked by a "green rage." But the love of nature would be corrupted if it transmuted into malevolent hatred of humanity which acted to give new energy and expression to an array of human vices and failings—callousness, enmity, recklessness, self-righteousness, and vengefulness.

7. CONCLUSION

All forms of misanthropy involve critical and negative appraisal of humankind, especially if rooted in an acute apprehension of the entrenchment and ubiquity of vices and failings in our forms of life. A misanthropic vision can be expressed in many ways, only some of which are characterized by feelings of hatred and dispositions to violence. Alongside Kant's Enemy and Fugitive, there can be more activist and quietist ways of enacting misanthropy that have little, if any, role for hate and violence. Much more has to be in place for misanthropy to take those darker forms, something that is clear in the case of the radical eco-misanthropy of Earth First! Misanthropy takes a plurality of culturally specific forms, depending on its particular etiology. Although it can take the form of an inchoate "hatred of humanity," it can take other forms, too—less hateful, and more sophisticated—even if embracing a critically charged stance on humankind can increase our susceptibility to indiscriminate feelings of hatred. The worry of Shklar and Williams that misanthropy leads to hatred therefore ignores the complex varieties of misanthropy and the various moderating commitments and conditions that may be at work.

Since moral dogmatism and obdurate zeal are dangers built into many evaluative stances, the sensible thing for a philosophical misanthrope is to strive to be self-critically alert. Someone shifting into a misanthropic vision of humanity should be actively cautious about the temptations to be provocative, radical, and self-righteously assured of one's status as a member of the uniquely courageous moral elect. Hatred can be powerful and intoxicating—but, without due care, it may well energize our vices and failings. If this is right, then what is crucial is appreciation that misanthropy brings its own vices and failings, and that recognizing and navigating them is central to the misanthropic predicament.

ACKNOWLEDGMENTS

I am grateful to the Editor, Noell Birondo, for the invitation and his helpful comments, to David E. Cooper and Simon James for helpful comments on an earlier draft, and to Sasha Garwood for helpful discussions of misanthropy and an impeccable commentary on the final draft.

NOTES

1. Contemporary conceptions of misanthropy often tie it to some doctrine of human nature. For arguments against that, see Cooper (2018, chap. 1) and Kidd (2020b).

2. Shklar, for instance, describes a type of misanthrope who condemns the human world in its current state for its poor contrast with "some inner vision of a transformed humanity" located "in the past or the distant future" (Shklar 1984, 194).

3. References to Kant are to *Critique of Practical Judgment* (CPJ), *Lectures on Anthropology* (LA), *Lectures on Ethics* (LE), *Religion within the Boundaries of Mere Reason* (R), and *Conflict of the Faculties* (SF). As is the convention, the lectures on anthropology include the name of the student notetaker.

4. References to Schopenhauer are to *Parerga and Paralipomena* (PP), *The Two Fundamental Problems of Ethics* (TFP), and *The World as Will and Representation* (WWR).

REFERENCES

Abbey, Edward. 1988. *Desert Solitaire: A Season in the Wilderness.* Tucson: University of Arizona Press.
Abbey, Edward. 1990. *A Voice Crying in the Wilderness (Vox Clamantis en Deserto): Notes from a Secret Journal.* New York: St Martin's Press.
Bari, Judi. 1991. "Why I Am Not a Misanthrope." *Earth First! Journal* 2: 25.
Beiser, Frederick C. 2016. *Weltschmerz: Pessimism in German Philosophy, 1860–1900.* Oxford: Oxford University Press.
Bendik-Keymer, Jeremy. 2006. *The Ecological Life: Discovering Citizenship and a Sense of Humanity.* New York: Rowman & Littlefield.
Bookchin, Murray and Dave Foreman, eds.1991. *Defending the Earth*: A Debate. Montréal and New York: Black Rose Books.
Callicott, J. Baird. 1998. "'Back Together Again' Again." *Environmental Values* 7: 461–75.
Callicott, J. Baird. 1999. *Beyond the Land Ethic: More Essays in Environmental Philosophy.* New York: SUNY Press.
Cassirer, Ernst. 1945. *Rousseau-Kant-Goethe.* Princeton: Princeton University Press.
Cooper, David E. 2018. *Animals and Misanthropy.* Abingdon: Routledge.
Cronon, William. 1998. "The Trouble with Wilderness, or, Getting Back to the Wrong Nature." In *The Great Wilderness Debate*, edited by J. Baird Callicott and Michael Nelson, 471–98. Athens, GA: University of Georgia Press.
Curry, Patrick. 2006. *Ecological Ethics: An Introduction.* Cambridge: Polity.
Dienstag, Joshua Foa. 2009. *Pessimism: Philosophy, Ethic, Spirit.* Princeton: Princeton University Press.
Doherty, Brian. 2005. *Ideas and Action in the Green Movement.* London: Routledge.
Frierson, Patrick. 2010. "Kantian Moral Pessimism." In *Kant's Anatomy of Evil*, edited by Sharon Anderson-Gold and Pablo Muchnik, 33–57. Cambridge: Cambridge University Press.
Gerber, Lisa. 2002. "What Is So Bad about Misanthropy?" *Environmental Ethics* 24: 41–55.
Gibson, Andrew. 2012. *Misanthropy: The Critique of Humanity.* London: Bloomsbury.
Grenberg, Jeanine. 2005. *Kant and the Ethics of Humility: A Story of Dependence, Corruption, and Virtue.* Cambridge: Cambridge University Press.
Israelsen, Andrew. 2019. "And Who Is My Neighbor? Kant on Misanthropy and Christian Love." *The Heythrop Journal* 60 (2): 219–32.
Jacquette, Dale. 2014. "Socrates on the Moral Mischief of Misology." *Argumentation* 28 (1): 1–17.
James, Simon P. 2013. "Finding—and Failing to Find—Meaning in Nature." *Environmental Values* 22 (5): 609–25.
James, Simon P. 2014. "'Nothing Truly Wild is Unclean': Muir, Misanthropy, and the Aesthetics of Dirt." *Environmental Ethics* 36 (3): 357–63.
Kant, Immanuel. 1992–. *Conflict of the Faculties* in Akademie Edition *Gessamelte Schriften* (Ak), vol. 7. Berlin: De Gruyter, 1992–.

Kant, Immanuel. 1996. "Religion Within the Boundaries of Mere Reason." In *Religion and Rational Theology*, edited by Allen W. Wood and George di Giovanni, 39–215. Cambridge: Cambridge University Press.

Kant, Immanuel. 1997. *Lectures on Ethics*. Edited by Peter Heath and J. B. Schneewind. Translated by Peter Heath. Cambridge: Cambridge University Press.

Kant, Immanuel. 2000. *Critique of the Power of Judgment*. Edited by Paul Guyer. Translated by Paul Guyer and Eric Matthews. Cambridge: Cambridge University Press.

Kant, Immanuel. 2012. *Lectures on Anthropology*. Edited by Allen W. Wood and Robert B. Louden. Translated by Robert R. Clewis, Robert B. Louden, G. Felicitas Munzel, and Allen W. Wood. Cambridge: Cambridge University Press.

Keller, David R., ed. 2010. *Environmental Ethics: The Big Questions*. Oxford: Wiley-Blackwell.

Kidd, Ian James. 2020a. "Animals, Misanthropy, and Humanity." *Journal of Animal Ethics* 10 (1): 66–72.

Kidd, Ian James. 2020b. "Humankind, Human Nature, and Misanthropy." *Metascience* 29: 505–508.

Kidd, Ian James. 2021. "Gardens of Refuge." *Daily Philosophy*, October 6, 2021. https://daily-philosophy.com/.

Lee, Martha F. 1995. *Earth First! Environmental Apocalypse*. Syracuse: Syracuse University Press.

Manes, Christopher. 1991. *Green Rage: Radical Environmentalism and the Unmaking of Civilization*. Boston: Little Brown.

McLaughlin, Andrew. 1995. "For A Radical Ecocentrism." In *The Deep Ecology Movement: An Introductory Anthology*, edited by Alan R. Drengson and Yuichi Inoue, 257–80. Berkeley, CA: North Atlantic Books.

Midgley, Mary. 1984. *Wickedness: A Philosophical Essay*. London: Routledge & Kegan Paul.

Molière. 2008. *The Misanthrope, Tartuffe, and Other Plays*. Translated by Maya Slater. London: Penguin.

Naess, Arne. 1973. "The Shallow and the Deep, Long-range Ecology Movement." *Inquiry* 16: 95–100.

Nash, Roderick. 1982. *Wilderness and the American Mind*. New Haven: Yale University Press.

Regan, Tom. 1983. *The Case for Animal Rights*. Los Angeles: University of California Press.

Rousseau, Jean-Jacques. 1969. *Emile, ou de l' education*. Edited by Bernard Gagnebin and Marcel Raymond. Paris: Gallimard.

Salwén, Håkan. 2014. "The Land Ethic and the Significance of the Fascist Objection." *Ethics, Policy & Environment* 17 (2): 192–207.

Schopenhauer, Arthur. 1969. *The World as Will and Representation*, 2 vols. Translated by E. F. J. Payne. New York: Dover.

Schopenhauer, Arthur. 1994 [1851]. *Parerga and Paralipomena*, 2 vols. Translated by E. F. J. Payne. Oxford: Clarendon Press.

Schopenhauer, Arthur. 2010 [1841]. *The Two Fundamental Problems of Ethics.* Translated by David E. Cartwright and Edward E. Eerdman. Oxford: Oxford University Press.

Shklar, Judith. 1984. *Ordinary Vices.* Harvard: Harvard University Press.

Swift, Jonathan. 1843. *The Works of Jonathan Swift, Containing Interesting and Valuable Papers, Not Hitherto Published, in Two Volumes.* London: Henry G. Bohn.

Taylor, Charles. 1992. *Sources of the Self: The Making of the Modern Identity.* Cambridge: Cambridge University Press.

Taylor, Gabriele. 2006. *Deadly Vices.* Oxford: Oxford University Press.

Taylor, Paul. 1992. "The Ethics of Respect for Nature." *The Animal Rights/ Environmental Debate: The Environmental Perspective*, edited by Eugene C. Hargrove, 95–121. New York: State University of New York Press, 1992.

Trimble, Stephen, ed. 1995. *Words from the Land: Encounters with Natural History Writing.* expanded edition. Reno and Las Vegas: University of Nevada Press.

Trullinger, Joseph. 2015. "Kant's Neglected Account of the Virtuous Solitary." *International Philosophical Quarterly* 55 (1): 67–83.

Williams, Bernard. 1985. "Resisting the Avalanche." *London Review of Books* 7 (10) (6 June): 6.

Wilson, Catherine. 2014. "Kant on Civilization, Culture, and Moralisation." In *Kant's Lectures on Anthropology*, edited by Alix Cohen, 191–210. Cambridge: Cambridge University Press.

Wittgenstein, Ludwig. 1998. *Culture and Value.* Edited by George Henrik von Wright in collaboration with Heikki Nyman. Revised by Alois Pichler. Translated by Peter Winch. Oxford: Blackwell.

Chapter 5

A Tradition Grounded in Hate
Racist Hatred and Anti-Immigrant Fervor
Grant J. Silva

Hatred is not a given; it is a struggle to acquire hatred, which has to be dragged into being, clashing with acknowledged guilt complexes. Hatred cries out to exist, and he who hates must prove his hatred through action and the appropriate behavior. In a sense he has to embody hatred. This is why the Americans have replaced lynching by discrimination.

—Franz Fanon[1]

I imagine one of the reasons people cling to their hates so stubbornly is because they sense, once hate is gone, they will be forced to deal with pain.

—James Baldwin[2]

1. INTRODUCTION

If searching for a clear picture of group-directed or social-identity-based hatred, look no farther than anti-immigrant fervor occurring in developed or "first-world" nations throughout the world today. Besides providing a glimpse of hatred in action, this fervor affords insight into the nature of *racist* hatred, or so I will argue in this chapter. Typically accompanied by feelings of contempt, anger, and resentment, the racist dimensions of anti-immigrant sentiment can be found in the reasons offered by many staunch "pro-border" advocates as to why immigrants, asylum-seekers, and refugees, especially those from the decolonizing and developing parts of the world, must be kept out of countries like the United States. Beyond tropes of "illegality" and lawfulness and the incessant need for border security, at the root of much anti-immigrant sentiment is a sense of loss, the fear of difference, and anxieties regarding cultural alienation, all of which are feelings that generate a great deal of hate. Delve deeper into this reasoning and one quickly realizes that the animosity directed toward migrants,[3] much like the hatred visited upon racialized minorities throughout the history of the United States, has less to do with the hated *other* and more to do with an insecure *self* or, for that matter, a self that can only be secure insofar as it is capable of hating.

In order to substantiate these claims, the second part of this chapter offers an overview of group-directed or social-identity-based hatred.[4] I focus on hatred's affective-intentional structure, examine the nature of hate crime, and explain how contempt for hate targets (and not necessarily anger-based hatred) drives most group-directed hatred. The third part of this chapter provides my argument for how anti-immigrant sentiment in the United States constitutes the legacy of the sociopolitical paradigm of white supremacy (see Mills 2017). Following the feminist scholar and writer Sarah Ahmed (2014), my goal is to conceptualize hatred as a social and cultural practice that often amounts to a tradition demanding to be kept alive in one way or another.

As I see it, the creation of hate crime, antidiscrimination laws, and the general disavowal of explicit acts of racism in the United States has not so much pushed instances of racist hatred underground or eliminated it as much as these have channeled this attitude into directions that force it to disassociate from the history of racialized violence in the United States. If hatred were to materialize in a straightforwardly "racist" manner, it would risk severe legal and social consequences. These consequences stymie hatred's expression, thus leaving individuals who have internalized a hateful disposition without a means of being who they are, or of continuing the traditions through which they find meaning and a sense of belonging. Anti-immigrant fervor, especially in its legalistic and border security guise, sidesteps the history of racialized violence in the United States, particularly antiblack violence, and avoids the pitfalls of situating race or, for that matter, racism as the cause of hatred (after all, it claims, its concern is with "illegals"). This fervor therefore acquires the ability to portray itself as a form of justified disdain or contempt, a type which provides a home for the feelings and concerns that drive the act of hatred—a home that one need not be ashamed of since it is "patriotic," so the thought goes, to prioritize one's nation ahead of the well-being of others.

Before moving ahead, three things need to be made clear. First, on my account, while human cognitive and emotional faculties make possible the ability to hate in general, the kind of hatred I am concerned with is learned behavior. Hatred has to be taught and, more importantly, modeled such that one comes to rely upon it when trying to make sense of feelings, anxieties, and concerns that are rather natural to have. I therefore do not believe that any race, nationality, or social group is inherently or essentially hateful. Second, I am *not* suggesting that hate-based violence targeting racialized minorities in the United States is "over" or a thing of the past. Sadly, as of the writing of this chapter, racial violence, particularly anti-Asian violence, is on the rise in the United States (later, I offer some reasons why). Instead, my goal is, third, to use anti-immigrant sentiment as an opportunity to reverse the optic and directionality through which racism is examined (a project I embarked upon earlier: see Silva 2019). I also recognize that were it not for the racial difference that immigrants, refugees, and asylum-seekers from the global South or war-torn regions of the world represent in the eyes of dominant U.S. racial imaginary, the "crisis" at the border would not exist. Yet, as I argue later, to focus on the racial difference of migrants, much like focusing on the race of the victim(s) when it comes to hate crime, is to head in the wrong direction when examining the nature of *racist* hatred.

Expressions of group-directed hatred often rely upon externalizing techniques to make themselves appear as *reactions to* and not *instigators of* social tension. The idea of "race" has long been one of these techniques; so too, now, is "illegality." In either instance the act of hating emanates from a collective attitude that stands in need of a hated other as a fixed pole by which hateful individuals orient their identity and build their sense of community (cf. Szanto 2018). This chapter thereby examines the psychological dependencies and the confidence placed in the act of hating that afflict societies throughout the world today.

2. ON GROUP-DIRECTED HATRED

Nothing calls to mind the idea of hatred like instances of group-directed violence. While one might "hate" grading papers, an unexpected bill, or even trips to the dentist, the sense of hatred that inspires lynching, genocide, displacement and forced relocation, internment, mass shootings, and even hate crimes registers something more than an extreme form of dislike. Acts like these are not just horrendous in their own right, to many they mark a degree of moral depravity that fringes upon evil. In order to make sense of these acts—that is, if sense can be made of them at all—one needs an equally vicious motivational source. Within the spectrum of human emotion, hatred is that which best fits the bill. It combines the necessary admixture of head and heart, so to speak, that captures the emotional investments and agential commitment necessary for the above actions to be possible.

Whereas some emotions have the tendency to overcome an individual, result in the loss of control, and are easily manipulated (for instance, grief, rage, or pity), hatred is the type of complex emotion in which a person maintains some level of intentionality or present mindedness throughout the act of hating. By "act" I do not mean to limit hatred to single event or particular action; as Thomas Szanto writes, hatred often "lingers" more than it erupts (2018, 454). Even if it is the case that during a bout of hatred one is seething, unsettled, and perhaps even "enraged," a hateful person consciously holds onto negative feelings and purposively sets out to harm or devalue their intended target when acting upon their hatred. Hatred is not accidental. Szanto (2018) refers to this as hatred's affective-intentional structure. For him what distinguishes hatred from other affective phenomena is the degree of intentionality attached to it. Describing hatred as an attitude, he writes, "Attitudes don't just passively (affectively) register certain external facts or occurrences (as bodily sensations do), nor do they simply react to them. Having an affective attitude is a response, or a form of position-taking, to affective significances for a subject" (Szanto 2018, 457). Actions performed out of a sense of hate may be emotionally charged and inspired by events outside of one's control: after all, as an antagonistic emotion, hatred is a reaction to something external to the self (Brogaard 2020, 12). Nevertheless, while one's affect may focus on a specific object of concern, hatred still amounts to a decision or choice. It is a form of "position-taking" in relation to one's claimed affect.

Hatred's affective-intentional structure assists in explaining why many people focus on this attitude in order to understand group-directed or social-identity-based violence. Hate crime, for instance, is a category of criminal behavior that is usually accompanied by additional charges and more severe sentencing due to the fact that it is performed out of a sense of intentional malice, prejudice, or disdain for victims on account of their perceived racial or ethnic membership. To be more precise, it is the intentional *moral* disvalue of persons or groups invested into acts of hate that explains why hate crimes maintain a heightened legal status (Van Bavel et al. 2018).[5] In their famous study, sociologists Jack Levin and Jack McDevitt (1998) identified hate crimes driven by four main motivations: thrill-seeking, claims of self-defense, retaliatory attacks, and "mission-driven" hate crimes, that is, hate crimes enacted from an ideological commitment. Of the four, thrill-seeking behavior accounts for most reported hate crimes (Shanmugasundaram 2018). While one might think this undermines the sense in which "hate" actually inspires hate crime, such a take glosses over the distinction between contempt-driven and anger-based hatred, a distinction I substantiate later. On top of that, it is interesting, to say the least, that *as* thrill-seeking behavior, hate crimes are bonding exercises through which a sense of comradery is formed (with one's friends or within a community of haters), a point that supports my claim about hatred constituting a tradition.

It is important to underscore—and this segues to a larger point later on—that hate crimes are not *caused* by the race, ethnicity, gender, or sexuality of the victim. I bring this point up now because most definitions of hate crime house a causal dynamic in which group-identity, especially that of the target or victim, "works only as a cause, rather than also being an effect of the crime," as Ahmed writes (2014, 556). For instance, U.S. Code, Title 18, Section 249 defines a hate criminal as follows:

> Whoever, whether or not acting under color of law, willfully causes bodily injury to any person or, through the use of fire, a firearm, a dangerous weapon, or an explosive or incendiary device, attempts to cause bodily injury to any person, because of the actual or perceived race, color, religion or national origin of any person.

In the above definition, the word "because" is where the trouble arises. It suggests that had it not been for the group-identity of the victim, the crime might not have happened or at the very least the crime would not be infected with hate. In the context of hate crimes involving race, the sociologist Karen E. Fields and historian Barbara J. Fields (2014) refer to this as "racecraft," the magic that transpires when racism, an action the aggressor *does*, transforms itself into race, something the target of that racism *is*, "in a sleight of hand that is easy to miss" (Fields and Fields 2012, 17). Racecraft occurs when the *idea* of race assumes ideological proportions in relation to racist *action*, when race is made to stand in for racism. The idea of racecraft thus helps to explain how group-directed hatred strives to externalize the source of hate, thereby making hatred appear as a reaction to and not the instigator of social tension, a move that bears the potential to mitigate blameworthiness.[6]

In order to avoid the production of racecraft, the professor of law and justice Key Sun suggests that the legal definition of hate crime ought to specify "the hate offender's mental state, including (1) the required criminal intent (mens rea) and (2) the offender's cognitive distortions." Sun says that this definition would stand "in contrast to the position that suggests that difference in group memberships related to the offender and the victim are the causality for hate crime" (Sun 2006, 598). He also notes that the "offender's cognitive distortions and prejudice involve misrepresenting the self's responsibility and intergroup reality and using the distinctiveness of the victim (e.g., ethnicity, race, religion, sexual orientation) to rationalize and justify the offense(s)" (Sun 2006, 598). Sun holds that psychologists and others should focus less on "group difference" as the source of hate crime and more on how "social learning environments, economic conditions, and other social variables influence the hate offenders' motivations" (Sun 2006, 601). For him, childhood trauma, a history of mistreatment, and even rigid forms of thinking are psychological variables requiring more consideration—and I would add to this list maligned identity-formations that are dependent on hate itself. Sun's intervention is all the more important in light of the tendency for hateful individuals to blame their victim for acts of hate—three out of the four motivations for hate crime offered above are capable of doing this—particularly when grotesque stereotypes or negative character appraisals portray hate targets as in some way deserving of it (Fischer et al. 2018, 313). Since victims of hate crime demonstrate "significantly more symptoms of depression, anger, anxiety, and posttraumatic stress," and even attribute blame to themselves at a higher rate (Sun 2006, 602), clinical interventions for victims stand to benefit by focusing on what motivates haters themselves. In particular, it is important to encourage victims to focus on the hater's dispositions when it comes to ascribing blame, lest they start to internalize the hatred they experienced by seeing the fault as their own and viewing their own group-identity in a negative light.

Following Sun's lead, one of the chief motivators of group-directed or social-identity-based hatred is the sense in which something is being taken away or jeopardized by hate targets. Ahmed expresses this point when she explains that hate frequently works through a narrative "generating a subject that is endangered by imagined others whose proximity threatens not only to take something away from the subject (jobs, security, wealth), but to take the place of the subject" (Ahmed 2014, 43). This something can be real, as Ahmed notes, or imagined. Often times, it is a loss opportunity, failed expectations, or even undelivered entitlements that hate targets take the blame for.

The lynching of African Americans in the United States offers an example. According to the theologian James H. Cone (2013), the purpose of lynching was to put black people back in their place and to restore the racial order/hierarchy at the base of white supremacy. Whereas early on in the westward expansion of the United States "lynching was not regarded as an evil thing but a necessity—the only way a community could protect itself from bad people out of reach of the law," the lynching of black America "marked an important turning point in the history and meaning of lynching." Coming on the heels of the enfranchisement of black Americans in 1867, "most southern whites were furious at the very idea of granting ex-slaves social, political, and economic freedom." The Ku Klux Klan (KKK), for instance, started as "a vigilante group whose primary purpose was to redeem the South and thereby ensure that America remained a white man's country." For founding members of the KKK, "it was one thing to lose the war to the North but quite another to allow ignorant, uncivilized 'niggers' to rule over whites or even participate with them in the political process" (Cone 2013, 4). Lynching was a means of recouping the political and legal *standing* once exclusively reserved for whites in full citizenship (see Beltrán 2020, 44). The primary objective was to remind black Americans of their subservient place *within* the socioeconomic structure. Lynching was "the white community's way of forcibly reminding blacks of their inferiority and powerlessness" (Cone 2013, 7).

The sense of loss that motivates group-directed hatred is made worse by social turmoil and economic uncertainty. In terms of the first, take the rise of anti-Asian hate accompanying the Covid-19 global pandemic.[7] While the origins of the SARS-CoV-2 virus still currently remains uncertain, at the time of the outbreak in early 2020, political leadership in the United States was already placing blame upon China as the source of the virus, particularly the Wuhan Institute of Virology. The first known outbreak, after all, was in Wuhan. Consequently, monikers such as "Kung Flu," "Chinese Flu," and "the China Virus" began circulating online and in the media. This racialized language was frequently used by the president of the United States himself when addressing the public. While business shuttered, schools closed, hospital beds filled up, and tensions heightened, people began looking at each other as potential carriers of the virus. This fear of others, however, acquired new meaning in the repeated attempts to blame China, part of the political leadership's attempt to skirt responsibility for its negligence in the early days of the pandemic. This led many to become particularly fearful of not only Chinese people but anyone of East Asian descent, a fear leading to resentment, blame, and hate. It is because of "them," the thought went, that one must now wear a mask, practice safe distance, get inoculated, and put up with additional government intrusion into our lives, a type of guilt via ethnic or racial association.

In terms of economic uncertainty, the sense of loss that leads to group-directed hatred was recently elucidated by the legal scholar and law professor Ian Haney López (2019). His team found that economic pessimism and the potential loss of intergenerational wealth, especially in terms of leaving something to one's children or the thought of their future job prospects, lead to increased racial resentment, "the sense of losing ground compared to others, especially to [racial or ethnic] groups perceived as underserving" (Haney López 2019, 59). Easily manipulated by politicians seeking to leverage hatred as fuel for their candidacy or political platform, this resentment can be a powerful tool. In a passage that Haney López quotes (and that bears repeating here in full), the sociologist Arlie Hochschild captures this resentment in her book *Strangers in Their Own Land: Anger and Mourning on the American Right* (2016):

> You are patiently standing in the middle of a long line stretching toward the horizon, where the American Dream awaits. But as you wait, you see people cutting in line ahead of you. Many of these line-cutters are black—beneficiaries of affirmative action or welfare. Some are career-driven women pushing into jobs they never had before. Then you see immigrants, Mexicans, Somalis, the Syrian refuges yet to come. As you wait in this unmoving line, you're being asked to feel sorry for them all. You have a good heart. But who is deciding

who you should feel compassion for? Then you see President Barack Hussein Obama waving the line-cutters forward. He's on their side. In fact, isn't he a line-cutter too? How did this fatherless black guy pay for Harvard? As you wait your turn, Obama is using the money in your pocket to help the line-cutters. He and his liberal backers have removed the shame from taking. The government has become an instrument for redistributing your money to the undeserving. It's not your government anymore; it's theirs. (Haney López 2019, 62)

Hochschild's words depict the sense of dwindling opportunities and victimization that often engenders disdain for certain groups. Haney López relies upon these words to explain how exploiting this animus can turn many voters toward political agendas that prey upon fear, anger, and resentment—a point I find fascinating since while it might be the case that hatred cannot be accidental, it is the type of complex emotion that can be easily manipulated.

Notice that in Hochschild's words and Haney López research two senses of "hatred/hate" become visible. Both are pertinent to my overview of nature of group-directed hatred. On the one hand, there is the animosity and anger that comes about because of the feeling that others are getting ahead of you and taking what is rightfully yours. This "hotter," more malevolent sense of hatred tends to be described as the narrower meaning of this term (Brogaard 2020, xiii and 33–34). It constitutes the image of hatred most associated with overt acts of racial terror and violence. On the other hand, a "wider" sense of hatred becomes particularly apparent when so-called line-cutters are described as "undeserving." This second sense of hatred is contempt-driven and differs from the anger-based form insofar as it tends to manifest as the blatant disregard or devaluation of the well-being of a group or person. In the above passage, a preestablished and already-existing "wider" sense of contempt-based hate leads to the narrower, hotter feeling.

While instances of the narrower understanding of hatred all too often manifest in group-directed or social-identity-based hatred, especially as violence, most instances of group-directed hatred are contempt-driven, or so I contend. Although many instances of hate crimes, for instance, might not arise from feelings of intense animosity toward the victim(s) (Levin and McDevitt 1998, 90), the fact that racialized minorities or immigrants are the kinds of person one can take pleasure in tormenting ("thrill-seeking") rests upon this sense of contempt.

Group-directed contempt need not arise from the belief that the targets of hatred are in some way inferior or less than human such that hatred of them is warranted. This marks the difference between my understanding of group-directed hatred and that of others who believe that central to the sense of contempt is the notion that hate targets deserve to be hated. For instance, the philosopher Berit Brogaard (2020) explains that to contemn a person means that "we judge, or condemn, them for their flawed character" or "look down on a person for vices they possess—vices tied to repugnant practices, such as gluttony, sloth, lust, pride, envy, greed, and wrath" (Brogaard 2020, 34). Similarly, Agneta Fischer et al. found that the ascription of malicious intent or an underlying and unchangeable malevolent nature works well to generate hate feelings (2018, 310). Targets of hatred are frequently described as fundamentally corrupt, immoral, "bad hombres," criminals, individuals prone to violence and assault, "nasty" people, and so on. Szanto refers to this process as hatred's "collectivizing" nature. The act of hating lumps together the targets of hatred in a generalizable way that then serves as a reference point not only for creating a sense of "we" (a community of haters) but also offering a continual justification for seeing this group in a negative light, and thereby offering a means of perpetuating the act of hating. This explains why it is often said that hatred calls for the complete destruction or annihilation of the hate target (Fischer et al. 2018, 311), a point I do not necessarily agree with.[8]

On my view, it is entirely possible to recognize an individual or group as equal if not at least deserving of a certain degree of moral respect (as the law or morality dictate) and still contemn against them. That is what makes the act of hating so wrong. The professor of practical theology Dr. Chanequa Walker-Barnes (2020) demonstrates this point in "Prayer of a Weary Black Woman." Generating quite the stir, in her prayer Walker-Barnes asks God to help her "hate White people" (2020, 69). Hatred, in her prayer, amounts to the ability to "stop caring about them, individually and collectively." She continues, "I want to stop caring about their misguided, racist souls, to stop believing that they can be better, that they can stop being racist" (Walker-Barnes 2020, 69). Hatred, for Walker-Barnes, is the ability to disregard, the opposite of care, the opposite of being invested in what the white people she has in mind think and do. She is not asking for violence or harm to come to her intended hate targets. Instead, she's simply asking for the ability to disinvest in them. Walker-Barnes reminds us that this prayer is not meant for all white people. White anti-racist allies are excluded as are ardent racists (2020, 70). Both are committed to their ideals and values (or ways of devaluing in the case of the latter). The white people Walker-Barnes wants to hate are those who purport to be good, nice folk, but really mask their racism behind liberal ideals or phony forms of Christianity. She does not recognize the white people she has in mind as less than human or undeserving of moral consideration—she is seeking permission from God to *stop* caring for them. Instead, it is *her* frustrations with the white people she has in mind that drive the desire to hate. From my point of view, what upsets many individuals about this prayer, especially those who did not read past the first line, was the fact that Walker-Barnes was, in a sense, asking God for the ability to do as they do: hate in this contempt-based way.

Not to care or to care insufficiently about a person's well-being means that they are deserving of more consideration and yet one precisely denies them this. Justifying or rationalizing hate-based contempt is where ascriptions of inferiority come in. They enter, however, the way racecraft does. That is to say, it is *because* you are inferior or in some way different that I hate you. People are born into hate traditions or ways of contemning such that their identity and actions take shape within preexisting forms of devaluation and social hierarchy that often correspond with group-identity. These preexisting social relations have a way of claiming one's affect and often supply an assortment of rationalizations for why one can disregard the wellbeing of others, but they are often second to the act of hating itself. Although hatred may not be the type of emotion that allows one to recall the precise moment one started feeling hatred toward a person or group, it does not require the type of process by which one is led to hate *after* reflecting on whether or not their target is superior, inferior, or equal. The feeling of hatred seems to be more immediate than the justification and rationalization of it. For this reason, I think that what motivates group-directed hatred the most is this sense of contempt mixed with fear and the range of anxieties mentioned above: the sense of loss or being "left behind," concerns regarding cultural alienation or being a minority in one's own land, and the desire for status or power that is quickly dissipating.

This point about the fear of difference leading to feelings of hate is not new. It has become somewhat commonplace to assume that hatred is caused by a lack of understanding or unfamiliarity, as in people come to hate that thing or those persons they do not understand or know. Often ascribed to Ibn Rushd (Averroës, 1126-1198 CE), this idea is frequently put in the formula: "ignorance leads to fear, fear leads to hate, and hate leads to violence. This is the equation" (see Lerner 1974, 16). In many ways, this formula is correct. Uncertainty or unfamiliarity with a person or group rouses suspicion, the need for caution, and even invites prejudgment (as in expecting the worst from strangers). These feelings generate fear which in turn causes aversive tendencies leading one to despise a person or entire social groups. We despise them because they expose our vulnerabilities and point out the limits of who we are and what we know.

If there is an aspect of group-directed hatred which is often overlooked, it is that hatred is learned behavior. That is to say, while the fear that inspires hatred is natural, the specific shape it takes—"hatred"—is not. Like other emotions, hatred is a resource for individuals and groups to make sense of their feelings toward objects and other persons. This is why my own discussion of the moral psychology of hatred reversed the direction scholars tend to look when examining the nature of group-directed hatred. My discussion has tried to focus attention "not only on those who have been injured but on the political and affective desires and racial imaginaries of 'those who *generate* injury,'" as the political theorist Cristina Beltrán (2020, 34, emphasis in original) writes, herself borrowing from the thoughts of Hagar Kotef. In the next section, I provide more detail about how hatred can become a resource that helps individuals and communities make sense of who they are.

3. ANTI-IMMIGRANT SENTIMENT AND WHITE SUPREMACY AS A TRADITION

Drawing from Ahmed's (2014) account of the sociality of emotions, this section explains how it is the case that emotions are not simply mental states or internal feelings but attitudes that "circulate" in communities and between individuals, products of the dialectical interplay between our internal states and those ways of thinking about emotions prevalent in our society. More specifically, I contend that there are individuals and communities throughout the world today who have come to depend upon and "trust in" hatred, as Szanto (2018) writes. This sense of dependence or trust, as I will explain, is not just practical but also ideological. In a community that cannot exist without contempt for others, there is as much "value" in the act of hating as there is in the idea of hatred.

Once a hateful disposition takes hold in a community or among a group of individuals it becomes a variable in the calculus determining their identity. As such, it must be proven through action and deed, as Franz Fanon writes in the epigraph above. Although one might be able to suppress the feeling of hatred for some time, doing so becomes increasingly difficult as this sentiment requires an outlet, "it has to be embodied," a facet of hatred that is necessary for it to spread. After all, expressing one's hatred becomes easier when others share in it. Hatred, in this way, often amounts to a tradition or way of life that demands continuation, for if it were to be let go, little else would be left and people might not recognize themselves anymore.

In suggesting that hatred can be a "tradition" I am saying, in part, that "emotions are partially constrained and defined by culture" (Brogaard 2020, 3). As the psychologist Lisa Feldman Barrett puts it, emotions are biologically evident *and* socially constructed, they depend upon "socially shared conceptual knowledge that perceivers use to create meaning" (2012, 1). Barrett's thoughts regarding the nature of emotions fits nicely alongside Ahmed's claim that emotions should not be regarded exclusively as psychological states but social and cultural practices (Ahmed 2014, 9). Ahmed questions both "inside-out" and "outside-in" approaches to emotions. The former begins introspectively with human interiority and "psychologizes" emotions. Any sense of "sociality" here requires one to express *their* feelings and see if others feel the same way. Emotions move outward on this model. Conversely, the idea that "emotions are assumed to *come from without and move inward*" (Ahmed 2014, 9, emphasis in original) is equally problematic. Ahmed is cautious to avoid claiming that all that matters is the "outside," a move that would assume that "the crowd," as she terms it, has feelings and these feelings constitute our individual emotional states. Instead, her point is that there is a dialectical interplay between "the outside" and "the inside." On the one hand, this interplay affords us the concepts and language required to make sense of how we feel internally. On the other hand, this language allows us to communicate these feelings with others, thus contributing to our group life. Emotions, in this sense, are proof of our intersubjectivity.

Moreover, given that few things can bind individuals like a common threat or enemy, hatred is the type of emotion through which community can be formed and social ties can be strengthened. In reality, as I explained earlier, it is the feelings of insecurity and fear that unites a community of haters (to admit that, however, would mean that the hatred comes from within and not without). Nevertheless, the problem with this type of "community" is that it can never be at peace and will continue to kick an inevitable identity crisis down the road. It must therefore keep the hatred going in order to maintain social cohesion.

Continuing my analogy from earlier, as in algebra and other branches of mathematics, variables are placeholders for quantities or expressions that may vary or change but are nonetheless integral to an equation as a whole. As a variable, hatred is bound by external constraints and the extent to which hateful persons are willing to suffer the consequences of public displays of hatred. This is why, if social mores and, more importantly, law, effectively proscribe the ability to lynch, people in the United States replace it with discrimination, as Frantz Fanon notes earlier. Once racial discrimination is prohibited, hatred moves on to something else. This section tracks that something else. I argue that anti-immigrant sentiment maintains the same affective focus that motivated past instances of racial violence in the United States. This focus—white racial security and social standing—is the middle term that unites the history (and present) of racialized violence in the United States with the resurgence of anti-immigrant fervor. In order to make sense of what I mean by an affective focus, I return to Szanto once again.

Drawing from contemporary phenomenology, Szanto breaks down the affective-intentional structure of emotions into three parts: the target of an emotion, the formal object of an emotion, and the focus of an emotion. The *target* of an emotion "is any correlate object that a given emotion is directed at and evaluates and that elicits an affective response" (Szanto 2018, 461). As an example, take my fear of being stung by wasps. In this case, wasps are the "target" of my emotion. The *formal object* of an emotion is

> not the object simpliciter that a particular emotion is directed at. Rather, it is the correlate that the type of emotion tracks. It is in virtue of the formal object that a particular emotion construes the target (e.g., refugees) as having a particular type of evaluative property (e.g., odiousness). (Szanto 2018, 462)

In the case of hatred, the formal object is what makes a target "hateworthy" or "odious," two evaluative terms connected to the feeling of hatred. In the case of my fear of being stung by wasps, the formal object would be "fearfulness" or the need for caution that accompanies being in the presence of something dangerous. The formal object connects the target of the emotion(s) it stirs in a way that is shaped by an emotion's focus. The *focus* of an emotion is

> the background object of concern that links the evaluative property to the target and is hence definitive of the formal object of the emotion. . . . The focus is what renders intelligible how and why the target is affectively significant for the subject, or why the emotion has the formal object it has.

A focus is "carved out against the background of all that matters to the subject" (Szanto 2018, 462). It brings to light why a particular target has the affective weight or significance it does for a subject, thus rendering my concern not a mere judgment or an "emotional reaction" but a felt-evaluative response.

In my wasp example, fearfulness emanates from concerns I have for my body. The focus is my desire not to be stung or feel pain. In the case of group-directed hatred, its unique nature is such that both the target and the formal object are "blurry" (Szanto 2018, 463–64). The "hateworthiness" of hate targets arises not from the target themselves—in fact, the targets are interchangeable insofar as they are depicted in a way that generates the evaluative properties typically connected to the feeling of hatred—but from the insecurities, fears, inadequacies, and even *the need for hatred* itself that constitutes "all that matters to the subject," as Szanto mentioned earlier. Rarely (if ever) is the affective focus of hatred concerned with the actual targets of hatred themselves. Instead, hate targets are a reflective medium upon which the hater projects their own emotional (and social and political) investments. The hateful person thus needs the target of hatred as a foil. This is part of what Szanto terms the "negative dialectics" of hatred.

This phenomenon of "negative dialectics" comes out of the attachment many people have to the very act of hating itself. As Szanto puts it, "Hatred gets its affective power for free, as it were, namely from a commitment and, in particular, a shared commitment to the attitude [of hatred] itself" (2018, 455). This is the sense in which, as Fanon writes, "hatred cries out to exist." Once hatred becomes a part of who a person or a group is, they become dependent on the act of hating and need a target that can easily be "collectivized." This process of collectivization gives hateful persons a "them," which in turn generates a "we" (Szanto 2018, 470). With hatred, the "them" is almost always fungible and can be replaced by anyone who is capable of threatening the "we." It is the "we" or "us" who really matter. Hatred in this form takes the shape of a relationship, a dependency of the "we" on the target of hatred (Szanto 2018, 470). Through the act of hating, one structures a relationship not only with the target of one's hatred, but more importantly with oneself and one's own community of haters (Alford 2006, 236). This relationship need not be real, and, indeed, it often is not in group-directed contexts. Ahmed writes, "Hatred is a negative attachment to an other that one wishes to expel, an attachment that is sustained through the expulsion of the other from bodily and social proximity" (Ahmed 2014, 55). Few things are capable of this sense of expulsion like "the border." Unlike segregation, in which laws were construed to "make difference legal," as the Rev. Dr. Martin Luther King Jr. put it, immigration law does not need to concoct racial difference as a justification. The state of being an "alien" in relation to the nation's citizen already does this. It is a legal category that, at least superficially, does not rest on racial fantasy.

Yet as much as a people might need hatred in this sense, as well as the target of hatred, they also often need to think of themselves as above or beyond the act of hating, as odd as that might sound. This is where the distinction between contempt-based and anger-driven hatred becomes relevant again. Hatred more easily transforms into a way of life or tradition, or so I will argue, when the contempt-based form of hatred takes hold of a community. This is why the narrower, "hotter" meaning of hatred captures popular opinion, and why few people are accustomed to think of themselves as hateful (in the wider, contempt-based form), especially when group-directed or social-identity-based hatred intersects with histories of racism.

To spell this out, one reason why the experience of hatred often goes unnoticed, especially in the United States, is because of the role it plays in the "national psyche."[9] This psyche situates hatred in a special place, and few things call it to mind like a nation's history of racial violence. Within the U.S. psyche, the close association between hatred and racial violence is not accidental. It is a consequence of the attempts to deal with what the Mexican philosopher Jorge Portilla (2020 [1952]) deemed "the Spiritual Crisis of the United States." For Portilla, this crisis amounts to the need to preserve the image of the collective innocence of this country amid the evil its citizens have committed. Portilla describes this innocence as the unfamiliarity with or foreignness of evil: "He is innocent who is not defiled by evil in general or by sin in particular. An innocent world will thus be that world in which evil has not penetrated, where evil has not corrupted the root of life itself" (Portilla 2020 [1952], 178).

In order to resolve one aspect of this crisis, namely that connected to its long history of racial antipathy, the U.S. psyche needs anger-based hatred to reside at the causal root of racial violence. Without this sense of hatred providing the spark that ignites the flames of racist activity, many Americans cannot resolve the cognitive dissonance they experience when forced to consider their nation's history of racism in tandem with its claims to moral exceptionalism. "Hatred" thus serves as a disassociation technique that offers individuals and communities the ability to compartmentalize and even evade responsibility for the racism and structural injustice they have come to depend upon. Confronted with such tension—that is, torn between a reality that does not square with one's imagining of it—the idea of hatred becomes one of the levees keeping inner psychic chaos at bay. Similar to the theological notion of "privation," the concept of hatred is thus a convenient emotive attitude to situate at the core of racial violence, since it allows one to compartmentalize it in the present. Anger-based hatred assumes the role of a secularized form of "evil." It becomes a mechanism used to explain atrocities and heinous acts that do not square with the innocent image of their nation. Vitriolic examples of hatred offer a containment strategy that helps to shape and define an innocent image of the United States by pointing to what it is not, therefore making evil extraordinary. With this framing, "America" is not hateful. Those who engage in hateful behavior have betrayed the ideals of the nation.

Anti-immigrant sentiment avoids this whole process, since exclusive forms of citizenship provide a rationale for differential treatment based on a political classification, not any form of racial categorization. In reality, though, political membership is just as problematic as a reason for disregarding the moral equality of human being. This is why pro-border adherents wrap their claims in the garb of legality and illegality. Naked appeals to law are all they have. Migrants can be targeted from this viewpoint because of their legal transgressions. They "deserve" negative treatment, even when their "transgression" is seeking political asylum. Borders here become a literal monument to their ability to disregard and not care for those they exclude. And even though racialized targets are central to this narrative, to focus on that issue heads in the wrong direction, for it is really white racial standing that drives anti-immigrant sentiment.

Whereas contempt-based hatred might be already present in the divide between the citizens and noncitizen, there are aspects of anti-immigrant fervor that are undoubtedly crueler. Cristina Beltrán (2020) captures this sense of hate in her book *Cruelty as Citizenship: How Migrant Suffering Sustains White Democracy*. According to Beltrán, the ideal of citizenship in the United States amounts to a right to dominate others. It is not only that targeting migrants "makes [certain individuals] feel stronger, freer, and more agentic," she says, but that it also transforms "acts of racialized violence into heroism, democratic redemption, civic engagement and virtuous sovereignty" (Beltrán 2020, 23). In his manifesto, Patrick Crusius—the man who shot and killed 22 people and injured 24 others at a Walmart in El Paso, Texas, on August

3, 2019—wrote that "I am simply defending my country from cultural and ethnic replacement brought on by an invasion." Targeting mainly "immigrant looking" Latinx people, he continues, "My motives for this attack are not at all personal." Similar motivations also laid behind three other 2019 mass shootings: the July 29 garlic festival massacre in Gilroy, California; the April 27 synagogue attack in Poway, California; and the March 15 assaults on two mosques in Christchurch, New Zealand.

From Beltrán's perspective, what immigrants threaten to take away is the "right" to oppress. This "right" is erroneously grounded in the freedom of speech, or the Second Amendment to the U.S. Constitution, hence the reason why the language of citizenship is so important. Along these lines, reactionary attacks on political correctness (from "anti-woke" culture) in the United States and elsewhere are expressions of frustrated identity-formation. At stake is the ability of individuals who have come to internalize a hateful disposition to be who they are and to enjoy the hateful traditions to which they belong without suffering any negative social or political consequences. These are persons and communities whose identities are bound up with the act of hating. The fear of loss does not only mean having one's land overrun, or taken over by foreigners, as Crusius wrote. It also entails having one's hateful traditions and hateful ways of being upended for something that involves less hatred. If hate works when a subject imagines they are on the verge of losing something, and if that something is a hateful tradition and way of being, then the ability to hate and hold others in contempt will be what they cherish most. It should be of no surprise that trying to take away the ability to hate creates even more hate.

NOTES

1. Fanon (2008 [1952], 35–36).
2. Baldwin (1998, 75).
3. By "migrants" I mean the general category of persons or groups moving across national borders. This includes those seeking to immigrate into a new country ("immigrants"), those seeking asylum for a variety of reasons ("asylum-seekers"), and those forced to move because of such things as environmental catastrophe, food scarcity, bleak economic prospects, civil unrest, or war ("refugees"). Needless to say, from my point of view, tourists are not migrants.
4. Throughout this chapter, I prefer "group-directed" and not "intergroup" hatred. The latter conveys the notion that two or more groups are at odds with each other. Such an idea does not capture the asymmetrical power relations and long-standing histories of violence against minorities that tend to constitute the backdrop against which the kind of hatred I am concerned with in this chapter occurs.

5. When serving as a deterrent, hate crimes are intended to address the fact that their prevalence in society directly contributes to racial strife, thereby harming societies striving to achieve some degree of racial justice: another reason why additional charges and tougher sentencing are associated with them.

6. The legal defense in Derek Chauvin's trial for the murder of George Floyd turned to racecraft when suggesting that Floyd—who was pinned down by the police officer for 9 minutes and 29 seconds—died as a result of a preexisting heart condition and history of drug use. The legal defense called upon David Fowler, former chief medical examiner for the state of Maryland, to explain how in his assessment, Floyd's preexisting heart condition and history of drug use, conditions which are well-documented as afflicting U.S. African Americans, are what contributed to his death (and *not* Chauvin's knee on Floyd's back and neck for the entire duration of that time). The defense tried to pin this case on Floyd's race and not Chauvin's callous disregard for Floyd's life, thereby transforming the practice of racism into race.

7. Compared to the same time in 2020 anti-Asian hate crime increased 189% in the first quarter of 2021 (Center for the Study of Hate and Extremism). Since the coronavirus outbreak "32% of Asian adults say they have feared someone might threaten or attack them—a greater share than other racial or ethnic groups," 71% of U.S. adults "see a lot or some discrimination against Asian people," and "45% percent of Asian adults say they have experienced at least one of five specific offensive incidents since the start of the coronavirus outbreak" (Ruiz et al. 2021).

8. See my comments on lynching above—the complete annihilation of black people would have been detrimental to the southern slave-based economy.

9. My use of "psyche" refers to how nations are frequently described as having a collective mindset, a spirit, or even a soul (as in "the soul of a nation"). Typically capturing the range of ideas, values, attitudes, beliefs, and feelings prevalent among those persons who inhabit the racial, gender, cultural, and sexual norm, these national imaginings are frequently at odds with the complexity afforded by the sub- and multinational communities within them. Amid this limitation, analyzing the collective mindset of a nation offers valuable insight into how individual members of it imagine their social whole.

REFERENCES

Ahmed, Sarah. 2014. *The Cultural Politics of Emotion*. 2nd ed. Edinburgh: Edinburgh University Press.

Alford, C. Fred. 2005. "Hate is the Imitation of Love." In *The Psychology of Hate*, edited by Robert J. Sternberg, 235–54. Washington, DC: American Psychological Association.

Aristotle. 2009. *The Nicomachean Ethics*. Translated by David Ross. New York: Oxford University Press.

Baldwin, James. 1998. "Notes of a Native Son." In *James Baldwin: Collected Essays*, edited by Toni Morrison, 63–84. New York: Library of America.

Barrett, Lisa Feldman. 2012. "Emotions are Real." *Emotion* 12 (3): 413–29.

Beltrán, Cristina. 2020. *Cruelty as Citizenship: How Migrant Suffering Sustains White Democracy*. Minneapolis: University of Minnesota Press.
Bem, Daryl J. 1972. "Self-Perception Theory." *Advances in Experimental Social Psychology* 6: 1–62.
Brogaard, Berit. 2020. *Hatred: Understanding Our Most Dangerous Emotion*. New York: Oxford University Press.
Brudholm, Thomas and Brigid Schepelern Johansen. 2018. "Pondering Hatred." In *Emotions and Mass Atrocity: Philosophical and Theoretical Explorations*, edited by Thomas Brudholm and Johannes Lang, 81–103. New York: Cambridge University Press.
Center for the Study of Hate and Extremism, CSUSB. 2021. "Report to the Nation: Anti-Asian Prejudice and Hate Crime—City Data Chart" (June 1, 2021). https://www.csusb.edu/hate-and-extremism-center. Accessed June 27, 2021.
Cone, James H. 2013. *The Cross and the Lynching Tree*. New York: Orbis Books.
Fanon, Franz. 2008 [1952]. *Black Skin, White Masks*. Translated by Richard Philcox. New York: Grove Press.
Fields, Karen E., and Barbara J. Fields. 2014. *Racecraft: The Soul of Inequality in American Life*. New York: Verso.
Fischer, Agneta, Eran Halperin, Daphna Canetti, and Alba Jasini. 2018. "Why We Hate." *Emotion Review* 10 (4): 309–20. Reprinted in this volume, chap. 7.
Haney López, Ian. 2019. *Merge Left: Fusing Race and Class, Winning Elections, and Saving America*. New York: The New Press.
Kotef, Hagar. 2020. "Violent Attachments." *Political Theory* 48 (1): 4–29.
Lerner, Ralph. 1974. *Averroes on Plato's Republic*. Translated by Ralph Lerner. Ithaca: Cornell University Press.
Levin, Jack, and Jack McDevitt. 1998. "Hate Crimes." In *The Encyclopedia of Peace, Violence, and Conflict*, edited by Lester R. Kurtz, 89–101. 1st ed. New York: Academic Press.
Mills, Charles W. 2017. *Black Rights/White Wrongs: The Critique of Racial Liberalism*. New York: Oxford University Press.
Portilla, Jorge. 2020 [1952]. "The Spiritual Crisis of the United States." In *The Disintegration of Community: On Jorge Portilla's Social and Political Philosophy*, edited by Carlos Sanchez and Francisco Gallegos, 175–90. Albany: State University of New York Press.
Ramirez, Mark D. and David A. M. Peterson. 2020. *Ignored Racism: White Animus Towards Latinos*. New York: Cambridge University Press.
Ruiz, Neil G., Khadijah Edwards, and Mark Hugo Lopez. 2021. "One-Third of Asian Americans Fear Threats, Physical Attacks, and Most Say Violence against Them is Rising." *Pew Research Center*, April 21, 2021. https://www.pewresearch.org/fact-tank/2021/04/21/one-third-of-asian-americans-fear-threats-physical-attacks-and-most-say-violence-against-them-is-rising/. Accessed June 27, 2021.
Shanmugasundaram, Swathi. 2018. "Hate Crimes, Explained." *Southern Poverty Law Center*. https://www.splcenter.org/20180415/hate-crimes-explained. Accessed June 27, 2021.

Silva, Grant J. 2019. "Racism as Self-Love." *Radical Philosophy Review* 22 (1): 85–112.

Silva, Grant J. 2021. "On 'Ur-Contempt' and the Maintenance of Racial Injustice: A Response to Monahan's 'Racism and "Self-Love": The Case of White Nationalism'." *Critical Philosophies of Race* 9 (1): 16–26.

Staub, Ervin. 2005. "The Origins and Evolution of Hate, With Notes on Prevention." In *The Psychology of Hate*, edited by Robert J. Sternberg, 51–66. Washington, DC: American Psychological Association.

Sternberg, Robert J. 2005. "Understanding and Combating Hate." In *The Psychology of Hate*, edited by Robert J. Sternberg, 37–49. Washington, DC: American Psychological Association.

Sternberg, Robert J. and Karin Sternberg. 2008. *The Nature of Hate*. New York: Cambridge University Press.

Stikkers, Kenneth W. 2014. "'. . . But I'm not Racist': Towards a Pragmatist Conception of 'Racism'." *The Pluralist* 9 (3): 1–17.

Sun, Key. 2006. "The Legal Definition of Hate Crime and the Hate Offender's Distorted Cognition." *Issues in Mental Health Nursing* 27 (6): 597–604.

Szanto, Thomas. 2020. "In Hate We Trust: The Collectivization and Habitualization of Hatred." *Phenomenology and the Cognitive Sciences* 19: 453–80.

Van Bavel, J. J., J. L. Ray, Y. Granot, and W. A. Cunningham. 2018. "The Psychology of Hate: Moral Concerns Differentiate Hate from Dislike." Unpublished manuscript.

Walker-Barnes, Chanequa. 2020. "Prayer of a Weary Black Woman." In *A Rhythm of Prayer*, edited by Sarah Bessey, 69–72. New York: Convergent.

Chapter 6

"Woman-Hating" as Redescription

Kate M. Phelan

Intercourse is the pure, sterile, formal expression of men's contempt for women.
—Andrea Dworkin[1]

1. INTRODUCTION

Feminists sometimes speak of women as hated by men. On one level, we need only read Norman Mailer in order to understand exactly what feminists mean, and to think them right. But further thought complicates talk of woman-hating. Such talk ascribes to men a hostility toward women. In male-dominant society, however, a man properly desires a woman, marries her, makes love to, and lives in intimacy with her. In other words, he relates to her as an object of sexual or romantic *love*. "In no other situation," Sarah Hoagland says, "are people expected to love, identify with, and become other to those who dominate them to the extent that women are supposed to love, identify with, and become other to men."[2] Love is hate's opposite. Curiously, woman-hating appears at odds with the nature of the relations between men and women in male-dominant society. If it is, then it exists only as an aberration.

Kate Manne arrives at a similar conclusion, but via, I think, different reasoning. She argues that insofar as women fulfill their roles, men have no cause to hate them: "When it comes to the women who are not only dutifully but lovingly catering to his desires, what's to hate, exactly?"[3] It is therefore unclear how woman-hating could be rife within male-dominant society (45). I am arguing instead that the relations between men and women in male-dominant

119

society are relations of a certain sort of love, and that it is therefore unclear how men could be said to hate women, other than aberrationally.

What, then, might feminists mean? For when they speak of women as hated by men, they are speaking of a hatred that is not aberrational but systemic. In this paper, I offer a novel answer to this question. I argue that talk of woman-hating is best understood as what Richard Rorty terms "redescription."

2. WOMEN'S OPPRESSION

Feminists, radical feminists in particular, implicate sexuality and its conceptual sibling, romantic love, in men's oppression of women. Catharine MacKinnon says that "sexuality is the linchpin of gender inequality" (MacKinnon 1989, 113); Andrea Dworkin that "romantic love, in pornography as in life, is the mythic celebration of female negation" (Dworkin 1976, 105); Sarah Hoagland that heterosexualism "de-skills a woman, makes her emotionally, socially, and economically dependent, and allows another to dominate her 'for her own good' all in the name of 'love'" (Hoagland 2001, 67); Ti-Grace Atkinson that "the phenomenon of love is the psychological pivot in the persecution of women" (Atkinson 1974, 43); and Shulamith Firestone that "love, perhaps even more than childbearing, is the pivot of women's oppression today" (Firestone 1970, 126).

MacKinnon most fully explicates the place of sexuality in men's oppression of women. She argues that the molding of sexuality is the creation of the genders:

> The molding, direction, and expression of sexuality organizes society into two sexes: women and men. This division underlies the totality of social relations. Sexuality is the process through which social relations of gender are created, organized, expressed, and directed, creating the beings we know as women and men. (MacKinnon 1989, 3)

If the molding of sexuality is the creation of the genders, what does it create them as? Some people—male people—are socialized to eroticize dominance, and thereby become men, and others—female people—are socialized to eroticize subordination, and thereby become women. On this argument, men are just those who eroticize dominance and women those who eroticize subordination. MacKinnon says, "Sexuality is gendered as gender is sexualized. Male and female are created through the eroticization of dominance and submission" (MacKinnon 1989, 113).

This, MacKinnon observes, reveals as noncoincidental the dual meaning of "sex." If men are those who eroticize dominance and women those who eroticize subordination, then men's realization as men and women's as women is their realization as sexual beings. One is realized as a sexual being by satiating one's sexual desire, which one does in the act of sex. If men's realization as men and women's as women is their realization as sexual beings, and if one's realization as a sexual being occurs in the act of sex, then men's realization as men and women's as women occurs in the act of sex. Men and women become men and women—the sexes—in sex (MacKinnon 1989, 143).

On MacKinnon's theory, the relations of men qua men with women qua women are sexual. They are animated by, and consummated in the satiation of, sexual desire. If the relations of men qua men with women qua women are sexual, then it seems to me that we cannot describe them as hateful of women. In our vocabulary, "sexual" is a species of "love": to have sexual intercourse is to make love. Similarly, to desire is to feel attraction rather than aversion to. So, to describe men's relations with women as relations of hate is to describe relations of love as relations of hate, which is incoherent. If the relations of men qua men with women qua women are sexual, and if we therefore cannot describe them as hateful of women, then how can we speak of woman-hating?

3. A FIRST PASS

MacKinnon's theory does not leave us altogether unable to speak of woman-hating. Certain sexual relations are recognizable as abusive, hence the concept "sexual abuse." As an abuse is consistent with a feeling of aversion, these relations can be described as hateful of women. We can, then, speak of woman-hating. But in our vocabulary sexual abuse is not the sexual in its proper form.[4] It is either not sexual at all—a "crime of violence rather than passion,"[5] an "act of power, not sex"[6]—or a corruption of the sexual. It is perverse, pathological, and harmful, while the sexual is natural, healthy, and good.

If the relations of men qua men with women qua women are sexual, if only those sexual relations that are abusive can be described as hateful of women, and if sexual relations that are abusive are corruptions of the sexual, then those relations that can be described as hateful of women are corruptions of the relations of men qua men with women qua women. As such, they are aberrational, not systemic. This pass thus fails to account for woman-hating as a systemic phenomenon.

In addition, "sexual abuse" is defined in relation to "appropriate sexual use": the former is that which exceeds the latter. In male-dominant society, the appropriate sexual use of a woman is the conquest of her. As one who eroticizes subordination, a woman is one who is to be treated accordingly, and to be treated accordingly is to be conquered. If sexual abuse is that which exceeds appropriate sexual use, and if the appropriate sexual use of a woman is the conquest of her, then the sexual abuse of a woman is only what exceeds such conquest. It is not conquest itself. So, if we locate woman-hating in sexual abuse, then it precludes men's conquest of women. It seems to me that feminists should want woman-hating to encompass such conquest.

4. A SECOND PASS

Perhaps we can make use of the Marxian idea of ideology in order to account for woman-hating. This idea consists in two claims. First, the beliefs of the ruling class have become the prevailing beliefs; second, the beliefs of the ruling class justify the social arrangement.[7] The beliefs of the ruling class therefore form an *ideology*, a constellation of beliefs that obscures the real—unjust—nature of the social arrangement. Insofar as ideology *obscures* the real nature of the social arrangement, the idea of ideology permits a distinction between ideology and reality. So, perhaps we can argue that in the ideology of male dominance women are those who eroticize subordination, and that this ideology obscures a reality in which women do not eroticize subordination. If women do not eroticize subordination, then men's conquest of women constitutes a sexual abuse rather than appropriate sexual use. The relations of men qua men with women qua women are thus in reality sexually abusive rather than sexual.

If the relations of men qua men with women qua women are sexually abusive, then they are consistent with a feeling of aversion. They are therefore coherently describable as hateful of women. This pass avoids both of the above problems. First, if the relations of men qua men with women qua women are hateful of women, then woman-hating is systemic. Second, if men's conquest of women constitutes a sexual abuse rather than appropriate sexual use, then sexual abuse encompasses conquest, and so too woman-hating.

On reflection, however, this pass too is unsatisfactory. Women may not eroticize subordination, but so long as men are enthralled to ideology, so long as they believe that women do eroticize subordination, they shall dominate women and, crucially, they shall regard this domination as respectful of women's natures. Insofar as they regard this domination as respectful, they cannot be said to be acting from hatred.

Perhaps men are enthralled to ideology only on the level of the conscious. That is, perhaps their conscious belief that women eroticize subordination conceals an unconscious belief that women are full human beings, and hence their conscious regard of domination as respectful of women an unconscious regard of domination as disrespectful of women. If they unconsciously regard domination as disrespectful of women, then in dominating women they can be said to be acting from a hatred of women.

I find this rather unconvincing. We attribute to the unconscious precisely so that the conscious can then neither verify nor falsify. But what can verify or falsify our attribution to the unconscious? Our freedom to attribute what we wish to the unconscious makes the claim that men unconsciously believe that women are full human beings a little too convenient.

This claim appears all the more convenient when we consider that feminists have long argued that men do not consider women human beings. Marilyn Frye explains well what they mean. She distinguishes between two senses of humanity—biological humanity and full personhood—and argues that although men consider women human in the first sense, they do not consider them human in the second:

> The personhood of which I am speaking here is "full" personhood. I am speaking of unqualified participation in the radical "superiority" of the species, without justification by individual virtue or achievement—unqualified membership of that group of beings that may approach all other creatures with humanist arrogance. Members of this group are to be treated not humanely but with respect. It is plain that not everybody, not even almost everybody, agrees that women belong to this group. (Frye 1983, 48–49)

For feminists to then claim that men unconsciously believe that women are full human beings appears disingenuous, contrived to salvage talk of woman-hating.

To say that the relations of men qua men with women qua women are sexually abusive is to say that the apparently sexual is in reality the sexually abusive. A further problem emerges: if the apparently sexual is in reality the sexually abusive, then nothing remains of "the sexual," in conjunction with which "the sexually abusive" exists. "Sexual" becomes a term with no referent. In order to avoid this problem, we might allow that some of the apparently sexual is sexual. But if the sexual is conquest, then to do this is to admit some conquest, presumably that in its mildest forms, into the concept "sexual." We now reencounter the problem identified earlier: if we locate woman-hating in sexual abuse, then it precludes conquest.

5. A THIRD PASS

Kate Manne's *Down Girl: The Logic of Misogyny* provides a third pass. Manne criticizes what the "naïve conception" (18) of misogyny is, as she terms it, according to which misogyny is "primarily a property of individual agents (typically, although not necessarily, men) who are prone to feel hatred, hostility, or other similar emotions toward any and every woman, or at least women generally, simply because they are women" (32). She identifies two problems with this conception. First, it leaves us unable to diagnose misogyny, as what lies behind a person's attitude, as a matter of deep psychological explanation, is often inscrutable (44). Second, it makes of misogyny an aberrational rather than systemic phenomenon, for, insofar as women conform to the norms of womanhood, men have no cause to hate them (47–48).[8]

Concluding that the naive conception is "hopelessly inadequate" (49), Manne sets out to develop an alternative conception. If the observation that women's conformity to the norms of womanhood leaves men no cause to hate them undermines one conception of misogyny, it also provides the material for another, better one, for it implies a possible cause of such hatred: women's departure from the norms of womanhood. Why is this departure a possible cause of hatred? Departure from the norms of womanhood is departure from a woman's prescribed role, the role of "man's attentive, loving subordinate" (57). In a man's eyes, a woman's departure from her prescribed role may, given what this role is, be her willful mistreatment of him: "Women's indifference becomes aversion; ignorance becomes ignoring; testimony becomes tattling; and asking becomes extortion" (58).

Manne thus arrives at a conception of misogyny as "the system that operates within a patriarchal social order to police and enforce women's subordination and uphold male dominance" (33). This conception avoids both of the above problems. First, it allows us to diagnose misogyny. On this conception, misogyny comprises the hostile social forces that function to police and enforce women's subordination (63). It is at work when these forces are at work. We can diagnose it, then, by determining whether these forces are at work, and we can do this more reliably than we can determine what lies behind a person's attitude, as a matter of deep psychological explanation. Second, it finds for misogyny a place within the system of male dominance, thereby making of it a systemic rather than aberrational phenomenon.

Manne provides a third possible conception of woman-hating. Although her conception may improve upon the first two, it is nevertheless problematic. First, on Manne's conception, women are hated because they deviate from womanhood, not because they simply are women. As Manne says, misogyny targets women who are "unbecoming" or "wayward," women who are "traitors to the cause of gender" (51). Manne acknowledges this objection:

> Misogynists can love their mothers—not to mention their sisters, daughters, wives, girlfriends, and secretaries. They need not hate women universally, or

even very generally. They tend to hate women who are outspoken, among other things.

No doubt the idea that I've just mooted will be resisted by some people. Misogyny must involve hating women as such, and for no further reason. So misogyny cannot just target some women, it might be insisted. (52)

She acknowledges it, however, only to dismiss it, saying that she "see[s] little motivation for this blanket insistence," an insistence that, she suspects, "draws strength from the unwarranted assumption that misogyny must resemble the most commonly—though often historically inaccurately—envisaged form of anti-Semitism, which is supposed to be levelled at the entire Jewish people in our entirety" (52). Manne appears to interpret the claim that misogyny must involve hating women as such as the claim that misogyny must involve hatred of every woman. I interpret it instead as the claim that misogyny must involve hating women for their womanhood. I therefore think Manne's suspicion mistaken and her dismissal hasty. When feminists speak of women as hated, they are often speaking of women as hated for no reason other than that they are women. Dworkin, for example, says,

> I learned something about the nature of the world which had been hidden from me before—I saw a systematic despisal of women that permeated every institution of society, every cultural organ, every expression of human being. And I saw that I was a woman, a person who met that systematic despisal on every street corner, in every living room, in every human interchange. (Dworkin 1976, 6)

And elsewhere,

> There are dirty names for every female part of her body and for every way of touching her. There are dirty words, dirty laughs, dirty noises, dirty jokes, dirty movies, and dirty things to do to her in the dark. Fucking her is the dirtiest, though it may not be as dirty as she herself is. Her genitals are dirty in the literal meaning: stink and blood and urine and mucous and slime. Her genitals are also dirty in the metaphoric sense: obscene. She is reviled as filthy, obscene, in religion, pornography, philosophy, and in most literature and art and psychology. (Dworkin 2007 [1987], 214)

It is not female people who deviate from womanhood who are dirty, who repulse, who inspire hatred, but the female person, or more accurately, the female body, as such. It is not for their departure from the norms of womanhood but for their sheer existence that women are hated. Manne claims as a virtue of her conception that it is consistent with recent feminist usage

(81). It may be. But it is evidently not consistent with all feminist usage. Of course, consistency with feminist usage is not necessarily, or perhaps not at all, a criterion for the success of a conception of misogyny. My concern is therefore not that Manne's conception is inconsistent with a certain feminist usage. Rather, it is that the notion that men hate women simply because they are women is significant, and that the loss of this notion is the loss of this significance.

Second, Manne's conception rests on the assumption that a woman's behavior is to men intelligible as resistance to the norms of womanhood. For example, Manne says,

> In view of some women's social roles in a patriarchal culture as men's attentive, loving subordinates, this suggests one obvious possibility to consider. A woman's *perceived resistance* to or violation of the norms and expectations that govern these social roles would naturally tend to provoke just these kinds of reactions. (49, emphasis mine)

In addition, she asks, "What could be a more natural basis for hostility and aggression than *defection* from the role of an attentive, loving subordinate?" (49, emphasis mine). Finally, she claims, "Women who *resist* or *flout* gendered norms and expectations may subsequently garner suspicion and consternation" (61, emphasis mine). Crucially, I think Manne's conception must rest on this assumption. That is, a man must experience a woman's behavior as an assault, upon his sense of self, upon his sense of the natural order, or upon his sense of the right and good, in order that this behavior might arouse in him hatred and a desire to punish. After all, punishment presupposes a transgression for which a person must be punished.

As Hoagland argues, however, a woman's behavior is not intelligible as resistance to the norms of womanhood. She says that "if we stop to reflect, it becomes clear that within the confines of the feminine stereotype no behavior counts as resistance to male domination" (Hoagland 1988, 40). If men hold a concept of "woman" as one fit for and fulfilled by caring for husband and home, then they cannot conceive of a woman's situation as a proper cause of discontentment and hence resistance, and so cannot understand a woman's behavior as resistance. Or, more accurately, they cannot understand it as rational resistance. They can understand it only as evidence either of irrationality or dysfunction. Hoagland illustrates this with an example: in Alix Kates Shulman's *Memoirs of an Ex-Prom Queen*, a housewife commits acts of "sabotage," such as packing a raw egg instead of a hard-boiled one in her husband's lunch, but her husband understands these acts not as attempts to defy him but as evidence of the foolishness that is typical of a woman (Hoagland 1988, 40).

What is the implication of this for Manne's conception of misogyny? If a woman's behavior is not intelligible as resistance to the norms of womanhood, then her departure from these norms is intelligible only as her failure to conform to them, and such failure is, I think, intelligible only as evidence of dysfunction.[9] For a woman to fail to conform to the norms of womanhood is for her to fail to be what she by her nature is. Such failure implies a dysfunction, a defect preventing her from functioning as by her nature she ought. Consistent with this, men have seen a woman's inability to have a vaginal orgasm, "spinsterhood," and lesbianism as each the symptom of a pathology—as frigidity or sexual inversion.[10] Perhaps most tellingly, they have seen feminists as women in need of a good fuck, as women whose anger is the product of their frustrated sexual desire. In each case, a woman does not conform to norms of womanhood—she either does not sexually submit to a man or does not experience pleasure in so submitting, and in each case she is seen as ill.

Manne sees a woman's departure from the norms of womanhood as a natural basis for male hostility (49). If such a departure is intelligible only as evidence of dysfunction, then I am not sure that it is, for I am not sure that a woman's perceived illness must arouse male hostility. Let us see whether it might.

6. CAN A WOMAN'S PERCEIVED ILLNESS AROUSE MALE HOSTILITY?

If a woman's departure from the norms of womanhood is intelligible only as evidence of dysfunction, then perhaps we can understand men's diagnoses of women as ill and subsequent attempts to cure them as their punishment of women for deviance. In fact, feminists have understood them thus. Phyllis Chesler says that "mental asylum procedures do threaten, punish, or misunderstand such women into a real or wily submission;"[11] Elaine Showalter that "labelling women campaigning for access to the universities, the professions, and the vote as mentally disturbed" is the "obvious" defense of a "patriarchal culture [that] felt itself to be under attack by its rebellious daughters" (Showalter 1987, 145); and Ann Wood that as

> disease was unconsciously viewed as a symptom of a failure in femininity, its remedy was designed both as a punishment and an agent of regeneration, for it forced her to acknowledge her womanhood and made her totally dependent on the professional prowess of her male doctor. (Wood 1973, 37)

This reconciles Manne's conception of misogyny with my claim that a woman's departure from the norms of womanhood is intelligible only as evidence of dysfunction.

But this understanding is problematic. If, in the male conceptual scheme, a woman's departure from the norms of womanhood is intelligible only as evidence of dysfunction, then those who hold this scheme—first and foremost, men—must see a woman who departs from the norms of womanhood as ill, "must" in that to see her otherwise is to reject this scheme. If men must see a woman who departs from the norms of womanhood as ill, then we can understand their diagnoses of women as ill as in fact as they appear: motivated by a belief that women are ill, not by a desire to retain a power that they are fearful of losing. In order to understand them as punishment for deviance, then, we shall have to engage in the very psychologizing that Manne seeks to avoid, locating the fear of losing power only on the unconscious level. We shall have to say that

> many doctors, despite the apparent conscious understanding shown in the analysis of Combe and Alcott, in practice tended unconsciously to see the neuralgic ailments of their female patients as a threatening and culpable shirking of their duties as wives and mothers,

and that the doctor "on some unacknowledged level, feared his female patient" (Wood 1973, 36–37).

This appears to ignore an important aspect of Manne's conception of misogyny: it focuses on what women *face*, rather than on what men *feel*. Manne says,

> Rather than conceptualizing misogyny from the point of view of the accused, at least implicitly, we might move to think of it instead from the point of view of its targets or victims. In other words, when it comes to misogyny, we can focus on the hostility women face in navigating the social world, rather than the hostility men (in the first instance) may or may not feel in their encounters with certain women—as a matter of deep psychological explanation, or indeed whatsoever. (59)

That a man's diagnosis of a woman as ill and subsequent attempt to cure her springs, from his perspective, from pity for her and a desire that she be well is not relevant. But what is relevant? Manne's answer is not so clear as it may seem. In speaking of "the point of view of its targets or victims," she suggests that what is relevant is that a woman experiences a man's behavior as hostile. But in speaking of "the hostility that women face in navigating the social world," she suggests that what is relevant is that a man's behavior is *in effect* hostile, that is, that this behavior serves to accomplish what hostile behavior necessarily does. On reflection, however, the latter collapses into the former, for it is only if a woman experiences a man's behavior as hostile that this behavior produces the effect of hostile behavior.

We may worry that if what is relevant is a woman's experience, then we cannot identify as misogyny what internalization of the male concept of "woman" has left women unable to experience as hostile. Manne, however, offers a solution to this problem: we may invoke a "'reasonable woman' standard," that is, we may ask "whether a girl or woman who the environment is meant to accommodate might reasonably interpret some encounter, aspect, or practice therein as hostile" (60). But a male-dominant environment, an environment an aspect of which is the male concept of "woman," can accommodate a woman who deviates from the norms of womanhood only as ill, and a man's reaction to such a woman only as an attempt to cure her. It cannot accommodate a man's reaction to such a woman as hostile, and so cannot accommodate a woman who experiences his reaction as hostile. Or, it can accommodate a man's reaction to such a woman as hostile only as an aberration, and so can accommodate a woman who experiences his reaction as hostile only as an aberration. On the "reasonable woman standard," misogyny is aberrational, not systemic.

Manne proposes a novel conception of misogyny: "the system that operates within a patriarchal social order to police and enforce women's subordination and uphold male dominance." This conception rests on an assumption: that a woman's departure from the norms of womanhood is a natural basis for male hostility. On first glance, this assumption appears valid: as the norms of manhood and womanhood place men in a position of power over women, a woman's departure from the norms of womanhood threatens male dominance. Reflection, however, reveals this departure as intelligible only as a symptom of illness, and men cannot, I think, find a symptom of illness threatening. Put simply, the male conceptual scheme voids women's departure from the norms of womanhood of the meaning in virtue of which it would arouse in men the emotions of hate or fear and the desire to punish.

Manne's conception of misogyny is intuitive, insofar as it is, because we hold a concept of "woman" as human being. Holding this concept, we see a woman as oppressed and we see her behavior as a response to this oppression, an attempt to resist it or a symptom of discontentment, both of which threaten male dominance. We then see men's behavior as a response to this threat, an attempt to suffocate it, an attempt to reinforce their dominance. But men do not hold this concept of "woman." Not holding this concept, they do not see a woman's behavior as threatening male dominance, and so their behavior cannot be described as a reaction to this threat. Manne's conception of misogyny is the result of projecting the feminist conceptual scheme onto men.

7. A FOURTH PASS

I have outlined three attempts to understand talk of woman-hating. On the first, a certain subset of men's relations with women, namely, those that are sexually abusive, are hateful of women. On the second, the entire set of men's relations with women, relations that appear sexual but are in reality sexually abusive, are hateful of women. On the third, men's reaction to women's departure from the norms of womanhood is hateful of women. I have argued that each attempt is flawed. The first allows a woman-hating that is aberrational rather than systemic. The second psychologizes men, attributing to them an unconscious belief that women are human beings. The third mistakenly assumes that a woman's departure from the norms of womanhood is intelligible as an action that threatens male dominance.

These attempts presume that talk of woman-hating is description. As I shall now argue, it is in fact, or it is better understood as, redescription. I am here employing Rortyian terminology. In this terminology, "description" denotes description of the world within the inherited vocabulary, as against "redescription," which denotes description of the world in a new vocabulary. Description is the use of the inherited vocabulary, redescription the invention of an altogether new vocabulary. To presume that talk of woman-hating is description is to presume that when feminists speak of woman-hating, they are speaking in the inherited vocabulary, which is to say, as this vocabulary permits. It is to presume that they are, in Wittgensteinian terminology, abiding by the rules of the inherited language-game. It is this presumption that is the source of our troubles in attempting to account for the phenomenon of woman-hating.

In the inherited vocabulary, "man" is one who eroticizes dominance and "woman" one who eroticizes subordination, or so MacKinnon argues. If a man is one who eroticizes dominance and a woman one who eroticizes subordination, then a man's conquest of a woman is the consummation of sexual relations, "sexual" in the sense of both relations between the sexes and relations that are erotic. In addition, "sexual" is, as I have said, a species of "love." If this is so, then we cannot speak in this vocabulary of the sexual, and hence of a man's conquest of a woman, and hence of the consummation of men's relations with women, as hateful of women. If we cannot speak of the consummation of men's relations with women as hateful of women, then we cannot speak of these relations as, in their proper form, hateful of women, and if we cannot speak of these relations as, in their proper form, hateful of women, then we cannot speak of woman-hating as a systemic phenomenon.

We can create a new concept, "sexual abuse." However, we can incorporate this concept into the inherited vocabulary only if it stands in a relation of opposition to the concept "sexual," for only if it stands in such a relation is it compatible with "sexual" as a species of "love." If a man's conquest of a woman is sexual, then a concept of "sexual abuse" that stands in opposition to a concept of "sexual" cannot refer to a man's conquest of a woman. This new concept does not allow us to speak of a man's conquest of a woman, and hence of the consummation of the relations between men and women, as hateful of women.

Insofar as feminists mean for "woman-hating" to name a phenomenon that is systemic, then, they must be speaking in a new vocabulary. In this vocabulary, a woman is the sort of creature that a man is, the sort of creature who desires to exert herself, to learn, to write, to participate in public life, in short, to impress herself upon the world. As Charlotte Brontë writes in *Jane Eyre*,

> Women feel just as men feel; they need exercise for their faculties, and a field for their efforts, as much as their brothers do; they suffer from too rigid a restraint, to absolute a stagnation, precisely as men would suffer; and it is narrow-minded in their more privileged fellow-creatures to say that they ought to confine themselves to making puddings and knitting stockings, to playing on the piano and embroidering bags. It is thoughtless to condemn them, or laugh at them, if they seek to do more or learn more than custom has pronounced necessary for their sex. (Brontë 1996, 125–26)

The claim that a woman is the same sort of creature as a man is unintelligible and thus unutterable in the inherited vocabulary, as Marilyn Frye illustrates beautifully. "The word 'woman,'" she says, "was supposed to mean *female of the species*, but the name of the species is 'Man.' The term 'female man' has a tension of logical impossibility about it that is absent from parallel terms like 'female cat' and 'female terrier'" (Frye 1983, 165, emphases in original). The claim that a woman is a member of the human species, as a man is, violates the rules of the inherited language-game.

In this new vocabulary, we can speak of woman-hating as systemic. If a woman is a member of the human species, then a man's conquest of her necessarily violates and degrades her. If a man's conquest of a woman violates her, and if x's violation of y implies x's disdain for y, then a man's conquest of a woman demonstrates his hatred for her. If a man's conquest of a woman demonstrates his hatred for her, and if this conquest is the consummation of sexual relations, then "intercourse is the pure, sterile, formal expression of men's contempt for women,"[12] and the relations of men qua men with women qua women are hateful of women. Woman-hating is systemic.

Notice that once the sexual itself becomes hateful of women, it is no longer a species of love. "Sexual" no longer occupies the place that it did in the inherited vocabulary. It no longer has the meaning that it had in that vocabulary. So, to say "the sexual is hateful of women" is in fact to say "the 'sexual' is hateful of women," where "sexual" is the term from the inherited vocabulary. Notice also that once the sexual becomes hateful of women, "woman" is no longer one who eroticizes subordination, no longer a man's opposite, no longer a not-human being. "Woman" no longer occupies the place that it did in the inherited vocabulary. It no longer has the meaning that it had in that vocabulary. For the sexual becomes hateful of women because "woman" becomes the sort of creature that man is, a human being. This may be seen as evidence that feminists are speaking in a new vocabulary. Considering the question of where one vocabulary ends and another begins, Rorty says,

> Roughly, a break of this sort occurs when we start using "translation" rather than "explanation" in talking about geographical or chronological differences. This will happen whenever we find it handy to start mentioning words rather than using them—to highlight the difference between two sets of human practices by putting quotation marks around elements of those practices. (Rorty 1989, 7)

In the inherited vocabulary, Dworkin's claim that "intercourse is the pure, sterile, formal expression of men's contempt for women" is either incoherent or metaphorical. Her critics hear it as incoherent (a lunatic's ravings). Her defendants, in contrast, hear it as a rhetorical formulation of such coherent literal claims as "under patriarchal conditions, women cannot genuinely consent to sexual relations," or, "sexual relations occur without women's consent more often than we realize." Both critics and defenders judge Dworkin's speech according to the rules of the inherited language-game. Although my sympathies lie with the defenders, I think it is the critics who come nearer to what Dworkin is doing, or what we ought to understand her as doing. Defenders find for Dworkin's speech a place within the inherited language-game, while critics do not. Defenders thereby nullify her speech as critics, I think, do not. That Dworkin's speech is, in the inherited vocabulary, incoherent allows that it may prove, in an alternative vocabulary, coherent.

We fail to hear Dworkin as speaking in a new vocabulary, insofar as we do, because this vocabulary has not yet displaced the inherited one, because feminists such as Dworkin are still in the process of redescribing, because we do not yet have a sufficiently developed vocabulary in which Dworkin's claims are at once literal and coherent. We feminists thus remain caught between two vocabularies, the inherited, which is to say patriarchal, and the new, which is to say, feminist, the former increasingly inadequate for our purposes, but the latter not yet able to bear our weight.

Manne attempts to find for "misogyny" a meaning within the inherited vocabulary. This attempt is doomed. A vocabulary in which "man" is one who eroticizes dominance, "woman" one who eroticizes subordination, and "sexual" a species of "love" is not one in which men qua men can be said to hate women qua women. To attempt to find for "misogyny" a meaning within this vocabulary is to attempt to find for a feminist tool a place within a patriarchal toolset. To succeed is to render it fit for patriarchal purposes, and thus unfit for feminist ones.

My examination of the first, second, and third passes revealed the difficulty of accounting for woman-hating as a systemic phenomenon: if the relations of men qua men with women qua women are sexual, and if "sexual" is a species of "love," then we can describe these relations as hateful of women only by ascribing to men a subliminal hatred of women. The understanding of "woman-hating" as redescription allows that woman-hating is systemic without psychologizing men. Let me elaborate. A vocabulary provides the rules that govern description of the world, govern in conjunction with the world itself, where "the world itself" is the world whose description this vocabulary countenances. The inherited vocabulary provides rules according to which we can describe a man's conquest of a woman only as an act of love, while the new vocabulary provides rules according to which we can describe it as an act of hate.

If a vocabulary provides the rules that govern description of the world, then we can evaluate a vocabulary with reference only to a description that a vocabulary permits. We can evaluate a vocabulary only with reference to a vocabulary. Vocabularies are incommensurable. Only if a set of rules governing description of the world, a set that transcended all vocabularies, existed would vocabularies be commensurable, for such a set of rules would permit a description independent of all vocabularies, against which we could evaluate them. Of course, as it is a vocabulary that provides the rules that govern description of the world, such a set of rules would be simply one more vocabulary, and thus not transcendent of all vocabularies.

If vocabularies are incommensurable, then we cannot noncircularly determine the superiority of a vocabulary with respect to its ability to represent the world. We cannot say that the feminist vocabulary is superior, in the sense of more correspondent to the world, than the patriarchal. If we cannot say this, then we shall be unable to say, if feminist redescription succeeds, if the feminist vocabulary replaces the patriarchal, that the sexual was, when we spoke in the latter, an act of hate, though we did not then realize it, and so we shall avoid having to say that though men spoke of loving women, and though they acted as men who loved women in such a semantic community, they deep down hated women.

On the other hand, we shall be unable to do otherwise, for to adopt the feminist vocabulary is to accept the rules that it provides, which is simultaneously to reject those that the patriarchal vocabulary provides. It is to see these rules as impediments rather than aids to the apprehension of truth, which is to see the description that these rules permit as illusion. Thus does a male physician's pity for a woman become his "pity," his attempt to cure her his attempt to "cure." Herein lies an explanation of our finding perverse the suggestion that men believed women ill, desired that they be well, and sought to cure them. Once we adopt the feminist vocabulary, we find the description that it permits true and finding this description true can see only what is reconcilable with it.

When, for example, we read "The Yellow Wallpaper," we see the female protagonist's presumed illness as a manifestation of discontentment, the source of which is the oppressiveness of marriage and motherhood. We therefore see her husband, a physician, who orders her to rest and forbids her to write, as attempting to reconcile her to her duty. In this light, we attend to certain aspects of the story: that her husband has chosen the room in which she recovers; that she does not like this room "a bit," that the windows in it are "barred," that "he hates to have [her] write a word," that if she does not pick up faster "he shall send [her] to Weir Mitchell," that he denies her request to visit Cousin Henry and Julia.[13] We not only attend to certain aspects of the story, but interpret them in certain ways: her room is a *prison*; her husband has his sister watch over her, so that she shall not escape; he *threatens* to send her to Weir Mitchell; he carries her upstairs, as though her body is his to move. This is to show that if ours is the feminist vocabulary, then we cannot but read "The Yellow Wallpaper" as the story of a man's attempt to "force [his wife] back to her feminine and maternal functions" (Wood 1973, 42). Consequently, we cannot but see the suggestion that her husband truly loves her, and that he seeks to cure her, as a distortion and denial of reality, and therefore as abhorrent. But if ours were not the feminist vocabulary, then we would attend to other aspects of the story: that her husband "loves [her] very dearly," that the house is "the most beautiful place," that it has a "delicious garden," that her room has "windows that look all ways, and air and sunshine galore," that while trying to persuade her husband to allow her to visit Cousin Henry and Julia, she begins to cry.[14] We would also interpret aspects of the story differently: her husband's love for her as genuine, her crying as justifying her husband's worry that she cannot bear a visit, this worry as motivating his denial of her request, this denial as an attempt not to control or deprive but to care for. My point is this: only because we speak in the feminist vocabulary is such an interpretation misinterpretation, is the suggestion that men believed women ill and sought to cure them perverse.

To be sure, the female protagonist of "The Yellow Wallpaper" does come to experience her husband's treatment of her as hostile, a fact suggested by her triumphant declaration, "I've got out at last . . . in spite of you and Jane!"[15] But this experience may mark an abandonment of the inherited vocabulary, rather than a discovery of the real nature of her husband's treatment of her. Interestingly, this experience coincides with her descent into madness.

Perhaps this is because to abandon the inherited vocabulary is, in the absence of an alternative, to fall into incoherence.

8. CONCLUSION

We feminists claim that women are oppressed. If the vocabulary in which feminists such as Dworkin speak replaces the inherited vocabulary, then such claims as "intercourse is the pure, sterile, formal expression of men's contempt for women" will cease to be metaphorical and become literal. The act that now fulfills women will become what violates them. What we feminists claim as women's oppression will be revealed as but the tip of the iceberg. To understand talk of woman-hating as redescription is thus to understand that we cannot yet comprehend the full horror of women's oppression.

NOTES

1. Dworkin (2007 [1987], 175).
2. Hoagland (1988, 67). Similarly, Andrea Dworkin says, "The nature of women's oppression is unique" because women "live with those who oppress them, sleep with them, have their children" (1974, 23).
3. Manne (2018, 47–48). All page references to Manne in the text are to this work.
4. Palmer, DiBari, and Wright (1999, 271–82).
5. Buchwald, Fletcher, and Roth (1993, 1).
6. Davies (1997, 133).
7. Marx and Engels (1970, 64–65).
8. Manne (2018, 47–48).
9. As Sarah Hoagland says, "The male-constructed concept of 'femininity' erases female resistance to male domination: a woman who resists male domination is mad, insane" (2001, 126).
10. For a discussion of sexual frigidity, see Jeffreys (1997, 165–85); for sexual inversion in women see Ellis (1908, 118–51).
11. Chesler (2018 [1972], 97).
12. Dworkin (2007 [1987], 175).
13. For these descriptions, see Gilman (1998, 5–10).
14. For these descriptions, see Gilman (1998, 4–10).
15. Gilman (1998, 19).

REFERENCES

Atkinson, Ti-Grace. 1974. *Amazon Odyssey*. New York: Link Books.

Brontë, Charlotte. 1996. *Jane Eyre*. London: Penguin Books.
Buchwald, Emilie, Pamela R. Fletcher, and Martha Roth. 1993. "Editors' Preface." In *Transforming a Rape Culture*, edited by Emilie Buchwald, Pamela R. Fletcher, and Martha Roth, 1–6. Minneapolis: Milkweed Editions.
Chesler, Phyllis. 2018 [1972]. *Women and Madness*. Chicago: Lawrence Hill Books.
Davies, Kimberly A. 1997. "Voluntary Exposure to Pornography and Men's Attitudes Toward Feminism and Rape." *Journal of Sex Research* 34 (2): 131–37.
Dworkin, Andrea. 1974. *Woman Hating*. New York: E. P. Dutton.
———. 1976. *Our Blood: Prophecies and Discourses on Sexual Politics*. New York: Perigee.
———. 2007 [1987]. *Intercourse*. New York: Basic Books.
Ellis, Havelock. 1908. *Studies in the Psychology of Sex*. 2nd ed., Vol. 2. Philadelphia: F. A. Davis.
Firestone, Shulamith. 1970. *The Dialectic of Sex: The Case for Feminist Revolution*. New York: William Morrow.
Frye, Marilyn. 1983. *The Politics of Reality: Essays in Feminist Theory*. Berkeley: Crossing Press.
Gilman, Charlotte Perkins. 1998. *The Yellow Wall-paper and Other Stories*. Oxford: Oxford University Press.
Hoagland, Sarah. 1988. *Lesbian Ethics: Toward New Value*. Palo Alto: Institute of Lesbian Studies.
———. 2001. "Resisting Rationality." In *Engendering Rationalities*, edited by Nancy Tuana and Sandra Morgen, 125–46. Albany: State University of New York Press.
Jeffreys, Sheila. 1997. "The Invention of the Frigid Woman." In *The Spinster and Her Enemies: Feminism and Sexuality 1880–1930*, 165–85. North Melbourne: Spinifex Press.
MacKinnon, Catharine A. 1989. *Toward a Feminist Theory of the State*. Cambridge, MA: Harvard University Press.
Manne, Kate. 2018. *Down Girl: The Logic of Misogyny*. New York: Oxford University Press.
Marx, Karl and Frederick Engels. 1970. *The German Ideology: Part One*. Edited by C. J. Arthur. New York: International Publishers.
Palmer, Craig T., David N. DiBari, and Scott A. Wright. 1999. "Is It Sex Yet?: Theoretical and Practical Implications of the Debate Over Rapists' Motives." *Jurimetrics* 39 (3): 271–82.
Rorty, Richard. 1989. *Contingency, Irony, and Solidarity*. New York: Cambridge University Press.
Showalter, Elaine. 1987. *The Female Malady: Women, Madness, and English Culture, 1830–1980*. London: Virago.
Wood, Ann Douglas. 1973. "'The Fashionable Diseases': Women's Complaints and Their Treatment in Nineteenth-Century America." *Journal of Interdisciplinary History* 4 (1): 25–52.

Chapter 7

Why We Hate

Agneta Fischer, Eran Halperin,
Daphna Canetti, and Alba Jasini

1. INTRODUCTION

In a comprehensive review of classic as well as more contemporary conceptualizations of hatred, Royzman et al. (2005) described hatred as the most destructive affective phenomenon in the history of human nature. These destructive implications of hatred on human life have been widely documented in several recent contributions (e.g., Halperin 2011; Levin and Nolan 2015a, b; Opotow and McClelland 2007; Sternberg 2005; Sullivan et al. 2016). This literature shows that hate has been defined in a variety of ways, a problem characteristic for emotions in general. Hate has been considered an emotional attitude (Ekman 1992), a syndrome (Solomon 1977), a form of generalized anger (Bernier and Dozier 2002; Frijda 1986; Power and Dalgleish 1997), a generalized evaluation (Ben-Ze'ev 2000), a normative judgment (McDevitt and Levin 1993), a motive to devalue others (Rempel and Burris 2005), or simply an emotion (Elster 1999). Despite these different views, it is remarkable that there is little theorizing about hate, although the topic seems to be getting increasing attention in recent years. Even more surprisingly, there is not much in-depth empirical research on hatred, especially not in psychology. Interestingly, other disciplines, such as sociology, political science, communication, and social justice research, have provided interesting new empirical data, in particular on hate crime and hate speech.

The fact that hate is an underresearched topic in psychology may be due to several factors. First, hate is a phenomenon that is complex to empirically investigate with the standard psychological methods and samples. The standard student population of the majority of psychological studies report that they have never experienced hate (e.g., Aumer et al. 2015; Halperin 2008). For example, Halperin (2008, Study 1) aimed to examine people's lay theories of hatred. For that purpose, he asked 40 Israelis to think of one event in their lives in which they felt hatred. All 40 interviewees immediately said that they had never experienced hatred. They further stated that they had felt extreme anger, that they knew other people who experienced hatred, and that they were aware of the prevalence of hatred in conflict zones. But to feel hatred toward other people? Not them. Ironically, some of the participants who said that they had never hated someone throughout their entire lives then described specific situations in the history of the Israeli-Palestinian conflict in which they had wanted to throw a bomb on a large Palestinian city, or situations in which they wanted to do everything to annihilate or destroy the Palestinians. These examples illustrate the social inappropriateness of hate and the unwillingness to acknowledge feeling such a destructive emotion.

Second, hate has never been conceived as a standard emotion and thus did not gain from the rising popularity of the psychological study of emotions in the past decades. For example, in most empirical investigations based on appraisal theories (e.g., Roseman 1984; Scherer 2005), one can find emotions such as dislike, anger, or contempt, but hate is systematically lacking (but see Fitness and Fletcher 1993; Halperin 2008). In this review, we will try to make up for this lack of attention, and analyze the literature on hate from different disciplinary perspectives and at different levels of analysis. We will start with defining the characteristics of hate, and addressing the question whether hate is an emotion or something else, or both. Second, we will move on to the analysis of hate at different social levels (from individual to intergroup). Third, we will analyze how and why hate spreads, including hate crimes and hate speech. Fourth, we will discuss the role of hate in society. Finally, we will end with a reflection on the role and function of hate at different levels of analysis and will then offer some future venues of research.

2. WHAT ARE THE CHARACTERISTICS OF HATE?

Most authors who have written on hate agree that it is a powerful negative emotional phenomenon (Aumer-Ryan and Hatfield 2007; Royzman et al. 2005; Sternberg 2003), although not all scholars would define it as an emotion. Hate is assumed to develop when others mistreat or humiliate someone, or whose deliberate actions have become an obstruction to someone's goals (Aumer-Ryan and Hatfield 2007; Baumeister and Butz 2005; Royzman et al. 2005; Sternberg 2003). Hate obviously shares characteristics with several other negative emotions, especially anger, contempt, or moral disgust (Fitness and Fletcher 1993; Frijda 1986; Halperin 2008; Oatley and Jenkins 1996). Indeed, hatred is partly characterized by features that are not unique to hatred. To make the demarcation with other emotions even more complex, it is highly likely that hate feelings are often accompanied by other negative emotions, maybe especially because hate is such an intense feeling. For example, individuals may report hate if appraising an event as contradicting their goals and interests (relevant to all negative emotions), perceiving the other's behavior as unjustified and unfair (characteristic of anger), morally inferior (characteristic of contempt), or morally nauseating (prototypical for disgust). In other words, anger, contempt, disgust, humiliation, revenge feelings, and hate can all be elicited in reaction to a similar event, namely when another's action is perceived as negative, intentional, immoral, or evil (Haidt 2003; Rozin 1999).

The question then is whether and how hate is different from these closely related emotions. We argue that we can theoretically distinguish these emotions on the basis of their appraisal patterns, action tendencies, and motivational goals. With respect to appraisals, hate is different from anger, because an anger target is appraised as someone whose behavior can be influenced and changed (Fischer and Roseman 2007; Halperin 2008; Halperin et al. 2011). A hate target, on the contrary, implies appraisals of the other's malevolent nature and malicious intent. In other words, hate is characterized by appraisals that imply a stable perception of a person or group and thus the incapability to change the extremely negative characteristics attributed to the target of hate (Allport 1954; Royzman et al. 2005; Schoenewolf 1996; Sternberg 2003). Its appraisals are targeted at the hate target itself, rather than at specific actions carried out by that target (Ortony et al. 1988). While we feel anger because a certain action by a certain person or group is appraised as immoral, unfair, or unjust, if that very same person changed his or her behavior, the levels of anger would be reduced and the person would be forgiven. However, the entire configuration of hatred appraisals focuses on the innate nature, motives, and characteristics of the target itself and therefore a momentary change in certain behavioral patterns will not necessarily diminish levels of hatred. One hates one's father because he is perceived as a bad father in one's entire youth, not just once. An individual hates his wife because she has betrayed him and humiliated him deeply and repeatedly. In such cases, there is nothing the hate target can do to make up or repair. The other *is* malicious, not just acts maliciously. This assessment also contributes to feelings of powerlessness, which have often been reported as a characteristic condition in the development of hate (Sternberg 2005). Indeed, Fitness and Fletcher's (1993) prototype analysis of hate (vs. anger, jealousy, and love) shows that the concept of hate includes low levels of control, high levels of obstacles, and intense unpleasantness, because one feels badly treated, unsupported, humiliated, ignored, or uncared for. This sense of powerlessness may be fed by the appraisal that hate targets are dangerous and may execute their malicious intentions at any time.

In short, on the basis of preliminary evidence we propose that when individuals experience hate, they typically perceive their hate target as having malicious intentions and being immoral, which is accompanied by feelings of lack of control or powerlessness. Such appraisals are not the result of one specific action, but of a belief about the stable disposition of the hated person or group. This stable and dispositional attribution of negative characteristics to the target of one's emotion can also be found in appraisals of contempt (see also Halperin 2008; Jasini and Fischer 2018) and disgust (Russell and Giner-Sorolla 2011). In the case of contempt, however, the target of one's emotion is seen as inferior (Fischer and Giner-Sorolla 2016), and in the case of disgust, appraisals are more specifically related to violations of a moral code in relation to what happens with one's own body, such as bodily contamination (Fischer and Giner-Sorolla 2016). Appraisals of humiliation are more specific than those of hate, entailing the appraisal of a specific act as extremely derogating and a threat to one's self-worth (see, for example, Mann et al. 2016), which is also the case for feelings of revenge (see Seip 2016). In sum, the core set of appraisals of hate seems to be the attribution of stable and malicious intentions to the target, accompanied by appraisals of danger and feelings of powerlessness.

However, the main difference that make hate stand out from other negative emotions can be especially found in its action tendencies and emotivational goals. According to Roseman et al. (1994), an emotivational goal reflects what the emotion tries to bring about, and thus drives the emotional experience. Action tendencies are very closely associated with emotivational goals as they reflect the emotional impulse to act on a specific goal (see also Rempel and Burris 2005). The coercion goal of anger, for example, is closely associated with the tendency to attack someone (either verbally or physically), and the exclusion goal of contempt is associated with the tendency to ignore or look down on someone (Roseman et al. 1994). The notion of an emotivational goal can implicitly be found in others' theorizing as well. White (1996), for example, describes hatred as the desire to harm, humiliate, or even kill its object—not always instrumentally, but rather to cause harm as a vengeful objective in itself. Bar-Tal (2007) also suggested that hatred is a hostile feeling directed toward another person or group that consists of malice, repugnance, and willingness to harm and even annihilate the object of hatred. Whereas anger implies a coercion goal, that is, the motive to change another person by attacking, confronting, or criticizing, contempt implies an exclusion goal (Fischer and Roseman 2007), motivating individuals to exclude others from their social environment (Halperin 2008; Halperin et al. 2012; Jasini and Fischer 2018). Adopting a social functional perspective on emotions (e.g., Fischer and Manstead 2016), we propose that the emotivational goal of hate is not merely to hurt, but to ultimately eliminate or destroy the target, either mentally (humiliating, treasuring feelings of revenge), socially (excluding, ignoring), or physically (killing, torturing), which may be accompanied by the goal to let the wrongdoer suffer (Ben-Ze'ev 2008). Although actions and expressions related to hate, anger, contempt, disgust, humiliation, or revenge can be similar, their emotivational goals are different (see figure 7.1). Anger has the emotivational goal to change the target (e.g., by attacking), contempt has the goal to socially exclude (e.g., by avoiding or derogating), and revenge has the goal to restore the equity in suffering and deter (Seip 2016). Humiliation has shown to have different goals, depending on the specific context: to withdraw and protect oneself (Mann et al. 2016) or to rehumiliate, that is, take revenge.

How exactly the emotivational goal of hate is translated into a specific action will differ, depending on why someone has developed hate and what the relation between the victim and perpetrator is. The best way to eliminate the parent one hates, for example, is to completely ignore them and ban them entirely from one's life, whereas the best way to destroy hated CEOs may be to derogate, ridicule, and scorn them. In extreme occasions, violence or actual murder may be a viable option, but if this is not feasible, then one can cherish feelings of revenge. We will come back to the relationship between hater and the hated later in this review.

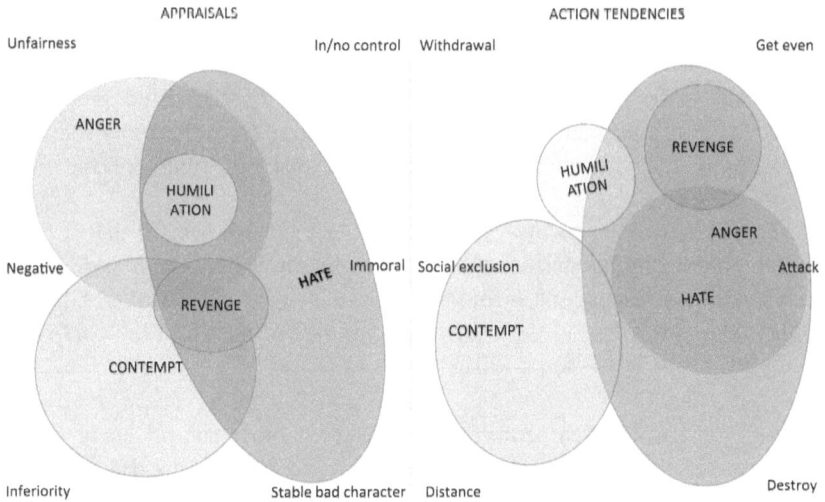

Figure 7.1 The overlap of appraisals and action tendencies, characteristic of anger, contempt, hate, humiliation and revenge.

3. LONG-TERM SENTIMENT OR AN EMOTION?

Scholars of hatred have continually debated the question of whether hatred is an emotion, a motive (Rempel and Burris 2005), or an (emotional) attitude or syndrome (Royzman et al. 2005). This debate is driven by the fact that one of hate's core characteristics is that it generally lasts longer than the event that initially evoked it. The enduring nature of hatred is based in the appraisals that are targeted at the fundamental nature of the hated group. Given that hate is often not a reaction to a specific event, and not limited to a short period of time, the question is raised whether hate actually is an emotion, or rather an emotional attitude or sentiment (Allport 1954; Aumer-Ryan and Hatfield 2007; Frijda 1986; Frijda et al. 1991; Halperin et al. 2012; Royzman et al. 2005; Shand 1920, as cited by Royzman et al. 2005; Sternberg 2005). In the past two decades, scholars (e.g., Fischer and Giner-Sorolla 2016; Halperin 2008; Sternberg 2003) have resolved this contradiction between emotions and sentiments by suggesting that some "emotions" can occur in both configurations—immediate and chronic, and thus can be conceived of as a (short-term) emotion as well as a (long-term) sentiment. In-depth interviews by Halperin (2008) with people who were asked to describe their own subjective experience of hatred indeed suggest that more than half of the participants report an ongoing emotional experience (i.e., an enduring sentiment), while the remainder focused on a more acute event of hate (Halperin 2008). Halperin et al. (2012) describe the sentiment hate, specifically in intergroup contexts, as a stable and familiar "hating" emotional attitude ("chronic hatred"), which organizes people's social world and helps strengthening the connection to the in-group ("in-group love") at the expense of various out-groups ("out-group hate"). To prevent future painful offenses by the hated group, the goal of the hate sentiment is to eliminate this group from their environment, for example, through an absolute separation from members of the other group.

Everyday observations also suggest that hate is so powerful that it does, not just temporarily but permanently, destroy relations between individuals or groups. An illustration comes from a story of a 20-year-old Kosovar Albanian woman who was asked to describe an experience of hatred in the context of a study by Jasini and Fischer (2018):

> I was 10 years old when Serbian paramilitary men broke into my house with violence. They had guns in their hands and they approached my dad and my brothers and asked them all the money we had in the house. They threatened to kill them all if the family did not leave the house immediately. A few hours after this horror moment, my family and I left the village to seek refuge in the

Albanian territory. *Even now, ten years after the Kosovo war, I still hate the Serbians and can't forget their hatred for us, nor their maltreatment of my family, relatives and neighbors.* I often talked about this event with my family members and friends, but never with Serbian people. (our emphasis)

Hate can thus remain long after an incident, and therefore can take a different form than a short-term emotional reaction to a specific event (like anger or disgust).

The emotion hate (also referred to as "immediate hate"; Halperin et al. 2012) is much more urgent and occurs in response to significant events that are appraised as so dramatic that they lead to the kind of appraisals (e.g., "the out-group is evil by nature") and motivations (e.g., "I would like it to be destroyed") that are usually associated with hatred. This intense feeling is often accompanied by unpleasant physical symptoms and a sense of fear and helplessness (Sternberg 2003, 2005). It provokes a strong desire for revenge, a wish to inflict suffering, and, at times, desired annihilation of the out-group. Studies by Halperin et al. (2012) unequivocally show that people are capable of short-term hate, following an unusual, mostly destructive, and violent event. In that very short period of time, they attribute the negative behavior of the out-group to its innate evil character.

The two forms of hatred are related, yet distinct, and one fuels the occurrence and magnitude of the other. Frequent incidents of the emotion hate may make the development of the sentiment more probable (see also Rempel and Burris 2005). At the same time, the lingering of hate as a sentiment constitutes fertile ground for the eruption of hate. Chronic haters, who encounter their targets or the consequences of their targets' actions, most likely react with immediate hatred. These people evaluate almost any behavior of the hate target through the lens of their long-term perspective that the hate target is malevolent. As such, haters are probably more susceptible than others to systematic biases, such as the fundamental attribution error (Ross 1977). What follows is that the mere presence, mentioning, or even internal recollection of the hated person or group can fuel hate as a sentiment. At the same time, the causal mechanism can work the other way as well. Repeated events of immediate hatred can very easily turn the hatred feeling into an enduring sentiment. Indeed, it is only natural that after repeated violent events of that kind, it becomes very difficult for people to forget earlier instances, and such feelings remain present for longer periods of time. In a way, hatred is an emotion that requires more time to evolve, but once it happens it takes much longer to dissolve, and it will always leave scars.

4. HATE AT DIFFERENT SOCIAL LEVELS OF ANALYSIS

Hate at an Interpersonal Level

One important factor in the development of hate, compared to most other negative emotions, is the relationship between the person who hates and the target of this hate. In the previous section, we have described the goal of hate to eliminate or destroy. Interestingly, at an interpersonal level, the relationship between hater and hated can be intimate. Studies by Aumer et al. (2016), for example, show that when individuals were asked to report on a person they currently love but at one time hated in the past, in contrast with a person they loved and never hated, they report in both cases on persons they know very well, such as family members, romantic partners, or colleagues. However, not surprisingly, the quality of the current relationship with the person, who was once hated, was shown to be characterized by less intimacy and love, and more hate. Indeed, in another study of hate and love in close relationships, hated persons were found to be perceived as less open, less agreeable, less conscientious, and less emotionally stable than loved ones (Aumer et al. 2015). Thus, although at an interpersonal level hated persons are often intimates, suggesting that love and hate are not necessarily diametrically opposed (Ben-Ze'ev 2008), the quality of the relationship with a person one once hated is less satisfactory (Aumer-Ryan and Hatfield 2007; Rempel and Burris 2005).

This more negative quality of relationships in which hate is involved is not restricted to marital or family contexts, but can also occur in work contexts, where hate has been found to be associated with experiences of humiliating and demeaning treatment (Fitness 2000; Fitness and Fletcher 1993). This is especially the case when such treatment comes from others who are considered as more powerful than oneself (Fitness 2000). It may be expected that recurrent experiences of humiliation, ridicule, or public shame by a partner or coworker may contribute to the development of intense hate toward them. In addition, previous hate feelings toward the other may leave traces of hurt feelings and resentment, which may put a strain on the relationship. These different lines of research thus suggest that past occurrences of hate seem to linger on in current relationships and are not forgotten, nor completely forgiven. From an emotion theoretical perspective this makes sense, because we can only have intense and extreme emotions such as love and hate when the objects of these emotions touch upon our concerns (Frijda 1986). In other words, we cannot love or hate persons we are indifferent to. Although we maybe would like or pretend not to care, and to easily forgive or forget, we do care about the neglecting, aggressive, or disgusting character of another person, especially if we once loved this person.

When moving from an interpersonal to an intergroup level, it is interesting to observe that we do not need to know the persons we hate. It is very well possible to hate groups because of what they represent (in terms of power, values, past behaviors, identity). People may hate Germans for what they did during World War II, even though they do not know any German involved in these atrocities. People may hate homosexuals or lesbians because they think that they are deviants from human nature, even though they do not know any such person. The hatred of groups, thus, does not require a personal connection with a member of this group. In such cases, there is only a symbolic relationship with a group member on the basis of one's perception of this person as part of a negative out-group.

Hate at an Intergroup Level

Similar to other intergroup emotions, intergroup hate is an emotion experienced on behalf of one's own group and targeting the out-group. Intergroup emotions are instigated by events that advance or threaten the in-group (Mackie et al. 2000). For instance, if group members perceive that their ingroup is unjustly treated or humiliated by another group, they may experience negative emotions toward out-group members as well as form negative attitudes about them. In addition, the strength of identification with the in-group may contribute to the intensity of intergroup emotions, with high compared to low identifiers generally reporting stronger emotional experiences (Gordijn at al. 2006; Iyer and Leach 2009; Yzerbyt et al. 2003).

Intergroup hatred is directed at a particular out-group, aiming to eliminate the group (e.g., Halperin 2008, 2011; Halperin et al. 2009, 2011). Hate at the intergroup level requires a clear distinction between the in-group and the out-group, and is facilitated by the perception that the out-group is a rather homogeneous entity. The perception of out-group homogeneity is essential for people to be able to generalize from a negative behavior of a single outgroup member to appraisals targeted at the entire out-group. For example, a Palestinian who suffered from an abusive behavior of an Israeli soldier in a military checkpoint will develop hate toward all Jews only to the extent that she believes that all Jews are the same, and that the behavior of that one soldier actually represents the innate characteristics of the entire Jewish people (for similar ideas, see Er-rafiy and Brauer 2013; Simon and Mummendey 1990). Especially a loathed out-group that has attacked the interests of the group makes the in-group identity salient and is most likely to become the target of one's hate.

Studies on intergroup hate show very similar patterns of appraisals and motives to those that we have reported for interpersonal hate. In a study on the appraisals of hate and two related emotions (anger and fear), Halperin (2008,

Study 2) provided Israeli participants with a questionnaire that included a detailed description of four emotionally conflicting scenarios (e.g., a terror attack, intergroup violent event in a nightclub), followed by a manipulation of the cognitive appraisals of the protagonist in the story regarding five dichotomous appraisal dimensions: (a) just/unjust event, (b) out-group/circumstances were responsible, (c) intentional/unintentional harm, (d) out-group is evil/not evil, and (e) low/high coping potential. After reading the scenario and the protagonist's appraisals, participants were asked to rank the extent to which the protagonist experienced hatred, fear, and anger (separately) in response to that event. The results support the assumption that hate has two unique appraisals: out-group harm is intentional and due to their stable, evil character. On the other hand, the attribution of responsibility to the out-group and the appraisal that the event was unjust were found for both hatred and anger, and the appraisal of low coping potential (powerlessness) was found for both fear and hatred. Jasini and Fischer (2018) found a similar pattern of appraisals for intergroup hate in their study in another specific intergroup context, namely in Kosovo. The study was conducted with Albanian Kosovars who suffered ethnic cleansing by Serbian (para)militaries during the Kosovo War (1998–1999). They asked Albanian participants to imagine an interpersonal assault carried out by Serbian individuals, and then to rate the emotions and appraisals in response to the event. They found that—after controlling for anger—the intensity of hate was positively associated with appraisals of malicious intent and immorality, and marginally with powerlessness.

Intergroup hate can also be characterized by specific emotivational goals and action tendencies. Jasini and Fischer (2017) found that hate was positively associated with the goal to take revenge and to exclude the other, and with the tendency to attack (and not to forgive or withdraw). This is in line with the findings from Halperin (2008, Study 1). Participants in this study (83.3%) stated that they would have wanted something very bad to happen to the hated group and its members. In another study (Halperin 2008, Study 3), Jewish Israelis were asked for their emotivational goals and action tendencies in reaction to certain Palestinian actions. The results showed that group-based hatred is characterized by specific emotivational goals mentioned earlier: to do harm to, to remove, and to even eliminate the out-group. Such goals are accompanied with specific action tendencies such as the tendency to attack and not forgive (Jasini and Fischer 2018) or the tendency to engage in a violent action toward the hated people, up to a point where respondents supported the killing of members of the out-group (Halperin 2008, Study 1). Still, in the latter study with Israeli participants, only a few participants (16.6%) reported the actual execution of a violent action. The three most common actions reported by the participants were complete detachment from the object of the hatred (83.3%), delight at the failure of the hated other (36.6%;

see also Smith and van Dijk 2018; van Dijk and Ouwerkerk 2014), and political action taken against the other (56.6%). In short, intergroup hate follows the pattern of interpersonal hate and is characterized by appraisals of harm or malicious intent on the part of the out-group, reflecting their evil nature. This can lead to the goal to take revenge and to eventually eliminate the out-group from one's environment. The bodily aspect of collective hatred seems less salient than the cognitive and motivational elements, although we assume it may sometimes also include unpleasant physical symptoms (Sternberg 2003, 2005), particularly when the hate is collectively experienced, for example, during a mass demonstration or a sports event.

Behaviorally, hate can lead to actual attempts to eradicate the out-group (White 1996). Extensive research has demonstrated that, in some situations, there is a connection between hate and its various active political manifestations, such as out-group exclusionism (Leader et al. 2009), terrorism (Sternberg 2003), the motivation to fight and kill in battle (Ballard and McDowell 1991), and hate crimes (Berkowitz 2005). We should note, however, that the (behavioral) expression of hate can differ, depending on the relation between in-group and out-group, the (violent) history between the two groups, the specific incidents that have taken place, the dominant (negative) narratives about the out-group, and the possibility to act upon one's hate. For example, one can be motivated to destroy the out-group out of perceived self-defense, driven by fear, or one can hate a powerless out-group, which may be accompanied by contempt and could lead to actions to completely ban the group from one's environment. Still all these forms of hate seem to share the common goal to eliminate the hate target, either physically or socially. In other words, while fear can sometimes lead to *flight* rather than *fight* tendencies and anger can lead to constructive rather than destructive corrections (see Fischer and Roseman 2007; Halperin 2011; Halperin et al. 2011; Reifen Tagar et al. 2011), hatred will always motivate people toward destructive action. The belief in stable, extremely negative characteristics implies that there is no merit in trying to correct or improve the out-group's behavior, and as such, only more extreme reactions seem applicable.

How Hate Spreads

There is abundant evidence that many emotions can be experienced at both an individual and group level. Yet, not all emotions have the same potential to transcend from the individual to the group or collective level. We think that hatred can more easily go through a transformation from individual to group level than other negative emotions; some will even claim that it is the most "group-based" emotion. Aristotle succinctly states that whereas anger is customarily felt toward individuals, hatred is often felt toward groups (see also Ben-Ze'ev 1992). One reason for this can be found in the core characteristics and the nature of hate. We have argued and shown that hate is based on the generalized attribution of an action to the basic traits and features of a person. In other words, the specific antecedent event of one hateful incident may become less important over time, and the character of the person or group becomes the sole reason for the hate. Generalizing these characteristics to members of a group further enables a parsimonious justification of one's hate. This facile transition of hatred from the interpersonal level to the group level makes it a pivotal agent in group-based political dynamics in general and in intergroup conflicts in particular.

There are three factors that further contribute to the flourishing of hate specifically at the intergroup level. First, hate seems often shared among in-group members (see Jasini and Fischer 2018). According to Rimé (2009), the extent of sharing one's emotions is influenced by the intensity of the emotional experience, and the primary targets of sharing generally are close family members and friends. In contexts where intergroup relations are tense, groups share collective narratives about their own group and other groups. For example, previous studies on social sharing have found that people who are victims of violence and ferocities and thus experience collective trauma often share their emotional experience with other group members (Rimé 2009). In intractable conflicts, collective narratives are dominated by the memory of past victimization and by ongoing intergroup violence (Bar-Tal et al. 2009; Canetti et al. 2017; Noor et al. 2012; Vollhardt 2012). Thus, collective victimhood evokes sharing one's feelings about the target of hate with similar others. Knowing that other in-group members experience an event in a similar way further reinforces the experience and expression of one's own emotions (see also Manstead and Fischer 2001). The sharing of strong negative emotions can in turn strengthen feelings of collective victimhood that may make the original feeling of hate even more intense and enduring (see also Bar-Tal et al. 2007; Kuppens et al. 2013). Thus, sharing past negative emotional experiences caused by an out-group increases the probability for the development of intergroup hatred (see also Jasini and Fischer 2018).

Second, while collective victimhood keeps the memory of hate alive across generations, it may also direct the appraisal of future events. Accumulated group knowledge on the immoral and violent behavior of an out-group affects the evaluation of future behavior, thereby confirming the sentiment that the out-group is a homogeneous malicious entity. In the eyes of those who see themselves as part of a transgenerational victimized group, the out-group is malicious, even though they did not personally suffer from the out-group behavior, or only for a relatively short time. The fact that the out-group's behavior is considered consistent across generations reflects on its innate negative characteristics. Moreover, shared appraisals on similar emotional events reinforce the emotional fit between individuals and their cultural group (De Leersnyder et al. 2015), as does identification with the group (Delvaux et al. 2015). In turn, the emotions also influence self-categorization, suggesting that similar emotions strengthen feelings of belonging to the same group (Livingstone et al. 2011; Porat et al. 2016).

A final and third interesting aspect of hatred that makes it more susceptible to become an intergroup sentiment that spreads fast is the fact that it can increase in the absence of any personal interaction between the hater and members of the hated group. According to Jasini and Fischer (2018), the lack of personal interactions with the targets of one's hate further diminishes chances of perspective taking from the side of the victim. Allport (1954) already mentioned the lack of direct interaction as one of the most powerful engines behind hate and prejudice. According to his approach, supported by studies in the framework of contact theory (e.g., Pettigrew and Tropp 2006), lack of direct interaction amplifies hate because the negative appraisal of the malicious character of the group will never be reappraised or contradicted by other information. For example, since Israel completed the construction of the separation wall, Jewish Israelis do not need to suppress their hate toward the Palestinians anymore, because the wall prevents direct encounters with individual Palestinians. Thus, Israelis are not confronted anymore with exceptions to the Israeli view of Palestinians and the hateful image of the Palestinians can easily remain intact. This does not necessarily mean that social interactions with hated group members automatically reduce hate. However, under the right circumstances, haters may learn more about the motives and circumstances of the hated group's actions, which could result in some perspective taking.

Hate Crimes and Hate Speech

One specific way in which intergroup hate spreads in a society is through hate crimes. According to Levin and McDevitt (2008), "Hate crimes are criminal offenses motivated either entirely or in part by the fact or perception that a victim is different from the perpetrator." In most cases, this difference is not based on individual characteristics, but on social identities, such as being black, woman, lesbian, or Muslim. The word "hate crime" is fairly recent and was used in the United States in the late 1980s to describe a racial incident in New York where a black man was killed for no apparent reason. Since then, there has been much debate about hate crime, which has recently led to a new field of research in some countries referred to as "hate studies" (Chakraborti and Garland 2015). Hate crimes are based on stereotypes, prejudice, or extreme negative sentiments about certain groups, and generally also targeted at visible social groups, such as blacks, Jews, Native Americans, or homeless people. The goal of hate crimes is to communicate a certain message to the group that the haters want to terrify or eliminate.

An important feature of hate crimes is that the victims generally have not done anything specific: they are terrorized for who they are, not for what they have done. This makes the victims feel powerless and unable to control the situation because changing their behavior or attitudes would not help. Levin and McDevitt (2008) distinguish between four types of hate crimes that are based on the offender's motivations: thrill, defense, retaliation, and mission. Whereas the first type is a form of thrill-seeking (mostly by groups of teenagers), the second motivation is based on anger and fear, and is considered a strategy to defend a way of living against intruders. This type of crime is mostly committed by single persons who feel threatened, for example, by a black family who moves into a white neighborhood, or a homosexual teacher hired by a school. The retaliatory third type of hate crime also seems to involve actual hate and is seen as an act of revenge against previous hate crimes or terrorist attacks. For example, after the terrorist attacks in September 2001, there was a 1.6% increase in anti-Muslim hate crimes reported to local police departments in the United States. Finally, the last motivation for hate crimes is the mission, which is less frequent and is defined by the fact that the perpetrator is on a moral mission to destroy out-group members who are not considered human.

In another line of research, hate crimes have been associated with a threatened belief in a just world (Lerner 1980). The just world belief implies that individuals generally believe that the world is a fair place to live in, and that justice is being done such that people get what they deserve. When an individual becomes the victim of a hate crime on the sole basis of his or her group identity, observers may start restoring their belief in a just world by derogating the victim (see also Sullivan et al. 2016). More importantly, the absence of punishment signals that the violence not only against one individual but against a whole group is justified.

Whereas hate crimes can occur in many forms, it is obvious that the rise of the Internet and the use of social media have been crucial in spreading hate, because hate messages now have a worldwide audience. The number of organized hate groups and hate-advocating sites has increased, and so has the exposure of potential victims to hate messages. In a recent study on the exposure of young adults to hate messages in four different countries (United States, Finland, United Kingdom, and Germany), Hawdon et al. (2017) found that 53% of the Americans, 48% of the Fins, 39% of the British, and 30.5% of the Germans had been exposed to hateful messages in the past 3 months. The authors explain this country difference on the basis of differences in hate speech laws. These are almost nonexistent in the United States, whereas there are relatively strict antihate speech laws in Germany. This question has indeed evoked a debate on the most efficient legislation with regard to hate crime. According to some scholars (e.g., Cavadino 2014), the emphasis on the punishment of hate crime has not reduced it, nor helped the victims, and therefore other ways to prevent hate crimes may be more successful. The problems with hate crime law are obviously also related to the fact that it is unclear whether victims always report hate crime. Most researchers assume underreporting, either because people do not expect to be taken seriously or because they ignore and deny their feelings related to the incident as a way of coping with it, or because of fear, or simply because they expect the perpetrators will not be punished anyway (Perry 2003). Research relating hate crime to the belief in a just world, however, clearly suggests that the absence of punishment may increase hate and hate crimes because it signals that the victim and even the whole group to which the victim belongs deserves this fate. This consequence is especially present for hate crimes because, in contrast with other crimes, the absence of punishment emphasizes the justification of the hatred.

Hate in Politics and Society

Some characteristics of a culture or society form fertile grounds for the development of hate. In his book on the roots of evil—genocide and mass killing—Staub (1989) argues that, first of all, difficult life conditions such as extreme economic problems leading to poverty of large groups of people, but also political, criminal, or institutional violence, facilitate evil intentions. The second set of features refers to culture, especially the rigidity or adaptability of a society. The more rigid the cultural values in a society, the more difficult it is to cope with changes or disturbances of one's traditional values and ways of life. According to Staub (1989), this may lead to scapegoating, trying to protect oneself and one's group to defend one's way of life, safety, health, and values. Blaming others helps to fulfill these needs in times of chaos and uncertainty, and this forms the basis for the development of hate toward groups in society that are seen as the cause of all problems. Other characteristics, such as strong leaders, strong respect for authority, nationalism, and a slow progression of devaluing out-groups, are the further ingredients for the slow but steady development of societal hate (Staub 1989). Waller (2002) refers to this latter set of characteristics as collective potentiation, the social augmentation of individual actions in a group, whether good or bad. In the case of hate, it may refer to all the characteristics of a society or culture at a specific point in time when the devaluation of an out-group may turn into real hate, and activate its associated goals to annihilate that group.

Under such conditions, the initial development of hate can be a consequence of short-term conflict-related events, but then may automatically result in support for initiating violent actions and for further escalating the conflict. That is also the reason that Staub (2005) and others (e.g., Petersen 2002; Volkan 1997) have pointed to hate as the most dominant emotion in past and recent mass murders and genocide (see also Mishra 2017). If one is convinced of the destructive intentions of the out-group and feels total despair regarding the likelihood that the out-group will change its ways, the violent alternative may seem the only reasonable and successful way out. Indeed, research has shown that feelings of hatred may increase the tendency to support extreme military action toward out-groups (e.g., Halperin 2011). The perception of increased threat is a powerful amplifier of hatred. Ongoing terrorist attacks elicit stress, fear, and uncertainty (Canetti et al. 2014), and become fertile ground for increasing hate for groups perceived as responsible for the turmoil. Additionally, the aftermath of such events demonstrates that perceived security threats prevail over other issues, such as individual rights and freedoms (Canetti-Nisim et al. 2008).

Hate has also been described as part of a broader societal sentiment coined "ressentiment" (Betz 1994; but see Salmela and von Scheve 2017) in theories on the growing support of right-wing populism. These scholars consider hate as part of a cluster of negative emotions. In particular, feelings of insecurity and shame can easily be transformed into anger, resentment, and hate toward other groups, like immigrants, refugees, or the political elite (Salmela and von Scheve 2017). However, whereas various negative emotions may play a role in mobilizing people to support out-group derogation and even violence, and to oppose compromises for peace and forgiveness, we think that intergroup hate is the most powerful one. There are two main reasons for this. First, hate is associated with very low expectations for positive change and with high levels of despair, and as a consequence, its associated political action tendencies are by definition destructive rather than constructive. If one does not believe that positive change in the out-group's violent and immoral behavior is possible, then constructive political reactions—like negotiations, compromises, gestures, or even apologies, which are usually meant to establish more friendly relations—seem just irrelevant (see also Tausch et al. 2011). In addition to that, the emotional goal associated with hate, namely to destroy or eliminate the out-group, also leads to one-sided political actions that do not leave any room for positive or constructive change. This is apparent from the hate speech spread by ISIS, who describes their online propaganda as "the Internet army" (Shaaban 2015).

Hate can even be a destructive force in the midst of peace negotiations. Two studies found that individuals who experienced short-term episodes of hatred in times of negotiations in the Middle East expressed an emotional goal of harming and eliminating the opponent (Halperin 2008). They likewise tended to reject any positive information regarding the opponent (i.e., lack of openness) and opposed the continuation of negotiations, compromise, and reconciliation efforts (Halperin 2011). Importantly, given that hatred is associated with a fundamental negation of the out-group as a whole, and not merely of the group's concrete actions or behavior, those who feel hatred toward the out-group oppose even the smallest gestures and symbolic compromises, thus refusing to even entertain new ideas that may lead to peace. Two experimental studies conducted in 2011 on the eve of an important peace summit between Israelis and Palestinians show that inducing anger toward Palestinians increased support for making compromises in upcoming negotiations among those with low levels of hatred, but decreased support for compromise among those with high levels of hatred (Halperin et al. 2011).

There is also evidence that hate fuels political intolerance. Political intolerance is the support or willingness to denounce basic democratic values and equal rights of individuals who belong to a defined out-group in a particular society (Gibson 2006; Stouffer 1955) and is considered one of the most problematic phenomena in democratic societies. Results of four large-scale nationwide surveys among Jews in Israel showed that intergroup hatred is the most important antecedent of political intolerance. It has a stronger effect in the face of heightened existential threat and is especially present among politically unsophisticated individuals—that is, those lacking exposure to political information, intellectual capacity, or efforts to obtain and understand political information (Halperin et al. 2009).

The question is what makes hate so persistent and prevalent in politics, more so than anger or fear. Hatred seems an effective, simple, political tool that is commonly used by politicians to attain in-group solidarity and political benefits and/or out-group exclusion. Campaign ads, canvassing, and slogans based on collective hatred are the bread and butter of successful campaigns because the message is simple and emotionally appealing (Hutchings et al. 2006; Lazarsfeld et al. 1944). Hatred has been employed in a number of local and national political campaigns in Israel, Europe (Mudde 2005), and the United States (Kaplan and Weinberg 1998). The simple and extreme nature of hatred increases its recurrence in the political realm (Leader et al. 2009). The intensity, swiftness, and superficiality of current political communication in many countries enforce cues, symbols, and extreme emotions such as hatred (Galtung and Ruge 1965; Kinder and Sears 1985).

Notwithstanding the context of moral values, hatred may be problematic from a political perspective. From a leadership perspective, fine-tuning of the exact patterns of hatred is almost impossible; hence, hate rhetoric can backlash. On the one hand, the use of hate rhetoric may attract *traditional voters*, encouraging them to reconsider their typical support as they search for new paths to channel their group-based hate and opt for more extreme political representation. On the other hand, the use of hatred to mobilize *new voters* may enhance their support for their own traditional parties (Halperin et al. 2012).

5. CONCLUSION

Hate is elicited in reaction to very negative transgressions by another person or group. It can be an emotional reaction to a specific event (i.e., immediate hate), but it often occurs as a sentiment (long-term emotion), generalizing from just one event to the nature of a group or person. Especially extreme transgressions may result in a plethora of negative emotions, like contempt, disgust, anger, humiliation, or revenge, and thus the question is to what extent and how hate differs from other emotions. We think that there is overlap between these negative emotions, but we can still theoretically distinguish them on the basis of unique patterns of appraisals and emotivational goals. This does not mean that daily lives are neatly carved up according to these theoretical categories, especially because these emotions may often be elicited in reaction to the same events, and thus may occur either simultaneously or sequentially. On the basis of research on interpersonal and intergroup hate, we suggest that the unique appraisals of hate are a stable, dispositional attribution of malicious intentions, in combination with the appraisal that the target is seen as dangerous and that one feels powerless (see figure 7.1). The emotivational goal associated with hate is to destroy the hate target, whether physically, socially, or symbolically. This goal is associated with the aforementioned appraisals and is different from the goals of contempt (social exclusion), disgust (distancing oneself), revenge (getting even), humiliation (withdrawal), or anger (attack). Still all these emotions can occur together with hate and each of them can become associated with the sentiment hate.

From a functional perspective, hate is part of a self-defense system by attempting to eliminate the target of one's hate. In an intergroup context, one's group identity is threatened by an out-group member, and self-defense implies defense of one's group membership. Hate seems particularly prone to spreading at this intergroup level because it helps us to defend ourselves by strengthening the ties with our in-group and putting all the blame for insecurity and violence elsewhere. Because hate is based on the perception of a stable, malevolent disposition of the other person, haters perceive little room for constructive change, and therefore there seem only radical options left to act upon one's hate. In the case of most emotions, the fulfillment of the emotivational goal reduces the emotion. For example, one may seek revenge in order to get even in suffering, and once this has been established, feelings of revenge decrease (see also Seip et al. 2014). In the case of hate, this means elimination of the target. This leaves the question whether hate can be changed or downregulated. We think that this is difficult, and the only way to regulate hate would be to reappraise the malevolent intentions of the out-group as stable and as a result of their identity or character. Trying to explain the hated target's actions in terms of circumstances rather than nature would be a first step. In the same vein, merely being angry, devoid of hate, would be a much more constructive emotion because its intensity can be decreased if the target apologizes or changes their behavior. Whether we can downregulate hate, and how it relates to perspective taking, empathy, and forgiveness are interesting and socially relevant venues for future research.

REFERENCES

Allport, Gordon W. 1954. *The Nature of Prejudice*. Reading: Addison-Wesley.

Aumer, Katherine, Anne Cathrine Krebs Bahn, and Sean Harris. 2015. "Through the Looking Glass, Darkly: Perceptions of Hate in Interpersonal Relationships." *Journal of Relationships Research* 6 (4): 1–7.

Aumer, Katherine, Anne Cathrine Krebs Bahn, Courtney Janicki, Nicolas Guzman, Natalie Pierson, Susanne Estelle Strand, and Helene Totlund. 2016. "Can't Let It Go: Hate in Interpersonal Relationships." *Journal of Relationships Research* 7 (2): 1–9.

Aumer-Ryan, Katherine, and Elaine Hatfield. 2007. "The Design of Everyday Hate: A Qualitative and Quantitative Analysis." *Interpersona* 1 (2): 143–72.

Ballard, John A., and Aliecia J. McDowell. 1991. "Hate and Combat Behavior." *Armed Forces & Society* 17 (2): 229–41.

Bar-Tal, Daniel. 2007. "Sociopsychological Foundations of Intractable Conflicts." *American Behavioral Scientist* 50 (11): 1430–53.

Bar-Tal, Daniel, Lily Chernyak-Hai, Noa Schori, and Ayelet Gundar. 2009. "A Sense of Self-Perceived Collective Victimhood in Intractable Conflicts." *International Review of the Red Cross* 91 (874): 229–77.

Bar-Tal, Daniel, Eran Halperin, and Joseph De Rivera. 2007. "Collective Emotions in Conflict Situations: Societal Implications." *Journal of Social Issues* 63 (2): 441–60.

Baumeister, Roy F., and David A. Butz. 2005. "Roots of Hate, Violence, and Evil." In *The Psychology of Hate*, edited by Robert J. Sternberg, 87–102. Washington, DC: American Psychological Association.

Ben-Ze'ev, Aaron. 1992. "Emotional and Moral Evaluations." *Metaphilosophy* 23 (3): 214–29.

———. 2000. *The Subtlety of Emotions*. Cambridge: The MIT Press.

———. 2008. "Hating the One You Love." *Philosophia* 36 (3): 277–83.

Berkowitz, Leonard. 2005. "On Hate and Its Determinants: Some Affective and Cognitive Influences." In *The Psychology of Hate*, edited by Robert J. Sternberg, 155–83. Washington, DC: American Psychological Association.

Bernier, Annie, and Mary Dozier. 2002. "Assessing Adult Attachment: Empirical Sophistication and Conceptual Bases." *Attachment and Human Development* 4 (2): 171–79.

Betz, Hand-Georg. 1994. *Radical Right-Wing Populism in Western Europe*. London: Macmillan.

Canetti, Daphna, Julia Elad-Strenger, Iris Lavi, Dana Guy, and Daniel Bar-Tal. 2017. "Exposure to Violence, Ethos of Conflict, and Support for Compromise: Survey in Israel, East Jerusalem, West Bank, and in Gaza." *Journal of Conflict Resolution* 61 (1): 84–113.

Canetti, Daphna, Eric Russ, Judith Luborsky, James I. Gerhart, and Stephen E. Hobfoll. 2014. "Inflamed by the Flames? The Impact of Terrorism and War on Immunity." *Journal of Traumatic Stress* 27 (3): 345–52.

Canetti-Nisim, Daphna, Gal Ariely, and Eran Halperin. 2008. "Life, Pocketbook, or Culture: The Role of Perceived Security Threats in Promoting Exclusionist Political Attitudes toward Minorities in Israel." *Political Research Quarterly* 61 (1): 90–103.

Cavadino, Michael. 2014. "Should Hate Crime Be Sentenced More Severely?" *Contemporary Issues in Law* 13 (1): 1–18.

Chakraborti, Neil, and Jon Garland, eds. 2015. *Responding to Hate Crime: The Case for Connecting Policy and Research*. Bristol: Policy Press.

De Leersnyder, Jozefien, Michael Boiger, and Batja Mesquita. 2015. "Cultural Differences in Emotions." In *Emerging Trends in the Social and Behavioral Sciences: An Interdisciplinary, Searchable, and Linkable Resource*, edited by Robert A. Scott, Marlis Buchmann, and Stephen M. Kosslyn. E-book. New York: Wiley.

Delvaux, Ellen, Loes Meeussen, and Batja Mesquita. 2015. "Feel Like You Belong: On the Bidirectional Link Between Emotional Fit and Group Identification in Task Groups." *Frontiers in Psychology* 6: 1106. DOI: https://doi.org/10.3389/fpsyg.2015.01106.

Ekman, Paul. 1992. "An Argument for Basic Emotions." *Cognition and Emotion* 6 (3–4): 169–200.

Elster, Jon. 1999. *Alchemies of the Mind: Rationality and the Emotions*. Cambridge: Cambridge University Press.

Er-rafiy, Abdelatif, and Markus Brauer. 2013. "Modifying Perceived Variability: Four Laboratory and Field Experiments Show the Effectiveness of a Ready-to-be-used Prejudice Intervention." *Journal of Applied Social Psychology* 43 (4): 840–53.

Fischer, Agneta H., and Roger Giner-Sorolla. 2016. "Contempt: Derogating Others While Keeping Calm." *Emotion Review* 8: 346–57.

Fischer, Agneta H., and Antony S. R. Manstead. 2016. "Social Functions of Emotion and Emotion Regulation." In *Handbook of Emotions*, edited by Lisa Feldman Barrett, Michael Lewis, and Jennette M. Haviland-Jones, 424–39. 4th ed. New York: Guilford Press.

Fischer, Agneta H., and Ira J. Roseman. 2007. "Beat Them or Ban Them: The Characteristics and Social Functions of Anger and Contempt." *Journal of Personality and Social Psychology* 93 (3): 103–15.

Fitness, Julie. 2000. "Anger in the Workplace: An Emotion Script Approach to Anger Episodes Between Workers and Their Superiors, Co-workers and Subordinates." *Journal of Organizational Behavior* 21 (2): 147–62.
Fitness, Julie, and Garth J. O. Fletcher. 1993. "Love, Hate, Anger and Jealousy in Close Relationships: A Prototype and Cognitive Appraisal Analysis." *Journal of Personality and Social Psychology* 65 (5): 942–58.
Frijda, Nico H. 1986. *The Emotions: Studies in Emotions and Social Interaction.* Cambridge: Cambridge University Press.
Frijda, Nico H., Batja Mesquita, Joep Sonnemans, and Stephanie van Goozen. 1991. "The Duration of Affective Phenomena or Emotions, Sentiments, and Passions." *International Review of Studies on Emotion* 1: 187–225.
Galtung, Johan, and Mari Holmboe Ruge. 1965. "The Structure of Foreign News: The Presentation of the Congo, Cuba and Cyprus Crises in Four Norwegian Newspapers" *Journal of Peace Research* 2 (1): 64–90.
Gibson, James L. 2006. "Overcoming Apartheid: Can Truth Reconcile a Divided Nation?" *The Annals of the American Academy of Political and Social Science* 603 (1): 82–110.
Gordijn, Ernestine H., Vincent Yzerbyt, Daniël Wigboldus, and Muriel Dumont. 2006. "Emotional Reactions to Harmful Intergroup Behavior." *European Journal of Social Psychology* 36 (1): 15–30.
Haidt, Jonathan. 2003. "The Moral Emotions." In *Handbook of Affective Sciences*, edited by Richard J. Davidson, Klaus R. Scherer, and H. Hill Goldsmith, 852–70. Oxford: Oxford University Press.
Halperin, Eran. 2008. "Group-Based Hatred in Intractable Conflict in Israel." *Journal of Conflict Resolution* 52 (5): 713–36.
———. 2011. "Emotional Barriers to Peace: Emotions and Public Opinion of Jewish Israelis about the Peace Process in the Middle East." *Peace and Conflict: Journal of Peace Psychology* 17 (1): 22–45.
Halperin, Eran, Daphna Canetti, and Shaul Kimhi. 2012. "In Love With Hatred: Rethinking the Role Hatred Plays in Political Behavior." *Journal of Applied Social Psychology* 42 (9): 2231–56.
Halperin, Eran, Daphna Canetti-Nisim, and Sivan Hirsch-Hoefler. 2009. "The Central Role of Group-Based Hatred as an Emotional Antecedent of Political Intolerance: Evidence from Israel." *Political Psychology* 30 (1): 93–123.
Halperin, Eran, and James J. Gross. 2011. "Intergroup Anger in Intractable Conflict: Long-term Sentiments Predict Anger Responses During the Gaza War." *Group Processes and Intergroup Relations* 14: 477–88.
Halperin, Eran, Alexandra G. Russell, Carol S. Dweck, and James J. Gross. 2011. "Anger, Hatred, and the Quest for Peace: Anger Can Be Constructive in the Absence of Hatred." *Journal of Conflict Resolution* 55 (2): 274–91.
Hawdon, James, Atte Oksanen, and Pekka Räsänen. 2017. "Exposure to Online Hate in Four Nations: A Cross-National Consideration." *Deviant Behavior* 38 (3): 254–66.
Hirsch-Hoefler, Sivan, Daphna Canetti, and Ami Pedahzur. 2010. "Two of a Kind?: Voting Motivations for Populist Radical Right and Religious Fundamentalist Parties." *Electoral Studies* 29: 678–90.

Hutchings, Vincent L., Nicholas A. Valentino, Tasha S. Philpot, and Ismail K. White. 2006. "Racial Cues in Campaign News: The Effects of Candidate Strategies on Group Activation and Political Attentiveness among African Americans." In *Feeling Politics*, edited by David P. Redlawsk, 165–86. New York: Palgrave Macmillan.

Iyer, Aarti, and Colin Wayne Leach. 2009. "Emotion in Inter-Group Relations." *European Review of Social Psychology* 19 (1): 86–125.

Jasini, Alba, and Fischer, Agneta H. 2018. *Characteristics and Social Determinants of Intergroup Hate*. Unpublished manuscript.

Kaplan, Jeffrey, and Leonard Weinberg. 1998. *The Emergence of a Euro-American Radical Right*. New Brunswick: Rutgers University Press.

Keltner, Dacher, and Jonathan Haidt. 1999. "The Social Functions of Emotions at Four Levels of Analysis." *Cognition and Emotion* 13 (5): 505–21.

Kinder, Donald R., and David O. Sears. 1985. "Public Opinion and Political Action." In *Handbook of Social Psychology*, edited by Gardner Lindzey and Elliot Aronson, 659–741. 2nd ed. New York: Random House.

Kuppens, Toon, Vincent Y. Yzerbyt, Sophie Dandache, Agneta H. Fischer, and Job van der Schalk. 2013. "Social Identity Salience Shapes Group-Based Emotions through Group-Based Appraisals." *Cognition & Emotion* 27 (8): 1359–77.

Lavi, Iris, Daphna Canetti, Keren Sharvit, Daniel Bar-Tal, and Stevan E. Hobfoll. 2014. "Protected by Ethos in a Protracted Conflict? A Comparative Study among Israelis and Palestinians in the West Bank, Gaza, and East Jerusalem." *Journal of Conflict Resolution* 58 (1): 68–92.

Lazarsfeld, Paul F., Bernard Berelson, and Hazel Gaudet. 1944. *The People's Choice: How the Voter Makes Up His Mind in a Presidential Campaign*. New York: Columbia University Press.

Leader, Tirza, Brian Mullen, Diane and Rice. 2009. "Complexity and Valence in Ethnophaulisms and Exclusion of Ethnic Out-Groups: What Puts the 'Hate' into Hate Speech?" *Journal of Personality and Social Psychology* 96 (1): 170–82.

Lerner, Melvin J. 1980. *The Belief in a Just World: A Fundamental Delusion*. New York: Plenum Press.

Levin, Jack, and Jack McDevitt. 2008. "Hate Crimes." In *The Encyclopedia of Peace, Violence, and Conflict*, edited by Lester R. Kurtz, 89–102. 2nd ed. New York: Academic Press.

Levin, Brian, and James J. Nolan. 2015a. "The Evolving World of Hate and Extremism: An Interdisciplinary Perspective—Part 1." *American Behavioral Scientist* 59 (12): 1643–45.

Levin, Brian, and James J. Nolan. 2015b. "The Evolving World of Hate and Extremism: An Interdisciplinary Perspective—Part 2." *American Behavioral Scientist* 59 (13): 1635–36.

Livingstone, Andrew G., Russell Spears, Antony S. R. Manstead, Martin Bruder, and Lee Shepherd. 2011. "We Feel, Therefore We Are: Emotion as a Basis for Self-Categorization and Social Action." *Emotion* 11: 754–67.

Mackie, Diane M., Thierry Devos, and Eliot R. Smith. 2000. "Intergroup Emotions: Explaining Offensive Action Tendencies in an Intergroup Context." *Journal of Personality and Social Psychology* 79 (4): 602–16.

Mann, Liesbeth, Allard R. Feddes, Bertjan Doosje, and Agneta H. Fischer. 2016. "Withdraw or Affiliate? The Role of Humiliation During Initiation Rituals." *Cognition and Emotion* 30 (1): 80–100.
Manstead, Antony S. R., and Agneta H. Fischer. 2001. "Social Appraisal: The Social World as Object of and Influence on Appraisal Processes." In *Appraisal Processes in Emotion: Theory, Methods, Research*, edited by Klaus R. Scherer, Angela Schorr and Tom Johnstone, 221–32. Oxford: Oxford University Press.
McDevitt, Jack, and Jack Levin. 1993. *Hate Crimes: The Rising Tide of Bigotry and Bloodshed*. New York: Plenum Press.
Mishra, Pankaj. 2017. *Age of Anger: A History of the Present*. New York: Farrar, Straus and Giroux.
Mudde, Cas. 2005. "Racist Extremism in Central and Eastern Europe." *East European Politics and Societies* 19 (2): 161–84.
Noor, Masi, Nurit Shnabel, Samer Halabi, and Arie Nadler. 2012. "When Suffering Begets Suffering: The Psychology of Competitive Victimhood Between Adversarial Groups in Violent Conflicts." *Personality and Social Psychology Review* 16: 351–74.
Oatley, Keith, and Jennifer M. Jenkins. 1996. *Understanding Emotions*. Malden: Blackwell.
Opotow, Susan, and Sara I. McClelland. 2007. "The Intensification of Hating: A Theory." *Social Justice Research* 20 (1): 68–97.
Ortony, Andrew, Gerald L. Clore, and Allan Collins. 1988. *The Cognitive Structure of Emotions*. Cambridge: Cambridge University Press.
Perry, Barbara. 2003. "Where Do We Go from Here? Researching Hate Crime." *Internet Journal of Criminology* 3: 45–47.
Petersen, Roger D. 2002. *Understanding Ethnic Violence: Fear, Hatred, and Resentment in Twentieth-Century Eastern Europe*. Cambridge: Cambridge University Press.
Pettigrew, Thomas F., and Linda R. Tropp. 2006. "A Meta-Analytic Test of Intergroup Contact Theory." *Journal of Personality and Social Psychology* 90 (5): 751–83.
Porat, Roni, Eran Halperin, Ittay Mannheim, and Maya Tamir. 2016. "Together We Cry: Social Motives and Preferences for Group-Based Sadness." *Cognition and Emotion* 30 (1): 66–79.
Power, Mick, and Tim Dalgleish. 1997. *Cognition and Emotion: From Order to Disorder*. Hove: Psychology Press.
Reifen Tagar, Michal, Christopher M. Federico, and Eran Halperin. 2011. "The Positive Effect of Negative Emotions in Protracted Conflict: The Case of Anger." *Journal of Experimental Social Psychology* 47 (1): 157–64
Rempel, John K., and Christopher T. Burris. 2005. "Let Me Count the Ways: An Integrative Theory of Love and Hate." *Personal Relationships* 12 (2): 297–313.
Rimé, Bernard. 2009. "Emotion Elicits the Social Sharing of Emotion: Theory and Empirical Review." *Emotion Review* 1: 60–85.
Roseman, Ira J. 1984. "Cognitive Determinants of Emotion: A Structural Theory." *Review of Personality and Social Psychology* 5: 11–36.

Roseman, Ira J., Cynthia Wiest, and Tamara S. Swartz. 1994. "Phenomenology, Behaviors, and Goals Differentiate Discrete Emotions." *Journal of Personality and Social Psychology* 67 (2): 206–21.

Ross, Lee. 1977. "The Intuitive Psychologist and His Shortcoming: Distortions in the Attribution Process." In *Advances in Experimental Social Psychology*, edited by Leonard Berkowitz, 174–214. New York: Academic Press.

Royzman, Edward B., Clark McCauley, and Paul Rozin. 2005. "From Plato to Putnam: Four Ways to Think about Hate." In *The Psychology of Hate*, edited by R. J. Sternberg, 3–35. Washington, DC: American Psychological Association.

Rozin, Paul. 1999. "The Process of Moralization." *Psychological Science* 10 (3): 218–21.

Russell, Pascale Sophie, and Roger Giner-Sorolla. 2011. "Moral Anger is More Flexible than Moral Disgust." *Social Psychological and Personality Science* 2 (4): 360–64.

Salmela, Mikko, and Christian von Scheve. 2017. "Emotional Roots of Right-Wing Political Populism." *Social Science Information* 4: 567–95.

Scherer, Klaus R. 2005. "What are Emotions? And How Can They be Measured?" *Social Science Information* 44 (4): 695–729.

Schoenewolf, Gerald. 1996. "The Couple Who Fell in Hate: Eclectic Psychodynamic Therapy with an Angry Couple." *Journal of Contemporary Psychotherapy* 26 (1): 65–71.

Seip, Elise C. 2016. "Desire for Vengeance: An Emotion-Based Approach to Revenge." Unpublished doctoral thesis. University of Amsterdam, Amsterdam, The Netherlands.

Seip, Elise C., Mark Rotteveel, Lotte F. van Dillen, and Wilco W. van Dijk, W. W. 2014. "Schadenfreude and the Desire for Vengeance." In *Schadenfreude: Understanding Pleasure at the Misfortune of Others*, edited by Wilco W. van Dijk and Jaap W. Ouwerkerk, 227–41. Cambridge: Cambridge University Press.

Shaaban, Eslam. 2015. *Controlling the Other Edge of Social Media, Hate Speech and Terrorism Propaganda*. Retrieved from https://papers.ssrn.com/sol3/papers.cfm?abstract_id=2589254.

Simon, Bernd, and Amélie Mummendey. 1990. "Perceptions of Relative Group Size and Group Homogeneity: We Are the Majority and They Are All the Same." *European Journal of Social Psychology* 20 (4): 351–56.

Solomon, Robert C. 1977. "The Rationality of the Emotions." *The Southwestern Journal of Philosophy* 8 (2): 105–114.

Staub, Ervin. 1989. *The Roots of Evil: The Origins of Genocide and Other Group Violence*. New York: Cambridge University Press.

———. 2005. "The Origins and Evolution of Hate, with Notes on Prevention." In *The Psychology of Hate*, edited by R. J. Sternberg, 51–66. Washington, DC: American Psychological Association.

Sternberg, Robert J. 2003. "A Duplex Theory of Hate: Development and Application to Terrorism, Massacres, and Genocide." *Review of General Psychology* 7 (3): 299–328.

———. 2005. "Understanding and Combating Hate." In *The Psychology of Hate*, edited by Robert J. Sternberg, 37–49. Washington, DC: American Psychological Association.

Stouffer, Samuel A. 1955. *Communism, Conformity, and Civil Liberties: A Cross-Section of the Nation Speaks its Mind*. Livingstone: Transaction.

Sullivan, Alison C., Aaron C. H. Ong, Stephen T. La Macchia, and Winnifred R. Louis. 2016. "The Impact of Unpunished Hate Crimes: When Derogating the Victim Extends into Derogating the Group." *Social Justice Research* 29: 310–30.

Tausch, Nicole, Julia C. Becker, Russell Spears, Oliver Christ, Rim Saab, Purnima Singh, and Roomana N. Siddiqui. 2011. "Explaining Radical Group Behavior: Developing Emotion and Efficacy Routes to Normative and Non-Normative Collective Action." *Journal of Personality and Social Psychology* 101 (1): 129–48.

Van Dijk, Wilco W., and Jaap W. Ouwerkerk, eds. 2014. *Schadenfreude: Understanding Pleasure at the Misfortune of Others*. Cambridge: Cambridge University Press.

Volkan, Vamik. 1997. *Bloodlines: From Ethnic Pride to Ethnic Terrorism*. New York: Farrar, Straus and Giroux.

Vollhardt, Johanna Ray 2012. "Collective Victimization." In *Oxford Handbook of Intergroup Conflict*, edited by Linda R. Tropp, 136–57. New York: Oxford University Press.

Waller, James. 2002. "Perpetrators of Genocide: An Explanatory Model of Extraordinary Human Evil. *Journal of Hate Studies* 1 (1): 5–22.

White, Robert S. 1996. "Psychoanalytic Process and Interactive Phenomena." *Journal of the American Psychoanalytic Association* 44 (3): 699–722.

Yzerbyt, Vincent, Muriel Dumont, Daniel Wigboldus, and Ernestine Gordijn. 2003. "I Feel For Us: The Impact of Categorization and Identification on Emotions and Action Tendencies." *The British Journal of Social Psychology* 42 (4): 533–49.

III

HATE, ETHICS, AND RATIONALITY

Chapter 8

Good Hate

Damian Cox and Michael P. Levine

1. INTRODUCTION

Is it ever a good thing to hate another person? The first step in answering this is to get a little clarity about the kind of hate in question. The term "hate" is used so freely in casual conversation—one hates a brand of pickle, a movie, or a new building—that it loses some of its currency. But the term is deeply ambiguous and retains its power to shock when appropriately disambiguated. To hate a brand of pickle is merely to dislike it strongly. To hate a person is to want something in particular: it is to find them intolerable; it is to wish, in some sense, for their downfall. We will need to be more precise about the characteristic motivational goals of such hatred, but the term "downfall" serves well in a first pass at what is peculiar about hatred of persons. Personal hatred is directed at both individual persons and groups of persons. We concentrate on individuals. We are looking at individuals encountered in one's life, even if remotely: family members; personal enemies; bosses; administrators; the police officer who torments you; the neighbor who mocks you; the politician who sends your country to war through lies; the genocidal killer you learn about, awaiting trial in the Hague; and so on. We ask whether it is ever good to hate such people. To suppose that all hate is bad in some way, or immoral, seems to be less jarring or surprising than supposing that all happiness or all love is good. This is not so.

Hate can be experienced as a passing emotion, but the most important forms of it are something more than this. In "The Historicity of Psychological Attitudes: Love Is Not Love Which Alters Not When It Alteration Finds," Amélie Rorty says, "There is a set of psychological attitudes—love, joy, perhaps some sorts of desire—that are individuated by the character of the subject, the character of the object, and the relation between them" (1988,

121). While these psychological attitudes may (and typically do) include emotions, they are different from emotion. On Rorty's account, love is not an emotion but a psychological attitude. It will at times involve emotion, and the kinds of emotion involved will characterize the nature of the love. Much the same can be said about hate. It too is a psychological attitude "individuated by the character of the subject, the character of the object, and the relation between them," and it too typically involves emotions, for example, hostility and resentment, that characterize the hate involved.[1]

We are taught early on that hate is bad (both in itself and bad for us) and there is no shortage of explanations as to why it is bad. Aaron Ben-Ze'ev gives a typical answer for what he terms "enduring hate"—hate that dominates in one's life: "When hate is not merely a temporary eruption but a constant feature, it distorts the agent's behavior and attitudes. As such, its moral value worsens with maturity" (2018, 322). While this seems uncontroversial, such dominating, enduring hate is rarer than other kinds of hate, in particular the focus of this chapter: hate directed for a while at a particular individual. Are there cases in which such a psychological attitude directed at a person in one's life is, on balance, a good thing? When might such hate be good, or what might be meant by good hate? Here are three possibilities.

First, and most generally, one may think that good hate is hating someone in circumstances that are emotionally appropriate. Good hate is fitting hate and the person hated must be worthy of hate. To rightly judge hateworthiness, in the circumstances, one must be correct about what the circumstances are, about the facts of the matter, and the circumstances must warrant the hate. Even though reasonable disputes may arise about hateworthiness, it is important that relevant facts exist that settle the issue.

We may not always be able to choose who it is that we hate, though we can at times influence such attitudes. Nonetheless, apparent inescapability of hate does not automatically confer appropriateness on the hate. Hating someone because they accidentally step on your foot, or even if they intentionally step on your foot, is inappropriate. Hating the police because they issue you a ticket (even if unwarranted) or hating a person that walks past you smoking a cigarette are not appropriate attitudes. Hating someone who tortures you, or who is guilty of genocide; hating someone who says or promotes harmful and hateful things about one's race, gender, gender identification, or sexual preferences; hating someone who promotes violence or endangers others for no good reason; hating someone who treats those around them as mere objects to be used, manipulated, and dispensed with are or at least may be appropriate. Hate might be directed at those in power over us—politicians, managers, petty administrators—particularly when they act with indifference, hypocrisy, laziness, vindictiveness, when, for example, they lie and cheat their way to an easy life. Whether liars and cheats, the petty and "stupid" are hateworthy depends in part on what it is they are lying and cheating or being petty and stupid about, along with the consequences of their actions. None of this makes hateworthiness purely subjective. It indicates that while there may be some people that we can more or less agree are appropriate objects of hate, in other cases it will not be clear.

We do not need psychoanalytic theory to tell us (though it does), that a principal reason why we often hate people who are not hateworthy is because, when we find ourselves hating someone, we imaginatively project onto that person properties that make them worthy of our hate thus justifying the hate we feel. When we hate (as when we are prejudiced toward a person, race, or gender) it is often because we see something in that person's character or attitudes that we recognize and find problematic in ourselves. We may see them or imagine them worse than they (probably) are. This is a defense mechanism of sorts. We do not wish to hate, or be seen to hate, inappropriately. To do so would conflict with the way in which we see ourselves or wish to see ourselves (e.g., as just). We therefore see to it that, at least in our minds, we are not unjust haters. We generally regard the objects of our hate as hateworthy.

The second way in which we might interpret the concept of good hate is as follows. Hate may sometimes play a role in a flourishing life: as a kind of self-defense, a marshaling of the resources of affective empathy, and as a kind of self-honesty. It may at times be psychologically, personally, socially, and politically good for us, and can serve important functions in all these areas. To further an analogy with love, a person incapable of hate may be, like a person incapable of love or strong affection, not merely a truncated or marginalized human being, but also psychologically problematic in various ways. The idea, in short, is that hate plays important roles in our psychic economy.

Much as with love, if hate is to be "good for us," to serve our well-being, it seems that it would have to also be, much if not most of the time, appropriate in the circumstances. We might get lucky, as we sometimes do, but it is difficult to see how hating an inappropriate person or hating inappropriately by hating too much or too little can further our ends. This is not meant to deny the received wisdom that far more often than not, and at times even when it is justified and appropriate, hate's role is negative. In various ways and on various fronts, it generally does us and others more harm than good. It causes unhappiness in ourselves and others. The reasons for this, as depicted in literature and film, are varied. One reason is that our psychological attitudes are often not discrete. They inform or seep into one another. A life in which hate dominates or plays a prominent part will be one in which other attitudes, feelings, and emotions are affected. It will affect one's loves, one's friendships, the attitudes one has to work and life generally. It is difficult to see how a life dominated by hate can be a happy life or serve our well-being in other ways. There are good reasons why we tend to disdain and avoid those who have hate-filled lives and admire those who do not. And yet, the possibility remains that hate sometimes plays a positive role in our lives.

The third way in which hate may be a valuable part of human experience is as an essential moral emotion. Hate, as Simone de Beauvoir (1946, 2004) claimed, may be foundational to justice in some sense. Whatever else may be involved, justice and morality, Beauvoir claims, may not even be possible without hate. As Blake Smith (2019, 5) puts it, "Not only are we responsible for the violence and death our hate engenders, [Beauvoir] claimed, but our hate is the only thing that can make violence and death legitimate. Justice without hate is a farce." In Beauvoir's words,

> Hate is not a capricious passion. It denounces an abominable reality and imperiously demands that this reality be eradicated from the world. One does not hate a hailstorm or a plague, one hates only men, not because they are material cause of material damage, but because they are conscious authors of genuine evil. A soldier who kills in combat is not to be hated, because he is obeying orders and because there is a reciprocity between his situation and the situation of his foes. Neither death nor suffering nor captivity are abominable in themselves. An abomination arises only at the moment that a man treats fellow men like objects, when by torture, humiliation, servitude, assassination one denies them their existence as men. Hatred grasps at another's freedom insofar as it is used to realize the absolute evil that is the degradation of a man into a thing. And it calls immediately for revenge that strives to destroy evil at its source by reaching the freedom of the evildoer. (Beauvoir 2004, 248)

Hate, then, may be an unavoidable aspect of what it is to take our moral condition seriously. Its positive role is to assert the necessity of respect for persons, the absolute hold of this principle upon us. Its negative role is to direct vengeance against those who without excuse profoundly violate this respect. To put it crudely, a failure to hate evildoers is a failure to take absolute evil seriously.

In the remainder of this paper, we explore these three ways in which hate of persons might be considered a good thing: hate as fitting attitude, hate as support for a flourishing life, hate as a necessary moral emotion/psychological attitude. The relations between the three claims also need to be considered. Hate as a necessary moral emotion appears to support its standing as support for a flourishing life: life is lacking something important if it is bereft of the capacity, when appropriate, to experience a fundamental moral emotion. It also presupposes the reality of fitting or appropriate hate since an inappropriate attitude cannot be the legitimate expression of a moral stance. (Even where a person is found to be an appropriate object of hate, it generally would not be the case that all aspects of the person are hateworthy or that one who is currently a hateworthy object either always has been so or always will be so.) By contrast, the first two bases for judging hate do not entail Beauvoir's claim that hate is a necessary attendant of justice. It may be that hate is both appropriate in some circumstances, and a good thing for a person in some circumstances, without its being necessary for justice. Indeed, true justice may require a sterner and more remote view of things in which all emotions of hate are replaced with a concern for the greater good. Again, the idea that an attitude of hate may sometimes be fitting does not imply that it is good for us. And the fact that hate may be good for us, serve useful purposes, does not strictly entail that the hated person must be worthy of hate. Hate may sometimes be good for us, after all, even if often misguided (as it surely is).

Because the relationship between each of our suppositions is complex, we examine them independently of each other. In the next section, we consider the fittingness conditions for the kind of hate we have in view. In section 3, we consider the possible role personal hate might play in a flourishing life by examining a fictional case of its absence. We discuss the HBO series *Succession* (2018–). This series revolves around four siblings (with various hangers-on) whose main life-failure appears to consist in a failure to hate their father. In section 4, we examine more closely Beauvoir's arguments that hate is implicit in the demands of justice.

2. APPROPRIATE HATE

When is it appropriate to hate someone?[2] To answer this question, we need to look more closely at the nature of the attitude of hate. Personal hate is a psychological attitude that centers on extreme negative judgments about another's character. But this feature is shared by other negative emotions, such as contempt and moral disgust. As Fischer, Halperin, Canetti, and Jasini set it out (Fischer et al. 2018), hate differs from other negative emotions primarily in terms of characteristic action tendencies and emotivational goals. They write,

> According to Roseman et al. (1994), an emotivational goal reflects what the emotion tries to bring about, and thus drives the emotional experience. Action tendencies are very closely associated with emotivational goals as they reflect the motivational impulse to act on a specific goal (see also Rempel and Burris 2005). . . . We propose that the emotivational goal of hate is not merely to hurt, but to ultimately eliminate or destroy the target, either mentally (humiliating, treasuring feelings of revenge), socially (excluding, ignoring), or physically (killing, torturing), which may be accompanied by the goal to let the wrongdoer suffer (Ben-Ze'ev 2008). (Fischer et al. 2018, 311)

The idea that hatred has a characteristic goal and that goal is destruction or elimination of its object has considerable prima facie plausibility. But the way Fischer et al. develop the idea is problematic.[3] Destruction, they note, may be mental, social, or physical, but the range of proffered examples is much too broad to encapsulate the idea of destruction or elimination. How is physically torturing a person emblematic of a wish to destroy them? Torturers want something from their victims—information, confession, suffering, vivid and visceral realization of their violations (real or pretend)—but physical destruction is not ordinarily among them. Of course, it is possible to torture another in order to *mentally* destroy them in some sense, but that is not characteristic of either the torturer or the hater. Also consider the goal of humiliation. This may be characteristic of hate, but what is its relation to destruction or elimination? To humiliate another is not to seek to socially eliminate or destroy them. It is typically aimed at another's social diminishment (taking them down a peg or two) as well as their suffering (it has got to hurt). What we need for our purposes is a more conceptually disciplined and precise account of the characteristic emotivational goals of personal hate.

Of course, it is possible to want your enemies to die, but generally only in extreme circumstances. Writing of the occupation of France during World War II, Beauvoir notes, "Since June 1940 we have learned rage and hate. We have wished humiliation and death on our enemies" (2004, 246). But hating a malicious boss or a racist neighbor is not the same thing as hating Nazis. And even in extreme circumstances, the death of one's enemies is most often a failure to secure the goals of hate. Again, Beauvoir sets this point out vividly.

> The death of Hitler frustrated us: one wished that he had remained alive to realize his ruin, in order to "understand." . . . The moment when Mussolini cries "No, no" in front of the firing squad satisfies hate far more than the moment when he collapses beneath the bullets. (2004, 250)

Building on Beauvoir's point, let us say that the emotivational goal of personal hate is the conscious, painful downfall of the object of hate. We may wish a hated boss fired; a lying politician found out, their career ruined; an abusive ex-partner shamed, guilt-ridden, distressed, lonely. Furthermore, the wished-for demise of an object of hate must be consciously *appreciated* by them. We may wish them to suffer, but not arbitrarily. We wish for them to understand what they have been like and what they have done and to suffer because of it. Characteristically, we want them to think of themselves and see themselves as we think of them and see them.

Because personal hate targets character rather than action, it tends to generate unrealistic wishes. If one has judged an enemy right, as befitting an attitude of hate, then they are perhaps unlikely to experience their own downfall in the longed-for spirit even if it arrives. Their hateworthy character may tend to get in the way. A surviving Hitler would not have surveyed his downfall as a judgment upon himself. He would have continued in his delusional belief that the German people had let him down, that the downfall is entirely theirs: it is their defeat (not his), and they deserve all the suffering and humiliation that is to follow from it. In more mundane circumstances, a bullying and abusive boss is unlikely to experience their demise as a fitting consequence of their bullying and abusive ways (though of course they might). More likely, they will think themselves the victim of office ressentiment and political correctness.

It is important that personal hate is directed at character rather than action: one hates a person because of what they are or have become; actions are targets of hate primarily on the basis of what they reveal about a person's character. To say "I do not hate you, I hate what you have done" is to refuse personal hate. It is to attempt (perhaps disingenuously) to rise above personal hate. This is important for the fittingness or appropriateness of attitudes of hate since it is unfitting to hate a person on the basis of a single act when that act is wholly out of character. A loyal and sincere friend who lets you down once is not a fitting object of hate. By contrast, a hypocritical putative friend (a "frenemy") who undermines you at important points in your life and succeeds in ruining your relationships with others might just be a fitting object of hate.

If we are right that personal hate implies a judgment of character and is attended by a wish for the painful and self-appreciated downfall of the hated person, then we have the materials to set out conditions of appropriateness or fittingness of attitudes of personal hate. Someone is a fitting object of personal hate only when the suppositions of the attitude, in the circumstances, are fully met. For the person to genuinely be a fitting object of hate, the suppositions have to be correct, not imagined or projected. A person is hated because of their character: for example, a hated boss is taken to be lazy, vindictive, bullying, unempathetic, and without remorse. This implicit judgment, then, must be accurate. A misunderstood boss, demanding and exacting, but doing her best in a difficult situation, knowing that incompetent or uncooperative employees threaten the sustainability of the entire work group, is not a fitting object of hate. No matter how tempting it is for employees to take out their frustrations upon her, or how comforting it is to direct distress outward toward the perceived source of one's trials rather than at one's own failures, hate is inappropriate. It is inappropriate whenever the character judgment at its base is wrong or unjustified. Whether hate is appropriate is not simply a matter of opinion.

It is possible that a person hate another on the basis of an unjustified belief about their character—say, a self-serving guess about the origins of their own misery—even though reality in fact lines up this way. Say an employee comes to hate their boss on the unreasonable supposition that the boss is targeting them out of personal animosity. On all the available evidence the boss is responding to the hater's incompetence and laziness. (The hater *is* lazy and incompetent and ought to have worked this out for themselves.) The hate in this case is inappropriate even if it were the case that the boss does indeed harbor a well-hidden animosity toward the hater and targets them accordingly. The epistemic condition for appropriate hate is not mere truth of the implicit character judgment. Nor is it mere justification of implicit character judgment. Consider a case in which someone justifiably concludes that their neighbor is racist and shows racist disdain and prejudice toward them. They see the neighbor react with apparent disgust as their children play in the yard; they see the neighbor spurn any attempt at friendly interactions; they also see the neighbor treat people of their own ethnicity well. They cast about and find no other plausible explanation of the neighbors' attitude. Eventually, they come to hate the neighbor—perhaps not deeply, but acutely. In situations like these, judgments of racism are often right, but they are also fallible. It might be the case that the neighbor is suffering from grief and is very withdrawn from people he does not know well (including his immediate neighbor, but not others in the street he has known for many years). Even if a judgment of racism is justified on the available evidence, it is not appropriate hate. It is based on a mistake; it is an injustice. Appropriate hate is not the same thing as hate epistemically justified in the circumstance. Thus, the epistemic condition on appropriate hate is not true belief, not justified belief, but knowledge.[4] If we are right about this, hate can be sincerely felt on the basis of justified judgment and yet not be a fitting attitude. Our emotional attitudes are fallible in this way, just as our beliefs are.

Appropriate hate is based on knowledge of character, but what sort of character? In the quote earlier, Beauvoir emphasizes the Kantian judgment that objects of appropriate hate reduce persons to objects, deny their standing as persons, their consciousness, freedom, and subjectivity, and treat them as tools to be made use of or dispensed with without concern. Hate is a reaction to abomination, and "an abomination arises only at the moment that a man treats fellow men like objects" (2004, 248) This is a convincing identification of basic kinds of evil, but a richer "aretaic" description of the character of those who are fitting objects of hate is ultimately required. There are ways of treating persons as objects that are not obviously hateful. There are lies one might tell or manipulations one might enact that undermine one's integrity to a degree without one deserving the hatred of others. Both character and consequence count, and although the kinds of character that constitute fitting objects of personal hatred are varied, they are each, in distinctive ways, profoundly harmful. The racist who undermines the dignity and social position of others; the bully who harms the security and well-being of others; the cheating partner who prioritizes adventure and lust over love and commitment, and thus damages the happiness and self-respect of loved ones are all patterns of behavior that arise out of character traits such as selfish hypocrisy, defensive aggression, greed, indifference, shallowness, narcissistic pride, and so on. It is beyond the scope of our chapter to give an exhaustive account of the kinds of character and kinds of behavior patterns that potentially warrant hatred (and such an account would in any case be exhausting and perhaps unprofitable to read), but the intuitive idea is reasonably clear. A hateworthy form of character is despicable: harmful in a way that derides and undermines the personhood of others.

Finally, let us consider one last constraint on appropriate hatred. To be appropriate, personal hate must be based on knowledge of character and its effects. It must be a response to real and profound damage caused by despicable character. But what connection should the hater have to be hated? Is it appropriate only to hate those who have harmed ourselves and our loved ones? This seems too restrictive. Is it appropriate to hate those who we only learn about remotely? Is it appropriate to hate a stranger based on reports about their character and behavior? What about hating politicians from another country—even noisy and destructive ones like Donald Trump or Jair Bolsonaro? Might it be right to complain of another's hatred: "Why do you hate this person? They have nothing to do with you." One way to express this point is to ask whether we fail sometimes to have appropriate standing to hate others. The appropriateness of our hatreds depends in part upon the appropriateness of the wishes attendant on them. For example, are ordinary Australian citizens, people with no ties to Brazil, appropriately placed to wish for Jair Bolsonaro's conscious, painful downfall? That depends on whether it is their business or not, whether, that is, the wish would be an unwarranted intrusion upon the affairs of others.

To sum up, personal hate is appropriate or fitting on our account if it is based on knowledge of despicable character, the profoundly harmful behavior that comes from it, and its attendant wishes are themselves appropriate for the hater in their own circumstances. None of this amounts to a demonstration that the hate thus generated is good in a more substantive sense. It sometimes makes emotional sense to hate; it is not always based on an error of judgment; it is not always a foolish or inappropriate attitude. On the other hand, it may not be doing us or anybody else any good. It may be an empty indulgence at best and a destructive force at worst. Even if it is, in some sense, fair, it may not be a good thing to experience and it may not serve our best interests. Hate has its pleasures (which is why villains make such good business at the box office), but it is also often a painful and disturbing thing to experience. Its negativity is hard to contain; it is hard to quell once its work is done; it is a dangerous emotion. A habit of confecting hatred for despised individuals can easily spill over into wholly unjustified hatred of groups. To say that hate *may be* fitting, then, is not yet to pass judgment about its value. So let us turn to this question next.

3. THE ROLE OF HATE IN A FLOURISHING LIFE

In the HBO series *Succession* (2018–), four siblings fight among themselves and with others for control of their family business. Not just any business, Waystar RoyCo is a global media and hospitality empire worth billions (also up to its corporate neck in unacknowledged debt). The principal interest in the series lies in the unfolding characters of the siblings: Kendall Roy (Jeremy Strong), Siobhan "Shiv" Roy (Sarah Snook), Roman Roy (Kieran Culkin), and, peripherally, Connor Roy (Alan Ruck). Over them all, looms the monstrous figure of their father Logan Roy (Brian Cox). It is a dark comedy and revels not only in power infighting, but in the humiliations visited upon the adult children of Logan Roy.

They are an unpleasant bunch, each projecting a singularly unattractive and distinct personality. Kendall is, in his power-hungry way, lost, gormless, frat-boy-rude, vulnerable, and desperate for his father's approval.[5] Shiv is conniving and untrustworthy, smarter than her brothers, her father's favorite; her principal flaw is hubris. Roman is a purely comic invention, permanently out of his depth, adolescent, smirky, shallow, pitiless, sexually dysfunctional: quite a mess (played with brilliant tenacity by Kieran Culkin). The other sibling, Connor, is yet another fine comic invention. A remarkably stupid and delusional character, he has at least the sense to *try* to stay out of the family's affairs as much as possible. There are various others hanging around all the power and wealth on offer (it is an ensemble work, with a principal cast list of 11).

So, what has gone wrong with this family? Excessive wealth and privilege have not helped of course. In the first episode, for example, the family fly out to a park to play softball in celebration of Logan's 80th birthday. Roman offers a local kid one million dollars if he can hit a home run and then delights in his failure to do so. (The kid comes close.) But excessive wealth and power only goes so far in explaining the family's deficits. It explains their callous indifference to the needs of others, their arrogance and rudeness. But it does not explain the core failure of each of Logan Roy's children's lives. Roman desperately wants to be a player but cannot play; he wants to be taken seriously but has no idea of what it would take to be taken seriously. Shiv is to marry a repulsive and nakedly greedy fool of a man. For all her talent, she is a political operative of the most venal, uninteresting sort. Kendall is the closest the series comes to a tragic, rather than farcical, figure. (He nonetheless furnishes many moments of brilliant farce.) What the three main siblings share—Connor can be left to the side in this discussion, as he is in life—is a ferocious dependency on their father and their father's approval.

Logan Roy is a monstrous figure, not because he is permanently hostile, grumpy, dishonest, self-serving, manipulative, greedy for power, and arrogant—he is all these things—but because he plays with his children's affections mercilessly and has clearly done so their entire lives. Shiv, being the father's obvious favorite, is a complex case, but Kendall and Roman are products of an emotionally abusive father, alternatively demanding fealty, supplying affection and withdrawing it, depriving his sons of stable love and respect throughout their childhood. The series title sequence—the only available scenes of the siblings' childhood—provides a clear presentation of this. A father-son portrait—a satisfied child, an attentive father, hand-in-hand—is taken only for the father to immediately withdraw with a distracted scowl, leaving the child (presumably Kendall) looking hurt and bewildered but not, it seems, surprised. (It has surely happened to him before, many times, in many ways.) Shiv, Kendall, and Roman's mother is a rarely mentioned and remote figure. It is not made clear what role she played in their childhoods. Based on their personality outcomes, and the awkwardness of their adult encounters with her, we might not think she helped much.

Given their limited emotional, social, and intellectual resources, what might have helped these three characters—from adolescence into adulthood—to address the core deficits of their lives? One does not overcome childhood emotional neglect and manipulation easily. But a prerequisite is to deal with the emotional abuse suffered: see it for what it was, confront the source of it, and if there is no hope of accommodation or recognition there (and it seems surely that there is not in this case) then find a way to overcome its effects. Instead, the children spend their lives circling their father, trying different ways of appeasing, solicitating, manipulating him, escaping from him; mostly trying in a hopelessly quixotic way to secure his affection and respect. Logan Roy professes affection, sometimes displays it (especially to Shiv), but these seem to be pantomimes of love. Logan's concern with the family appears real, but it is mostly a concern with dynasty, not with the individual lives of his children.

So, given that there is no emotional recourse through Logan Roy, and given that there never was, what can these people do to free themselves of his malign influence on their lives? The obvious answer is to leave: to get out of the business, leave the wealth and power and privilege behind, and make a life for themselves. At the beginning of Season One, Shiv is half trying this as (in his way) is Connor. But they are both soon drawn back into the circle.

It seems that none of Logan Roy's children have the emotional resources to simply leave. There is unfinished emotional work to do. But what work?

There are basically two kinds of attitudes one might develop in circumstances like these: stoic or "cool" attitudes and engaged or "hot" attitudes. A stoic response would be to develop a lofty indifference to the claims of the father and thus free oneself from his grip. The strongest emotional expression of this attitude is what we dub "stoic contempt." If the children could learn to feel such a contempt for their father, they may yet have a chance of living flourishing lives of their own. But this kind of attitude is very difficult to acquire. Stoic contempt requires an attitude of condemnation that is not hateful, but, perhaps, at most, pitying or loftily compassionate. It requires an objective and unconcerned appraisal and a consequent withdrawal. Some may manage this, and it is a handy way of dealing with impossible people, but what if it is out of our emotional range, as it surely is with the siblings of *Succession*? Kendall, Shiv, and Roman, in their individual circumstances, need accessible emotions—emotions that can be felt, reinforced, secured, acted upon by people of limited emotional recourses. Stoic contempt is not always—or indeed very often—available to the victims of emotional abuse. An alternative is engaged or "hot" emotions. In this case, hate. The children of Logan Roy needed to come to hate him at some point in their lives; their failure to do so condemned them to circling his emotional black hole and never quite managing to get free of it. It would be a good thing for them if they came to hate him and acknowledge that hate.

Succession illustrates one possible role for hate in a flourishing life. In the right circumstances, hate can facilitate emotional and practical escape from an intolerable situation. Emotional and practical dependence on a hateworthy person is likely to blight one's life. Escape from such a situation requires considerable emotional resources: the lucidity to see what is wrong and the motivational strength to do something about it. In the right circumstances, the right kind of hate will provide these. Of course, it is possible to do the work of escape in other ways, with other emotional resources. As we mentioned earlier, stoic contempt is one possibility. It can yield lucidity and motivate distantiation. But stoic contempt requires lucid appraisal of the malignancy of another without attendant hostility toward them. It is a hard thing to pull off; a person who could respond to Logan Roy in such a way is perhaps unlikely to be raised by him.

For this reason, it is important to consider what we have called accessible emotional attitudes when considering the role of attitudes in a flourishing life. The accessibility of emotional attitudes is a function of character and circumstance: ideally, a person may do best by responding to a situation with a particular emotion, but they may also find that emotion inaccessible. Emotions are not ordered up like menu items, they are largely automatic interpretative (not wholly cognitive) responses to feeling. They can be influenced (enhanced or diminished) in various ways, but not manufactured at will. Emotional attitudes toward other people, by contrast, are longer-term states that may be cultivated up to a point. For example, we may cultivate critical attitudes to another by unstinting concentration on what a person has done, by critically undoing facile excuses for their behavior, by refusing to turn a blind eye to what they themselves reveal about their inner attitudes and motivations, and so on. This kind of work can form the basis for an evolving emotional attitude toward a person. Both contempt and hate, like love, can be cultivated in this way. We plant the seed, we water and fertilize the plant, but we cannot give it life. Whether or not it grows and how strongly it grows is not ultimately up to us. Since cultivation of emotional attitudes is not fully up to us, some emotional attitudes are accessible and others not. Hate is, often enough, accessible where stoic distantiation is not. This is likely true in the case of the *Succession* siblings, and in many other situations. Although hate is often an accessible emotional attitude, it need not represent a permanent state of affairs. Time and distance may diminish Kendall, Shiv, and Roman's feelings of outright hostility toward their father and more admirable emotional attitudes can come to replace hate. But the process, for them, would have to start with hate.

To live a flourishing life requires good fortune, as Aristotle acknowledged, but it is perhaps unwise to import too much good fortune into one's conception of a flourishing life. Enough good fortune would deprive us of the need for hate, either by ensuring we experience no occasion fitting it or ensuring we have both the character and strength of will to make do with less hateful alternatives such as stoic contempt, pity, or compassion when we encounter circumstances appropriate to hate. However, this amounts to a great deal of good fortune. The lives of those not so blessed can also flourish, and hate may play an ineliminable role in such flourishing. In this sense, personal hate may be good because of the various roles it may play (we have explored one) in a flourishing life. The hostility and destructive wishes of hate need not be a good thing in themselves—and all else being equal, it would be better not to experience them—but sometimes our hate saves us from what is worse.[6]

4. HATE AS A NECESSARY MORAL EMOTION

The third sense in which personal hate may be good is the role it might play in morality and a sense of justice. What is the relationship between hating evil people and being a just person? Thomas Hurka sets out several fundamental principles of his virtue ethics in terms of hate. He says (2001, 16),

(HG) If *x* is intrinsically good, hating *x* (desiring or pursuing *x*'s not obtaining or being pained by *x*'s obtaining) for itself is intrinsically evil.

Since hating is an inappropriate response to intrinsic goods, (HG) makes it intrinsically evil. Thus, (HG) makes it intrinsically evil for person B to desire or seek for itself the destruction of A's pleasure or to be pained by A's pleasure. A parallel clause concerns the intrinsic goodness of *hating for itself what is evil*, (HE, emphasis in the original):

(HE) If *x* is intrinsically evil, hating *x* for itself is intrinsically good. (Emphases in original)

Hurka makes it clear that his principles apply only to states of affairs. Personal hatred is a very different matter. Whereas the emotivational status of hating state of affairs is the elimination of the state of affairs (elimination of the pain, for example), and the hatred is felt as a pain (e.g., the pain of one person's thinking of another's pain), the case of personal hatred is, as we have argued in section 2, very different. Personal hatred is experienced as hostility (agitation, distress experienced on contemplation of another, combined with negative representations of the other) and emotivationally tends toward wish for conscious, painful downfall of the object of hate. The easy path to eliminative wishes is for the most part blocked in the case of personal hatred. Nonetheless, can similar principles apply to appropriate personal hate? Consider the following, where *p* is a person:

(PHG) If *p* is intrinsically good, hating *p* is intrinsically evil.
(PHE) If *p* is intrinsically evil, hating *p* is intrinsically good.

What might be said for such principles? For our purposes, the most important point conveyed by Hurka's original formulation, one that survives their translation from states of affairs to persons, is the expressive content of the principles. For example, to hate a person who has willfully and joyously done irreparable harm to others or oneself is (ideally) to give vivid, emotionally honest expression to a fundamental value. A failure to hate evil may be a failure to take evil fully seriously at an emotional level. It may be to treat evil as merely a problem to be overcome, not as a phenomenon to be lamented and a battle to be fought.

But there is a problem. If to hate a person is to wish their painful downfall, then it clearly falls foul of another pair of Hurka's principles (2001, 15):

(BE) Pain, false belief, and failure in the pursuit of achievement are intrinsically evil.
(LE) If *x* is intrinsically evil, loving *x* for itself is also intrinsically evil.

Hurka's principles, BE and LE, constitute a plausible, if bare, expression of the conventional view of vengeance. To love another's pain is wrong. As we saw in section 1, Beauvoir sets out a different view of the value of vengeance. She argues that it is a necessary feature of justice. Beauvoir's view is subtle, however. Marguerite La Caze sets it out as follows:

> For [Beauvoir], revenge aims at getting the perpetrator to understand in a practical, Heideggerian sense "the process by means of which our entire being realizes a situation" (EE [2004] 248). The evil cannot be remedied by the torturer feeling what their victim felt. Torturers must understand in a concrete and genuine way that the victims are also free like themselves. Beauvoir sees this as reestablishing the reciprocity between the perpetrator and victim, and argues that vengeance is justified as a response in the extreme cases of reducing others to a thing because it reestablishes the reciprocity that was destroyed by the crime. This reciprocity should not be seen as simply inflicting a like suffering on the perpetrator. In vengeance perpetrators are reminded of their thing-like aspect while at the same time the victims' consciousnesses are affirmed. (La Caze 2015, 191)

As a ground for the legitimacy of vengeance—in some situations, not many—hate functions as a wish for the reestablishment of genuine reciprocity. This wish for reciprocity validates the hate. Hate is not a wish for another's suffering and harm per se. It is a wish for a phenomenological realization of justice in which the perpetrator suffers and comes to accept, not some bland truth about their wrongdoing, but the inner meaning of it. The perpetrator—experiencing the reduction of their freedom, the diminishment of their dignity as a consciousness—comes to realize the assault on another's freedom implicit in their actions. They come "to understand" as Beauvoir puts it (2004, 248). In hate, as Beauvoir has it, the victim of a perpetrator's efforts to reduce them to a mere thing develops a wish to have the perpetrator understand, and the wished-for lived experience of the perpetrator's punishment is a complex mix of pain and realization: realization through pain; validation of the victim through the resulting understanding.

In this way, Beauvoir suggests that hate has important moral work to do. The work is phenomenological rather than practical, and centers on the reestablishment of lived reciprocity between those who hate on appropriate grounds and the people they hate. However, as La Caze clearly establishes (2015, 190–95), there is something paradoxical in this project of vengeance and Beauvoir is keenly alert to it. A perpetrator is free to interpret their punishment in any number of ways. It does not matter whether it is a gentle or fierce punishment, a short-lived or lifelong punishment. The attempt to control the perpetrator's consciousness is itself a denial of their reality as free persons and it founders on the inevitability of this freedom.

If vengeance is not a satisfactory goal in most circumstances—if it is an implausible attempt to control the consciousness of another by making them suffer—then how might it validate the emotion which animates it? It seems that the moral work of hate is expressive rather than practical. To hate a hateful person in a morally valid way is to wish for them to come to understand the reality of what they have been doing, the reality of their character and its effects on those vulnerable to it, in an appropriate way. This appropriate way involves suffering, and the aim of the suffering is to forestall easy conversions and pat acceptance of what is wrong in the hateful person's life and to ensure that the lived experience of the penitent is fitting to the seriousness of what they have been and what they have done.

A person hated who comes to feel intense, long-standing, and painful remorse for the effect they have had on others loses much, if not all, of their hateworthiness—though not their immorality. This suggests that some of the moral work done by good hate is to express the value of remorse. Of course, not all hate expresses such a thing. We have argued that the characteristic emotivation of hate is a wish for the painful, self-appreciated downfall of the object of hate, but this does not equate to a wish for remorse. Much hate is an elaborate form of hostility: unjustified, selfish, and possibly sadistic. But when hate is good, from a moral point of view, it is directed at reestablishing the reciprocity between free individuals and expresses the value of the remorse that must attend such a thing.

Beauvoir provides an account of the moral value of hate that is based on her existentialism and focuses on the wish implicit in a longing for vengeance: the wish that reciprocity between free individuals be properly restored. Justice is an, often impossibly difficult, attempt at such restoration and hate expresses this wish with greater force and honesty than other emotions. If this is correct, what are we to make of hatred of figures from the past? Because there is no possibility of restored reciprocity between the hateworthy dead and their victims, the dead are not practically sensible objects of vengeance. We can tear down their statues and write ferocious books about them, but we cannot in fact hold them to account. Does it make sense, today, to hate Adolf Hitler or Cecil Rhodes? What is the moral value or purpose of such hate?

Attitudes of hate are appropriate, we argued in section 2, only if the wishes attendant upon the hate are themselves appropriate. And since the wish characteristic of personal hate is the painful, self-appreciated downfall of the object of hate, these wishes can never be fully satisfied for the dead. (Tearing down a statue of Cecil Rhodes, for example, contributes to the downfall of his reputation, but he is no longer around to feel the pain of it.) This does not mean that such wishes are inappropriate or ridiculous. It means that the work they do is expressive and psychological. They work to express the moral seriousness with which we respond to what the hateworthy have done and what they have been. The corresponding wishes are only satisfiable substitutionally: a statue of Rhodes torn down substitutes for both the individual and the symbolic order he presided over. It might be that a fully realized moral response to evil requires both an expression of hostility toward the hateworthy dead and a wish that is open only to substitutional satisfaction. It may not be enough to walk away from past evils—particularly those whose effects are still with us—with lofty contempt or disinterested impartial judgment. Hate may be a necessary response if we are to inhabit our moral commitments with full and honest emotion.

The films of Quentin Tarantino offer a striking example of the substitutional wish fulfillment of morally directed hate. In *Once Upon a Time in Hollywood* (2019) Tarantino revisits the 1969 murders of Sharon Tate, Wojciech Frykowski, Jay Sebring, and Abigail Folger by members of the Mason Family. He reimagines the events of that night so that Mason's plans are thwarted and the would-be killers are humiliated and slaughtered. The film is based on a presumption that the audience knows its events are false. It is a self-consciously counterfactual exercise. The wishes it satisfies are not just wishes for the avoidance of evil and the restoration to life of Sharon Tate (the director's love object), but for violent and humiliating vengeance on those who in fact murdered her. In Tarantino's hands, counterfactual vengeance visited upon the Mason Family is gleeful, and he exploits his audience's vulnerability to the pleasures of sadistic wish fulfillment. We do not suggest that Tarantino's way with vengeance is well-realized from a moral point of view, but Tarantino has a point. If vengeance has moral work to do in our response to present evils, it has work to do in our response to the past and that work is symbolic, substitutional, and counterfactual.

Counterfactual vengeance is at the core of much of Tarantino's oeuvre. In *Inglourious Basterds* (2009) he revels in the vengeance that a band of Jewish resistance fighters visit upon Nazi murderers; Hitler is burned alive in a cinema fire. In *Django Unchained* (2012) a freed slave takes out bloody (very bloody) vengeance upon a racist slave-owning plantation owner and his cronies. These films successfully exploit the role that fantasy plays in our moral response to evil. Tarantino's exploitation of vengeful wishes may be problematic because he tends to mix together symbolic moral crusades against past evils with indulgent, cheapening evocations of sadistic glee, but the characteristic wishes of vengeance might for all this still be a part of what it is to respond wholeheartedly to evil. The moral work of hate, then, may include an expression of hostility to evil and the vengeful wishes characteristic of hate. Even if such wishes are granted only substitutional satisfactions, they may be part of what it is for us to fully realize our hostility to evil.

Commenting on the trials and executions she discusses in *An Eye for an Eye*, Beauvoir says, "It is our values, our reasons to live that are affirmed by their punishment. . . . The thirst for revenge . . . answers to one of the metaphysical requirements of man" (2004, 246–47). Hate somehow affirms and sustains values essential to living and so is essential to justice. We have argued in this section that hate does this by expressing the significance of the wrongs done by the hateful, the value of a reestablished reciprocity between victim and perpetrator, and the value of remorse as a moral response to profound moral failure. For a system of ethics and justice to get off the ground one has to care and have a regard and concern for issues of right and wrong. Personal feelings are not merely indicative of such regard and concern, they are essential to it. Without them there just could not be an ethical framework. Hate, as well as love or caring, may be foundational and necessary in this respect.

5. CONCLUSION

Despite what may be seen as central tenets of Buddhism and Christianity, it would be exceedingly difficult, if not impossible, to show that a psychological attitude of hate is never appropriate to any circumstances. It is after all fitting at least by definition in a range of circumstances. To be the least bit plausible, the religious claim would need to be understood as, or reduced to, the view that we should never act on our hate because doing so is always detrimental to us and diminishing of us. Alternatively (and relatedly), it could be claimed that hate—even when appropriate in the circumstances—should always be repressed, again, because hating is always detrimental and diminishing.

In this chapter we have surveyed ways in which this claim may simply be wrong. Although hate is detrimental much of the time—it is, for the most part, an odious emotion—it may well play important roles in a flourishing life and it may be fundamental to moral thought, feeling, and action.

NOTES

1. Comparisons between love and hate and their relations have long been commonplace. See Freud (1915) for a complex discussion set in the context of aspects of his psychoanalytic theory.

2. We will use the terms "appropriate" and "fitting" interchangeably. The question of whether this amounts to a justification of the attitude will be discussed at the end of the section.

3. Fischer et al. are trying to capture the emotivational goals of hate as a generic species of both emotion and attitude, and this probably explains the inclusiveness of their categorization. Perhaps it is better to discuss distinct forms of hate independently of the generic concept.

4. We do not mean to commit ourselves to an analysis of knowledge as justified true belief. This point is compatible with various accounts of knowledge.

5. At least until the conclusion of Season Two. Season Three has been announced but not completed at the time of writing, and we have no knowledge of any succeeding seasons. Our discussion is based on the first two seasons.

6. For further discussion see Richard Hamilton's contribution to this volume, chapter 11.

REFERENCES

Arp, Kristana. 2004. "Introduction to de Beauvoir's 'An Eye for an Eye'." In *Philosophical Writings*, edited by Margaret A. Simons, 239–44. Urbana: University of Illinois Press.

Beauvoir, Simone de. 2004. "An Eye for an Eye." In *Philosophical Writings*, edited by Margaret A. Simons, 245–60. Urbana: University of Illinois Press.

Ben-Ze'ev, Aaron. 2008. "Hating the One You Love." *Philosophia* 36 (3): 277–83.

———. 2018. "Is Hate Worst When It Is Fresh? The Development of Hate Over Time?" *Emotion Review* 10 (4): 322–24.

Fischer, Agneta, Eran Halperin, Daphna Canetti, and Alba Jasini. 2018. "Why We Hate." *Emotion Review* 10 (4): 309–20. Reprinted in this volume, chap. 7.

Freud, Sigmund. 1915. "Instincts and their Vicissitudes." In *The Standard Edition of The Complete Psychological Works of Sigmund Freud*, Vol. 14 (1914–1916), translated by James Strachey in collaboration with Anna Freud, first published 1957. London: Hogarth Press. Hogarth Press.

Hurka, Thomas. 2001. *Virtue, Vice, and Value*. Oxford: Oxford University Press.

La Caze, Marguerite. 2015. "The Time of Possible and Impossible Reciprocity: Love and Hate in Simone de Beauvoir." In *Thinking About Love: essays in contemporary continental philosophy*, edited by Diane Enns and Antonio Calcagno. University Park: Pennsylvania State University Press.

Rempel, John K. and Christopher T. Burris. 2005. "Let Me Count the Ways: An Integrative Theory of Love and Hate." *Personal Relationships* 12 (2): 297–313.

Rorty, Amélie O. 1988. "The Historicity of Psychological Attitudes: Love Is Not Love Which Alters Not When It Alteration Finds." In *Mind in Action: Essays in the Philosophy of Mind*, edited by Amélie O. Rorty. Boston: Beacon Press, 121–34. First published in *Midwest Studies in Philosophy* X (1986): 399–412.

Roseman, Ira J., Cynthia Wiest, and Tamara S. Swartz. 1994. "Phenomenology, Behaviors, and Goals Differentiate Discrete Emotions." *Journal of Personality and Social Psychology* 67 (2): 206–221.

Smith, Blake 2019. "In Praise of Hate." *Tablet Magazine*, August 18, 2019. https://www.tabletmag.com/jewish-arts-and-culture/289639/in-praise-of-hate.

Succession, Seasons One and Two. 2018–. Showrunner: Jesse Armstrong. HBO, June 3, 2018.

Tarantino, Quentin, dir. 2009. *Inglourious Basterds*. Los Angeles: Universal Pictures.

———. 2012. *Django Unchained*. Los Angeles: Columbia Pictures.

———. 2019. *Once Upon a Time in Hollywood*. Los Angeles: Columbia Pictures.

Chapter 9

Hateful Actions and Rational Agency

Mary Carman

1. INTRODUCTION

We typically think of hate as a problematic and extreme emotion.[1] News is full of crimes driven by hate and we may wish not to own up to our own personal hates. Yet, there may be times when hate is an appropriate response to others (see Murphy 1988; Bell 2011). Take an example that Sisonke Msimang discusses in her memoir *Always Another Country* (2017) about growing up in a family politically exiled from South Africa during apartheid. While recollecting time her family spent in Nairobi in Kenya, she narrates an encounter as a young girl with a street boy who steals her bike. When caught by a man and a crowd of onlookers, the street boy is forced to apologize to her—but not until after he is knocked around by the crowd. He does apologize. However,

> he doesn't mean it. He is saying it because he has been caught and because he has been forced to, but he hates me. . . . He stares at me with naked rage. He is sorry that I am rich and that he is poor and he is not moved by my tears or my vulnerability. (Msimang 2017, 92–94)

As the story continues, Msimang in fact forgives the young boy. For her, "there is nothing that can be done about his hatred because he is right. People like me own the world and it is all an accident of birth and circumstance. . . . Why shouldn't he be outraged?" (Msimang 2017, 92). Later, when telling the story to her parents' friends she chooses not to "tell them that he judged me and did not ask for forgiveness because none was needed" (Msimang 2017, 94). This is a powerful example because Msimang is reflecting on how, in some sense, she was indeed hateworthy and the young boy's hate, so typically negative, was nevertheless appropriate.

185

At the same time, however, hate motivates actions of quite characteristic types. As Agneta Fischer et al. (2018) note, the "emotivational" goal of hate appears to be not merely to hurt the target of hate, but to destroy them or let them suffer. For the sake of example, suppose that the young boy stole the bike in the first place *because* he hated the young girl, where his emotivational goal was to let her suffer. In the spur of the moment, he acted intentionally but without further reflection: he was led by his hate. Even if we grant that his hate could be appropriate, such types of action immediately raise questions about their moral status and we should also ask questions about their rational status. Specifically, can we act rationally when being led by hate in this kind of way?

Jean Hampton (1988) argues that many of our actions motivated by hate will be rationally problematic because they will be self-defeating. In malicious hate, for instance, the hater engages in actions that aim at letting the opponent suffer by degrading the opponent and making the hater appear better in comparison. But, in the process, those actions also succeed in diminishing the hater's own presumed status along with the opponent's. Suppose the young boy's hate is a malicious hate of this kind. If he spends his time bad-mouthing the young girl, he may succeed in diminishing her status but only at the expense of diminishing his own—if he is any better than someone so low, that is no achievement. Nevertheless, Hampton does allow that another kind of hate—a moral hate where one hates a person or group for a moral wrong with which they are identified—is not self-defeating in the same way because it does not involve an aim of downranking another. The young boy's hate is perhaps best interpreted as an example of moral hate. But what if hate and hateful actions of even the moral sort are rationally problematic in a deeper sense, not by being self-defeating but by hate's just not being the right kind of emotion by which we can be seen to act rationally?

A central feature of rational agency is that rational agents can and do guide their actions by what they take to be reasons. While being able to guide one's actions by reasons has traditionally been thought to require the involvement of a belief or judgment, such a position has been increasingly challenged to allow other kinds of mental states to play important guiding roles, including emotion. Indeed, and as I explain in more detail in the next section, provided that certain conditions are met, an emotional agent can see the emotional considerations as pro tanto reasons favoring an action and thereby guide her action by reasons, where a pro tanto reason is a reason that is non-decisive and can, on balance, be defeated by other reasons. Drawing on this framework for emotional actions in general, I nevertheless argue in the rest of the chapter that there is something inherently problematic to being led by hate because hateful actions cannot be done in light of reasons in the right kind of way to meet the conditions for guiding an action by reasons when acting emotionally. To make this argument, I draw on Thomas Szanto's (2020) analysis of the affective-intentional nature of hate and explore the implications it has for hateful actions. Before proceeding, however, three quick notes are needed about hate itself and the kinds of hateful actions with which I will be concerned.

First, the kind of hate under focus here is not the strong but simple aversion we might have to a whole range of things, such as my hate for broth. This is what Hampton calls "simple hate" and it is distinct from more complex forms of hate, like moral hate or malicious hate. When asking if we can rationally guide our actions when being led by hate, then, I am not looking at the rational status of my avoidance of broth because I have a strong aversion to it but rather actions relating to moral hate, such as Hampton's example of the kid who beats up the bully out of moral hate, or actions relating to malicious hate, like my slashing your car tires.

Second, I take hate typically to be an affective attitude, as distinct to other affective phenomena such as episodic emotions (Ben-Ze'ev 2000; Brudholm 2010; Kauppinen 2015; Szanto 2020). Affective attitudes involve patterns of attention and affect toward their objects where, as Antti Kauppinen helpfully describes, affective attitudes are ways of

> relating to someone or something that disposes one to have different emotions in different situations, to want certain things, to focus attention on certain things, to deliberate in certain ways, and possibly to make use of evidence in certain ways. (Kauppinen 2015, 1721)

As an affective attitude, hate isn't just one way of being and it is closely related to but distinct from episodic emotions like anger and the young boy's "naked rage," or other affective attitudes like resentment. It is worth noting that some instances of hate can be more episodic and short-term in nature (Fischer et al. 2018), but this is compatible with understanding paradigmatic hate as a longer-term affective attitude.

Third, my focus is on cases where one is motivated to act by the hateworthy considerations without necessarily reflecting on what to do—one is "led by" hate. In a moment of opportunity, say, the kid beats up the bully, or the young boy steals the bike, or I slash your car's tires. None of us reflect on what we are doing, although our actions are still intentional in that they are under our control and we are aware of what it is that we are doing. When I refer to "hateful actions" or "being led by hate," these are the kinds of actions that I have in mind. This is important because, in arguing that hateful actions cannot be done in light of reasons in the right kind of way, I am not thereby rejecting that hate may still have a role in rational agency in other ways, such as by drawing our attention to things that matter to us, thereby enabling us to engage in further reflection.

What, then, can we say about hate, hateful actions, and rational agency? I start by introducing a working framework for how emotions can form part of our rational agency and against which we can measure hate and hateful actions.

2. A FRAMEWORK FOR EMOTIONS AND RATIONAL AGENCY

A central feature of rational agency is that rational agents can and do guide their intentional actions by what they take to be reasons, where intentional action is action that is under one's control and awareness as something that one does.[2] In this chapter, I assume and do not defend both that we can act intentionally when acting emotionally without the involvement of a belief or judgment, and that we need not understand guiding one's actions as necessarily requiring a belief or judgment.[3] The task is to explore how hate could play such a guiding role. In this section, I therefore present a general framework for how emotions can fit into our conceptions of rational agency, a framework which we can apply to hate and hateful actions. Two ideas are central to this framework. The first is that emotions can be responses to reasons. The second is that, because emotions are part of a wider pattern of response, they can provide prima facie support for actions. This allows that when acting emotionally we can stand in the right kind of relation to reasons to guide our actions by those reasons.[4]

There is, however, an important precondition. As Karen Jones (2003) argues, guiding actions by reasons in the right kind of way for acting rationally at a minimum requires that a rational agent is someone who is able to critically reflect on her reasons and actions, is disposed to do so when needed, and is disposed to allow those reflections to guide her subsequent behavior (see also Scanlon 1998). If the person is also committed to being a rational agent, as most of us are, then as a rational agent she must be committed to monitoring, cultivating, and regulating the mechanisms that underlie those dispositions to ensure that she can trust them. As I discuss in this section, emotions can be responses to reasons and can be such mechanisms. If so, then if we are rational agents and want to place trust in our emotions as responses to reasons, we at the very least need to be committed to monitoring, cultivating, and regulating our emotions. We must reflectively accept that our emotions, or perhaps only certain emotions, are sufficiently reliable as responses to the kinds of considerations we take to be our reasons.

Now, in the philosophy of action, a distinction is made between different types of reasons, where two such types are normative and motivating reasons.[5] Normative reasons are considerations that count in favor of an action independent of an agent's perspective (Scanlon 1998; Alvarez 2017). They are reasons for which we ought to act or reasons that can justify an action. In contrast, motivating reasons are considerations that an agent takes as (normative) reasons that count in favor of an action. When an agent acts on her motivating reasons, she is said to "act in light of" that reason, where motivating reasons are sometimes referred to as "agential reasons," "the agent's normative reason," "possessed reason," or other similar terms (Alvarez 2017).[6]

The picture of rational agency whereby an agent guides her actions by reasons is one that focuses on the motivating reasons of an agent, as the agent can only guide her action by the reasons of which she takes herself to be aware. Even so, motivating and normative reasons are intricately connected because, from the perspective of the agent, motivating reasons are taken to be normative reasons. That is, the agent takes the motivating reasons to be reasons that count in favor of and justify an action.

Can emotions fit into a picture of rational agency that centralizes guiding action by motivating reasons? An initial consideration for taking emotions seriously is that they are intentional. "Intentional" here is not the sense in which actions are intentional, but rather the sense in which emotions are "about" something and are not mere feelings. Indeed, this is a defining feature of all affective phenomena (Ben-Ze'ev 2010). Emotions, taken generally to include a range of affective phenomena including affective attitudes, typically have a target at which they are directed.[7] If I am afraid of the slithery-looking shape in the grass, for instance, my fear is directed at and about the target, the slithery-looking shape in the grass. However, the target is also apprehended as being a certain evaluative way. To continue with the simple example, my fear is about the slithery-looking shape *as being dangerous to me*. My fear, then, is not just about the target but also about what is called the "formal object," the evaluation or appraisal in virtue of which the emotion is intelligible as the emotion it is. It is because I apprehend the object as dangerous that my emotion is intelligible as fear. In what follows, I refer to this intentional content of an emotion as the "emotional considerations."

The intentionality of emotion is relevant when we turn to questions of rational agency. As various philosophers have highlighted, emotions can be responses to reasons. Unlike cognitive states like perception, we can and do ask for someone's reasons for why they have the emotion that they do. If I am afraid of the object in the grass, for instance, you can ask *why* I am afraid, where you are asking for the reasons in light of which my response makes sense as the response it is. In answering your question, I might explain that I think that the object is a snake or point out features of the object that would make it dangerous. If it turns out that I knew that the object was a garden hose all along or if I explain my fear by saying that the object is aesthetically beautiful, not only would my emotion be unintelligible as fear, but I would have failed to show how my emotion was a response to the considerations I took to be reasons.

Further, the intentional content of emotion can be appropriate by being fitting or inappropriate by not being fitting (D'Arms and Jacobson 2000). An emotion is fitting when what it presents really is the case, where the target really does instantiate the formal object. This has led some philosophers to argue that emotions can *track* reason-giving considerations, which is why they can be a mechanism that underlies our dispositions as rational agents (Arpaly 2002; Jones 2003). Here, the claim that emotions can be fitting is different to the claim that emotions can be responses to reasons. If, say, I am afraid of the garden hose because I thought it was a snake, my fear would not be fitting because the garden hose is not dangerous. My emotion would misfire in tracking danger. But if I really did think it was a snake, my emotion will still be a response to considerations I took to be reasons.

In any event, the intentional nature and potential fittingness of emotion set the scene for how emotions can fit into a picture of rational agency. Once we also acknowledge that emotions have an affective force that is not just a motivational edge exhausted by somatic changes or an action tendency, the details of the scene start to emerge.

Emotions can and do frequently consume and direct our attention toward the target of our emotion and the ways in which it stands in relation to the things we care about. They can do this because emotions, including affective attitudes, are a form of responding to how our cares and concerns are apprehended as being affected, which is something of significance to ourselves (Frijda 1986; Clore 1994; Helm 2001; Roberts 2003; Brady 2013). That is, the apprehension of our cares and concerns as being affected is the apprehension of significant considerations that are plausibly taken as pro tanto reasons for our responding in certain ways. Szanto makes a similar point with regard to affective attitudes, where, as he writes, "attitudes don't just passively (affectively) register certain external facts or occurrences (as bodily sensations do), nor do they simply react to them" (Szanto 2020, 457). Instead, they are a form of position-taking in response to things of significance, which are apprehended as pro tanto reasons.

For instance, suppose that I care about my financial security. Because the looming job cuts at my place of work pose a threat to my financial security, something that is of significance for me, I am afraid about those job cuts and what they mean to me. If I really am being affected in this kind of way, that is a significant reason-giving consideration and I ought to respond appropriately, such as with fear. As such, my emotion has affective force with a normative bearing because it is a response to considerations of significance that are apprehended as pro tanto reasons to respond. Or take an example that Jean Moritz Müller gives where, for him, responding emotionally can be understood as complying with a prompt. In his example of anger in response to a colleague's condescending look, he describes how

> it is because you care about being treated respectfully that you cannot but be angry in light of your colleague's condescending look. Given what is at stake, you owe it to yourself qua subject of this concern to respond as prompted. (Müller 2021, 13)[8]

Accepting that an emotion has affective force, however, is not the same as accepting that an emotion is appropriate, as Müller also highlights, or even the same as reflectively endorsing the background sets of cares and concerns. Rather, an emotional experience pushes us to take the emotional considerations seriously because of their significance, but not necessarily because of their truth (Carman 2018a). Because of that seeming significance, emotions can be difficult to ignore even when we judge that our emotion is inappropriate or wrong or even that we ought not to care about the things that we do seem to care about. As such, if emotions are to play a role in our rational agency where we are to guide our actions by the considerations we take to be reasons, we need to be able to trust that our emotions are sufficiently reliable as responses to the kind of things that we take to be reasons. This is why the precondition from earlier, that we monitor, cultivate, and regulate our emotions, is of vital importance for a full picture of emotions within rational agency.

Now, where normative reasons can be called on to justify an action and motivating reasons can be called on to explain why an agent so acted from the agent's perspective, if we are looking at whether an agent is responsive to what they take to be reasons, we are concerned with motivating reasons. If on top of that emotions can be responses to reasons and our emotional responses are responses to considerations that strike us with affective force because of our background cares and concerns, they are responses to reason-giving considerations that could also be motivating reasons for action. When we are looking at actions, however, we want an account of how the emotional considerations can be seen not just as reasons making an emotional response intelligible but also as reasons favoring a specific action. That is, we still need to show that we stand in relation to the reasons and the action in the right kind of way, where we see *those* considerations as reasons for *that* action and not some other action.

A first thing to emphasize here, then, is that emotions form patterns of response in virtue of our having background set of cares and concerns.[9] In particular, if we have a set of cares and concerns, then we can respond in a variety of ways to how they are impacted in different situations. Earlier, I introduced the concepts of the target and the formal object of an emotion, but we now need another important concept: the *focus* of an emotion. The focus of an emotion, as Bennett Helm describes, is a background object that has import or significance for the subject, one which helps to make sense of why the target of the emotion has import or significance for a particular person.[10] The focus is what makes sense of why a certain subject apprehends a particular target as instantiating a particular formal object. It is also what helps to explain the affective force of an emotion, where the formal object would otherwise remain an abstract evaluative notion that we do not engage with affectively. It is because I am committed to and care about my financial security, for instance, that I apprehend the looming job cuts as something dangerous to me and experience fear in the first place. Indeed, to have an experience of fear *is* to be committed to the import of the focus of my emotion, my financial security, which is what Helm calls the focal commitment of an emotion and which is why we can make sense of why I appraise the looming job cuts as something potentially dangerous to me at all.

If I am committed to the import of, and care about, my financial security, then I ought to respond in a range of other ways when my financial security is impacted upon because my background care about my financial security can be the focus of other related emotions, such as my relief when I pass through the period unscathed, or my excitement in response to a new lucrative job offer. Suppose that I pass through the period of job cuts unscathed but feel no relief. Unless there are countervailing considerations, we can meaningfully question whether I really did care about my financial security or whether, perhaps, it is no longer top of my priorities. In other words, if I do not respond in ways that are aligned with being committed to the import of the focus of my emotion and how my financial security is affected, we have a basis to question whether it really is (or still is) something that I care about.

In a similar fashion, parts of the patterns of response could be actions. Through the focal commitment, of being committed to the import of the focus of an emotion, not only will I be disposed to undergo other related emotions, but I will also be disposed to act in ways related to how I apprehend my cares and concerns being affected. Think of it as a tree: our cares and concerns form the trunk and branching out are different kinds of responses that are related to each other in virtue of being committed to the same cares and concerns—emotions, actions, even beliefs and judgments. This allows us to see the emotional considerations as pro tanto reasons for an action of a particular type when undergoing an emotional experience without necessarily involving a belief or judgment about what to do, where the action relates to the cares and concerns and how they are apprehended as being affected.

We have not yet completed the picture, however. To guide our actions by those emotional considerations seen as reasons, we also need to be able to see the considerations as indeed *the* reasons for which we ought to act. This need not involve a belief or judgment that the emotional considerations are the reasons for which we ought to act, so long as two further conditions are met for guiding our actions by reasons when acting emotionally (Carman 2018a, 57–59).

The first is that, for an agent to guide her actions emotionally, she must be aware of the emotional considerations that form the pro tanto reasons for acting. She cannot just act on the motivational edge of her emotion. After all, reasons are reasons *for* something, where the relation between the reason and what it is supposed to be a reason for is of importance. If I cannot identify what my emotional considerations are—perhaps I have a general feeling of uneasiness but cannot pin down what the uneasiness is about—we cannot see the emotional considerations (what are they?) as favoring a particular action. I might still do something like go for a run to alleviate my emotional discomfort, but my reason that favors so acting is the reason of being in emotional discomfort, not the emotional considerations themselves.[11]

Further, seeing the emotional considerations as pro tanto reasons may be sufficient for guiding an action in a good case, but it is not sufficient in a bad case where there is a conflict between reasons. For instance, we typically think of akratic actions, actions where we act against our best judgment, as rationally problematic, and frequently akratic actions are driven by emotions. On the story offered so far, we would nevertheless apprehend the emotional considerations as pro tanto reasons for acting in a particular way even when acting akratically. To rule out such actions as being rationally guided, we must introduce a second condition: the agent must see the considerations as the reasons for which she should act. This need not require that she reflectively endorse the considerations *as* reasons before acting, so long as she would have endorsed the considerations given what she was aware of at the time. Given what the agent was aware of at the time, we might ask, would she have endorsed her action for those reasons? In a good case where there is no conflict between reasons, it is likely that she would. In a bad case where there is conflict between reasons, she may not have endorsed the emotional considerations and would not have guided her action by her reasons. In fact, as a rational agent she should be disposed to reflect critically on the conflicting reasons in such a scenario anyway. And in a case of akratic action where she judges another reason to be what she should act according to, then she really would not endorse the emotional considerations as her reasons for acting.

While I have only skimmed over the details of this framework, we are at least in a position now to turn to hate and hateful actions and to assess how they fare.

3. THE MESSINESS OF HATE

To assess the rational status of hateful actions, we need to examine whether hate, like other emotions, can be a response to reasons, how hate might feature in patterns of response, and whether the conditions for guiding an emotional action by reasons can be met. In this section, I draw on Szanto's analysis of the affective intentionality of hate to unpack these aspects of hate in more detail. Hate, as we shall see, is a messy emotion. Because of this, I argue in the rest of the chapter that hateful actions cannot be done in light of reasons in the right kind of way. Before we get there, though, let us start by thinking a bit more sympathetically about how hate *could* fit into our framework of rational agency.

The patterns of response that form a crucial part of the framework are dependent upon the emotional subject's having a set of background cares and concerns. This is a feature that hate, as an affective attitude, shares. As Fischer et al. discuss with reference to hate, the object of the emotion has to impact our cares and concerns in some way: "We cannot . . . hate persons we are indifferent to" (Fischer et al. 2018). Or, as Szanto describes in a discussion of hate, "Having an affective attitude [such as hate] is a response, or a form of position-taking, to affective significances for a subject" (Szanto 2020, 457).

Remember our example from Msimang's memoir, of the young boy who steals her bike. "He is sorry that I am rich and that he is poor," she writes, "and he is not moved by my tears or my vulnerability" (Msimang 2017, 94). It is plausibly because the young boy cares about being treated fairly, say, that he hates those who treat him unfairly or, perhaps more saliently in this example, those who represent a wider system or set of values by which he is treated unfairly. What is critical here is that his hate is a form of responding to the significance that his standing in relation to others, embodied in the young girl, has for him, because of other things that he cares about. This is also an example of how hate, like other emotions, can plausibly be a response to reasons. We can meaningfully ask someone for their reasons for hating.

In our example, the *target* of the boy's hate is quite clearly the young girl. He apprehends the young girl as being a certain way, as being hateworthy. Hateworthiness, then, is the *formal object* of hate (Szanto 2020). For the young boy, his hate is about the young girl, the target, as being hateworthy, and it is because he apprehends her in this negative way that his hate is intelligible as hate. If the *focus* of hate is something that has import or significance for the subject and what makes a particular target hateworthy for that subject, the focus of the young boy's hate may be something like being treated fairly. It is in virtue of caring about being treated fairly that the target, the young girl who threatens his fair treatment, also has import or significance for him and is evaluated as hateworthy.

If the above is correct, then the young boy's hate just is his being committed to the import of the focus, which is the focal commitment of his hate. Because of his being committed to the import of the focus, the young boy ought to respond in related ways when he apprehends the same focus, the same care or concern through which he is committed by his hate, as being affected in other ways. If some of those ways of responding are actions, then it is possible that he can see the hate considerations as pro tanto reasons favoring certain actions without the involvement of a belief or judgment about what to do. Further, if he monitors, cultivates, and regulates his emotion by reflecting on the things he hates and agrees that his hate does typically reflect what he considers reasons, if he is aware of the specific emotional considerations that are the pro tanto reasons for acting, and if he sees those considerations as reasons for which he should act, then it is possible that he even guides his actions by reasons when being led by hate.

But is this really what is happening? We need to look more closely at the target, formal object and focus of hate, which is where Szanto's (2020) analysis of the affective-intentional nature of hate becomes pertinent. Szanto's analysis highlights the role of cares and concerns in an attitude like hate and, crucially, he argues that hate is different to other emotions in the way that hate's target and focus feature.[12] Two of the core claims that he defends are, first, that the focus of hate is inherently "blurred" because the formal object of hate is global in nature and the target of hate shifts and, second, that with hate we are committed to the attitude itself. If this is correct, then actions done out of hate are unlikely to meet the conditions for guiding our actions by reasons when acting emotionally, as I will now argue.

Let us start with the first of Szanto's core claims, that the focus of hate is "blurred," by which he means that it is uninformative. Earlier, I suggested that the focus of the young boy's hate could be something like being treated fairly. This seems like a clear background care that has import or significance for the young boy. However, we need to remember that the focus of an emotion, as the focus and not just as something that the person cares about, is supposed to make the connection between the formal object and a particular target informative. And it is here, in making the connection informative, that the focus becomes blurred, because of both the nature of the formal object and the nature of the target. Let us work through these.

The formal object of hate is something like "hateworthiness" where hate involves a negative evaluation or set of appraisals that is typically of a person, social group, a "type" of person or a proxy for a group or "type," ideologies or other social facts (Szanto 2020, 461), and it involves a negative evaluation of that person, group, or social fact *as a whole*. Because of this, hate is classed as a *globalist* affective attitude, where the negative evaluation making up the formal object is global in nature. Saying that the negative evaluation is global in nature is saying that "the negative aspects are so fundamental that other traits become insignificant" (Ben-Ze'ev 2000, 382). Or, following Aurel Kolnai (1998, 591), we can say that hate is essentially "substantival" and directed at the target as a whole entity and not at specific features. This sets up an important contrast with related emotions, such as anger. Whereas anger is typically understood to be in response to and about some action that someone has performed, hate is instead about the person themselves. As Fischer et al. describe, "Hate is characterized by appraisals that imply a stable perception of a person or group" where "the other *is* malicious, not just acts maliciously" (Fischer et al. 2018, 310, emphasis in original).

So, in our example, the target of the street boy's hate is the young girl. However, his hate is not about something nasty the girl did but about the young girl as a whole: he hates her *because* she is rich and thereby representative of a social system in which he is systematically treated unfairly. Her wealth and what she represents is so fundamental that the fact that she is also distressed and had been minding her business is insignificant. His perception of her as rich and representative of an unfair system is a stable perception of her, regardless of her other features.

What we also see here is how the target can shift. In this example, the young girl is presented as hateworthy and as the target of the boy's hate *because of what she represents*. This is something that Sarah Ahmed draws attention to when she writes, "Hate may respond to the particular, but it tends to do so by aligning the particular with the general," "I hate you because you are this or that," where the "this" or "that" evokes a group that the individual comes to stand for or stand in for" (Ahmed 2014, 49; cited in Szanto 2020, 466). However, if a particular individual is the target of hate because she is apprehended as being hateworthy in virtue of standing for or standing in for a hateworthy group, then the target could potentially "be substituted by any other who does or simply is such-and-such" (Szanto 2020, 466). Szanto is concerned with group-based hate, which is the hate for other social groups or members of other social groups, but similar things can be said of interpersonal hate. Because of the globalizing nature of hate, even if someone initially caused one harm, say, the target becomes hateworthy because they are "that" kind of person who does those kinds of things (lies, cheats, harms, etc.) and becomes substitutable with others of that kind. Imagine that the young boy in our example stole the bike because of his hate, as a group-based hate. He hated the young girl before they even interacted because of what she represents, and if another young rich girl had gone by with a shiny bike, he would have hated her, too. Imagine, now, the same scenario as an instance of interpersonal hate. Suppose that the young boy was not a poor street kid but in fact one of the young girl's rich classmates, who steals her bike as a prank. After the way he is treated by those who come to the young girl's rescue—kicked around, bullied—he may come to hate her for her indirect involvement in his mistreatment. However, his hate then generalizes. He doesn't hate her because of something she did, as she is not the one who treated him badly, but because she is one of "those," where "those" are the people who have treated him unfairly and where the target of his current hate becomes substitutable with others of that kind.

If the formal object is global and if the target can shift and be substitutable, then the focus becomes blurred or uninformative. The background care is not blurred—the young boy's caring about being treated fairly is a clear and important value—but the care's status as *the focus* of hate is blurred. Take our young boy. The target of his hate, in this instance, is the young girl, who he apprehends as hateworthy, while the focus of his hate is being treated fairly. Quite generally, the focus does indicate that the target is hateworthy by being a threat to his background care. However, while the young girl may be a proxy for a social group or social system that has features that treat the young boy unfairly, she herself is not a determinate target of his hate and is substitutable with other targets. The focus fails to inform us why *this* young girl instantiates the global evaluation of hateworthiness because it fails to make sense of why the young girl, minding her own business, impacts his care for being treated fairly to the extent that her standing as a proxy for a wider group makes her many other features insignificant in an assessment of her.

What are the implications of this analysis so far? It is here that we turn to Szanto's second core claim, which is that hate involves a commitment to the attitude itself.

Through the focal commitment of the emotion, the agent ought to respond in ways that are commensurate with the ways in which the focus of the emotion is affected. If the young girl in fact treats the boy with respect and care, in other words his background care for being treated fairly is promoted, he ought to stop hating her. However, because his hate is global and the target shifting, he pays little attention to the specific actions or features of the current target. For this reason, Szanto concludes that hate "doesn't commit the hater to anything (specific)" (Szanto 2020, 472). This is not to say that the young boy is not otherwise committed to being treated fairly, or to claim that the focus of his hate is something other than being treated fairly. Rather, it is to deny that his hate *is itself* a commitment to the focus, what should be the focal commitment. If this is right, and if the focal commitment is what usually provides an emotion with its affective force, what grounds the affective force of hate that motivates the kinds of actions it does?

It is here that Szanto proposes that "hatred gets its affective power for free, as it were—namely from the *commitment* to the attitude" (Szanto 2020, 472, emphasis in original). While hate might arise because of the way in which the target is apprehended as affecting the focus, the actions and direction of attention it motivates are spurred on by being committed to maintaining that hate rather than by responding to changes in the ways in which the focus is affected. This picks up on the way in which feelings of hate can be self-feeding as something we nurture, like a kind of schadenfreude, where, as Szanto also highlights, hate is an attitude we frequently share with others. We bond with others over shared hates, whereby we define ourselves and our own in opposition to what we do not want to be. We care about hating, together with others.

This is a plausible picture of hate, capturing how it can become disconnected from its targets and be self-feeding. If it is correct, it has important implications for hateful actions, to which we can now turn.

4. IMPLICATIONS FOR HATEFUL ACTIONS

Hate has a blurred focus, a shifting target and a global formal object. Hate involves a commitment to hate itself. How do these features of hate impact the status of hateful actions, those actions we perform when we are led by hate? Earlier I introduced one precondition for being a rational agent, that we cultivate, regulate, and monitor our emotions, and two conditions for emotionally guiding our actions by reasons: (a) we must be aware of the emotional considerations to see the considerations *as* reasons for a particular action and (b) we must see the considerations as the reasons for which we ought to act. This precondition and these conditions need to be met in the case of hateful actions. But are they?

To be a rational agent, our hater needs to be committed to monitoring, cultivating, and regulating the mechanisms that underlie her disposition to critically reflect on her reasons and actions, to reflect when needed, and to allow those reflections to guide her actions. Among such mechanisms are her emotions. If she is committed to monitoring, cultivating, and regulating her emotions, she can come to trust that her emotions do more often than not align with what she takes to be reasons, but where some emotions might be better than others. Hate, however, is a nebulous phenomenon in that we frequently deny experiencing hate, most likely because of the social sanctioning of such a negative attitude (Fischer et al. 2018; Szanto 2020). If so, then it seems that we fail to acknowledge the nature of the emotion we undergo, and so will overlook how the focus may be blurred because of the shifting target and global formal object. If we do not acknowledge that our very reaction is one of hate, we may overlook how the considerations we take to be reasons could be misrepresented. Cultivating and monitoring our emotions at the very least requires that we own up to the emotions that we have.

Nevertheless, when we do admit to hating we can monitor, cultivate, and regulate an emotion like hate. Even so, monitoring our hate reactions would pressure us to identify why we find a target hateworthy, a global negative evaluation. Once we start to look closely, the difficulty of identifying the features specific to the target that makes it hateworthy to the extent that those features outweigh other potentially countervailing features should become apparent. Further reflection on *why* we continue to hate and are insensitive to changes in how our background focus is affected would cast doubt on the reliability of hate as a mechanism that can underlie the dispositions we need as rational agents. Thus, it is doubtful that a rational agent would place trust in hate as a reliable response to what we take to be our reasons at all.

Note that I am not rejecting that there can still be reasons for why we hate. The young girl, for instance, may be representative of an unjust system, where Msimang's reflections draw attention to how the boy's hate is responding to something of grave concern. As she writes, "People like me own the world and it is all an accident of birth and circumstance" where "he judged me and did not ask for forgiveness because none was needed" (Msimang 2017, 92, 94). Reflecting on our hates—and even the hates of others, as Msimang does—may still serve an important role by directing our attention to considerations that have a bearing on matters of great significance. Monitoring our hate will draw attention to how it cannot be trusted as a reliable response to reasons by itself but monitoring our hate may still give us insight anyway.

Let us, though, suppose that the precondition can be met for the sake of considering how we might apply the framework introduced earlier for guiding our actions by reasons when acting emotionally. What was core to the framework was that emotions are parts of patterns of response, where the background cares and concerns make sense of what we respond to emotionally as well as the affective force of the emotion. Those cares and concerns are captured by the emotion's focus, whereby because we are committed to the focus, we ought to respond in certain ways, which sets the scene for meeting the two conditions for guiding our action by reasons when acting emotionally. How well does hate fare?

Let us start with the second condition this time around, which is the condition that the agent see the emotional considerations as *the* reasons for which she ought to act. Here, the tendency to deny experiencing hate rears its head again. If we nevertheless experience hate and see the hate considerations as reasons favoring an action, a peculiar form of akratic action can arise. By denying that we experience hate, we deny that the target is hateworthy. Yet, the hateworthiness of the target is what stands in relation to the kinds of actions we take where, as Fischer et al. (2018) discuss, hate typically motivates destructive actions precisely because of its global nature. Even if we misinterpret our emotion as, say, anger, we still reject that the hateworthiness on which we do act is our reason. As such, we act on reasons whose rational authority we deny, and in that sense the action is akratic.

By contrast, if we own up to our hate, we may still be able to meet this second condition. The real problem arises with placing hate within patterns of response and meeting the first condition, which is that the agent is aware of the considerations that favor the action. Remember, guiding an action by a reason requires that we see *these* considerations as favoring *this* action, which requires some specificity in terms of what it is that we are aware of and how it favors a specific action, where being part of a pattern of response plays an important role.

As we have seen, hate is not itself a commitment to the focus, even though we might be committed to the focus in other ways. If hate were, then we ought to be responsive to the ways in which that focus is affected but, because hate is global and the target shifting, we pay little attention to the specific actions or features of the target that might affect the focus in other ways. So, by lacking that focal commitment through hate, the subject is not thereby committed to patterns of response based on how the focus is affected. Yet, the connections within a pattern of response were what allowed us to see the emotional considerations as pro tanto reasons for an action forming part of that pattern when undergoing an emotional experience without necessarily involving a belief or judgment about what to do, and so to guide our actions by reasons when acting emotionally in the first place. I suggested earlier that we understand the background cares and concerns that inform an emotion as forming the trunk of a tree, with the branches the various responses. With hate, we may have the tree, but the branches are broken or, instead of branches, we have a creeping ivy—dependent on the trunk but somewhat disconnected.

Further, while we may be aware of the hateworthiness of the target, we need not be aware of any feature specific of that target by which the target, and not a substitutable other, is impacting the focus. This is because the target of hate shifts and the formal object is global in nature. If the young boy cares about being treated fairly, for instance, that care alone fails to inform why this girl, here and now, instantiates hateworthiness, a global evaluation of her that necessarily involves a prioritization of her as a proxy for a certain group over all the other features that she has. The kind of considerations he is aware of—her hateworthiness—is too general to favor a particular and specific action directed at destroying *this young girl* or allowing *this girl* to suffer as part of responding to how the focus is affected, especially once we recognize that hate does not form patterns of response arising from a focal commitment.

The commitment to hate itself muddies the picture even more. Hate still has a focus which, while blurred, helps to relate the target to the formal object. It is because the young boy cares about being treated fairly that we can begin to make sense of why he finds the young girl hateworthy because of what she represents, even if the target can shift and even if he is insensitive to other features of the girl. When experiencing hate, it presents with affective force whereby we take the considerations of hateworthiness as reasons favoring an action. But in truth, our hate does not commit us to the focus, else we ought to be sensitive to changes in the ways in which the care making up the focus is affected. Instead, it commits us to maintaining the attitude of hate itself. If so, then we are deceived about what we are committed to, suggesting that we misunderstand the nature of our own hateful actions. If we nevertheless act on our hate, we are more likely to be acting in light of the nature of having the attitude of hate, such as to maintain it, rather than in light of some insight in the emotion's intentional content, those emotional considerations of hateworthiness. The emotional considerations could delineate what kind of action choices would be successful in maintaining the state, and in that way explain why hate typically motivates destructive actions, but are not the reasons in light of which we ultimately act.

Overall, it is unlikely that a rational agent, committed to monitoring, cultivating, and regulating her emotions, would trust her hate as reliably responding to the things she takes as her reasons. It is further unlikely that either of the two earlier conditions are met for guiding actions by reasons when acting emotionally.

5. CLOSING REFLECTIONS

While we do typically think of hate as problematic and extreme, it may sometimes be an emotion that indicates important considerations and even be an appropriate response to others who have done us harm or who stand for things that are indeed hateworthy. Msimang's example of the young street boy's hate is an example of how we can be sympathetic to another's hate and recognize that it may very well be grounded on important and significant concerns. Nevertheless, I have argued that hateful actions cannot meet conditions for rationally guiding our actions when acting emotionally.

If we take seriously Szanto's argument that the focus of hate is blurred and that hate "doesn't commit the hater to anything (specific)" (Szanto 2020, 472), then the very nature of hate is such that we cannot guide our hateful actions by reasons in the right kind of way for rational agency. The focus of hate is blurred because the target of hate shifts and the formal object is global, with the result that the focus fails to make the connection between the target and the formal object fully informative. This has implications for whether the precondition and conditions for rational agency, at least on the framework adopted in this chapter, can be met. Because of hate's very nature, a rational agent committed to monitoring, cultivating, and regulating her emotions ought to reject hate as something that can be trusted as a reliable response to the things she takes to be reasons. Hate fails to form part of a wider pattern of response such that the agent can see the hate considerations as reasons favoring a certain action in a way compatible with her rational agency.

Nevertheless, while hateful actions look to be rationally problematic when measured against a framework for guiding one's actions by reasons, there might still be a place for hateful actions within a wider picture of how rational agents do sometimes act. I will end with some suggestions along these lines.

Keep in mind that, while the focus of hate is blurred, it does still help to relate the target of hate to the formal object of hate at least somewhat, especially once we recognize that the reason why the target shifts is because the target typically stands in for a wider group that is seen to be hateworthy. So, the target is hateworthy in general in virtue of being a representative of or a proxy for a wider group that is hateworthy. As a proxy for a wider group, the target's hateworthiness as one of "those" would still be connected to the hater's actions, but symbolically. If so, then we could examine hateful actions as a type of symbolic action, where exploring analogies between hateful actions and other types of symbolic action could potentially be fruitful. For instance, expressive actions are frequently symbolic actions. Take an example of such expressive action: Jane's tearing at Joan's eyes in a photograph out of anger (Hursthouse 1991, 59). In this example, the photograph of Joan is a proxy for Joan and Jane acts expressively with no clear reason for her action. We might think that expressive actions are "arational" (Hursthouse 1991)—neither rational nor irrational—or alternatively that they are done for a distinct kind of *expressive reason* whereby the agent acts to "do justice to the import of the situation" (Bennett 2021, 17). Could something similar be said for hateful actions?

There are of course important differences between expressive actions and hateful actions. In expressive actions the action is symbolic whereas with hateful actions the target is symbolic, and with an expressive action like Jane's expression of anger, Jane may not want to harm Joan herself but if she were acting out of hate, she may very well want to harm the hated group that Joan represents. Even so, expressive actions may still offer an informative alternative approach to explore the way in which the hateworthy considerations one is aware of through one's hate connect to the actions one performs. There may thus, after all, still be a place for hateful actions within a full picture of the how rational agents do sometimes act on their hate without compromising their status as rational agents.

NOTES

1. I use "emotion" here to refer collectively to a range of related affective phenomena, including affective attitudes like hate.

2. "Intentional" in this sense is different to "intentional" in the sense that relates to emotion, as I discuss later in this section. To avoid confusion between the different senses of "intentional," I will simply refer to "intentional action" as "action" from here on.

3. For how emotional actions can be intentional, see Pacherie (2002). For a challenge to the centrality of belief in conceptions of rational action, see Arpaly and Schroeder (2012), and for the possibility for other kinds of states, like imagination, to play a belief-like role, see Velleman (1996).

4. I will only give an overview of the framework here as my focus will be on applying the framework to hate. For a more detailed defense of the ideas in this section, see Carman (2018a).

5. Normative and motivating reasons have dominated the literature but those like Maria Alvarez (2017) argue that we ought to identify a third type of reason, explanatory reasons. I will not be concerned with explanatory reasons here.

6. Normative reasons are typically taken to be facts, whereas there is controversy about whether motivating reasons are also facts or are instead psychological states of the agent. I will not take a stance on this debate here.

7. Typically—but not always. Moods plausibly do not have a particular target, although they are still intentional.

8. As Szanto (2020) suggests with hate, and as Müller (2021) argues in detail for emotion in general, this is an important way in which an emotion can be active and not passive as we often think of them.

9. The following discussion draws on Bennett Helm's account of emotions as felt evaluations. See Helm (2001).

10. Helm actually defines the formal object of an emotion in terms of targets and focus. Using the example of fear, he writes, "We can understand danger, the formal object of fear in terms of the target being a threat to the focus of the emotion such that it is the import of the focus that makes intelligible the resulting import of the target" (Helm 2001, 69).

11. For more on the relation between the affective discomfort of an emotion and reasons, see Carman (2018b).

12. Szanto's interest is specifically in group-based hate—hate for other groups—rather than interpersonal hate, but I think his insights can be extended to hate in general.

REFERENCES

Ahmed, Sara. 2014. *The Cultural Politics of Emotions*. 2nd ed. Edinburgh: Edinburgh University Press.

Alvarez, M. 2017. "Reasons for Action: Justification, Motivation, Explanation." In *The Stanford Encyclopedia of Philosophy*, edited by Edward N. Zalta. https://plato.stanford.edu/archives/win2017/entries/reasons-just-vs-expl/.

Arpaly, Nomy. 2002. "On Acting Rationally Against One's Best Judgment." In *Unprincipled Virtue: An Inquiry into Moral Agency*, 33–65. Oxford: Oxford University Press.

Arpaly, Nomy and Timothy Schroeder. 2012. "Deliberation and Acting for Reasons." *Philosophical Review* 121 (2): 209–239.

Bell, Macalester. 2011. "Globalist Attitudes and the Fittingness Objection." *The Philosophical Quarterly* 61 (244): 449–72.

Ben-Ze'ev, Aaron. 2000. *The Subtlety of Emotion*. Cambridge, MA: MIT Press.

———. 2010. "The Thing Called Emotion." In *The Oxford Handbook of Philosophy of Emotion*, edited by Peter Goldie, 63–94. Oxford: Oxford University Press.

Bennett, Christopher. 2021. "The Problem of Expressive Action." *Philosophy* 96 (2): 1–24.

Brady, Michael. 2013. *Emotional Insight: The Epistemic Role of Emotional Experience*. Oxford: Oxford University Press.

Brudholm, Thomas. 2010. "Hatred as an Attitude." *Philosophical Papers* 39 (3): 289–313.

Carman, Mary. 2018a. "Emotionally Guiding Our Actions." *Canadian Journal of Philosophy* 48 (1): 43–64.

———. 2018b. "How Emotions Do Not Provide Reasons to Act." *Philosophia* 46 (3): 555–74.

Clore, Gerald. 1994. "Why Emotions Require Cognition." In *The Nature of Emotion*, edited by Paul Ekman and Richard J. Davidson, 181–91. Oxford: Oxford University Press.

D'Arms, Justin and Daniel Jacobson. 2000. "The Moralistic Fallacy: On the 'Appropriateness' of Emotions." *Philosophy and Phenomenological Research* 61 (1): 65–90.

Fischer, Agneta, Eran Halperin, Daphna Canetti, and Alba Jasini. 2018. "Why We Hate." *Emotion Review* 10 (4): 309–20. Reprinted in this volume, chap. 7.

Frijda, Nico H. 1986. *The Emotions: Studies in Emotions and Social Interaction*. Cambridge: Cambridge University Press.

Hampton, Jean. 1988. "Forgiveness, Resentment and Hatred." In *Forgiveness and Mercy*, edited by Jean Hampton and Jeffrie Murphy, 35–87. Cambridge: Cambridge University Press.

Helm, Bennett. 2001. *Emotional Reason: Deliberation, Motivation, and the Nature of Value*. Cambridge: Cambridge University Press.

Hursthouse, Rosalind. 1991. "Arational Actions." *Journal of Philosophy* 88 (2): 57–68.

Jones, Karen. 2003. "Emotions, Weakness of Will, and the Normative Conception of Agency." In *Philosophy and the Emotions*, edited by Anthony Hatzimoysis, 181–200. Cambridge: Cambridge University Press.

Kauppinen, Antti. 2015. "Hate and Punishment." *Journal of Interpersonal Violence* 30 (10): 1719–37.

Kolnai, Aurel. 1998. "The Standard Modes of Aversion: Fear, Disgust and Hatred." *Mind* 107 (427): 581–95.
Msimang, Sisonke. 2017. *Always Another Country*. Cape Town: Jonathan Ball.
Müller, Jean M. 2021. "The Spontaneity of Emotion." *European Journal of Philosophy*, pp. 1–19. DOI: https://doi.org/10.1111/ejop.12625.
Murphy, Jeffrie. 1988. "Hatred: A Qualified Defense." In *Forgiveness and Mercy*, edited by Jean Hampton and Jeffrie Murphy, 88–110. Cambridge: Cambridge University Press.
Pacherie, Elisabeth. 2002. "The Role of Emotions in the Explanation of Action." *European Review of Philosophy* 5: 53–92.
Roberts, Robert. 2003. *Emotions: An Essay in Aid of Moral Psychology*. Cambridge: Cambridge University Press.
Scanlon, T. M. 1998. *What We Owe to Each Other*. Cambridge, MA: Harvard University Press.
Szanto, Thomas. 2020. "In Hate We Trust: The Collectivization and Habitualization of Hatred." *Phenomenology and the Cognitive Sciences* 19: 453–80.
Velleman, J. David. 1996. "The Possibility of Practical Reason." *Ethics* 106 (4): 694–726.

Chapter 10

Trashing and Tribalism in the Gender Wars

Holly Lawford-Smith

I have been watching for years with increasing dismay as the Movement consciously destroys anyone within it who stands out in any way. I had long hoped that this self-destructive tendency would wither away with time and experience. Thus I sympathized with, supported, but did not speak out about, the many women whose talents have been lost to the Movement because their attempts to use them had been met with hostility. . . . [But] the Movement has not learned from its unexamined experience. Instead, trashing has reached epidemic proportions. Perhaps taking it out of the closet will clear the air.

—Jo Freeman[1]

1. SISTERHOOD IS POWERFUL. IT KILLS. MOSTLY SISTERS.[2]

Kathleen Lowrey is one of the more recent feminist women to have been "canceled," dismissed from her position as undergraduate programs chair and subject to intense criticism online. In a recent account, she writes, "I will start with what was most personally distressing about this experience. Almost all of my most enthusiastic public attackers were feminist academic women . . . many of whom I had known and been friendly with for years" (Lowrey 2021, 757). Lowrey's observation is that what played out in her case was largely a matter *between* feminist women. *Canceling* is a broad social phenomena that is not sex-specific. *Trashing* is the more specific phenomena that refers to what happened to Lowrey.[3]

In 1976, Jo Freeman wrote an article for *Ms.* magazine, titled "Trashing: The Dark Side of Sisterhood." She told the stories of her trashings, attacks by other women in the feminist movement on "[her] character, [her] commitment, and [her] very self." This was the essay that bought trashing, as a concept, into the mainstream among feminists. Freeman reports that the article "evoked more letters from readers than any article previously published in *Ms.*, all but a few relating their own experiences of being trashed." Clearly she hit a raw nerve, and created an impulse among the women in the movement to say *Yes, this happened to me!* and more importantly, *What is it about? Why is this happening?*[4]

On Freeman's own account, trashing is not merely disagreement, conflict, or opposition. Rather, it is "a particularly vicious form of character assassination," that is "manipulative, dishonest, and excessive," and is done not with the motivation of exposing disagreement and resolving differences, but in order "to disparage and destroy." It is a behavior that comes from hatred, contempt, anger, or other negative emotions between women.[5] It is worth quoting Freeman's examples of the tactics used to trash at length:

> Trashing can be done privately or in a group situation; to one's face or behind one's back; through ostracism or open denunciation. The trasher may give you false reports of what (horrible things) others think of you; tell your friends false stories of what you think of them; interpret whatever you say or do in the most negative light; project unrealistic expectations on you so that when you fail to meet them, you become a "legitimate" target for anger; deny your perceptions of reality; or pretend you don't exist at all.[6]

One of the revelations of Freeman's essay is the confusion that trashing causes women in the feminist movement. Despite previous experience with political conflict, it got under her skin. She says it took her years to understand why. Her conclusion is that

> the Movement seduced me by its sweet promise of sisterhood. It claimed to provide a haven from the ravages of a sexist society; a place where one would be understood. It was my very need for feminism and feminists that made me vulnerable. I gave the movement the right to judge me because I trusted it. And when it judged me worthless, I accepted that judgement.

Feminist trashing hit Freeman hard, as it still hits some women hard today, because it comes from a source not only not expected, but so dissonant with women's expectations that it is hard to believe or understand. Women are implored by feminism to choose women, to fight for women, and yet when they do, they are attacked by women, and betrayed by women. Mary Daly, in her canonical book *Gyn/Ecology*, talks about women being "woman-identified," "choos[ing] to be present to each other," saying "no" to men and "yes" to women (Daly 1988, xii–xiii). Janice Raymond declared in *A Passion for Friends* that "the best feminist politics proceeds from a shared friendship" (Raymond 1986, 9). Andrea Dworkin describes the achievement of consciousness-raising groups during the second wave, writing that "women discovered each other, for truly no oppressed group had ever been so divided and conquered" (Dworkin 1974, 20). It may be perplexing that members of *any* social justice movement treat each other badly, but it is *particularly* perplexing for this to happen within feminism, the whole point of which is for women to stand for women.

Freeman herself became convinced, over time and after hearing from countless movement women about their experiences, that "trashing was not an individual problem brought on by individual actions; nor was it a result of political conflicts between those of different ideas; it was a social disease." It arose from the feminist movement's commitment to the ideal of "sisterhood," which said that every woman was a sister. The reality of dislike and other complicated dynamics between individual women made them unable to conform to the ideal of sisterhood by *treating* all women as sisters. The ideal forced the behavior underground, which at least partly explained its subtlety and perniciousness.

Is Freeman right about what explains trashing? Is it the impossibility of living up to the ideal of "sisterhood" that creates hatred between women[7] in the feminist movement? Or is there a better explanation to be had? That question will be the focus of this paper. I'll present a range of potential explanations, some offered already in the literature and some new, and assess their plausibility. Along the way I'll be trying to work out whether trashing is a *novel* phenomenon, unique to feminist movement, or a feature of any social justice movement, or indeed, just a feature of social life.[8]

2. WOMEN HATING WOMEN

I'll discuss 11 independent explanations of trashing, all of which are competitors to Freeman's explanation (although which need not be exclusive to it). These are (a) tribalism, (b) anti-hierarchy, (c) internalized misogyny, (d) misdirected rage, (e) unresolved trauma, (f) who's attracted to feminism, (g) status hierarchies/power grabs, (h) overzealous moralism, (i) performative moralism, (j) resentment (justified), and (k) feminine socialization and expected social roles. Then I'll return to Freeman's explanation: (l) the ideal of sisterhood. Any of these might explain particular instances of trashing, and any combination might overdetermine or exacerbate it in a particular feminist community.

a. Tribalism

Freeman described being subjected to a particularly nasty form of trashing, a behavior we now call "gaslighting," in her case having others deny that they are mistreating her while in fact mistreating her, causing her to doubt her own sanity. She writes:

> One woman, in private phone conversations, did admit that I was being poorly treated. But she never supported me publicly, and admitted quite frankly that it was because *she feared to lose the group's approval*. She too was trashed in another group. (my emphasis)

Women who disapprove of how a member is being treated are here unwilling to do anything about it, lest they find themselves at odds with the group, too.

bell hooks makes a similar point about group dynamics within feminism. She wrote that

> many splinter groups who share common identities (e.g., the WASP working class, white academic faculty women, anarchist feminists, etc.) . . . endeavor to support, affirm, and protect one another while demonstrating hostility (usually through excessive trashing) towards women outside the chosen sphere. (hooks 2000, 47)

And she goes on to say that this is nothing new:

> Bonding among a chosen circle of women who strengthen their ties by excluding and devaluing women outside their group closely resembles the type of personal bonding among women that has always occurred under patriarchy—the one difference being the interest in feminism. (hooks 2000, 47)

hooks locates this behavior among *women* but not among *feminists* in particular. The latter is just a version of the former.

If tribalism is the explanation of trashing, then trashing may not have very much to do with the particular woman being trashed. Rather, how she is treated is simply a *signal* to others, its primary purpose being the redrawing of in-group/out-group lines, and a communication of loyalty and allegiance to the in-group. Geoffrey Brennan, Lina Eriksson, Robert Goodin, and Nicholas Southwood (2013) discuss the signaling effect of adherence to particular norms. (Their discussion is instructive here whether we run it through norms or not. For example, we might say there's a *norm* for this feminist group to trash that one, for example, during the second wave, for lesbian separatist feminists to trash heterosexual feminists,[9] or we might set norms to the side and simply ask, what is signaled by individual lesbian separatist feminists when they trash heterosexual feminists?)

They talk about "a teenager who dresses in black, dyes her hair, and wears skull jewellery" (Brennan et al. 2013, 157). In doing so, she signals belonging to the group who dress that way: first emphasizing her similarity to others in the group, which is a signal to them, and second emphasizing her difference from those outside the group or in the "mainstream," which may have the effect of cutting her off from them. This makes her signal act as a credible commitment:

> Were she able to go off and interact with someone else instead whenever the group tried sanctioning her, there would be a real risk that she might betray the group. Sending a credible signal of her affiliation with the group that at the same time makes it hard for her to leave the group makes her a more trustworthy member of it. (Brennan et al. 2013, 157)

We can say exactly the same thing about trashing. When a lesbian separatist publicly trashes a heterosexual feminist, she doesn't *only* attack that particular woman. She also sends a signal. The signal goes back to her own in-group, the lesbian feminists, and emphasizes the fact of her belonging, and it goes out to all of the out-groups, not only the heterosexual feminists but everyone else too. The heterosexual feminists in particular will be likely to "cut her off" for this behavior, and this ensures that she cannot go to them when the lesbian feminists attempt to sanction her. The same may be true of other feminists groups adjacent in values to the heterosexual feminists. This in turn makes her a more reliable member of the lesbian feminist group.[10]

In-groups built out of identities may be even more at risk for trashing based in tribalism. Writing for *The Guardian*, Jill Filipovic (2013) speculates that "identity-based movements may be particularly susceptible, precisely because of our personal investment in them." She identified feminism as one such movement, saying,

> Feminism isn't just a general ideology for making the world a better place: it's a very specific ideology of liberation for the actors of the movement. It's personal by definition. Challenges to the movement, or the sense that other women are somehow doing feminism wrong, can feel like personal affronts. For feminists, your work often feels like a reflection of who you are, and the critiques even more so. (Filipovic 2013)

This is still group-based, because it's about *we, women*, but the explanation is that our personal investment in the movement explains our sensitivity to criticism, or to others' differing approaches, and that this in turn may at least partially explain the extravagance of our negative treatment of one another.

b. Anti-Hierarchy

The Redstockings, a radical feminist group based in New York, wrote in their 1969 manifesto, "We are committed to achieving internal democracy.

We will do whatever is necessary to ensure that every woman in our movement has an equal chance to participate, assume responsibility, and develop her political potential" (Redstockings 1969). Democracy here was seen as the opposite of hierarchy, and a reaction to it, a commitment to doing things differently, and better.

It was a noble goal; but the feminist commitment to anti-hierarchy seems to have had some undesirable effects. Freeman quotes a speech by Anselma dell'Olio read at the Congress to Unite Women, where she talks about the personal attacks she witnessed in the feminist movement, including character assassinations and purging women from the movement entirely. Dell'Olio asks, "And whom do they attack?"

> Generally two categories—some women are unlucky to fall into both—achievement or accomplishment of any kind would seem to be the worst crime. . . . Do anything, in short, that every other woman secretly or otherwise feels she could do just as well—and baby, watch out, because you're in for it.
>
> If you are in the first category (an achiever) you are immediately labelled a thrill-seeking opportunist, a ruthless mercenary, out to get her fame and fortune over the dead bodies of selfless sisters who have buried their abilities and sacrificed their ambitions for the greater glory of Feminism. Productivity seems to be the major crime—but if you have the misfortune of being outspoken and articulate, you are accused of being power-mad, elitist, fascist, and finally the worst epithet of all: A MALE-IDENTIFIER, AAARRGGG![11]

Dell'Olio describes the phenomenon colloquially referred to as "tall poppy syndrome"; when an individual excels at something, others feel the need to "cut her down to size" in order to restore equality. While equality is important, the feminist movement will be handicapping itself if it suppresses achievement and accomplishment in feminist women, traits that could be better used to drive the movement forward. Phyllis Chesler writes that she's sure trashing has driven away many talented women from feminism. She wrote of the early second wave that "individual petty jealousies and leaderless group bullying were frightening and ugly. Mean girls envied and destroyed excellence and talent. In short, they ate their most gifted leaders" (Chesler 2018, 183).

Nancy Hartsock quotes dell'Olio from the passages above to make the point that leadership qualities in women have been confused, by women in the feminist movement, with that woman *wanting to be a leader*, and this in turn has been interpreted as her having the desire to dominate others. Firm commitments against hierarchy and domination then lead movement women to reject any women who have leadership qualities. Hartsock criticizes this practice, saying, "Women have not recognized that power understood as energy, strength, and effective interaction need not be the same as power that requires the domination of others in the movement" (Hartsock 1974; quoted in hooks 2000, 91).

It is perfectly comprehensible why there would be a strong reaction among feminist women to a perceived trait of desire for domination. Some feminists saw feminism as a microcosm for wider society, an "experiment in living" working out ways to live according to different values than characterized the mainstream.[12] The domination of women by men was one of the central problems identified by feminists, a problem which they worked to find ways to challenge. It is therefore not surprising that there would be sensitivity about the presence of domination within feminist communities. The problem, of course, comes when domination is misdiagnosed, because it is confused with traits that have superficial commonalities with it, but are ultimately constructive (as leadership is).

And regardless of feminist women's propensity to confuse leadership qualities with a desire for domination, there is still a question of the best way to eliminate domination (i.e. *even if* that was what it was). It might be more constructive for the group to discuss its concerns with a particular feminist woman and to try to negotiate with her from a place of mutual respect, rather than to simply trash her in the hope that she is either shamed into submission or drops out of the movement entirely.

c. Internalized Misogyny

Misogyny is hatred of women, or at least, hatred of women who are not "good women"—women who conform to sex-based norms for what a woman should be like.[13] Andrea Dworkin wrote in *Woman-Hating*, published almost 50 years ago, that women

> have begun to understand the extraordinary violence that has been done to us, that is being done to us: how our minds are aborted in their development by sexist education; how our bodies are violated by oppressive grooming imperatives; how the police function against us in cases of rape and assault; how the media, schools, and churches conspire to deny us dignity and freedom; how the nuclear family and ritualized sexual behavior imprison us in roles and forms which are degrading to us. (Dworkin 1974, 20)

She says that through consciousness-raising groups "we [women] began to see ourselves clearly, and what we saw was dreadful" (Dworkin 1974, 21). In a world full of cultural messaging about the inferiority of women relative to men, and where important institutions are marked by sex discrimination (e.g., the low rates of prosecution for rape that Dworkin mentions, which remains the case today), it is hardly surprising that women themselves may have internalized woman-hate.

Audre Lorde, writing about the civil rights struggle, says that in any move for liberation, "we must move against not only those forces which dehumanize us from the outside, but also against those oppressive values which we have been forced to take into ourselves" (Lorde 1984, 135). This is an important point: a people that has been oppressed does not face only external pressure, from outsiders who treat them badly, but also faces internal pressure, because individuals will to some extent have *internalized* outsiders' ideas about themselves. We have to reject the views of outsiders *and* reconceive ourselves. She writes,

> If our history has taught us anything, it is that action for change directed only against the external conditions of our oppressions is not enough. In order to be whole, we must recognize the despair oppression plants within each of us—that thin persistent voice that says our efforts are useless, it will never change, so why bother, accept it. And we must fight that inserted piece of self-destruction that lives and flourishes like a poison inside of us, unexamined until it makes us turn upon ourselves in each other. But we can put our finger down upon that loathing buried deep within each one of us and see who it encourages us to despise, and we can lessen its potency by the knowledge of our real connectedness, arcing across our differences. (Lorde 1984, 142)

If we don't do that, we are at risk of treating each other the way that outsiders treat us, and thereby being a perpetrator of our own group's oppression. Could this be the explanation of trashing—the simple idea that feminist women are treating each other with contempt and disrespect following cultural cues about how it is appropriate to treat women?

Freeman dismisses this explanation of trashing as "facile,"[14] saying, "It obscures the fact that trashing does not occur randomly." She says it's more common in some feminist groups than others, and that this needs an explanation and makes general group self-hatred insufficient. She says,

> It is much more prevalent among those who call themselves radical than among those who don't; among those who stress personal changes than among those who stress institutional ones; among those who can see no victories short of revolution than among those who can be satisfied with smaller successes; and among those in groups with vague goals than those in groups with concrete ones.

I am not aware of any empirical research on trashing that would back up this claim of Freeman's, although it is an intriguing claim and would have interesting implications if true. We can accept that this is what she observed at the time, without accepting that it is an accurate characterization of the dynamics across the whole feminist movement. Without confirmation of those differences, the objection is highly speculative. So I will leave internalized misogyny on the table as an explanation of trashing.

d. Misdirected Rage

In a talk given at the Malcolm X Weekend at Harvard University in 1982, Lorde quoted Malcolm X having said he had "begun to discuss those scars of oppression which lead us to war against ourselves in each other rather than against our enemies" (Lorde 1984, 135).[15] This same phrase, "ourselves in each other," showed up in the quote from Lorde in (c) above, "self-destruction . . . makes us turn upon ourselves in each other." What did Malcolm X mean by it?

Lorde understands it as referring to "those closest to us who mirrored our own impotence" (Lorde 1984, 135–36). As members of an oppressed group, we lack power in particular ways, and we see this clearly in each other in a way that reflects back to us what we are most frustrated about in our own situation. And because we are *right there* while those who oppress us are not, the anger and frustration that we feel about what we see can easily be directed at those from our own groups, rather than at those who cause our group's marginalization. Instead, Lorde says, we must "focus our rage for change upon our enemies rather than upon each other" (Lorde 1984, 135).

This phenomenon is distinct from internalized misogyny, because it is one thing to hate other women *because they are women* (or because they are not "good women"), another to hate them because they are similarly impotent in the face of oppression, and conveniently right there, available to be the recipients of other women's frustration.

In Lorde's view, we spare each other from misdirected rage by knowing who the "we" is. For feminist women, this means knowing who *women* are. This allows us to "use our energies with greater precision against our enemies rather than against ourselves" (Lorde 1984, 137). When feminist women are clear in the knowledge that we stand for women, we will make sure that we don't spend our time attacking women, and rather focus on those who are the enemies of women[16] (or that which is the enemy of women, when the "enemy" is structural or institutional).[17]

Is trashing just misdirected rage, and something that could be ameliorated with a clear understanding of who feminists are *for* and who/what they are *against*? It's not clear whether the latter would resolve trashing per se, although it might transform trashing (a phenomenon between women) into canceling (a general phenomenon, that would in this case be between women and men). That is to say, we might shift the target of the rage without changing how that rage is expressed. If Lorde's claim is just that it is better for the target to be "the oppressor" than one's fellow oppressed, then that might be right. But if the question is *why is there trashing at all, and how do we get rid of it, because it's horrible*, then the proposed solution might not help much. Misdirected rage does seem a useful explanation though, in terms of capturing the otherwise perplexing phenomena of highly acrimonious infighting over very small differences, rather than directing rage at bigger and what would seem to be more threatening differences. (A current example is the trashing of gender critical feminists by mainstream feminists, when surely anti-feminists are the much more important enemy).[18]

Freeman also favors misdirected rage as an explanation of trashing (although she "doubt[s] that there is any single explanation to trashing").[19] She says,

> I have never seen women get as angry at other women as they do in the Movement. In part this is because our expectations of other feminists and the Movement in general are very high, and thus difficult to meet. We have not yet learned to be realistic in our demands on our sisters and ourselves. *It is also because other feminists are available as targets for rage.* (My emphasis)

She explains that rage is a logical response to oppression, and that it needs an outlet, but that outlet cannot be men, because women have learned that when they direct rage at men they can be hurt. Men are distant, "the system" is vague, but women are near. Thus "their rage is often turned inward." Freeman says that this can create a sense of power, a feeling of having "done something," because trashing hurts women and those women often leave the movement. She speculates that this will be especially appealing to women who focus on revolution rather than reform, because they are less likely to have the feeling of having "done something" in the course of ordinary activism.

e. Unresolved Trauma

According to the World Health Organization, 35% of women worldwide have experienced intimate partner violence, or sexual violence (WHO 2013; cited in VicHealth 2017). To give some detail on just one country, in Australia, the greatest contributor to the disease burden for women between 18 and 44 years old is male intimate partner violence.[20] Australian women, in significant numbers, have experienced physical violence (34%), sexual violence (19%), and physical and/or sexual violence from male perpetrators (39%). Ten percent of Australian women have experienced violence from male strangers (as opposed to men known to them), and 17% have been stalked by a man. Eighty-one percent of the women who had experienced male violence in a 12-month period experienced more than one violent incident (VicHealth 2017, 7). One of the social and economic costs of violence against women is homelessness. Thirty-six percent of the 92,000 people seeking assistance from government-funded homelessness agencies were fleeing domestic violence, and the estimated cost of the health impact on women is $21.7 billion dollars a year (VicHealth 2017, 11). There is also female trauma not captured in these figures, associated with, for example, childhood sexual abuse, trauma associated with pregnancy (e.g., miscarriages and stillbirths), trauma associated with body image (anorexia, bulimia, cutting, anxiety, depression), and the impacts of workplace sexual harassment and bullying, and everyday sexism.

Why mention all of this? The underlying thought is that there is a serious cost to being a member of an oppressed group, a group that is—as women are—subject to exploitation, violence, and cultural imperialism[21] at the hands of men and male-dominated culture. People who have experienced trauma are carrying a high psychological and emotional (and sometimes physical) burden, and therefore may have less resources available to manage interpersonal conflict. They may have individual triggers that are hard for others to anticipate, or for them to know well enough to warn others of. Thus one explanation of trashing comes from the fact of women being members of an oppressed group in the first place. Reduced resources to manage conflict and greater numbers of triggers for that conflict may result in a tinderbox-type situation for infighting.

If this explanation is accurate, then we should expect to see similar tensions in other oppressed groups, in particular those oppressed along race or class lines.[22] The explanation does not make trashing *unique* to feminism, unless there is more to be said about the specific shape this response to trauma takes in the context of women together attempting to work for liberation from their common oppression.

f. Who's Attracted to Feminism

Chesler's description of feminism in her memoir *A Politically Correct Feminist* stands out because it gives an unflattering, albeit cheerful, description of the women in the feminist movement at the time: "In our midst was the usual assortment of scoundrels, sadists, bullies, con artists, liars, loners, and incompetents, not to mention the high-functioning psychopaths, schizophrenics, manic depressives, and suicide artists. I loved them all" (Chesler 2018, 3). The subtitle of her book continues this theme: *Creating a Movement with Bitches, Lunatics, Dykes, Prodigies, Warriors, and Wonder Women*. Like

(e) above, this offers us an explanation of trashing that is "upstream" from feminism itself. Here, it's not about the content of feminist theory or movement, or about women as an oppressed group, or about between- and within-group dynamics. Rather, it's about the individuals who tend to be *attracted to* feminist activism in the first place. If the feminist movement attracts some number of women who are especially volatile in interpersonal interactions, then this may explain both the quantity and quality of trashing within the feminist movement.

We can strengthen Chesler's observation by thinking about the alternative motivations women might have for participation in feminist activism, quite aside from a simple commitment to the cause of feminism itself. Women might come to feminist activism looking for new friends, new lovers, companionship, a sense of belonging, a shared understanding of negative life experiences (e.g., male violence), a new interest/hobby, excitement (e.g., participating in civil disobedience or protests),[23] and more. Because these are personal motivations, it can be personally disappointing when things don't work out as anticipated.

Imagine that a small group of women get together to push back against proposed legislation, working on coordinating meetings with members of parliament, opinion pieces for the media, and a public awareness–raising sticker campaign. Suppose that all the women except one are there because they oppose the law, and their standard of success is strong resistance to the law, while one woman is there to make new friends. Conflict within the group may be harder for this last woman to deal with, because it is more personally disappointing to her if the relationships do not develop in the direction she had hoped they would. Similarly, a woman who seeks a sense of belonging may be distressed by a group dynamic in which she does not feel accepted or supported. Frustration, needing an outlet, may tip over into trashing.

Further, because feminist activism is generally antagonistic, certain personality traits will do better than others—people who are combative, argumentative, self-assured, and even aggressive will do well against *opponents* of feminism, and therefore advance the feminist cause, but those same personality traits may create interpersonal difficulties between movement women. It is important not to confuse conflict with abuse at this point, however—this explanation is compatible with high conflict, but high conflict can exist without trashing (Schulman 2019). Disagreements need not be personal, but trashing is personal.

g. Status Hierarchies/Power Grabs

Trashing over issues of race within the Instagram knitting community made headlines in 2019. A knitting designer, Karen Templer, had written a blog post describing her longing to visit India, mentioning a friend from her youth who had offered for her to accompany the friend and her family on a trip there. Templer wrote, "To a suburban midwestern teenager with a severe anxiety disorder, that was like being offered a seat on a flight to Mars" (Moore 2019). Her blog filled up with angry comments accusing her of colonialism, imperialism, exploiting the emotional labor of her Indian friends, crying "white women's tears," and "othering." As she responded to criticisms she was accused of being "defensive and dismissive." One Instagram knitting activist "warned her white knitter friends that if they stayed silent and didn't speak up against racism then they would be considered 'part of the problem'" (Moore 2019). Another knitter who spoke up against the mobbing of Templer, Maria Tusken, was then targeted, losing thousands of followers and having her livelihood directly targeted. The editor of a British knitting magazine tweeted "don't be sucked in by her and people like her. . . . Don't give them your money" (Moore 2019).

James Lindsay, author of *Cynical Theories*, describes such activist campaigns as "a power grab thinly clothed as a civil rights movement" (Moore 2019). What this means is that people who have previously not had social power, or as much social power, are able to make a "grab" for that power through the guise of social justice. A person of color knitter with fewer Instagram followers can call out a white knitter with greater numbers of Instagram followers, and by taking the position of the moral authority can gain new followers, and in cases where social media profile corresponds to small business success, can make more money. The same dynamics can play out when the rewards are not so quantifiable, too, for example, in simply improving reputation or standing within a social group.

It is part of the history of women's oppression that women have been denied status and recognition; this may make women's groups more susceptible to power grabs, because power can be "grabbed" more effectively from other women, where it is less secure, than from men, where it is more secure. (This is not to ignore the possibility of power grabs between men and women, it is simply to bracket it as less relevant to the theme of trashing.) One of the rationales for women's spirituality during the second wave of feminism was to give women status and recognition, through formal roles like "priestess," in recognition of what they had been denied by male-dominated society (see, for example, Budapest 1980).

Jill Filipovic appears to agree with this idea, saying of trashing that "it happens because we've internalized a narrative of scarcity: we act as though we're fighting for crumbs" (Filipovic 2013). She says that criticizing other feminists is "safe"; it allows women to position themselves as good feminists and to avoid becoming targets themselves in the way that they might if they put out new ideas. But she thinks this is "not because we're catty or mean or somehow predisposed to cliquishness and competition. It's because we're starving" (Filipovic 2013). It is the predicament that women are in that creates the preconditions for trashing. If feminist women had the freedom to express themselves without becoming targets, there would, paradoxically, be less trashing.

h. Overzealous Moralism

Barbara Ryan, writing about second wave radical[24] feminists, noted that "volatile divisions" developed around different feminist orientations:

> Separatist feminists accused heterosexual feminists of being male-identified; Marxist feminists charged that all women's groups were bourgeois; socialist feminists considered radical, lesbian, and separatist feminists to be man-haters; and radical feminists dismissed women who continued to be associated with the organized (male controlled) left. (Ryan 2013, 55–56)

She asks, "Why were the battles over ideological definitions and the emphasis on ideological purity so intense?" (Ryan 2013, 60). The answer she offers depends on the importance of ideology to social movements more generally.

In Ryan's view, multiple theories can contribute to the same overall ideology, but adherents of a particular theory can come to see it as definitive and this can create disputes over ideological purity. Who is committed to the superior theory? Who is the best feminist? Instead of taking a pluralist view of theory and focusing on a shared commitment to the same ideology, "the movement found itself with competitive models of 'right thinking'" (Ryan 2013, 61). Ryan says that this was an inheritance of leftist groups: "Radical feminist women reacted against the male chauvinism they found in leftist groups of the 1960s era; nevertheless, they borrowed heavily from them, including the practice of promoting dogmatic positions on correct thinking" (Ryan 2013, 61). Commitments to specific theories were used as a means to creating feminist identities, which had the effect of separating feminist women from each other, and distancing them from "ordinary" women. In Ryan's view, feminists became "ideologues rather than social change agents" (Ryan 2013, 64).

It's not clear whether this is a more or less expected outcome of creating and disseminating theory and ideology, or whether "becoming ideologues" was something that the second wave feminists fell into when they might have not done. If it's the former, then we have an *explanation* of feminist infighting, in terms of adherence to a specific theory being confused for ideological disagreement, and policed as such. For example, the overall ideology of feminism might be centered on women's liberation, and some women might theorize that as requiring legal reforms, others as requiring revolution. Then instead of taking a pluralistic approach—*we're all working for the same overall goal*—women who subscribe to one theory or the other might decide that their theory is definitive, and so begin to confuse subscription to alternative theory with dissent from the overall ideology. *You work for legal reform, so you don't really stand for women's liberation.* But if it's the latter, something that feminists might have avoided, by taking a more pluralistic approach, then we still don't have an explanation of feminist infighting. We'll need to know why the second wavers—and why feminists today—made this mistake, and why they let their ideological differences become a means to create their identities, rather than forming their identities in other ways, or relative to a broad and pluralistic commitment to advancing women's equality or women's liberation.

Randall Collins writes in the collection *Passionate Politics* that the kind of emotional solidarity that comes out of highly mobilized social movements creates feelings of morality. He writes that the group

> generates its own standards of right and wrong. The highest good becomes commitment to the group and sacrifice of individual selfishness in its service; those who are outside the group, or worse yet, oppose it, are morally tagged as unworthy, evil, or inhuman. (Collins 2009, 28)

Emotions are amplified within collectives; feelings of outrage, anger, and fear grow much stronger (Collins 2009, 29). On this explanation, trashing is a by-product of the moral emotions, a response to the sense that out-groups are violating the in-group's standards of moral rightness. The sort of social sanctioning we might ordinarily reserve for serious interpersonal moral violations is then seen as appropriately directed at ideological opponents.

Gavin Haynes approaches this issue differently, saying that ideological purity policing is in fact not about morality. He think it's about *purity*, and this is a relative concept: people try to demonstrate that they are *more* pure than each other.[25] This creates what he calls a "purity spiral," which is what we see in the dynamics of escalating conflict such as happened in the knitting community, and are happening in the context of other disagreements too.[26] It is "a process of moral outbidding," using self-censorship and loyalty tests to "weed out its detractors long before they can band together. In that sense . . . its momentum can be very difficult to halt" (Haynes 2020a). On social media, individuals stand to "benefit enormously from taking on the status of a thought leader—from becoming a node that directed moral traffic" (Haynes 2020a). These incentives push in the direction of joining the purity spiral.

Even when it comes to those not motivated to seek the benefits of demonstrating purity, the incentives push people toward neutrality, rather than intervening in an attempt to stop the spiral. By intervening you make yourself a target, and risk becoming the means by which others can display their own purity, by sanctioning you. It may well be that many more people are motivated to avoid being sanctioned than they are to achieve the benefits of having demonstrated purity, but these two things together amount to purity spirals being hard to stop.

Haynes's idea is also important because it explains why *minor* disagreement is policed with such force, which can be a confusing aspect of trashing. Why, we might wonder, are feminists spending so much emotional energy on sanctioning each other over fairly insubstantial disagreements, when they have so much greater moral and ideological opposition to confront?[27] The purity spiral explanation has an answer to this, supplied by Timur Kuran in an interview with Haynes. Kuran observes that

> people who are trying to prevent members of society from speaking the truth will often punish minor criticisms. . . . Simply to send the message to the rest of society that no dissent will be tolerated and no attempt to form an opposing group—even one that differs only slightly from the status quo—will be tolerated. If you allow minor differences, you allow people to coordinate around minor differences, and that can encourage even greater opposition. If people get that sense, then the whole process can unravel. (Haynes 2020a)

Haynes thinks the solution to purity spirals is to *notice* that they are about purity, not morality, and call that out early. On this explanation, trashing is not a unique phenomenon, it's just the name we give to overzealous moralism when it occurs in the context of feminist activism.

i. Performative Moralism

From its name, this explanation might sound similar to what we've just been talking about in (h). But it's different in its intention, and how reflective those who participate in it are likely to be able to be. Performative moralism is moral behavior performed in order to secure particular signaling effects, where these effects may be desired independently of the signaler's actual beliefs or preferences. That's what sets it apart from overzealous moralism, which is generally sincerely felt. (Although, as discussed in the case of purity spirals, sometimes what looks like overzealous moralism can be done out of fear of sanctions for *not* doing it, and in that case it may be closer to performative moralism).

For example, a feminist woman working to oppose double mastectomies in girls under the age of 18 might think that it is *strategically* best to work only with left-leaning political groups on this issue, because this reduces the likelihood of other left-leaning people writing the cause off as "conservative" or "religious" (e.g., about the purity and sanctity of the female body, or preserving the role of motherhood with breastfeeding, rather than about reducing unnecessary surgeries and preventing future regret). In order for this strategy to succeed, however, it may not be enough that she simply work with left-leaning groups and get on with things. It may be that occasionally, when other feminist women associated with this issue work with conservative-leaning groups, she has to denounce them for doing so *in order to send the signal that she is committed to left-leaning groups only*. Denouncing what she is *against* is an easy way to send a clear signal of what she is *for*.

Whether or not it is acceptable for feminists to work with non-left groups is one of the major fault lines in feminism today, and disagreements over it have been a major cause of trashing (generally by the left-purists against the feminists who are open to alliances across the political spectrum). It is an intriguing possibility, however, that in this instance trashing is not about tribes, not about woman-hating, not about genuine moral disapproval, not about any of the other explanations, but just about being a convenient way to advance one's political goals. Left-purist feminists *couldn't* just appear fine with all their feminist colleagues allying with non-left groups, because that very appearance would undermine their commitment. If you're a left-purist then you're vehemently *not* able to take the line that different feminist women will do things differently—at least, not publicly.

There may be performative moralism on other issues, too. Whenever one's commitment to certain values can be signaled by one's disapprobation of others, and where a public signal of commitment to those initial values is likely to advance one's cause, we might expect to see that disapprobation. Another example of where this explanation might be in play is in the feminist conflict over the assertion that "trans women are women!" This is a conflict in which there is a lot of what looks like trashing going on. But in fact, it might be that trashing those who *deny* that "trans women are women!" is a way to signal support for transwomen as a group, and *that* is the real goal that is being advanced by the trashing.[28] This explanation is like tribalism—discussed in (a) above—in the sense that there need not be any real emotion underwriting the trashing, and in fact it need not have much to do with the women being trashed at all. They are mere vehicles for a larger public communication.

j. Resentment (Justified)

In (b) we discussed the fact that trashing is often directed at feminist leaders. Focusing on this point allows us to explore another explanation, that is more focused on the emotion of *envy* or *resentment* between women. Writing about the way mothers sabotage each other when it comes to breastfeeding, Allison Dixley writes of envy,

> Admitting that one is envious is akin to declaring one's inferiority. This dark, intense, implacable and irrational emotion is painfully private and publicly feared. . . . It is characterised by tension and torment. The begrudging nature of envy stems from a preoccupation with one's own limitations and defects. (Dixley 2014, 163)

Could the same dynamic be behind at least some of the trashing in the feminist movement?[29]

There are some good reasons to think it could. They relate to the fact that while most women have a chance to participate in feminist activism in some form, there is an unequal chance for *recognition*. Feminist women with a social status that affords them public credibility may be given greater opportunities to speak for the movement (e.g., lawyers, doctors, academics, journalists), and subsequently receive greater recognition from other women for their contributions *to* the movement. It is perfectly reasonable for women who don't have this same access, but are making substantial contributions to feminist activism in other ways, to feel frustrated about the asymmetry in recognition. This dynamic is likely to be exacerbated in countries with stronger class hierarchies, because the women who have the social status that gives them the greater opportunity to speak for the movement may have (or be perceived to have) that status as a result of a more ingrained inequality of opportunity. (The UK and India are good examples of this, although very different in terms of the progress of feminist movement.)

Similarly, feminist women who don't have this kind of access *depend on* women who are so-placed to speak their concerns, to the media, to the public, to policymakers. This means there is a lot at stake if and when those higher-profile feminists make mistakes, or do things that other feminist women would not do, or think it inadvisable to do. Frustration and disappointment at not being represented in the right way may end up being expressed in trashing.

I have focused on *justified resentment* rather than resentment more generally. That is not because I don't think resentment more generally could be playing an explanatory role in trashing; likely it could. Rather it's because I think justified resentment is the more interesting and complex phenomena, one that the feminist movement could do more to accommodate. There are interesting questions to be asked about the exact nature of the responsibilities naturally emerging feminist leaders have to the women in the movements they're affiliated with, even when those movements are highly unorganized. Women in this position often seem to feel that they have *no* responsibility, that they speak only for themselves. But although they may *intend* to speak only for themselves, they will often be publicly understood to be speaking for the movement. That means their individual, unilateral actions can damage the movement, and that is something that all movement women have an interest in. Without more formal ways to influence spokeswomen, social sanctioning may be the only tool available, and if that happens through social media, with the associated dynamics of moral grandstanding,[30] it is likely to mean trashing.[31]

k. Feminine Socialization and Expected Social Roles

An alternative explanation than offered in (b) of why it is so often women taking leadership positions who are trashed, comes from thinking about the traits women leaders have as being norm-violating relative to ideals of femininity. Freeman notes that the overachiever is the assertive woman, and that assertiveness is a failure to perform femininity correctly. She speculates that women may be policing this norm-violation without conscious awareness that this is what's actually happening. In support of this explanation in terms of women's expected social role is Freeman's observation that "two different types of women are trashed," where one is the leader/achiever, but the other is the "mother."

What she means by "mother" is not literal mothers, but the supportive and self-effacing woman, the woman who is "constantly attending to others' personal problems," who "play[s] the mother role very well." She says the women who "look the part" for this role are expected to play it and then trashed when they refuse; women who play the role but cannot meet other women's impossibly high expectations for them are trashed when they fail to meet those expectations. Trashing is a tool used to pressure women to "conform to a narrow standard," and while this standard is "clothed in the rhetoric of revolution and feminism," "underneath [it] are some very traditional ideas about women's proper roles."

Audre Lorde also leans toward this type of explanation when she talks about members of the black community policing a specific version of blackness:

> We were poised for attack, not always in the most effective places. When we disagreed with one another about the solution to a particular problem, we were often far more vicious to each other than to the originators of our common problem. Historically, difference had been used so cruelly against us that as a people we were reluctant to tolerate any diversion from what was externally defined as Blackness. In the 60s, political correctness became not a guideline for living, but a new set of shackles. A small and vocal part of the Black community

lost sight of the fact that unity does not mean unanimity—Black people are not some standardly digestible quantity. In order to work together we do not have to become a mix of indistinguishable particles resembling a vat of homogenized chocolate milk. (Lorde 1984, 136)

This is an imposition of expected social role applied to blackness itself. Applied to women, it would suggest we should anticipate attacks between feminist women about "what is externally defined as womanhood." But as Lorde points out for blackness, we can be *unified* as women in the broad goal of achieving women's equality or women's liberation, without needing to have accomplished *unanimity* between all feminist women about feminist issues, including what womanhood consists in, what explains women's oppression, and what the right vision for a feminist future is. We do not need to make ourselves "the same" in order to be understood by men, or in order to work together. *Women* are not "some standardly digestible quantity," they are half the population of the world, and so can be expected to be incredibly diverse.

What is tragic about this explanation of trashing is that if it were motivating feminist women at the conscious level, they would surely repudiate it. Liberation from narrow ideas of femininity is a central concern of feminist movement; it would surely be deeply uncomfortable to confront the fact that we were imposing these roles on each other in the course of seeking that liberation.

1. The Ideal of Sisterhood

Freeman's own explanation of trashing was that it emerged from the ideal of sisterhood, which was impossible to live up to. bell hooks writes in *Feminist Theory* of "white" or "bourgeois" women liberationists' vision of sisterhood that

> their version of Sisterhood was informed by racist and classist assumptions about white womanhood, that the white "lady" (that is to say bourgeois woman) should be protected from all that might upset or discomfort her and shielded from negative realities that might lead to confrontation. Their version of Sisterhood dictated that sisters were to "unconditionally" love one another; that they were to avoid conflict and minimize disagreement; that they were not to criticize one another, especially in public. For a time these mandates created an illusion of unity, suppressing the competition, hostility, perpetual disagreement, and abusive criticism (trashing) that was often the norm in feminist groups. (hooks 2000, 45–47)

In hooks' view, trashing was actually *suppressed*, at least for a time, by the ideal of sisterhood. But as the view of womanhood the suppression of all conflict was based on became increasingly untenable, so too did the suppression, and trashing (and transparency about the lack of unity) reemerged.

Barbara Ryan also points to the ideal of sisterhood, but not as an impossible ideal that *caused* trashing, but as something that simply made trashing harder to bear:

> Because feminism is a movement that exhibits an important departure from other social movements, that is, it is led by women, there is an expectation that it should not be hierarchical, elitist, or controlling of adherents. Indeed, feminism is meant to value, support, and unite women. It was the expectation of "a haven from the ravages of a sexist society; a place where one would be understood" that led to despair when, for some participants, just the opposite occurred. . . . In repeated incidents of what became known as trashing, the sense of joy in women discovering themselves was dissipated. (Ryan 2013, 62)

If Ryan is right, then we still need an explanation of *why* trashing occurs, and undermines the hopes that women have for feminism. We'll have to draw on one of the other explanations to fill this in.

3. FINAL THOUGHTS

"Sisterhood" being an impossible ideal does not exhaust the plausible explanations of trashing within feminist activism; there are at least 11 other alternatives that may explain it, or overdetermine its existence. To me, the most intriguing explanations are those that take the sting out of trashing, either by focusing on its communicative/signaling effects, or by focusing on how it is one of the only tools available for the expression of dissatisfaction under anarchic conditions (the relationship between the "represented" constituency and the "representative" woman). But I have my own reasons for minimizing the extent of the genuine negative emotions behind trashing, given that I am routinely trashed myself.

We have not fully resolved the question of whether trashing is a unique phenomenon. Freeman denied that trashing was unique to feminism, seeing it as one form of the more general "use of social pressures to induce conformity and intolerance for individuality," which she saw as "endemic" across society. Ryan shared this view, writing about how "most movements experience factionalism, many collapsing under the weight of excessive infighting." She gives the civil rights movement, gay liberation movement, and leftist organizing as examples (Ryan 2013, 61). Lorde described dynamics within the black liberation movement that were parallel to trashing in the feminist movement.

Certainly the contemporary phenomena of "canceling," "mobbing," and "deplatforming" are conceptually close to trashing, and the dynamics of "woke culture," "cancel culture," "grandstanding," "virtue signaling," and "purity spirals"—all more general social dynamics—impact or feed into feminist trashing.[32] But I think it is useful to reserve a term for the feminism-specific phenomenon that Freeman first lifted the lid on, precisely *because* it has some plausible explanations that are specific to women as a group (e.g., internalized misogyny, internalized norms of femininity). I have not resolved whether trashing is about women in general or about feminist women in particular. Some explanations point to the former, and some to the latter. It would be illuminating to compare trashing within feminism with the dynamics between members of other social justice movements, and between people in other oppressed social groups. But that comparison will have to be a project for another time.

NOTES

1. Freeman (1976), archived at https://www.jofreeman.com/joreen/trashing.htm, no page numbers. All references to Freeman are to this article.

2. The phrase "Sisterhood Is Powerful" was coined by Kathie Sarachild in 1968; the longer "Sisterhood is powerful. It kills. Mostly sisters" was used by Ti-Grace Atkinson in her resignation from The Feminists (a New York feminist group that she had founded). See discussion in Faludi (2013) and Filipovic (2013).

3. Lowrey herself does not explain what happened in terms of trashing, nor focus much on the between-women aspect of it, after noting it. Her explanation is that this is part of a "New Ptolemaism" in universities. Ptolemaism involves "an inordinately complex model" that makes "all of the empirical data conform to a central, organizing false assumption" (Lowrey 2021, 757). The "New Ptolemaism" involves the flipping of hierarchical binaries; in the case that impacted Lowrey herself, flipping sex and gender. But this is an explanation more in line with that offered by the critics of critical theory, who see a certain approach being implemented across a range of areas relating to "identity" (e.g., Pluckrose and Lindsay 2020). So I will set Lowrey's explanation aside in what follows.

4. There are many individual testimonies from women about their own experiences of trashing in Phyllis Chesler's book *Women's Inhumanity to Women* (Chesler 2001).

5. For a discussion of some of the more positive uses of anger inside feminist organizing, drawing on examples from the New Zealand second wave, see Holmes (2004).

6. Freeman (1976); see also dell'Olio (n.d. but *c.* 1970s) for a similar description.

7. Let me be completely clear that when I say "between women" here, I mean "between *some* women." While it seems that many if not most feminist women experience trashing, it's not remotely the case that all feminist women trash or that feminist

women are trashed by all or most of the feminist women they know. (Freeman agrees with this when she says, "Although only a few women actually engage in trashing, the blame for allowing it to continue rests with us all"—see Freeman 1976.) There are many positive relationships among feminist women not characterized by any of the negative emotions I'm focusing on here. It's important to say this given the prevalence of the "catfight" narrative in understanding relationships between women, feminist women being no exception. For criticism of this narrative in the context of the series *Mrs. America* (2020), see (Brown 2020).

8. Cf. Lorde (1984, 135–36), who suggests there was a similar dynamic in the 1960s black community in the United States.

9. By "heterosexual feminists" here I mean *practicing* heterosexuals, so, non-separatist feminists. This dispute, originating during the second wave and still lingering in some quarters today, was about the practice of interacting with men—romantically, sexually, or in any other ways—rather than devoting one's energies to women alone, and not about the bare fact of one's sexual orientation. (The latter was treated with more skepticism than it is today, at least when the orientation was "heterosexual," given that feminine socialization was taken to include socialization into heterosexuality, and feminine socialization was seen as the mechanism by which women—female people—were oppressed).

10. A similar insight has been put forward in the discussion of slurs, with Geoff Nunberg suggesting that the use of a slur may be more about signaling in-group solidarity than it is about the individual or group being slurred (Nunberg 2017).

11. Dell'Olio (n.d.). Also quoted in Freeman (1976). I present the same passages that Freeman quotes, but from dell'Olio's original mimeograph. There are some minor differences in the wording.

12. See Mackay (2017) and discussion in Lawford-Smith (forthcoming, chap. 1).

13. Manne (2017) argues against the former and for the latter understanding of misogyny.

14. Freeman is not responding to Lorde, whose talk came later, but anticipating Lorde's *type* of explanation and rejecting it.

15. Lorde gave this explanation, and the one discussed in (c), in the course of explaining infighting in black communities in the 1980s. I'm applying her reasoning to women in (c) and (d).

16. The exception, of course, will be the case in which certain *women* are enemies of women, for example, in advocating for policies which harm women's interests. Just as knowing who the "we" is in the case of the black community wouldn't preclude fighting against black people who genuinely worked against black interests, knowing who the "we" is in the case of the community of women wouldn't preclude fighting against women who genuinely worked against women's interests. The trick is to have a broad enough understanding of "women's interests" that it permits disagreement (reasonable pluralism) among women about feminism, rather than justifying attacks against anyone who doesn't have our specific feminist view. The latter would risk justifying the trashing-filled status quo.

17. Freeman (1976) makes a similar point about locating the real enemy. She writes, "The collective cost of allowing trashing to go on as long and as extensively

as we have is enormous. We have already lost some of the most creative minds and dedicated activists in the Movement. More importantly, we have discouraged many feminists from stepping out, out of fear that they, too, would be trashed. We have not provided a supportive environment for everyone to develop their individual potential, or in which to gather strength for the battles with the sexist institutions we must meet each day. A Movement that once burst with energy, enthusiasm, and creativity has become bogged down in basic survival—survival from each other. Isn't it time we stopped looking for enemies within and began to attack the real enemy without?"

18. Gender critical feminism is an emerging feminist theory and movement that attempts to reorient feminism back to a focus on women as a sex caste, and works for the protection of women's sex-based rights. See discussion in Lawford-Smith (forthcoming).

19. Dell'Olio (n.d.) seems to agree that there is misdirected rage, and puts the point rather more colorfully: "I learned 3 1/2 years ago that women had always been divided against one another, were self-destructive and filled with impotent rage. I thought the movement would change all that. I never dreamed that I would see the day when this rage, masquerading as a pseudo-egalitarian radicalism under the 'pro-woman' banner, would turn into frighteningly vicious anti-intellectual fascism of the left, and used within the movement to strike down sisters singled out for punishment with all the subtlety and justice of a kangaroo court of the Ku Klux Klan."

20. Webster (2016), cited in VicHealth (2017). Two clarifications will be helpful here. Male intimate partner violence means violence perpetrated by male partners of women, including dates, boyfriends, and current or ex-cohabiting partners (VicHealth 2017, 5). The "disease burden" refers to "the combined toll of illness, disability and premature death" (VicHealth 2017, 11). The negative impacts on women's health of intimate partner violence include poor mental health, particularly anxiety and depression, alcohol and drug use, suicide, injuries, and homicide (Ayre et al. 2016; Webster 2016; both cited in VicHealth 2017, 11).

21. These are three of "five faces" of oppression, according to one understanding of oppression (Young 2014).

22. These groups are the most similar to sex in that they involved—historically, and to some extent still—an extraction of resources from the oppressed to the oppressor. For this conception of oppression see Atkinson (1974, 110).

23. There is some discussion of the excitement motivation for participating in social movement in Collins (2009, 29–30).

24. Note that her usage of "radical" here only means not of the mass feminist movement. The mass movement was the National Organization of Women (NOW), who were reformers. Ryan considers radical feminists, socialist feminists, and separatist feminists, all under the umbrella of "radical feminist." See Ryan (2013, 54–55).

25. Haynes (2020a). Justin Tosi and Brandon Warmke (2016) also write about this phenomenon, but they call it "ramping up," and "trumping up," as two of the forms that "moral grandstanding" takes. "Ramping up" is to make a slightly stronger claim than the person before you (e.g., about what kind of punishment someone deserves), "trumping up" is to declare a moral problem where there isn't one (Tosi and Warmke 2016, 205–6).

26. Haynes (2020a, b). See also discussion of purity spirals in Redfern and Whatmore (2020).

27. An alternative answer to this question is that the things feminists are expending energy sanctioning each other over are *not* insubstantial, even if they may appear to be at first glance. For example, for feminists who are extremely concerned about epistemic injustice against women—testimonial injustice, hermeneutical injustice, gaslighting, and so on—it will matter a lot that we believe women, affirm women's experience, give women's testimonies uptake. Feminists who don't do this, because they think some other project is more important (like stopping the harms that women need to testify to in the first place), or have significant worries with that approach (e.g., what happens when a woman's perception of her experience is distorted or exaggerated?), will be seen as compromising something at the very heart of the feminist project, and this may justify a strong reaction. Still, that need not mean trashing.

28. I have outlined this possibility elsewhere, see Lawford-Smith (2019).

29. There's an important disanalogy between the breastfeeding example and the feminist activism example. In the breastfeeding case, there are background ideas about what it means to be a *good woman*, informing the standards to which women aspire as mothers, the fulfillment (or otherwise) of which creates envy and resentment between women. But in the feminist activism case, it's not clear that the emergent leaders are *good women*. Indeed insofar as they violate many norms of femininity, they may be *bad women*. One way to resolve this tension is to say that the standards are relative to particular communities of women, so that within feminism what makes a *good woman* is recognition for contributions. Another way to resolve it is to say that feminism itself has been co-opted into an idea of being a *good woman* in the sense not relativized to particular communities, for example, because the "new good woman" is independent and sassy (in a sexy way, of course).

30. See note 25 above. In addition to ramping up and trumping up there's also piling on (also known as dogpiling), excessive emotional displays, and claims that something's moral wrongness is self-evident. See Tosi and Warmke (2016). Piling on, where many people join a chorus saying the same thing, can often *feel like* trashing simply because of the volume of criticism, even when what is being said or disagreed with itself has only moderate strength.

31. It is also worth noting the role of social media platforms in exacerbating this dynamic. Several women who are generally taken to be "spokeswomen" for gender critical feminism, for example, have had their social media accounts banned as part of an ideologically driven move to suppress gender critical feminist speech. This has the effect of cutting those women off from their informal constituencies, and making them less available for informal consultation and constructive criticism. I'm thinking in particular of Meghan Murphy of *Feminist Current*, who is banned from Twitter; and Kellie-Jay Keen-Minshull of *Standing for Women*, who at the time of writing was on her 3rd 30-day ban from Facebook, banned from advertising on Instagram, and banned permanently from change.org, teespring.com, Mumsnet, and Twitter.

32. Some of these examples come from Haynes (2020a).

REFERENCES

Atkinson, Ti-Grace. 1974. *Amazon Odyssey*. New York: Links Books.

Ayre, Julie, Miriam Lum On, Kim Webster, Michelle Gourley, and Lynelle Moon. 2016. *Examination of the Burden of Disease of Intimate Partner Violence Against Women in 2011: Final Report*. Sydney: ANROWS.

Brennan, Geoffrey, Lina Eriksson, Robert Goodin, and Nicholas Southwood. 2013. *Explaining Norms*. Oxford: Oxford University Press.

Brown, Mark. 2020. "Gloria Steinem Says TV Drama of 1970s Feminist History 'Ridiculous'." *The Guardian*, May 23, 2020.

Budapest, Zsuzsanna. 1980. *The Holy Book of Women's Mysteries*. Berkeley: Wingbow Press.

Chesler, Phyllis. 2001. *Women's Inhumanity to Women*. Chicago: Lawrence Hill Books.

———. 2018. *A Politically Incorrect Feminist*. New York: St. Martin's Press.

Collins, Randall. 2009. "Social Movements and the Focus of Emotional Attention." In *Passionate Politics: Emotions and Social Movements*, edited by Jeff Goodwin, James Jasper, and Francesca Polletta, 27–44. Chicago: University of Chicago Press.

dell'Olio, Anselma. n.d. "Divisiveness and Self-Destruction in the Women's Movement: A Letter of Resignation." Printed mimeograph, circa 1970s.

Dixley, Allison. 2014. *Breast Intentions: How Women Sabotage Breastfeeding for Themselves and Others*. London: Pinter & Martin.

Dworkin, Andrea. 1974. *Woman Hating*. New York: E. P. Dutton.

Faludi, Susan. "Death of a Revolutionary." *The New Yorker*, April 15, 2013.

Filipovic, Jill. "The Tragic Irony of Feminists Trashing Each Other." *The Guardian*, May 2, 2013.

Freeman, Jo. 1976. "Trashing: The Dark Side of Sisterhood." *Ms.*, April 1976. Retrieved from https://www.jofreeman.com/joreen/trashing.htm.

Hartsock, Nancy. 1998. "Political Change: Two Perspectives on Power." In *The Feminist Standpoint Revisited and Other Essays*. New York: Routledge.

Haynes, Gavin. 2020a. "How Knitters Got Knotted in a Purity Spiral." *UnHerd*, January 30, 2020. https://unherd.com/2020/01/cast-out-how-knitting-fell-into-a-purity-spiral/.

———. 2020b. "The Purity Spiral." *BBC Radio 4*, February 11, 2020. https://www.bbc.co.uk/programmes/m000d70h.

Holmes, Mary. 2004. "Feeling Beyond Rules: Politicizing the Sociology of Emotion and Anger in Feminist Politics." *European Journal of Social Theory* 7 (2): 209–227.

hooks, bell. 2000. *Feminist Theory: From Margin to Centre*. London: Pluto Press.

Lawford-Smith, Holly. Forthcoming. *Gender-Critical Feminism*. Oxford: Oxford University Press.

———. 2019. "How the Trans Rights Movement is Turning Philosophers into Activists." *Quillette*, September 20, 2019.

Lorde, Audre. 1984. "Learning from the 60s." In *Sister Outsider*, 134–44. Trumansburg: Crossing Press.

Lowrey, Kathleen. 2021. "Trans Ideology and the New Ptolemaism in the Academy." *Archives of Sexual Behaviour* 50: 757–60.

Mackay, Fiona. 2017. "Jane Mansbridge—A Quietly Dangerous Woman." *Dangerous Women Project*, March 8, 2017.

Manne, Kate. 2017. *Down Girl: The Logic of Misogyny*. Oxford: Oxford University Press.

Moore, Kathrine Jebsen. 2019. "A Witch-Hunt on Instagram." *Quillette*, February 17, 2019.

Nunberg, Geoff. 2017. "The Social Life of Slurs." In *New Work on Speech Acts*, edited by Daniel Fogal, Daniel Harris, and Matt Moss, 238–295. Oxford: Oxford University Press.

Pluckrose, Helen, and James Lindsay. 2020. *Cynical Theories: How Activist Scholarship Made Everything About Race, Gender, and Identity—and Why This Harms Everybody*. London: Swift Press.

Redfern, Katrin, and Richard Whatmore. 2020. "History Tells Us that Ideological 'Purity Spirals' Rarely end Well." *The Conversation*, July 1, 2020.

Ryan, Barbara. 2013. *Feminism and the Women's Movement*. Abingdon: Routledge.

Schulman, Sarah. 2019. *Conflict is Not Abuse*. Vancouver: Arsenal Pulp Press.

Tosi, Justin, and Brandon Warmke. 2016. "Moral Grandstanding." *Philosophy & Public Affairs* 44 (3): 197–217.

VicHealth. *Violence Against Women in Australia. An Overview of Research and Approaches to Primary Prevention*. Melbourne: Victorian Health Promotion Foundation.

Webster, Kim. 2016. *A Preventable Burden: Measuring and Addressing the Prevalence and Health Impacts of Intimate Partner Violence in Australian Women*. Sydney: ANROWS.

World Health Organization. 2013. *Global and Regional Estimates of Violence Against Women: Prevalence and Health Effects of Intimate Partner Violence and Non-Partner Sexual Violence*. Geneva: World Health Organization.

Young, Iris Marion. 1990. "Five Faces of Oppression." In *Justice and the Politics of Difference*, 39–65. Princeton: Princeton University Press.

Chapter 11

Hatred as a Burdened Virtue

Richard Paul Hamilton

No amount of cajolery can eradicate from my heart a deep burning hatred for the Tory Party. So far as I am concerned, they are lower than vermin.

—Aneurin "Nye" Bevan

1. INTRODUCTION

In her 2016 book on anger and forgiveness, Martha Nussbaum suggests that there are good reasons for supposing that hatred "is always a bad emotion to have" (Nussbaum 2016, 50). She makes this remark in passing, in the context of a much more extensive discussion of the role of anger in political life, in which she rejects her earlier view that anger may play some limited role in resisting oppression. Little wonder then that her assessment of hatred is even more damning. I disagree with her recent views on anger, but in this chapter I will be focusing on hatred. While most of the time we would be better off without it, in our politics as much as in our interpersonal relationships, there are some very specific circumstances in which hatred is not only morally permissible but virtuous.

My concern will be with political hatred though I do not think that one can draw a hard and fast distinction between the personal and the political.[1] I will be considering hatred that manifests itself as hard-heartedness: a refusal to forgive or mend bridges as an act of political defiance and particularly where hatred is what I will call "identity-preserving," where not to hate would place in peril one's identity as a particular kind of moral and political self.[2] Much will, therefore, turn on whether that identity is actually worth preserving. The world would clearly be better off without certain identities such as "irredentist US Confederate" or "Orangeman," though intuitions may differ on more controversial examples.[3] Where the identity in question is valuable or even innocuous, then fighting to preserve it can be noble.

Much also turns on what one means by "hatred." I do not think there is much hope for the traditional analytic philosopher's project of neatly tidying up our emotional discourse. Any attempt to define a complex and contested concept such as "hatred" is quickly liable to become arbitrarily stipulative and tacitly moralistic (Hamilton 2006). Rather, we can locate hatred in a cluster of "dark emotions" alongside anger and resentment which sometimes overlap and sometimes come apart. This does not mean that we cannot distinguish between different dark emotions but those distinctions will be drawn in practical contexts of use and will be inescapably bound up with our moral evaluations.[4]

One important distinction to draw is between hatred and a propensity to violence. One may think, as Aristotle apparently did, that hatred always wants the destruction of the hated object (Aristotle, *Rhetoric* 2.4, 1382a14). Whether this is a bad thing will largely depend upon whether violence is morally justified, but even where it is not, there is no reason to suppose that hatred need lead only to violence. There are other ways of hating someone than wishing their destruction. Hatred can also manifest itself in a refusal to entertain the possibility of any kind of relationship with someone and thus a common expression of hatred is hard-heartedness and a refusal to forgive. Precisely because forgiveness is what Miranda Fricker has called "a proleptic moral attitude," capable of creating relationships where none previously existed, someone may refuse to forgive and thereby also refuse the possibility of a relationship with the one who has wronged them (Fricker 2018).

This refusal to enter into relation with someone is part of what I mean by calling certain forms of hatred "identity-preserving." In an interpersonal setting, we are familiar with some of the patterns of abusive partners who gaslight and otherwise emotionally manipulate their partners into becoming complicit in their own abuse. These practices are concerned with distorting the abused partners' identity along the lines determined by the abuser. For someone in a situation of political oppression, they are already in a dyadic relation to their oppressors and the form their identity has taken is shaped to a considerable extent by the conditions of their oppression. Hatred may be the means whereby they remove themselves from that dyadic relation, assert their own identity, and take control of their ability to shape it in ways more conducive to their flourishing. Hatred thereby becomes a form of political resistance rather than mere rancor.

Resistance rarely comes without costs. It is therefore also worth noting that even if there are times when hatred can be virtuous, it resembles a peculiar class of virtues which Lisa Tessman has called "burdened virtues" (Tessman

2005). A burdened virtue is one where the circumstances of oppression mean that the normal connection between virtue and flourishing is severed and the fostering of certain character traits which are essential for survival and resistance may exert a considerable toll on the self. As my title suggests, it is possible for hatred to be virtuous and yet be accompanied by considerable regret. Either as participants or onlookers we might regret that someone is filled with hatred but this need not entail a negative moral evaluation. Regret may be directed at the situation that makes hatred necessary. It is the willingness of someone in such a situation to bear the burden of hatred that renders it "for the sake of the noble" and therefore virtuous.[5]

2. THE COMPLEX HATREDS OF JULIAN TUWIM

In 1944, following the annihilation of Polish Jewry, Julian Tuwim penned his masterpiece "My Żydzi Polscy" ("We Polish Jews"). This poetic essay is an extended meditation on an identity which is on the verge of obliteration, beset on the one side by resurgent Polish anti-Semitism and on the other by the calls of Zionism to abandon the false hope of assimilation and perform Aliyah. He writes, "Polak—bo moja nienawiść dla faszystów polskich jest większa, niż faszystów innych narodowości / I am a Pole because my hatred for Polish fascists surpasses my hatred of fascists of other nationalities" (Tuwim 1944).

Even though German Fascists were the architects of the Holocaust, Tuwim directs his hatred toward his fellow Poles. They are closer to him than the Germans and thus his reactions to them are more complex. Perhaps hatred is one of the characteristically Polish flaws that Tuwim claims to have inherited. Tuwim's hatred is constitutive of his identity, not as an amorphous person imbued with abstract dignity (much beloved by a certain kind of philosopher and theologian) but rather as a rich, complex, and ambivalent human being. In defiance of both the Polish anti-Semites and the Zionists (neither of whom have a high tolerance for ambiguity), Tuwim insists upon his right to be a Polish Jew and a Jewish Pole.

Contrast these lines from Tuwim with a more famous passage from the writings of George Orwell. Recounting his experiences fighting on the Republican side of the Spanish Civil War, Orwell describes the following scene:

> Early one morning another man and I had gone out to snipe at the Fascists in the trenches outside Huesca. Their line and ours here lay three hundred yards apart, at which range our aged rifles would not shoot accurately, but by sneaking out to a spot about a hundred yards from the Fascist trench you might, if you were

lucky, get a shot at someone through a gap in the parapet. Unfortunately the ground between was a flat beet-field with no cover except a few ditches, and it was necessary to go out while it was still dark and return soon after dawn, before the light became too good. This time no Fascists appeared, and we stayed too long and were caught by the dawn. We were in a ditch, but behind us were two hundred yards of flat ground with hardly enough cover for a rabbit. We were still trying to nerve ourselves to make a dash for it when there was an uproar and a blowing of whistles in the Fascist trench. Some of our aeroplanes were coming over. At this moment a man, presumably carrying a message to an officer, jumped out of the trench and ran along the top of the parapet in full view. He was half-dressed and was holding up his trousers with both hands as he ran. I refrained from shooting at him. It is true that I am a poor shot and unlikely to hit a running man at a hundred yards, and also that I was thinking chiefly about getting back to our trench while the Fascists had their attention fixed on the aeroplanes. Still, I did not shoot partly because of that detail about the trousers. I had come here to shoot at "Fascists"; but a man who is holding up his trousers isn't a "Fascist," he is visibly a fellow creature, similar to yourself, and you don't feel like shooting at him. (Orwell 2000 [1968], 253–54)

Passages such as this cement Orwell's reputation as a central figure in the literary conscience of the twentieth century. The glimmer of recognition of the Fascist's status as a fellow human being, even in the darkness of civil war, offers hope for something better. Despite the fact that Orwell spent the rest of his time in Spain shooting at Fascists, he has been recruited as an ally for those who advocate fighting Fascism with dialogue and reasonable debate. He joins an odd panoply of historical figures, including Gandhi, Martin Luther King Jr., and Nelson Mandela, who urge us to embrace love and forgiveness and reject hatred for fear of losing our own humanity.[6] But such a panoply has always been a liberal fiction which has ignored the broader context in which all of these movements took place. As Howard Curzer and others have noted, the achievements of all of these figures took place against the backdrop of often violent actions of others, and it is hard to disentangle how much progress was made by peaceful means and how much by force (Curzer 2017). For every Gandhi there is a Bhagat Singh, for every Martin Luther King Jr. there is a Malcolm X, and for every Nelson Mandela there is a Winnie.

If anything counts as virtuous hatred, it is hatred of Fascism, but Tuwim speaks of something stronger and potentially more problematic than hatred of an idea or even a movement. Tuwim hated Fascists. The example of Orwell seems to suggest that one can fight Fascism and yet still acknowledge that one's opponent remains a human being. Might we not think that in denying his enemies' humanity, Tuwim also risks losing some of his own? The idea that fighting Fascism may lead one to become indistinguishable from Fascists has resurfaced recently in debates around the antifa movement. "Antifa," which stands for "anti-Fascists," is a loose grouping of activists who believe in physically confronting Fascists and denying them a platform. Antifa activists are often confused with a small minority of "black bloc" activists who advocate violent direct action and who may well be *agents provocateurs*. Some professionally high-minded media pundits bemoan the decline of civility in public life and have claimed that opposing Fascists by force makes one just as bad as they are.

Yet how can someone like Tuwim be civil toward a group of people who deny his right to exist? The fundamental difference between Tuwim and those advocates of civil discourse (and even Orwell, his personal heroism notwithstanding) is that Tuwim has "skin in the game" in the way that they do not. As Aleksandar Hemon writes,

> Only those safe from fascism and its practices are likely to think that there might be a benefit in exchanging ideas with fascists. What for such a privileged group is a matter of a potentially productive difference in opinion is, for many of us, a matter of basic survival. The essential quality of fascism (and its attendant racism) is that it kills people and destroys their lives—and it does so because it openly aims so. (Hemon 2018)

Were Polish Fascists prepared to allow Tuwim physical security and the right to remain a Polish Jew, then peaceful coexistence, albeit at arm's length, may be possible. But Tuwim's very existence is anathema to them. Their assertion of a particularly narrow conception of Polish identity crowds out his, so his hatred is his way of making space for himself.[7]

3. LIMPHO HANI REFUSES TO FORGIVE

Sadly, Polish Fascism is not a historical footnote. The Law and Justice Party, which currently dominates the political scene in Poland, while not Fascist in the strict sense, has pandered to Fascist elements. Every November 11 National Independence Day marches have seen increasingly belligerent demonstrations by Fascist groups. Some of them carry banners bearing the image of Janusz Waluś, a Polish migrant to South Africa. In 1994 Waluś and Clive Derby-Lewis assassinated Chris Hani, one of the most outstanding leaders of the anti-apartheid struggle, in a deliberate attempt to provoke a race war and end South Africa's faltering transition from apartheid. The fact that South Africa did not descend into civil war is seen as a mark of the strength of the transition process. This transition process reached its high watermark in the Truth and Reconciliation Commission (TRC) which, drawing heavily on theories of restorative justice, sought an alternative to retribution. Victims and perpetrators came together in a cathartic encounter in which wrongs were acknowledged and forgiveness offered. It is generally considered a success and an example to be followed in conflict zones elsewhere, such as in the aftermath of the Rwandan Genocide.[8]

Chris Hani's widow, Limpho Hani, stands out in stark contrast to this consensus. She refuses (along with the family of Steve Biko) to forgive her husband's murderers and has actively opposed their parole applications (Msimang 2014). In 2016 she gave testimony against a fresh appeal by Clive Derby-Lewis, even though he was in failing health. Interviewed at that time, her words are striking: "I am not an animal. I am a human being" (Msimang 2016). They are striking not least because many highly sanitized philosophical discussions of forgiveness treat our ability to forgive rather than our refusal to do so as the hallmark of our humanity. For Hani, however, to forgive under these circumstances would be dehumanizing. It is crucial to note that neither Derby-Lewis nor Waluś have ever apologized, since both regarded themselves as soldiers and the TRC required acknowledgment rather than apology. To forgive in the absence of apology and remorse would give credence to their claim to be combatants rather than simple criminals.

These acts of dissent by Limpho Hani and the Bikos need to be situated in the broader South African context. The deal that the ruling African National Congress (ANC) made with members of the privileged white community was that they would not be held to full account for the crimes committed in their name, in return for their engagement with the new ANC-promoted Rainbow Nation. The Truth and Reconciliation moment was an attempt to assuage some of the anger that had built up in the black and colored communities. One of the particularly unfortunate aspects of the process is that it tended to lump together the experience of the oppressed and the oppressor: both were wounded by apartheid, both needed to find ways of moving on.

Had this process been conducted alongside widespread structural reform, it might have been laudable. In reality, the TRC was a substitute for it. The franchise is now open to all adult South Africans but the ANC's hegemony and complex system of patronage (to put matters politely) means that no genuine opposition exists. This might not have been such a tragedy, if the ANC had used their political monopoly to radically reform the fundaments of South African society. Instead, they used their dominance not to radically improve the living conditions of those South Africans who suffered most under apartheid but rather to ensure that South Africa continued to be a safe destination for international investment. The most graphic example of this came with the 2012 massacre of striking miners in Marikana, sanctioned at the highest levels of government, with images of police shooting unarmed civilians in scenes eerily redolent of the darkest days of apartheid.

Despite the formal end of apartheid in the early 1990s, three decades on South Africa remains the most unequal country in the world with grinding poverty alongside obscene wealth.⁹ Schools in black and colored communities lack basic facilities and HIV continues to take lives where elsewhere in the world, it has become just another manageable chronic health condition. The anger generated by this occasionally spills out as xenophobic attacks on other Africans and visible minorities, but it also reached a peak in 2015 to 2016 in the "Rhodes Must Fall" movement. This movement highlighted the fact that symbols of South Africa's colonial and apartheid past continued to be publicly visible, most notably in the form of statues of Cecil Rhodes in Cape Town and one of South Africa's most prestigious universities, which continues to bear his unfortunate name. All in all, it would seem that the Truth and Reconciliation process has done a much better job at assuaging the historical guilt of the white minority than addressing the grievances of the black and colored communities. This is the light in which we should view Limpho Hani's refusal to forgive Waluś and Derby-Lewis.

4. HATRED: VICIOUS AND VIRTUOUS

I propose that Julian Tuwim and Limpho Hani are virtuous haters. To defend this claim it will be necessary to distinguish virtuous hatred from its vicious manifestations. Vicious hatred involves a failure of practical reasonableness and in particular a failure to satisfy "*pros ton kairon*" criteria ("circumstances of the case"). Aristotle notes that while anger is aroused by particulars, "hate is directed also at types (everyone hates the thief and the sycophant)" (Aristotle, *Rhetoric* 2.4, 1382a6–7). One example of vicious hatred would therefore involve singling out the wrong type. For instance, hatred of Jews *qua* Jews is clearly vicious.

Often the vicious hater is aware of the unreasonableness of his hatred. Jean-Paul Sartre describes this phenomenon in one of the most famous passages from his (insightful but controversial) essay on anti-Semitism:

> If out of courtesy he consents for a moment to defend his point of view, he lends himself but does not give himself. He tries simply to project his intuitive certainty onto the plane of discourse. I mentioned awhile back some remarks by anti-Semites, all of them absurd: "I hate Jews because they make servants insubordinate, because a Jewish furrier robbed me, etc." Never believe that anti-Semites are completely unaware of the absurdity of their replies. They know that their remarks are frivolous, open to challenge. But they are amusing themselves, for it is their adversary who is obliged to use words responsibly, since he believes in words. The anti-Semites have the right to play. They even

like to play with discourse for, by giving ridiculous reasons, they discredit the seriousness of their interlocutors. They delight in acting in bad faith, since they seek not to persuade by sound argument but to intimidate and disconcert. If you press them too closely, they will abruptly fall silent, loftily indicating by some phrase that the time for argument is past. It is not that they are afraid of being convinced. They fear only to appear ridiculous or to prejudice by their embarrassment their hope of winning over some third person to their side. (Sartre 1976, 13–14)

As Sartre later suggests, part of the unreasonableness of the anti-Semite's hatred is that it has not been arrived at through rational means; his hatred has become constitutive of himself as a particular kind of self. Although Sartre does not use this vocabulary, we would say that the anti-Semite has become vicious.

There are other forms which vicious hatred might take. We are more than familiar with circumstances where legitimate hatred spills over into mindless violence. Others include occasions where hatred continues long after the original offence which provoked it has passed. It would be odd, for example, for a contemporary Irish person to hold a grudge toward Scandinavians because of the Viking slave trade but not for a contemporary African American still very much living with the unresolved harms of Anglo-American slavery to remain aggrieved. Were postapartheid South Africa to have lived up to even a small part of its promise, we might consider Limpho Hani's hatred unreasonable but under current circumstances it is not. Similarly, the causes which incited Julian Tuwim's hatred of Polish Fascists remain. Even today, Polish Fascists march on the streets of Warsaw carrying images of Janusz Waluś and visible minorities live in fear.

5. THE PERILS OF HARD-HEARTEDNESS

As W. B. Yeats wrote, "Too long a sacrifice / Can make a stone of the heart." Perhaps then, even when circumstances have not changed, even where apologies have not been proffered, it might be worthwhile forgiving unconditionally for no other reason than it preserves one's own humanity. This is the argument that has been made by Jessica Wolfendale. Hard-heartedness "can result in the adoption of aspects of the wrongdoer's moral outlook and so forgiveness is worth attempting for reasons unconnected to the wrongdoer's attitudes: reasons that arise from the kinds of moral agents we strive to be" (Wolfendale 2005). Wolfendale's argument is broadly situated within the Kantian tradition and like other Kantians she regards the act of forgiving as closely related to the notion of universal respect for persons. The *locus classicus* of modern Kantian accounts of forgiveness is P. F. Strawson's seminal essay "Freedom and Resentment," in which he defines forgiveness as "a participant moral attitude" (Strawson 1974). By forgiving, we remind the wrongdoer that they remain within the circle of morality.

Philosophical accounts of forgiveness generally distinguish between its conditional and its unconditional form. As the name suggests "conditional" forgiveness requires some sort of act of recompense on the wrongdoer's part whereas unconditional forgiveness does not. Based on this distinction, Hani's refusal to forgive can be seen as a type of conditional forgiveness in which the required conditions have not been met. Wolfendale argues that

> conditional accounts of forgiveness fall victim to several misconceptions based on the conflation of forgiveness with condoning, amnesty, or mercy and furthermore they place what Trudy Govier calls an unacceptable "burden of unforgivingness" on the victim. Effectively, under many conditional accounts of forgiveness the offender's behavior dictates when the victim may forgive.

By contrast, "unilateral accounts of forgiveness remove that burden from the victim and make a strong conceptual distinction between forgiveness, condoning, mercy, and amnesty" (Wolfendale 2005, 344). Forgiveness need not necessarily entail any of these. Nor need it entail reconciliation. In my example, I may forgive my toxic friend but also insist that we go our separate ways, acknowledging the risks entailed by resuming our friendship. Such a variety of forgiveness is done at my own behest and does not ask anything of the wrongdoer while still respecting his inherent humanity.

This may be all well and good for everyday infractions. A much greater challenge is posed by what Wolfendale calls "dehumanizing evil" among which the horrors of apartheid clearly belong. Such evil is directed at the victim, Wolfendale says,

> simply because they are a member of a despised group that is believed to be inherently inferior, whether that group is racial, sexual or political. In the eyes of the perpetrator of dehumanizing evil the victim's moral worth is defined entirely by their membership in the despised group: They are a Jew, a communist, a woman—and nothing more. (Wolfendale 2005, 345)

This description seems reasonable enough at face value but lacks nuance. Does the wrongness of dehumanizing evil consist in the fact that it targets individuals solely because they are members of a group or because it regards certain persons as inherently inferior? Would Tuwim's hatred count as an example of "dehumanizing evil" in Wolfendale's sense? She might respond that it would not, simply because hating Fascists *qua* Fascists is not evil. Yet

Tuwim hates Polish Fascists primarily because they belong to a group which he considers morally unworthy. The clear difference is that whereas Jews *qua* Jews have done nothing wrong, Fascists *qua* Fascists are a clear and present danger to anyone who does not fall within the bounds of their imagined folk community. There may be Fascists who are not active participants in the persecution of minorities but they are despicable nonetheless, since they provide moral and material support to, and so are still complicit in, harmful Fascist activities.

I have described Tuwim and Hani's hatred as identity-preserving but might we not regret that Hani and Tuwim are forced to preserve their identities in this way? At the start of her paper, Wolfendale cites the example of Jamie Bulger's mother. Bulger was the toddler brutally murdered by two youths in Liverpool in the early 1990s. Bulger's mother, Denise Fergus, writes that she is now "consumed with anger, hate, and fear" (cited in Wolfendale 2005, 344). This is clearly a tragedy and Fergus is as much the victim here as her son, but consider the details of the Bulger case. Jamie was murdered by children not that much older than himself who, following a tabloid inspired public frenzy and questionable judgments by senior politicians, were prosecuted as adults. The Bulger case struck such a nerve because it exposed our highly ambivalent cultural attitudes toward children: on the one hand innocent and vulnerable like Jamie, on the other malevolent forces of nature like his killers. The children in question came from an area of extreme social deprivation and themselves experienced childhoods of chaotic and neglectful parenting. How is it even possible for the restorative work of forgiveness to take place under such circumstances? As the Kantian tradition acknowledges, when we forgive, we recognize the other as a rational agent, but these acts were not the products of fully rational agents but rather young children.

If the process of rehabilitation has succeeded, then the adult versions of these children would not re-offend and indeed would regard this horrendous act with the same revulsion that we do. The public discourse attributed a preternatural level of agency and rationality to the children but at the same time it was also insinuated that they were the manifestation of some dark primal force. This insinuation, as Terry Eagleton points out, is a useful distraction from the social and economic conditions which may have contributed to their criminality. Eagleton also notes the vicious circularity in popular conceptions of evil:

> People do evil things because they are evil. Some people are evil in the way that some things are coloured indigo. They commit their evil deeds not to achieve some goal, but just because of the sort of people they are. But might this not mean that they can't help doing what they do? For the policeman, the idea of evil is an alternative to such determinism. But it seems that we have thrown

out a determinism of environment only to replace it with one of character. It is now your character, not your social conditions, which drives you to unspeakable deeds. And though it is easy enough to imagine an environment being changed—slums demolished, youth clubs set up, crack dealers driven out—it is harder to imagine such a total transformation when it comes to the question of human character. How could I be totally transformed and still be me? Yet if I happen to be evil, only such a deep-seated change will do. (Eagleton 2010, 4)

On an Aristotelian account, character is not something like "being indigo" but rather an ongoing project, something we cocreate alongside our peers. When something is deeply awry with our community our character is likely to be distorted in various ways. If, as seems likely, Jamie's killers were deeply malformed individuals, then the community to which they belonged share part of the responsibility for their acts. It is understandable, then, that many prefer to talk about evil as if it were an independent causal variable operating in a vacuum. But if their actions were the product of evil, something quasi-supernatural, what is there for Denise Fergus to forgive?

In making these observations my point is to emphasize the sheer complexity and ambivalence of Denise Fergus's attitudes. It is hard to know what to say about them. Yet Wolfendale contrasts Fergus's hard-heartedness with that of Mandela, and she confidently asserts that

Mandela forgave his unrepentant captors after 25 years in prison yet we do not think that he is morally *at fault* by his act of forgiveness. On the contrary we think he is exhibiting a moral virtue and we consider him to be morally praiseworthy. Similarly, while we might understand why Jamie Bulger's mother has not forgiven her son's murderers, we do not think her attitude is morally *virtuous* and we do not think she is a role model we should seek to emulate. (Wolfendale 2005, 352)

I do not share Wolfendale's confidence. The Mandela example is well-worn but it is every bit as complex and ambivalent as the Fergus example. It comes from his very skillfully constructed autobiography, which, like all political biographies, is first and foremost a political intervention. Mandela's forgiveness was undoubtedly sincere and heartfelt but it is much more than this. The story forms part of Mandela's elevation to the status of secular saint ("Madiba") in a deeply religious country and the optimistic narrative of the Rainbow Nation that he was striving to forge. Mandela's redemption mirrors that of his nation. The image of Madiba forgiving his jailors is symbolic of black and colored South Africans forgiving their oppressors.[10] However, as we have seen, the promise of the Rainbow Nation stalled, and not because of an unwillingness on the part of black and colored South Africans to follow his example. It has stalled because the process of reconciliation was a substitute for necessary structural changes rather than their conclusion. If anything, black and colored South Africans have forgiven too much.

Denise Fergus's hatred is not primarily political. Although working-class people in general, and working-class women in particular, are disproportionately represented as victims of crime, neither she nor her son were singled out as victims because of their socioeconomic status. What makes her continued refusal to forgive problematic is that the objects of her hatred are children, or were at the time of the murder, and thus are not in any obviously dominant position over her. They did not, for instance, exploit any special privilege to evade prosecution or mitigate their punishment. If anything, given our ambivalent attitudes to children discussed earlier, they were punished more severely than they otherwise might have been. Wolfendale rightly stops short of claiming that Denise Fergus's hard-heartedness is morally vicious. It falls into an intermediate category somewhere between praise and blame. I venture that it falls into the category of morally permissible hatred, but her hard-heartedness lacks the redeeming features that can make hatred virtuous: it lacks a broader context of political struggle, and if anything Fergus's identity is not preserved by it but spoiled.

The Bulger case certainly draws our attention to the perils of unforgiveness. Her insistence on holding onto her "hatred, anger, and fear" has ruined her life and possibly exacerbated her trauma. The hope would be that were she able to forgive her son's killers she might be able to achieve some peace. Her inability to forgive is itself a feature of the ongoing poignant tragedy of this case. But this thought should also lead us to be cautious of any simplistic causal story about the relationship between forgiveness and healing. It seems just as plausible that rather than being the precursor for such healing, Denise Fergus would need to already be a considerable way down that road before she reached a stage where she was able to forgive, in much the same way that Mandela was by the time he was able to forgive his captors. That is, the relationship between forgiveness and psychological healing is more likely a constitutive relationship rather than a causal one.

Wolfendale claims that the type of hard-heartedness shown by someone like Fergus "can destroy one's quality of life and one's self-image" and for that reason should be avoided. It is hard to know what to say about the Bulger case. Wolfendale's claim requires that the costs of not forgiving are greater than those of forgiving, and that may be true here. But what about the cases which I have singled out as possible instances of virtuous hatred? Would Limpho Hani and Julian Tuwim's lives have gone better without hatred? The cases are also complex and full of ambivalence, and my answer to this question will be correspondingly so. One thing seems obvious: Hani and Tuwim's lives would almost certainly have been better had they not encountered the circumstances which occasioned hatred. Nevertheless, given the inescapable fact that they did encounter these circumstances, their hatred is constitutive of the kinds of selves they became. To regret their circumstances is to implicitly wish that they were other than they were.

Lisa Tessman talks about burdened virtues in the context of "regretting the self one is." What if the identity-preserving hatred shown by Tuwim and Hani is essential to constituting themselves as resistors? Hani's refusal to forgive is also a refusal to accept that she is less human than her oppressors. Tuwim's hatred of Polish Fascists is a necessary condition for his resisting their attempt to deny him his complex identity as a Polish Jew. Tessman suggests that oppressive conditions often force one to adopt traits and attitudes which under normal circumstances would be harmful, and even though they enable one to survive and resist, they do so only while leaving a moral residue.

Tessman argues that one of the challenges of radical resistance movements is the need to overcome our natural inclinations toward such emotions as compassion. She discusses a historical assassination attempt which took place during a bitterly fought nineteenth-century strike. She recounts her moment of involuntary compassion toward the victim, which she later comes to see as regrettable, not

> because I supported political assassinations or any variety of political violence—I never did—but because my sense of even milder (but still radical) strategies of resistance was that they required anger, hatred, or at least a withholding of attention toward the oppressors; certainly, compassion for one's oppressors seemed inappropriate. (Tessman 2005, 117)

In our earlier example, one might argue that Orwell momentarily failed as an anti-Fascist fighter because of his inability to suppress compassion toward his enemies. If the defenders of Stalingrad had succumbed to similar feelings, then we would be inhabiting a very different world today. Resistance requires sacrifices, and part of that sacrifice may be a willingness to carry on with damage to one's character.

We can and should aspire to live in a world where such sacrifice becomes unnecessary. But it is the worst kind of wishful thinking to pretend that that world is our world. Perhaps all that is left to say in considering whether those born later will forgive the present generation is already contained in a poem by Bertolt Brecht (2003, 75):

> And yet we know:
> Hatred, even of meanness
> Contorts the features.
> Anger, even against injustice

Makes the voice hoarse. Oh, we
Who wanted to prepare the ground for friendliness
Could not ourselves be friendly.

But you, when the time comes at last
And man is a helper to man
Think of us
With forebearance.

NOTES

1. For instance, John Hacker-Wright has suggested to me that hating an unrepentant abusive parent or partner may be virtuous and I agree, but I also think it is important to remember that abuse and sexual violence are themselves features of an unjust political order and are often ways of enforcing that order, so even if a rebellion is a private one it remains a political act. I would like to thank John for his insightful comments on an earlier version of this paper along with David Coady, Dirk Baltzy, and other philosophers at the University of Tasmania who also gave useful feedback.

2. A fuller treatment of these themes can be found in Coulthard (2014), especially chap. 4, "Seeing Red: Reconciliation and Resentment."

3. The key criterion here is whether the assertion of one's identity impinges in a problematic way on another's. There are ways that someone born in the Southern United States can appreciate aspects of their heritage and culture without being a bigot and the same goes for Protestants in the Six Counties, but in both cases the dominant political manifestations of these identities require the exclusion of others.

4. For instance, someone may feel the need to distinguish between anger and hatred because we believe that the former is sometimes morally justified whereas the latter never is.

5. It might be argued that the sorts of hatred being discussed here are episodic, even if the episodes are lengthy ones and that once the circumstances occasioning the hatred disappear, the hatred will too. That means that hatred like this may not meet the test for an Aristotelian character trait, since it is not a stable feature of someone's character. However, the worry evinced by haters of hatred is that the emotion will become a stable feature of someone's character and thereby scar them for life. If this is a real possibility, then it is also possible for virtuous, identity-preserving hatred to become a stable feature of a person's character. Even if this were not the case, the term "virtue" seems the most plausible description from an ordinary language perspective. (For empirical data see Fischer et al. [2018, sect. 3], "Long-Term Sentiment or an Emotion?", reprinted as chapter 7 in this volume.)

6. In her recent discussion of anger and forgiveness, Nussbaum gives pride of place to Mandela who she rightly sees as superior to Gandhi. Yet, despite recognizing his distance from standard "transactional" accounts of forgiveness she seems to present South Africa's Truth and Reconciliation process as an unqualified success.

7. The same goes for those Zionists who would require him to be either Pole or Jew but not both, although his attitude toward them is rather less straightforward, presumably because they do not pose the same existential threat to him.

8. One important dissenting voice is Thomas Brudholm. See Brudholm (2008).

9. According to the World Bank as of 2019: https://edition.cnn.com/2019/05/07/africa/south-africa-elections-inequality-intl/index.html.

10. The fable should be set alongside Mandela's inability to forgive his wife's personal and political transgressions.

REFERENCES

Aristotle. 2006. *On Rhetoric: A Theory of Civic Discourse*. Translated by George A. Kennedy. New York and Oxford: Oxford University Press.

Brecht, Bertolt. 2003. "To Those Born Later." In *Bertolt Brecht: Poetry and Prose*, edited by Reinhold Grimm with the collaboration of Caroline Molina y Vedia, 70–75. New York: Continuum.

Brudholm, Thomas. 2008. *Resentment's Virtue: Jean Améry and the Refusal to Forgive*. Philadelphia: Temple University Press.

Coulthard, Glen Sean. 2014. *Red Skin, White Masks: Rejecting the Colonial Politics of Recognition*. Minneapolis: University of Minnesota Press.

Curzer, Howard. 2017. "The Philosophers' Anger: Review of Martha Nussbaum, *Anger and Forgiveness*." *Los Angeles Review of Books*, November 2, 2017.

Eagleton, Terry. 2010. *On Evil*. New Haven: Yale University Press.

Fischer, Agneta, Eran Halperin, Daphna Canetti, and Alba Jasini. 2018. "Why We Hate." *Emotion Review* 10 (4): 309–20. Reprinted in this volume, chap. 7.

Fricker, Miranda. 2018. "Ambivalence about Forgiveness." *Royal Institute of Philosophy Supplements* 84: 161–85.

Hamilton, Richard Paul. 2006. "Love as a Contested Concept." *Journal for the Theory of Social Behaviour* 36 (3): 239–54.

Hemon, Aleksandar. 2018. "Fascism is Not an Idea to Be Debated, It's a Set of Actions to Fight." *Literary Hub*. November 1, 2018. https://lithub.com/fascism-is-not-an-idea-to-be-debated-its-a-set-of-actions-to-fight/.

Msimang, Sisonke. 2014. "Limpho Hani, Clive Derby-Lewis, and the Power of Refusing to Forgive." *Daily Maverick*, June 11, 2014.

———. 2016. "You may Free Apartheid Killers But You Can't Force Their Victims to Forgive." *The Guardian*, March 11, 2016.

Nussbaum, Martha C. 2016. *Anger and Forgiveness: Resentment, Generosity, Justice*. Oxford: Oxford University Press.

Orwell, George. 2000 [1968]. "Looking Back on the Spanish War." In *The Collected Essays, Journalism and Letters, II: My Country Right or Left, 1940–1943*, 249–67. Boston: David R. Godine.

Sartre, J. P. 1976. *Anti-Semite and Jew*. Translated by George J. Becker. New York: Schocken Books.

Strawson, P. F. 1974. "Freedom and Resentment." In *Freedom and Resentment*, editor by Sonia Orwell, Ian Angus, 1–25. London: Methuen.
Tessman, Lisa. 2005. *Burdened Virtues: Virtue Ethics for Liberatory Struggles*. Oxford: Oxford University Press.
Tuwim, Julian. 1944. "We Polish Jews." Retrieved from http://www.polish-jewish-heritage.org/Eng/RYTM_Tuwim_Eng.htm.
Wolfendale, Jessica. 2005. "The Hardened Heart: The Moral Dangers of Not Forgiving." *Journal of Social Philosophy* 36 (3): 344–63.

Epilogue

An Imperial Passion

Noell Birondo

This idea is key for me: to separate ideas from their circumstances is to remove philosophy from its history. For me, history cannot exist without philosophy, nor philosophy without history.

—Leopoldo Zea[1]

Western imperialism has received many different types of moral-political justifications, but one of the most historically influential justifications appeals to an allegedly universal form of human nature.[2] In the early modern period this traditional conception of human nature—based on a Western archetype, for example, Spanish, Dutch, British, French, German—opens up a logical space for considering the inhabitants of previously unknown lands as having a "less-than-human" nature.[3] This appeal to human nature originally found its inspiration in the philosophy of Aristotle, whose ethical thought pervaded the work of European philosophers at the outset of the early modern period and the modern age of empire. Indeed some Spanish writers—most famously, Juan Ginés de Sepúlveda (b. 1494)—explicitly appealed to Aristotle's moral-political philosophy in order to justify the conquest of the Americas in the early sixteenth century, for instance, to justify war against the Aztecs and other indigenous peoples.[4] At the time of European arrival, the Aztec civilization was easily the greatest in Mesoamerica—and yet the Europeans generally considered the Aztec people to be "barbaric," that is, less-than-fully-human. Aztec human sacrifice has, of course, been paradigmatic for late twentieth-century moral philosophers interested in moral relativism and intercultural understanding (e.g., Taylor 2002; Williams 1972, 24–26).[5]

Despite Aristotle's association with the history of Western imperialism, the past 40 years in moral philosophy have seen an explosion of interest in Aristotle's ethics, especially the idea that the virtues are indispensable to a good human life. Today, proponents of an Aristotelian ethics can insist that Aristotle's appeal to human nature can easily allow for—and even celebrate—the wide variety of lifestyles found in different cultural-historical contexts, that it can allow for a more flexible conception of the ways in which human nature is realized in different cultures and historical moments. Several philosophers have even developed accounts of previously overlooked virtues that people will need under conditions of oppression or social marginalization, conditions that are often the result of intercultural imperialism (e.g., Tessman 2005; Medina 2013).

These recent developments flow naturally from an Aristotelian orientation,[6] and such developments should lead us to consider, further, whether the assumptions that enabled Western imperialism might linger enough today to influence contemporary conceptions of the virtues—for instance, unreflective assumptions about European cultural supremacy and American exceptionalism. My hypothesis is that such unreflective and deep-seated cultural prejudices have shaped the development of Western ethics in various ways—as already illustrated in Sepúlveda's appeal to Aristotelian "natural slaves"—and that such prejudices partially explain the felt need for an extra-ethical foundation for the virtues, one provided by a universal and morally determinative form of human nature.[7] An acknowledgment of the actual world-historical development of Western ethics would therefore be a first but crucial step toward developing a more modest, intercultural approach to moral philosophy—an approach that aims precisely, in its open-endedness and epistemological humility, to supersede any form of imperialism (cf. Beuchot 2005, 126–127).

What I suggest here, much more specifically, is that a consideration of the actual historical collision of these two radically distinct belief systems, Christian and Aztec, reveals the possibility—even in the early modern period—of a helpfully "dialogical" ethics, one that strains to understand, from within, the perspective of alien others. This dialogical ethics disavows an "epistemology of ignorance"—it disavows the need *not* to know, the motivation *not* to learn, something that is arguably essential to Eurocentrism and the racialized hatred it nurtures.[8]

1. THE AZTECS AS ALIEN OTHERS

In order to illustrate this kind of dialogical ethics, I will discuss one of the central arguments deployed by the Spanish friar Bartolomé de Las Casas (*b*. 1484) in defense of Aztec human sacrifice.[9] This defense was originally delivered in front of the Council of the Indies, a tribunal convened in 1550 by Charles I of Spain—Charles V of the Holy Roman Empire—in order to determine the fate of the native inhabitants of the Indies (our Americas). The question before the Council was whether waging war against the native inhabitants of the Indies was morally justified in order to convert them to the Christian faith. This question seemed urgent given the apparently barbaric nature of the Aztecs and other indigenous peoples—something most notably demonstrated by the religiously sanctioned practice of human sacrifice and the equally morbid practice (or so it was believed: see Pagden 1982, 80–90) of consuming the flesh of the sacrificial victims. Despite these apparently barbaric practices—which genuinely horrified sixteenth-century Europeans—Las Casas defends the rationality of the Aztec way of life.

The discussion here should not of course be thought to question the gruesome nature of Aztec human sacrifice. One recent historian, drawing on authoritative sources, offers this lurid description:

> In a typical ritual . . . the helpless individual was confronted with the sight of the great sacrificial stone, stained with blood, which also matted the hair of the magnificently adorned priests. Seized by these gory apparitions, the victim was stretched backwards over the stone altar, each limb extended by a priest so that the back was arched and the chest stretched taut and raised high toward the heavens. A fifth priest struck open the chest with an obsidian knife, excised the heart with knife and hands and raised the fertile offering to the heavens, displaying to the gods the sacrificial fruit.[10]

Las Casas addresses the question of whether it would be just to wage war against the Aztecs, in the name of Christianity, in order to end this practice and to spare the lives of the innocent victims. The answer he gives is "No."

Las Casas's defiant approach to these issues already shows in his response to a different Spanish pretext for war. According to this different justification, war against the indigenous peoples is justified because they are guilty of killing Christians and therefore guilty of thwarting the spread of Christianity. Las Casas provides a sharp response. It highlights the contemporary relevance of thinking through his arguments—for instance, their relevance in evaluating past and present U.S. policy toward indigenous peoples and their descendants.[11] In response to this initial pretext for war—that war is justified because the Indians kill Christians and prevent the spread of the Gospel—Las Casas responds that although the Indians have indeed killed Christians, they have not killed them *qua* Christians. Rather, the Indians kill Christians *qua* perpetrators of violence, theft, rape, torture, and murder. This insightful distinction is a distinction of which any Aristotelian can be justly proud. Its contemporary relevance should be obvious.

2. THE LIMITATIONS OF THE "NATURAL LIGHT"

Overall, Las Casas argues that the Aztec way of life "cannot be excused in the sight of God" (that the Mexica are not objectively correct about the propriety of human sacrifice) but that it "can completely be excused in the sight of men" (1974, 221). What this means is that no one can justifiably blame the Aztecs for their violent religious practices—but certainly not the Spaniards.[12] Thus the following line of inquiry, with which Las Casas opens his discussion of human sacrifice, is certainly intended to sting. Las Casas says that "it would not be right to make war on them for this reason." This is because

> it is difficult to absorb in a short time the truth proclaimed to them. . . . Why will they believe such a proud, greedy, cruel, and rapacious nation? Why will they give up the religion of their ancestors, unanimously approved for so many centuries and supported by the authority of their teachers . . . ? (Las Casas 1974, 221)

In this passage Las Casas gestures toward one of his main arguments here, which is that the Aztecs are committing what he calls a "probable" error. In explaining the nature of probable error Las Casas makes direct reference to Aristotle's *Topics* Book I. Las Casas insists that "as the Philosopher says, that is said to be probable which is approved by all men, either the majority of wise men or by those whose wisdom has the greatest following" (1974, 220–221). Our starting points in ethics can only amount to the best ethical judgments that we and our society have managed to arrive at so far—the ethical judgments that seem most evident to us. This will be a subject that, as a historical matter, merits our ongoing ethical reflection, especially as we encounter previously unfamiliar "out-groups."[13]

Las Casas also argues that it is not easy to convince even rational people to abandon their cultural heritage in a short amount of time, especially given *only* the resources provided by the "natural light of reason"—that is, without the further epistemological resources that Las Casas believes are provided by "faith, grace, and doctrine." Waging war on the Aztecs would therefore be unjustified, because "it is difficult to absorb in a short time the truth proclaimed to them." Here Las Casas emphasizes that the "natural light of reason" displays epistemological limitations—that in the absence of divine revelation, natural reason seems to provide justificatory reasons *in favor* of human sacrifice (cf. Beuchot 1998, 28–30).

Las Casas mentions three strategies for defending this radical conclusion. His avoiding the third strategy, in spite of its apparent argumentative force, must have been determined by facts on the ground.

First, Las Casas appeals to biblical and historical precedents of human sacrifice that seem to illustrate its consistency with natural reason. He cites biblical episodes apparently indicating that God sometimes requires (or permits) human sacrifice. He also cites episodes of human sacrifice from Western civilizations: for instance, among the Greeks, Romans, and even "our own Spaniards" (1974, 224).[14]

Second, Las Casas argues that natural reason seems even to *require* sacrificing humans to God. He proceeds by first establishing four principles (mostly by appeal to theological and philosophical authorities): (a) No nation is so barbarous that it does not have at least some confused knowledge of God. (b) People are led by natural inclination to worship God according to their capacities and in their own ways. (c) There is no better way to worship God than by sacrifice, which is the principle act of *latria* (adoration). (d) Offering sacrifice to the true God, or to the one who is thought to be God, comes from the natural law, whereas the things to be offered to God are a matter of human law and positive legislation (1974, chap. 35). From these principles Las Casas derives the conclusion of the natural light of reason (given that no earthly thing is more valuable than human life). He writes:

> Therefore nature itself dictates and teaches those who do not have faith, grace, or doctrine, who live within the limitations of the light of nature, that, in spite of every contrary positive law, they ought to sacrifice victims to the true God or to the false god who is thought to be true, so that by offering a supremely precious thing they might be more grateful for the many favors they have received. (Las Casas 1974, 234)

A similar conclusion might also be reached by direct appeal to Christianity, as follows.

Third, Las Casas might have emphasized—something he does indeed mention—that Christianity itself essentially involves human sacrifice (Las Casas 1974, 239; cf. Pagden 1982, 227, n. 198). Hence the activity of human sacrifice cannot, by itself, be any sign of barbarism and cannot be contrary to the natural light of reason. The charitable view would be that the Aztecs are only partially mistaken here (in absence of divine revelation), since the sacrificial debt has already been paid in the person of Jesus Christ. Moreover, as I myself would emphasize, if one takes seriously the Roman Catholic doctrine of transubstantiation—that the bread and the wine of the Eucharist are not mere representations of the body and the blood of Christ, but that they literally are the body and the blood of Christ—then Christianity also involves a form of cannibalism.

What each of these strategies demonstrates is the possibility of a radical form of hermeneutical charity even regarding the allegedly barbarous practices of the Aztec people. Gustavo Gutiérrez nicely summarizes this in his magisterial study of Las Casas. Gutiérrez writes:

By attending to the customs, lifestyles, and religious freedom of the Indians, [Las Casas] created the necessary conditions for a dialogue to be conducted in respect for both parties. In this manner of dialogue, reason, not undue pressure, makes possible an integral presentation of the gospel message: now that message is offered—without prejudice to the values of the one proclaiming it—for the free acceptance of each hearer.

Such a dialogue will respect the rational freedom of both parties. It will also involve, not only the giving of reasons, but also the taking of them:

> If evangelization is a dialogue, it will not exist without an effort to understand the position of one's interlocutor from within, in such a way that one may sense the vital thrust of these positions and grasp their internal logic. Neither will it be possible unless one is ready to give *as well as to receive*.[15]

This passage characterizes the dialogical approach that I would suggest (but without any appeal to the supernatural). Although we should certainly be wary, in intercultural contexts, of any appeal to "evangelization," Las Casas's radical hermeneutical charity advances the discussion here.[16] Las Casas demonstrates the central virtue involved in a philosophical version of what is known in Latin America as *mestizaje* (or "admixture")—a radical hermeneutical charity that constitutes a distinctive form of epistemic justice. This epistemic virtue disavows an epistemology of ignorance by recognizing and—where appropriate—encouraging philosophical admixture. This philosophical admixture will occur, in my view, in at least the following two ways. First, it will occur across spatio-cultural geography and between different philosophical, cultural, and academic communities. This is a kind of cross-pollination—something that seems to be more often lauded than practiced. Second, it will occur across world-historical time, as a result of one's own historical (i.e., "genetic") philosophical inheritance, an inheritance that shapes one's overall philosophical outlook, one's framework of thought. This is a kind of dialogue with the past.[17] In the final section I gesture toward a more rounded view of each of these.

3. EPISTEMIC JUSTICE IN WESTERN ETHICS

In the *Nicomachean Ethics*, Aristotle restricts the audience of his ethical lectures on the grounds that those who engage in moral philosophy must have been well brought up or brought up in good habits (*NE* I.4, 1095b4–6). What is less frequently noticed is that this requirement—to have appropriate ethical starting points and to have a character sufficiently well-formed that one is not swayed by, for instance, unruly desires (*NE* I.3, 1095a4–6)—is also one that applies to Aristotle himself, and to Aristotelian moral philosophers in general, since they are also engaged in the practice of moral philosophy. But in the aftermath of the Spanish conquest of Tenochtitlán and other parts of the Americas, Western moral philosophy did not generally embrace the dialogical approach advocated by Las Casas. I believe we need to trace the history of the damage done to Western ethics in the long historical interim.[18]

By way of analogy, consider an episode of European barbarism, recorded from the perspective of Aztec witnesses immediately before the fall of Mexico. In this episode, Spanish soldiers block the exits during a festive religious gathering, allowing the soldiers to massacre the participants. This gruesome episode seems to be taking inspiration from something in Homer and giving inspiration to something in George R. R. Martin—except that this actual historical episode involves gross violations of human dignity:

> And when they had closed them off . . . they then entered the temple courtyard to slay them . . . they surrounded those who danced whereupon they went among the drums. Then they struck the arms of the one who beat the drums; they severed both his hands, and afterwards struck his neck, [so that] his neck [and head] flew off, falling far away. . . . Of some, they struck the belly, and their entrails streamed forth. And when one in vain would run, he would only drag his entrails like something raw, as he tried to flee. . . .
>
> And the blood of the chieftains ran like water; it spread out slippery, and a foul odor rose from the blood. And the entrails lay as if dragged out. And the Spaniards walked everywhere, searching the tribal temples; they went making thrusts everywhere in case someone were hidden there. Everywhere they went, ransacking every tribal temple they hunted.[19]

Ultimately it is unclear whether Anglo-American moral philosophy has displayed an understanding of cultural others that has been *much* better than the understanding displayed in this historical episode. Whether intentionally or not, mainstream Anglo-American philosophy has been remarkably effective at securing its borders against what many of its practitioners consider to be alien influences. This includes influences from other cultures and from demographics other than the dominantly situated demographic in the profession, from other academic disciplines (for instance, history, sociology, and anthropology, although this is improving in some quarters), and from philosophical methodologies other than the methodologies developed within Anglo-American philosophy in the early- and mid-twentieth century and still insisted upon by some philosophers today as the defining mark of any genuine philosophy. Indeed, some philosophers seem to be eerily at home with the history of Western imperialism. This is a history that such philosophers seem to think can be neatly left in the past, in such a way that they—and their favored research projects—can continue to benefit from centuries of past injustice.

Obviously I cannot fully develop these suggestions here.[20] Instead of doing so, I will emphasize something that I think is utterly crucial for developing a plausible moral philosophy informed by an intercultural perspective. This is a radical form of cultural self-scrutiny, especially a scrutiny of the ethical and epistemic prejudices that are embedded within our social-historical framework of thought—a framework of thought that is of course usually taken for granted. It ceases to be taken for granted—or *can* do so—when it comes into contact with radically alternative frameworks, ones that are culturally or historically distant from our own current location. To put the point differently: contemporary moral philosophers need to pay greater attention to history in at least two senses. We need a better understanding of the history and the historicity of philosophy, an understanding of the former that is not willfully inaccurate and that disavows the arrogance of knowing only one's own philosophical tradition.[21] We also need a better appreciation of our current place in history and our cultural particularity—a critical understanding of the framework of thought that can of course seem inevitable to us. This would be a form of Western ethics that takes seriously those genealogical approaches that still remain *very* much against-the-current in contemporary moral philosophy. It would also be a form of moral philosophy that, in better appreciating our current (globalized, multicultural, postcolonial/neocolonial) place in history, strains to embody the virtues of epistemic justice.

NOTES

1. Zea and Maciel (1985, 11). Leopoldo Zea was one of the most influential philosophers in Mexico in the twentieth century. His most important work for my discussion here is Zea (1992 [1957]). In the 1985 interview with David Maciel, Zea describes certain negative U.S. perspectives on Mexican and Latin American philosophy as involving a kind of "imperial passion" (Zea and Maciel 1985, 12).

2. This closing chapter is a condensed and mildly revised version of Birondo (2020a), which was awarded the American Philosophical Association's 2019 Essay Prize in Latin American Thought. The chapter considers racialized hatred as a product of Western imperialism, underwritten by European appropriations of Aristotle and willful forms of ignorance. It is reprinted here with permission. References are listed in the General Bibliography.

3. Cf. Pagden (1982, chaps. 1–2), Alcoff (2017). On the earliest debates concerning the general capacity of the indigenous peoples of the Americas, see Hanke (1974, chap. 1).

4. Beuchot (1998, 28) mentions the Scottish philosopher John Major (Mair) (*b.* 1467) and the Spanish bishop Juan de Quevedo (*b.* 1450) as Sepúlveda's precursors in the appeal to Aristotelian "natural slaves." Cf. Hanke (1959, 14–16).

5. Alcoff (2017, 402) argues that the Eurocentrism involved here essentially involves an epistemology of ignorance: "Such a construction of barbarian identity removes any motivation to learn other ways or creeds. The claim that those designated are inferior and inadequate thinkers is not justified by a study and evaluation of different practices, customs, forms of religiosity, institutions, beliefs, and the like, but simply on the observation that a group is not-Christian or not-rational or *not-self*." She argues that Las Casas recognizes his own perspective *as* a perspective, and hence that he can "see the Other as having a substantive difference, and not simply as a 'not-self'" (2017, 405). Cf. Gutiérrez (1993, passim, and 188–189, quoted on p. 256 of the main text); Beuchot (1998, 26–36). See also Pagden (1982, chap. 4) on the move to considering the native peoples of the Americas to be "nature's children."

6. Philosophers who are explicitly indebted to Aristotle here include Tessman (2005) and Fricker (2007). Recent discussions of epistemic injustice are all ultimately indebted to the revival of Aristotelian ethics in the latter part of the twentieth century. In future work I aim to urge the importance of this genealogical fact for the future development of any plausible neo-Aristotelian ethics: such an ethics must *embody* epistemic justice.

7. By the phrase "Western ethics" I mean to capture both Western moral philosophy and Western morality, which I take to be largely symbiotic, even if there is no necessary causal influence between the two. It may be that elements of A and B are both made possible by, and nurtured in the soil of, a third and more basic element C, and thereafter A and B feed off each other in certain ways. Cf. Ameriks (2022) on Kantian dignity and the U.S. Declaration of Independence.

8. See Alcoff (2017, 402). Cf. Mills (2007); Pohlhaus (2012); Fricker (2016); Silva (2022).

9. To speak of the Aztecs here is perfectly appropriate, in spite of the fact that the conquest of Tenochtitlán (1521), the Aztec capital, antedates the debate between Las Casas and Sepúlveda at Valladolid (1550–1551). In the minds of sixteenth-century Europeans, nothing compared to what the Spaniards witnessed at Tenochtitlán. Here I am following the lead of Anthony Pagden, who notes that "the most famous of the Amerindian cannibals were, of course, the Mexica, whose spectacular bouts of human sacrifice were assumed to have been followed by orgiastic feasts on the flesh of the victims" (1982, 83).

10. Pennock (2008, 21); cf. *Florentine Codex* 2.2.

11. On the contemporary relevance of the Valladolid debate, see the excellent recent treatment in Santana (2019); see also the magisterial discussion of Las Casas in Gutiérrez (1993). The best short book on the debate in English—which encompasses both its prelude and its aftermath—remains Hanke (1959). See also the more detailed discussion in Hanke (1974).

12. For details, see Las Casas (1992). It has been long recognized that for rhetorical and political purposes (this was quite common) Las Casas engages in certain exaggerations of the devastation he documents, especially regarding magnitude (e.g.,

number of deaths). For contemporary discussions that significantly temper the "Black Legend" of unparalleled Spanish brutality, see Greer et al. (2007).

13. On Aristotle's method in ethics, Kraut (2008) provides a helpful overview, noting on Aristotle's behalf that when we engage in ethical inquiry, "it is reasonable to throw into the mixture of opinions that we take seriously not only the theories of those who have spent their lives studying the subject, but also the common moral consciousness, not only of our time and place, but of other times and places as well" (80).

14. For a helpful discussion of Las Casas's use of historical sources here, see Carman (2016, 285–288).

15. Gutiérrez (1993, 188–189, my emphasis). Gutiérrez finds a similar hermeneutical charity in the work, much later, of Sor Juana Inés de la Cruz (*b*. 1648): see Gutiérrez (1993, 525, n. 69). On the importance of taking as well as giving reasons in intercultural contexts, see Birondo (2017), to which the original version of this chapter (Birondo 2020a) is a kind of late addendum.

16. This seems to be the context in which to understand Alcoff's claim that in contrast to a Cartesian form of self-understanding, Las Casas is "groping toward a different self-understanding, in which one's own inclinations are analyzed in relation to their social context" (2017, 405). She immediately adds something that could be helpful for contemporary philosophers: "Within this approach, dialogic models of philosophical thought, especially those that can span cultures and belief systems, are non-negotiable necessities for the development of understanding." Castro (2007) and von Vacano (2012) reach rather harsher verdicts on Las Casas's evangelism. But neither author seems to me adequately to address Gutiérrez's painstaking case for the claim that a "single idea" governs Las Casas's *Apología*: "respect for the Indians' religious customs" (1993, 174).

17. Beuchot (2005) helpfully argues for the type of anti-presentism that I mention here. He argues that contemporary Mexican philosophers can benefit from a neo-Aristotelian outlook that appreciates the influence of cultural-historical tradition—he cites the work of Alasdair MacIntyre and Hans-Georg Gadamer (127). Beuchot reasonably asks, "If it is true that we live within a tradition, how can we advance in it or even oppose it if we do not have at least a minimum knowledge of it?" (114). The right hermeneutical balance can nevertheless be, in any specific context, difficult to strike: see O'Gorman (2017 [1960]) on understanding Aztec archeological artifacts, specifically the magnificent statue of Coatlicue in the National Museum of Anthropology in Mexico City.

18. The valuable collection of essays in Miller (2017) provides a good beginning here—it considers the historical reception of Aristotle's ethics—except that there is no consideration of the European encounter with the Americas or the Latin American world. A valuable corrective can be found in Aspe (2018).

19. *Florentine Codex* 12.20, 53–54.

20. The historiographical study in Park (2013), the polemic by Van Norden and Garfield (2017), and the work of Robert Bernasconi, Walter Mignolo, and Charles W. Mills (among others) have helpfully gotten the discussion going, as have recent attempts to generate "new histories of philosophy"—but see also Allais (2016) and Ameriks (2022) for helpfully more sympathetic views of the late eighteenth century

and Kant in particular. Recent work on Aztec ethics and Aristotle (Purcell 2017) and Aztec metaphysics (Maffie 2014) illustrates another type of void waiting to be filled.

21. Latin American philosophy provides an epistemological opportunity for Anglo-American philosophy: to scrutinize its own historical development from the radically alternative perspective of world-historical marginality. This theme in Latin American thought—the theme of marginality—has been especially emphasized in the work of Leopoldo Zea and Enrique Dussel. See, for instance, Zea (1992 [1957]) and Dussel (1995); see also Alcoff (2017) and Schutte (1993). On the dangers that can prevent dominantly situated individuals from taking advantage of such epistemological opportunities, see Mills (2007), Pohlhaus (2012), and Fricker (2016).

Bibliography

Abbey, Edward. 1988. *Desert Solitaire: A Season in the Wilderness.* Tucson: University of Arizona Press.
———. 1990. *A Voice Crying in the Wilderness (Vox Clamantis en Deserto): Notes from a Secret Journal.* New York: St Martin's Press.
Ahmed, Sara. 2014. *The Cultural Politics of Emotions.* 2nd ed. Edinburgh: Edinburgh University Press.
Alcoff, Linda Martín. 2017. "Philosophy and Philosophical Practice: Eurocentrism as an Epistemology of Ignorance." In *The Routledge Handbook of Epistemic Injustice*, edited by Ian James Kidd, José Medina, and Gaile Pohlhaus, Jr., 397–408. New York: Routledge.
Allais, Lucy. 2016. "Kant's Racism." *Philosophical Papers* 45 (1 and 2): 1–36.
Allport, Gordon W. 1954. *The Nature of Prejudice.* Reading: Addison-Wesley.
Alvarez, M. 2017. "Reasons for Action: Justification, Motivation, Explanation." In *The Stanford Encyclopedia of Philosophy*, edited by Edward N. Zalta. https://plato.stanford.edu/archives/win2017/entries/reasons-just-vs-expl/.
Alford, C. Fred. 2005. "Hate is the Imitation of Love." In *The Psychology of Hate*, edited by Robert J. Sternberg, 235–54. Washington, DC: American Psychological Association.
Ameriks, Karl. 2022. "Kant and Dignity: Missed Connections with the United States." In *The Court of Reason: Proceedings of the 13th International Kant Congress*, Vol. 1, edited by Beatrix Himmelmann and Camilla Serck-Hanssen, 27–48. Berlin: de Gruyter.
Aquinas, Thomas. 1981. *Summa Theologica.* Translated by the Fathers of the English Dominican Province. Westminster, MD: Christian Classics.
Aristotle. 1946. *Rhetorica.* Translated by W. Rhys Roberts. In *The Works of Aristotle*, edited by W. D. Ross, vol. 11. Oxford: Clarendon Press.
———. 2006. *On Rhetoric: A Theory of Civic Discourse.* Translated by George A. Kennedy. New York and Oxford: Oxford University Press.

———. 2009. *The Nicomachean Ethics*. Translated by David Ross. New York: Oxford University Press.

Arnold, Dan and Alicia Turner. 2018. "Why Are We Surprised When Buddhists Are Violent?" *New York Times*, March 5, 2018. https://www.nytimes.com/2018/03/05/opinion/buddhists-violence-tolerance.html. Accessed March 7, 2021.

Aronson, Harvey B. 1980. *Love and Sympathy in Theravāda Buddhism*. Delhi: Motilal Banarsidass.

Arp, Kristana. 2004. Introduction to de Beauvoir's "An Eye for an Eye." In *Philosophical Writings*, edited by Margaret A. Simons, 239–44. Urbana: University of Illinois Press.

Arpaly, Nomy. 2002. "On Acting Rationally Against One's Best Judgment." In *Unprincipled Virtue: An Inquiry into Moral Agency*, 33–65. Oxford: Oxford University Press.

Arpaly, Nomy and Timothy Schroeder. 2012. "Deliberation and Acting for Reasons." *Philosophical Review* 121 (2): 209–39.

Aspe Armella, Virginia. 2018. *Aristóteles y Nueva España*. San Luis Potosí: Universidad Autónoma de San Luis Potosí, Facultad de Ciencias Sociales y Humanidades.

Atkinson, Ti-Grace. 1974. *Amazon Odyssey*. New York: Link Books.

Aumer, Katherine, Anne Cathrine Krebs Bahn, and Sean Harris. 2015. "Through the Looking Glass, Darkly: Perceptions of Hate in Interpersonal Relationships." *Journal of Relationships Research* 6 (4): 1–7.

Aumer, Katherine, Anne Cathrine Krebs Bahn, Courtney Janicki, Nicolas Guzman, Natalie Pierson, Susanne Estelle Strand, and Helene Totlund. 2016. "Can't Let It Go: Hate in Interpersonal Relationships." *Journal of Relationships Research* 7 (2): 1–9.

Aumer-Ryan, Katherine, and Elaine Hatfield. 2007. "The Design of Everyday Hate: A Qualitative and Quantitative Analysis." *Interpersona* 1 (2): 143–72.

Ayre, Julie, Miriam Lum On, Kim Webster, Michelle Gourley, and Lynelle Moon. 2016. *Examination of the Burden of Disease of Intimate Partner Violence against Women in 2011: Final Report*. Sydney: ANROWS.

Baier, Annette. 1985. *Postures of the Mind: Essays on Mind and Morals*. Minneapolis: University of Minnesota Press.

Baldwin, James. 1992. *Another Country*. New York: Vintage.

———. 1998. "Notes of a Native Son." In *James Baldwin: Collected Essays*, edited by Toni Morrison, 63–84. New York: Library of America.

Ballard, John A., and Aliecia J. McDowell. 1991. "Hate and Combat Behavior." *Armed Forces & Society* 17 (2): 229–41.

Bari, Judi. 1991. "Why I Am Not a Misanthrope." *Earth First! Journal* 2: 25.

Barney, Rachel. 2020. "Becoming Bad: Aristotle on Vice and Moral Habituation." *Oxford Studies in Ancient Philosophy* 57: 273–308.

Barrett, Lisa Feldman. 2012. "Emotions are Real." *Emotion* 12 (3): 413–29.

Bar-Tal, Daniel. 2007. "Sociopsychological Foundations of Intractable Conflicts." *American Behavioral Scientist* 50 (11): 1430–53.

Bar-Tal, Daniel, Lily Chernyak-Hai, Noa Schori, and Ayelet Gundar. 2009. "A Sense of Self-Perceived Collective Victimhood in Intractable Conflicts." *International Review of the Red Cross* 91 (874): 229–77.
Bar-Tal, Daniel, Eran Halperin, and Joseph De Rivera. 2007. "Collective Emotions in Conflict Situations: Societal Implications." *Journal of Social Issues* 63 (2): 441–60.
Bartholomeusz, Tessa. 1999. "In Defense of Dharma: Just-War Ideology in Buddhist Sri Lanka." *Journal of Buddhist Ethics* 6: 1–16.
———. 2002. *In Defense of Dharma: Just-War Ideology in Buddhist Sri Lanka*. London: Routledge.
Bartky, Sandra Lee. 1990. "Shame and Gender." In *Femininity and Domination: Studies in the Phenomenology of Oppression*, 83–98. New York: Routledge.
Baumeister, Roy F., and David A. Butz. 2005. "Roots of Hate, Violence, and Evil." In *The Psychology of Hate*, edited by Robert J. Sternberg, 87–102. Washington, DC: American Psychological Association.
Beauvoir, Simone de. 2004. "An Eye for an Eye." In *Philosophical Writings*, edited by Margaret A. Simons, 245–60. Urbana: University of Illinois Press.
Beiser, Frederick C. 2016. *Weltschmerz: Pessimism in German Philosophy, 1860–1900*. Oxford: Oxford University Press.
Bell, Macalester. 2011. "Globalist Attitudes and the Fittingness Objection." *The Philosophical Quarterly* 61 (244): 449–72.
Beltrán, Cristina. 2020. *Cruelty as Citizenship: How Migrant Suffering Sustains White Democracy*. Minneapolis: University of Minnesota Press.
Bem, Daryl J. 1972. "Self-Perception Theory." *Advances in Experimental Social Psychology* 6: 1–62.
Bendik-Keymer, Jeremy. 2006. *The Ecological Life: Discovering Citizenship and a Sense of Humanity*. New York: Rowman & Littlefield.
Benjamin, Jessica. 1988. *The Bonds of Love: Psychoanalysis, Feminism, and the Problem of Domination*. New York: Pantheon Books.
Ben-Ze'ev, Aaron. 1992. "Emotional and Moral Evaluations." *Metaphilosophy* 23 (3): 214–29.
———. 2000. *The Subtlety of Emotions*. Cambridge: The MIT Press.
———. 2008. "Hating the One You Love." *Philosophia* 36 (3): 277–83.
———. 2010. "The Thing Called Emotion." In *The Oxford Handbook of Philosophy of Emotion*, edited by Peter Goldie, 63–94. Oxford: Oxford University Press.
———. 2018. "Is Hate Worst When It Is Fresh? The Development of Hate Over Time?" *Emotion Review* 10 (4): 322–24.
Bennett, Christopher. 2021. "The Problem of Expressive Action." *Philosophy* 96 (2): 1–24. DOI: https://doi.org/10.1017/S0031819120000467.
Berkowitz, Leonard. 2005. "On Hate and Its Determinants: Some Affective and Cognitive Influences." In *The Psychology of Hate*, edited by Robert J. Sternberg, 155–83. Washington, DC: American Psychological Association.
Bernier, Annie, and Mary Dozier. 2002. "Assessing Adult Attachment: Empirical Sophistication and Conceptual Bases." *Attachment and Human Development* 4 (2): 171–9.

Betz, Hand-Georg. 1994. *Radical Right-Wing Populism in Western Europe*. London: Macmillan.
Beuchot, Mauricio. 1998. *The History of Philosophy in Colonial Mexico*. Translated by Elizabeth Millán. Washington, DC: The Catholic University of America Press.
———. 2005. "The Study of Philosophy's History in Mexico as a Foundation for Doing Mexican Philosophy." In *The Role of History in Latin American Philosophy: Contemporary Perspectives*, edited by Arleen Salles and Elizabeth Millán-Zaibert, 109–29. Albany: State University of New York Press.
Birondo, Noell. 2017. "Virtue and Prejudice: Giving and Taking Reasons." In *Virtue's Reasons: New Essays on Virtue, Character, and Reasons*, edited by Noell Birondo and S. Stewart Braun, 189–202. New York: Routledge. First published in *The Monist* 99 (2016): 212–23.
———. 2020a. "The Virtues of Mestizaje: Lessons from Las Casas on Aztec Human Sacrifice." *APA Newsletter on Hispanic/Latino Issues in Philosophy* 19 (2): 2–8.
———. 2020b. "Patriotism and Character: Some Aristotelian Observations." In *Handbook of Patriotism*, edited by Mitja Sardoč. Cham: Springer.
Blair, James, Derek Mitchell, and Karina Blair. 2005. *The Psychopath: Emotion and the Brain*. Oxford: Blackwell.
Bodhi, Bhikkhu, trans. 2000. *The Connected Discourses of the Buddha: A New Translation of the Saṃyutta Nikāya*. 2 Vols. Boston: Wisdom Publications.
———, ed. 2005. *In the Buddha's Words: An Anthology of Discourses from the Pāli Canon*. Boston: Wisdom Publications.
———, trans. 2012. *The Numerical Discourses of the Buddha: A Translation of the Aṅguttara Nikāya*. Boston: Wisdom Publications.
Bommarito, Nicolas. 2011. "Bile and Bodhisattvas: Śāntideva on Justified Anger." *Journal of Buddhist Ethics* 18: 356–81.
Bonhoeffer, Dietrich. 1955. *Ethics*. Edited by Eberhard Bethge. Translated by Neville Horton Smith. New York: MacMillan.
Bookchin, Murray and Dave Foreman, eds.1991. *Defending the Earth: A Debate*. Montréal and New York: Black Rose Books.
Borges, Jorge Luis. 1999. "The Cruel Redeemer Lazarus Morell." In *Collected Fictions*, 6–12. Harmondsworth: Penguin.
Brady, Michael. 2013. *Emotional Insight: The Epistemic Role of Emotional Experience*. Oxford: Oxford University Press.
Brecht, Bertolt. 2003. "To Those Born Later." In *Bertolt Brecht: Poetry and Prose*, edited by Reinhold Grimm with the collaboration of Caroline Molina y Vedia, 70–75. New York: Continuum.
Brennan, Geoffrey, Lina Eriksson, Robert Goodin, and Nicholas Southwood. 2013. *Explaining Norms*. Oxford: Oxford University Press.
Brogaard, Berit. 2020. *Hatred: Understanding Our Most Dangerous Emotion*. New York: Oxford University Press.
Brontë, Charlotte. 1996. *Jane Eyre*. London: Penguin Books.
Brown, Mark. 2020. "Gloria Steinem Says TV Drama of 1970s Feminist History 'Ridiculous'." *The Guardian*, May 23, 2020.

Brudholm, Thomas. 2008. *Resentment's Virtue: Jean Améry and the Refusal to Forgive*. Philadelphia: Temple University Press.

———. 2010. "Hatred as an Attitude." *Philosophical Papers* 39 (3): 289–313.

Brudholm, Thomas and Brigid Schepelern Johansen. 2018. "Pondering Hatred." In *Emotions and Mass Atrocity: Philosophical and Theoretical Explorations*, edited by Thomas Brudholm and Johannes Lang, 81–103. New York: Cambridge University Press.

Buchwald, Emilie, Pamela R. Fletcher, and Martha Roth. 1993. "Editors' Preface." In *Transforming a Rape Culture*, edited by Emilie Buchwald, Pamela R. Fletcher, and Martha Roth, 1–6. Minneapolis: Milkweed Editions.

Budapest, Zsuzsanna. 1980. *The Holy Book of Women's Mysteries*. Berkeley: Wingbow Press.

Buddharakkhita, Acharya, trans. 1996. *The Dhammapada: The Buddha's Path of Wisdom*. 2nd ed. Kandy, Sri Lanka: Buddhist Publication Society.

Burnyeat, M. F. 1980. "Aristotle on Learning to be Good." In *Essays on Aristotle's Ethics*, edited by Amélie Oksenberg Rorty, 69–92. Berkeley: University of California Press.

Callicott, J. Baird. 1998. "'Back Together Again' Again." *Environmental Values* 7: 461–75.

———. 1999. *Beyond the Land Ethic: More Essays in Environmental Philosophy*. New York: SUNY Press.

Canetti, Daphna, Julia Elad-Strenger, Iris Lavi, Dana Guy, and Daniel Bar-Tal. 2017. "Exposure to Violence, Ethos of Conflict, and Support for Compromise: Survey in Israel, East Jerusalem, West Bank, and in Gaza." *Journal of Conflict Resolution* 61 (1): 84–113.

Canetti, Daphna, Eric Russ, Judith Luborsky, James I. Gerhart, and Stephen E. Hobfoll. 2014. "Inflamed by the Flames? The Impact of Terrorism and War on Immunity." *Journal of Traumatic Stress* 27 (3): 345–52.

Canetti-Nisim, Daphna, Gal Ariely, and Eran Halperin. 2008. "Life, Pocketbook, or Culture: The Role of Perceived Security Threats in Promoting Exclusionist Political Attitudes toward Minorities in Israel." *Political Research Quarterly* 61 (1): 90–103.

Carlsson, Ulrika. "Tragedy and Resentment." *Mind* 127 (508): 1169–91.

Carman, Glen. 2016. "Human Sacrifice and Natural Law in Las Casas's *Apologia*." *Colonial Latin American Review* 25 (3): 278–99.

Carman, Mary. 2018a. "Emotionally Guiding Our Actions." *Canadian Journal of Philosophy* 48 (1): 43–64.

———. 2018b. "How Emotions Do Not Provide Reasons to Act." *Philosophia* 46 (3): 555–74. DOI: https://doi.org/10.1007/s11406-017-9896-y.

Cassirer, Ernst. 1945. *Rousseau-Kant-Goethe*. Princeton: Princeton University Press.

Castro, Daniel. 2007. *Another Face of Empire: Bartolomé de Las Casas, Indigenous Rights, and Ecclesiastical Imperialism*. Durham: Duke University Press.

Cavadino, Michael. 2014. "Should Hate Crime Be Sentenced More Severely?" *Contemporary Issues in Law* 13 (1): 1–18.

Center for the Study of Hate and Extremism, CSUSB. 2021. "Report to the Nation: Anti-Asian Prejudice and Hate Crime—City Data Chart." June 1, 2021. https://www.csusb.edu/hate-and-extremism-center. Accessed June 27, 2021.

Césaire, Aimé. 1972 [1955]. *Discourse on Colonialism*. Translated by Joan Pinkham. New York and London: Monthly Review Press.
Chakraborti, Neil, and Jon Garland, eds. 2015. *Responding to Hate Crime: The Case for Connecting Policy and Research*. Bristol: Policy Press.
Chesler, Phyllis. 2001. *Women's Inhumanity to Women*. Chicago: Lawrence Hill Books.
———. 2018 [1972]. *Women and Madness*. Chicago: Lawrence Hill Books.
———. 2018. *A Politically Incorrect Feminist*. New York: St. Martin's Press.
Clore, Gerald. 1994. "Why Emotions Require Cognition." In *The Nature of Emotion*, edited by Paul Ekman and Richard J. Davidson, 181–91. Oxford: Oxford University Press.
Collins, Randall. 2009. "Social Movements and the Focus of Emotional Attention." In *Passionate Politics: Emotions and Social Movements*, edited by Jeff Goodwin, James Jasper, and Francesca Polletta, 27–44. Chicago: University of Chicago Press.
Condon, Paul et al. 2013. "Meditation Increases Compassionate Responses to Suffering." *Psychological Science* 24: 2125–7.
Cone, James H. 2013. *The Cross and the Lynching Tree*. New York: Orbis Books.
Cooper, David E. 2018. *Animals and Misanthropy*. Abingdon: Routledge.
Cooper, John M. 1996. "An Aristotelian Theory of the Emotions." In *Essays on Aristotle's Rhetoric*, edited by Amélie Oksenberg Rorty, 238–57. Berkeley: University of California Press).
———. 1999. "Contemplation and Happiness: A Reconsideration." In *Reason and Emotion: Essays on Ancient Moral Psychology and Ethical Theory*, 212–36. Princeton: Princeton University Press.
Corrigan, John. 2008. "Religious Hatred." In *The Oxford Handbook of Religion and Emotion*, edited by John Corrigan, 333–45. New York: Oxford University Press.
Coulthard, Glen Sean. 2014. *Red Skin, White Masks: Rejecting the Colonial Politics of Recognition*. Minneapolis: University of Minnesota Press.
Cronon, William. 1998. "The Trouble with Wilderness, or, Getting Back to the Wrong Nature." In *The Great Wilderness Debate*, edited by J. Baird Callicott and Michael Nelson, 471–98. Athens, GA: University of Georgia Press.
Curry, Patrick. 2006. *Ecological Ethics: An Introduction*. Cambridge: Polity.
Curzer, Howard J. 2002. "Aristotle's Painful Path to Virtue." *Journal of the History of Philosophy* 40: 141–62.
———. 2017. "The Philosophers' Anger: Review of Martha Nussbaum, *Anger and Forgiveness*." *Los Angeles Review of Books*, November 2, 2017.
Dalai Lama XIV. 1997. *Healing Anger: The Power of Patience from a Buddhist Perspective*. Ithaca: Snow Lion Publications.
———. 1998a. "Human Rights and Universal Responsibility." In *Buddhism and Human Rights*, edited by Damien Keown, Charles S. Prebish, and Wayne R. Husted, xvii–xxi. Richmond Surry: Curzon.
———. 1998b. "Humanity's Concern for Human Rights." In *Reflections on the Universal Declaration of Human Rights: A Fiftieth Anniversary Anthology*, edited by Barend van der Heijden and Bahia Tahzib-Lie, 101–6. The Hague: Martinus Nijhoff Publishers.

D'Arms, Justin and Daniel Jacobson. 2000. "The Moralistic Fallacy: On the 'Appropriateness' of Emotions." *Philosophy and Phenomenological Research* 61 (1): 65–90.
Davies, Kimberly A. 1997. "Voluntary Exposure to Pornography and Men's Attitudes Toward Feminism and Rape." *Journal of Sex Research* 34 (2): 131–7.
Deigh, John. 1966. *The Sources of Moral Agency*. Cambridge: Cambridge University Press.
———. 1999. "All Kinds of Guilt." *Law and Philosophy* 18 (4): 313–25.
De Leersnyder, Jozefien, Michael Boiger, and Batja Mesquita. 2015. "Cultural Differences in Emotions." In *Emerging Trends in the Social and Behavioral Sciences: An Interdisciplinary, Searchable, and Linkable Resource*, edited by Robert A. Scott, Marlis Buchmann, and Stephen M. Kosslyn. E-book. New York: Wiley.
dell'Olio, Anselma. n.d. "Divisiveness and Self-Destruction in the Women's Movement: A Letter of Resignation." Printed mimeograph, circa 1970s.
Delvaux, Ellen, Loes Meeussen, and Batja Mesquita. 2015. "Feel Like You Belong: On the Bidirectional Link Between Emotional Fit and Group Identification in Task Groups." *Frontiers in Psychology* 6: 1106. DOI: https://doi.org/10.3389/fpsyg.2015.01106 .
Diener, Ed and Carol Diener. 1996. "Most People are Happy." *Psychological Science* 7 (3): 181–5.
Dienstag, Joshua Foa. 2009. *Pessimism: Philosophy, Ethic, Spirit*. Princeton: Princeton University Press.
Dixley, Allison. 2014. *Breast Intentions: How Women Sabotage Breastfeeding for Themselves and Others*. London: Pinter & Martin.
Doherty, Brian. 2005. *Ideas and Action in the Green Movement*. London: Routledge.
Dow, Jamie. 2015. *Passions and Persuasion in Aristotle's Rhetoric*. Oxford: Oxford University Press.
Dreyfus, Georges. 1995. "Meditation as Ethical Activity." *Journal of Buddhist Ethics* 2: 28–54.
———. 2001. "Is Compassion an Emotion: A Cross-Cultural Exploration." In *Visions of Compassion: Western Scientists and Tibetan Buddhists Examine Human Nature*, edited by Richard J. Davidson and Anne Harrington, 31–45. New York: Oxford University Press.
Dussel, Enrique. 1995. *The Invention of the Americas: Eclipse of 'the Other' and the Myth of Modernity*. Translated by Michael D. Barber. New York: Continuum.
Dworkin, Andrea. 1974. *Woman Hating*. New York: E. P. Dutton.
———. 1976. *Our Blood: Prophecies and Discourses on Sexual Politics*. New York: Perigee.
———. 2007 [1987]. *Intercourse*. New York: Basic Books.
Eagleton, Terry. 2010. *On Evil*. New Haven: Yale University Press.
Ekman, Paul. 1992. "An Argument for Basic Emotions." *Cognition and Emotion* 6 (3–4): 169–200.
Ellis, Havelock. 1908. *Studies in the Psychology of Sex*. 2nd ed., Vol. 2. Philadelphia: F. A. Davis.
Elster, Jon. 1999. *Alchemies of the Mind: Rationality and the Emotions*. Cambridge: Cambridge University Press.

Er-rafiy, Abdelatif, and Markus Brauer. 2013. "Modifying Perceived Variability: Four Laboratory and Field Experiments Show the Effectiveness of a Ready-to-be-used Prejudice Intervention." *Journal of Applied Social Psychology* 43 (4): 840–53.

Faludi, Susan. "Death of a Revolutionary." *The New Yorker*, April 15, 2013.

Fanon, Franz. 2008 [1952]. *Black Skin, White Masks*. Translated by Richard Philcox. New York: Grove Press.

Fields, Karen E., and Barbara J. Fields. 2014. *Racecraft: The Soul of Inequality in American Life*. New York: Verso.

Filipovic, Jill. "The Tragic Irony of Feminists Trashing Each Other." *The Guardian*, May 2, 2013.

Firestone, Shulamith. 1970. *The Dialectic of Sex: The Case for Feminist Revolution*. New York: William Morrow.

Fischer, Agneta H., and Roger Giner-Sorolla. 2016. "Contempt: Derogating Others While Keeping Calm." *Emotion Review* 8: 346–57.

Fischer, Agneta, Eran Halperin, Daphna Canetti, and Alba Jasini. 2018. "Why We Hate." *Emotion Review* 10 (4): 309–20. Reprinted in this volume, chap. 7.

Fischer, Agneta H., and Antony S. R. Manstead. 2016. "Social Functions of Emotion and Emotion Regulation." In *Handbook of Emotions*, edited by Lisa Feldman Barrett, Michael Lewis, and Jennette M. Haviland-Jones, 424–39. 4th ed. New York: Guilford Press.

Fischer, Agneta H., and Ira J. Roseman. 2007. "Beat Them or Ban Them: The Characteristics and Social Functions of Anger and Contempt." *Journal of Personality and Social Psychology* 93 (3): 103–15.

Fitness, Julie. 2000. "Anger in the Workplace: An Emotion Script Approach to Anger Episodes Between Workers and Their Superiors, Co-workers and Subordinates." *Journal of Organizational Behavior* 21 (2): 147–62.

Fitness, Julie, and Garth J. O. Fletcher. 1993. "Love, Hate, Anger and Jealousy in Close Relationships: A Prototype and Cognitive Appraisal Analysis." *Journal of Personality and Social Psychology* 65 (5): 942–58.

Frankfurt, Harry. 1999. "Autonomy, Necessity, and Love." In *Necessity, Volition, and Love*, 129–41. Cambridge: Cambridge University Press.

Freeman, Jo. 1976. "Trashing: The Dark Side of Sisterhood." *Ms.*, April 1976. https://www.jofreeman.com/joreen/trashing.htm.

Freud, Sigmund. 1915. "Instincts and their Vicissitudes." In *The Standard Edition of The Complete Psychological Works of Sigmund Freud*, vol. 14 (1914–1916), translated by James Strachey in collaboration with Anna Freud, first published 1957. London: Hogarth Press. Hogarth Press.

———. 1915. "Mourning and Melancholia." *The Standard Edition of the Complete Psychological Works of Sigmund Freud*, vol. 14 (1914–1916), translated by James Strachey in collaboration with Anna Freud, first published 1957. London: Hogarth Press.

———. 1916. "Some Character-Types Met with in Psycho-Analytic Work." In *The Standard Edition of the Complete Psychological Works of Sigmund Freud*, vol. 14 (1914–1916), translated by James Strachey in collaboration with Anna Freud, first published 1957. London: Hogarth Press.

———. 1989. *Civilization and its Discontents*. Translated by James Strachey. W. W. Norton & Company.
Fricker, Miranda. 2007. *Epistemic Injustice: Power and the Ethics of Knowing*. New York: Oxford University Press.
———. 2016. "Epistemic Injustice and the Preservation of Ignorance." In *The Epistemic Dimensions of Ignorance*, edited by Rick Peels and Martijn Blaauw, 160–77. Cambridge: Cambridge University Press.
———. 2018. "Ambivalence about Forgiveness." *Royal Institute of Philosophy Supplements* 84: 161–85.
Frierson, Patrick. 2010. "Kantian Moral Pessimism." In *Kant's Anatomy of Evil*, edited by Sharon Anderson-Gold and Pablo Muchnik, 33–57. Cambridge: Cambridge University Press.
Frijda, Nico H. 1986. *The Emotions: Studies in Emotions and Social Interaction*. Cambridge: Cambridge University Press.
Frijda, Nico H., Batja Mesquita, Joep Sonnemans, and Stephanie van Goozen. 1991. "The Duration of Affective Phenomena or Emotions, Sentiments, and Passions." *International Review of Studies on Emotion* 1: 187–225.
Frye, Marilyn. 1983. *The Politics of Reality: Essays in Feminist Theory*. Berkeley: Crossing Press.
Galtung, Johan, and Mari Holmboe Ruge. 1965. "The Structure of Foreign News: The Presentation of the Congo, Cuba and Cyprus Crises in Four Norwegian Newspapers" *Journal of Peace Research* 2 (1): 64–90.
Ganeri, Jonardon. 2012. *The Self: Naturalism, Consciousness, and the First-Person Stance*. Oxford: Oxford University Press.
Garfield, Jay L. 2015. *Engaging Buddhism: Why It Matters to Philosophy*. Oxford: Oxford University Press.
———. 2017. "Mindfulness and Ethics: *Attention, Virtue, and Perfection*." In *A Mirror is for Reflection: Understanding Buddhist Ethics*, edited by Jake H. Davis, 203–22. New York: Oxford University Press.
Gerber, Lisa. 2002. "What Is So Bad about Misanthropy?" *Environmental Ethics* 24: 41–55.
Gereboff, Joel, Keith Green, Diana Fritz Cates, and Maria Heim. 2009. "The Nature of the Beast: Hatred in Cross-Traditional Religious and Philosophical Perspective." *Journal of the Society of Christian Ethics* 29 (2): 175–205.
Gibson, Andrew. 2012. *Misanthropy: The Critique of Humanity*. London: Bloomsbury.
Gibson, James L. 2006. "Overcoming Apartheid: Can Truth Reconcile a Divided Nation?" *The Annals of the American Academy of Political and Social Science* 603 (1): 82–110.
Gilman, Charlotte Perkins. 1998. *The Yellow Wall-paper and Other Stories*. Oxford: Oxford University Press.
Gombrich, Richard. 2009. *What the Buddha Thought*. London: Equinox Publishing.
Gordijn, Ernestine H., Vincent Yzerbyt, Daniël Wigboldus, and Muriel Dumont. 2006. "Emotional Reactions to Harmful Intergroup Behavior." *European Journal of Social Psychology* 36 (1): 15–30.
Gowans, Christopher W. 2003. *Philosophy of the Buddha*. London: Routledge.

———. 2010. "Medical Analogies in Buddhist and Hellenistic Thought: Tranquility and Anger." In *Philosophy as Therapeia*, Royal Institute of Philosophy Supplement 66, edited by Clare Carlisle and Jonardon Ganeri, 11–33. Cambridge: Cambridge University Press.
———. 2021. *Self-Cultivation Philosophies in Ancient India, Greece and China*. New York: Oxford University Press.
Graver, Margaret. 2002. *Cicero on the Emotions: Tusculan Disputations 3 and 4*. Translated and with Commentary by Margaret Graver. Chicago: University of Chicago Press.
———. 2007. *Stoicism and Emotion*. Chicago: University of Chicago Press.
Greer, Margaret R., Walter D. Mignolo, and Maureen Quilligan, eds. 2007. *Rereading the Black Legend: The Discourses of Religious and Racial Difference in the Renaissance Empires*. Chicago: University of Chicago Press.
Grenberg, Jeanine. 2005. *Kant and the Ethics of Humility: A Story of Dependence, Corruption, and Virtue*. Cambridge: Cambridge University Press.
Gutiérrez, Gustavo. 1993. *Las Casas: In Search of the Poor of Jesus Christ*. Translated by Robert R. Barr. Maryknoll: Orbis Books.
Haidt, Jonathan. 2003. "The Moral Emotions." In *Handbook of Affective Sciences*, edited by Richard J. Davidson, Klaus R. Scherer, and H. Hill Goldsmith, 852–70. Oxford: Oxford University Press.
Halperin, Eran. 2008. "Group-Based Hatred in Intractable Conflict in Israel." *Journal of Conflict Resolution* 52 (5): 713–36.
———. 2011. "Emotional Barriers to Peace: Emotions and Public Opinion of Jewish Israelis about the Peace Process in the Middle East." *Peace and Conflict: Journal of Peace Psychology* 17 (1): 22–45.
Halperin, Eran, Daphna Canetti, and Shaul Kimhi. 2012. "In Love With Hatred: Rethinking the Role Hatred Plays in Political Behavior." *Journal of Applied Social Psychology* 42 (9): 2231–56.
Halperin, Eran, Daphna Canetti-Nisim, and Sivan Hirsch-Hoefler. 2009. "The Central Role of Group-Based Hatred as an Emotional Antecedent of Political Intolerance: Evidence from Israel." *Political Psychology* 30 (1): 93–123.
Halperin, Eran, and James J. Gross. 2011. "Intergroup Anger in Intractable Conflict: Long-term Sentiments Predict Anger Responses During the Gaza War." *Group Processes and Intergroup Relations* 14: 477–88.
Halperin, Eran, Alexandra G. Russell, Carol S. Dweck, and James J. Gross. 2011. "Anger, Hatred, and the Quest for Peace: Anger Can Be Constructive in the Absence of Hatred." *Journal of Conflict Resolution* 55 (2): 274–91.
Hamilton, Richard Paul. 2006. "Love as a Contested Concept." *Journal for the Theory of Social Behaviour* 36 (3): 239–54.
Hampton, Jean. 1988. "Forgiveness, Resentment and Hatred." In *Forgiveness and Mercy*, edited by Jean Hampton and Jeffrie Murphy, 35–87. Cambridge: Cambridge University Press.
Haney López, Ian. 2019. *Merge Left: Fusing Race and Class, Winning Elections, and Saving America*. New York: The New Press.

Hanh, Thich Nhat. 2001. *Anger: Wisdom for Cooling the Flames*. New York: Riverhead Books.
———. 2005. *Being Peace*. Berkeley: Parallax Press.
Hanke, Lewis. 1959. *Aristotle and the American Indians: A Study of Race Prejudice in the Modern World*. Bloomington: Indiana University Press.
———. 1974. *All Mankind is One: A Study of the Disputation Between Bartolomé de Las Casas and Juan Ginés de Sepúlveda in 1550 on the Intellectual and Religious Capacity of the American Indians*. DeKalb: Northern Illinois University Press.
Harris, Ian. 2012. "Buddhism, Politics and Nationalism." In *Buddhism in the Modern World*, edited by David L. McMahan, 177–94. London: Routledge.
Hartsock, Nancy. 1998. "Political Change: Two Perspectives on Power." *The Feminist Standpoint Revisited and Other Essays*. New York: Routledge.
Hawdon, James, Atte Oksanen, and Pekka Räsänen. 2017. "Exposure to Online Hate in Four Nations: A Cross-National Consideration." *Deviant Behavior* 38 (3): 254–66.
Haynes, Gavin. 2020a. "How Knitters Got Knotted in a Purity Spiral." *UnHerd*, January 30, 2020. https://unherd.com/2020/01/cast-out-how-knitting-fell-into-a-purity-spiral/.
———. 2020b. "The Purity Spiral." *BBC Radio 4*, February 11, 2020. https://www.bbc.co.uk/programmes/m000d70h.
Heim, Maria. 2017. "Buddhaghosa on the Phenomenology of Love and Compassion." In *The Oxford Handbook of Indian Philosophy*, edited by Jonardon Ganeri, 171–89. New York: Oxford University Press.
Helm, Bennett. 2001. *Emotional Reason: Deliberation, Motivation, and the Nature of Value*. Cambridge: Cambridge University Press.
Hemon, Aleksandar. 2018. "Fascism is Not an Idea to Be Debated, It's a Set of Actions to Fight." *Literary Hub*, November 1, 2018. https://lithub.com/fascism-is-not-an-idea-to-be-debated-its-a-set-of-actions-to-fight/.
Hirsch-Hoefler, Sivan, Daphna Canetti, and Ami Pedahzur. 2010. "Two of a Kind?: Voting Motivations for Populist Radical Right and Religious Fundamentalist Parties." *Electoral Studies* 29: 678–90.
Hoagland, Sarah. 1988. *Lesbian Ethics: Toward New Value*. Palo Alto: Institute of Lesbian Studies.
———. 2001. "Resisting Rationality." In *Engendering Rationalities*, edited by Nancy Tuana and Sandra Morgen, 125–46. Albany: State University of New York Press.
Holmes, Mary. 2004. "Feeling Beyond Rules: Politicizing the Sociology of Emotion and Anger in Feminist Politics." *European Journal of Social Theory* 7 (2): 209–27.
hooks, bell. 2000. *Feminist Theory: From Margin to Centre*. London: Pluto Press.
Hurka, Thomas. 2001. *Virtue, Vice, and Value*. Oxford: Oxford University Press.
Hursthouse, Rosalind. 1991. "Arational Actions." *Journal of Philosophy* 88 (2): 57–68.
Hutchings, Vincent L., Nicholas A. Valentino, Tasha S. Philpot, and Ismail K. White. 2006. "Racial Cues in Campaign News: The Effects of Candidate Strategies on Group Activation and Political Attentiveness among African Americans." In

Feeling Politics, edited by David P. Redlawsk, 165–86. New York: Palgrave Macmillan.

Irvine, William B. 2006. *On Desire: Why We Want What We Want*. New York: Oxford University Press.

Irwin, Terence. 1985. "Permanent Happiness: Aristotle and Solon." *Oxford Studies in Ancient Philosophy* 3: 89–124.

Israelsen, Andrew. 2019. "And Who Is My Neighbor? Kant on Misanthropy and Christian Love." *The Heythrop Journal* 60 (2): 219–32.

Iyer, Aarti, and Colin Wayne Leach. 2009. "Emotion in Inter-Group Relations." *European Review of Social Psychology* 19 (1): 86–125.

Jacquette, Dale. 2014. "Socrates on the Moral Mischief of Misology." *Argumentation* 28 (1): 1–17.

James, Simon P. 2013. "Finding—and Failing to Find—Meaning in Nature." *Environmental Values* 22 (5): 609–25.

———. 2014. "'Nothing Truly Wild is Unclean': Muir, Misanthropy, and the Aesthetics of Dirt." *Environmental Ethics* 36 (3): 357–63.

Jasini, Alba, and Fischer, Agneta H. 2018. *Characteristics and Social Determinants of Intergroup Hate*. Unpublished manuscript.

Jeffreys, Sheila. 1997. "The Invention of the Frigid Woman." In *The Spinster and Her Enemies: Feminism and Sexuality 1880–1930*, 165–85. North Melbourne: Spinifex Press.

Jones, David H. 1966. "Freud's Theory of Moral Conscience." *Philosophy* 41 (155): 34–57.

Jones, Karen. 2003. "Emotions, Weakness of Will, and the Normative Conception of Agency." In *Philosophy and the Emotions*, edited by Anthony Hatzimoysis, 181–200. Cambridge: Cambridge University Press.

Kant, Immanuel. 1992–. *Conflict of the Faculties* in Akademie Edition *Gessamelte Schriften* (Ak), vol. 7. Berlin: De Gruyter, 1992–.

———. 1996. "Religion Within the Boundaries of Mere Reason." In *Religion and Rational Theology*, edited by Allen W. Wood and George di Giovanni, 39–215. Cambridge: Cambridge University Press.

———. 1997. *Lectures on Ethics*. Edited by Peter Heath and J.B. Schneewind. Translated by Peter Heath. Cambridge: Cambridge University Press.

———. 2000. *Critique of the Power of Judgment*. Edited by Paul Guyer. Translated by Paul Guyer and Eric Matthews. Cambridge: Cambridge University Press.

———. 2012. *Lectures on Anthropology*. Edited by Allen W. Wood and Robert B. Louden. Translated by Robert R. Clewis, Robert B. Louden, G. Felicitas Munzel, and Allen W. Wood. Cambridge: Cambridge University Press.

Kaplan, Jeffrey, and Leonard Weinberg. 1998. *The Emergence of a Euro-American Radical Right*. New Brunswick: Rutgers University Press.

Kauppinen, Antti. 2015. "Hate and Punishment." *Journal of Interpersonal Violence* 30 (10): 1719–37.

Keller, David R., ed. 2010. *Environmental Ethics: The Big Questions*. Oxford: Wiley-Blackwell.

Keltner, Dacher, and Jonathan Haidt. 1999. "The Social Functions of Emotions at Four Levels of Analysis." *Cognition and Emotion* 13 (5): 505–21.
Keng, Shian-Ling, Moria J. Smoski, and Clive J. Robins. 2011. "Effects of Mindfulness on Psychological Health: A Review of Empirical Studies." *Clinical Psychology Review* 31 (6): 1041–56.
Kenny, Anthony. 1992. *Aristotle on the Perfect Life*. Oxford: Oxford University Press.
Kidd, Ian James. 2020a. "Animals, Misanthropy, and Humanity." *Journal of Animal Ethics* 10 (1): 66–72.
———. 2020b. "Humankind, Human Nature, and Misanthropy." *Metascience* 29: 505–8.
Kidd, Ian James. 2021. "Gardens of Refuge." Daily Philosophy, October 6, 2021. https://daily-philosophy.com/.
Kinder, Donald R., and David O. Sears. 1985. "Public Opinion and Political Action." In *Handbook of Social Psychology*, edited by Gardner Lindzey and Elliot Aronson, 659–741. 2nd ed. New York: Random House.
Kolnai, Aurel. 1998. "The Standard Modes of Aversion: Fear, Disgust and Hatred." *Mind* 107 (427): 581–95.
Konstan, D. 2007. *The Emotions of the Ancient Greeks*. Toronto: Toronto University Press.
Kotef, Hagar. 2020. "Violent Attachments." *Political Theory* 48 (1): 4–29.
Kraut, Richard. 1989. *Aristotle and the Human Good*. Princeton: Princeton University Press.
———. 2008. "How to Justify Ethical Propositions: Aristotle's Method." In *The Blackwell Guide to Aristotle's Nicomachean Ethics*, edited by Richard Kraut, 76–95. Malden: Blackwell Publishing.
Kuppens, Toon, Vincent Y. Yzerbyt, Sophie Dandache, Agneta H. Fischer, and Job van der Schalk. 2013. "Social Identity Salience Shapes Group-Based Emotions through Group-Based Appraisals." *Cognition & Emotion* 27 (8): 1359–77.
La Caze, Marguerite. 2015. "The Time of Possible and Impossible Reciprocity: Love and Hate in Simone de Beauvoir." In *Thinking About Love: essays in contemporary continental philosophy*, edited by Diane Enns and Antonio Calcagno. University Park: Pennsylvania State University Press.
Las Casas, Bartolomé de. 1974. *In Defense of the Indians*. Translated by Stafford Poole. DeKalb: Northern Illinois University Press.
———. 1992. *The Devastation of the Indies: A Brief Account*. Translated by Herma Briffault. Baltimore: Johns Hopkins University Press.
Lavelle, Brooke D. 2017. "Compassion in Context: Tracing the Buddhist Roots of Secular, Compassion-Based Contemplative Programs." In *The Oxford Handbook of Compassion Science*, edited by Emma M. Seppälä et. al., 17–25. New York: Oxford University Press.
Lavi, Iris, Daphna Canetti, Keren Sharvit, Daniel Bar-Tal, and Stevan E. Hobfoll. 2014. "Protected by Ethos in a Protracted Conflict? A Comparative Study among Israelis and Palestinians in the West Bank, Gaza, and East Jerusalem." *Journal of Conflict Resolution* 58 (1): 68–92.

Lawford-Smith, Holly. Forthcoming. *Gender-Critical Feminism*. Oxford: Oxford University Press.

———. 2019. "How the Trans Rights Movement is Turning Philosophers into Activists." *Quillette,* September 20, 2019.

Lawrence, Gavin. 2011. "Acquiring Character: Becoming Grown-Up." In *Moral Psychology and Human Action in Aristotle*, edited by M. Pakaluk and G. Pearson, 233–83. Oxford: Oxford University Press.

Lazarsfeld, Paul F., Bernard Berelson, and Hazel Gaudet. 1944. *The People's Choice: How the Voter Makes Up His Mind in a Presidential Campaign*. New York: Columbia University Press.

Leader, Tirza, Brian Mullen, Diane and Rice. 2009. "Complexity and Valence in Ethnophaulisms and Exclusion of Ethnic Out-Groups: What Puts the 'Hate' into Hate Speech?" *Journal of Personality and Social Psychology* 96 (1): 170–82.

Lear, Jonathan. 2016. *Radical Hope: Ethics in the Face of Cultural Devastation*. Cambridge: Harvard University Press.

Lee, Martha F. 1995. *Earth First! Environmental Apocalypse*. Syracuse: Syracuse University Press.

Lerner, Melvin J. 1980. *The Belief in a Just World: A Fundamental Delusion*. New York: Plenum Press.

Lerner, Ralph. 1974. *Averroes on Plato's* Republic. Translated by Ralph Lerner. Ithaca: Cornell University Press.

Levin, Jack, and Jack McDevitt. 2008. "Hate Crimes." In *The Encyclopedia of Peace, Violence, and Conflict*, edited by Lester R. Kurtz, 89–102. 2nd ed. New York: Academic Press.

Levin, Brian, and James J. Nolan. 2015a. "The Evolving World of Hate and Extremism: An Interdisciplinary Perspective—Part 1." *American Behavioral Scientist* 59 (12): 1643–45.

———. 2015b. "The Evolving World of Hate and Extremism: An Interdisciplinary Perspective—Part 2." *American Behavioral Scientist* 59 (13): 1635–36.

Lindemann, Hilde. 2014. *Holding and Letting Go: The Social Practice of Personal Identities*. New York: Oxford University Press.

Livingstone, Andrew G., Russell Spears, Antony S. R. Manstead, Martin Bruder, and Lee Shepherd. 2011. "We Feel, Therefore We Are: Emotion as a Basis for Self-Categorization and Social Action." *Emotion* 11: 754–67.

Long, Anthony. 2011. "Aristotle on *Eudaimonia, Nous,* and Divinity." In *Aristotle's Nicomachean Ethics: A Critical Guide*, edited by Jon Miller, 92–114. Cambridge: Cambridge University Press.

Longuenesse, Béatrice. 2012. "Kant's 'I' in 'I ought to' and Freud's Superego." *Proceedings of the Aristotelian Society*, Supplementary Volume (86): 19–39.

Lorde, Audre. 1984. "Learning from the 60s." In *Sister Outsider*, 134–44. Trumansburg: Crossing Press.

Lowrey, Kathleen. 2021. "Trans Ideology and the New Ptolemaism in the Academy." *Archives of Sexual Behaviour* 50: 757–60.

Loy, David. 2009. "The Suffering System." *Lion's Roar*, July 1, 2009. https://www.lionsroar.com/the-suffering-system/ Accessed Dec. 10, 2020.

Mackay, Fiona. 2017. "Jane Mansbridge—A Quietly Dangerous Woman." *Dangerous Women Project*, March 8, 2017.
Mackie, Diane M., Thierry Devos, and Eliot R. Smith. 2000. "Intergroup Emotions: Explaining Offensive Action Tendencies in an Intergroup Context." *Journal of Personality and Social Psychology* 79 (4): 602–16.
MacKinnon, Catharine A. 1989. *Toward a Feminist Theory of the State*. Cambridge, MA: Harvard University Press.
Maffie, James. 2014. *Aztec Philosophy: Understanding a World in Motion*. Boulder: University Press of Colorado.
Manes, Christopher. 1991. *Green Rage: Radical Environmentalism and the Unmaking of Civilization*. Boston: Little Brown.
Mann, Liesbeth, Allard R. Feddes, Bertjan Doosje, and Agneta H. Fischer. 2016. "Withdraw or Affiliate? The Role of Humiliation During Initiation Rituals." *Cognition and Emotion* 30 (1): 80–100.
Manne, Kate. 2018. *Down Girl: The Logic of Misogyny*. New York: Oxford University Press.
Manstead, Antony S. R., and Agneta H. Fischer. 2001. "Social Appraisal: The Social World as Object of and Influence on Appraisal Processes." In *Appraisal Processes in Emotion: Theory, Methods, Research*, edited by Klaus R. Scherer, Angela Schorr and Tom Johnstone, 221–32. Oxford: Oxford University Press.
Marx, Karl and Frederick Engels. 1970. *The German Ideology: Part One*. Edited by C. J. Arthur. New York: International Publishers.
McDevitt, Jack, and Jack Levin. 1993. *Hate Crimes: The Rising Tide of Bigotry and Bloodshed*. New York: Plenum Press.
McLaughlin, Andrew. 1995. "For A Radical Ecocentrism." In *The Deep Ecology Movement: An Introductory Anthology*, edited by Alan R. Drengson and Yuichi Inoue, 257–80. Berkeley, CA: North Atlantic Books.
McRae, Emily. 2018. "The Psychology of Moral Judgment and Perception in Indo-Tibetan Buddhist Ethics." In *The Oxford Handbook of Buddhist Ethics*, edited by Daniel Cozort and James Mark Shields, 335–58. Oxford: Oxford University Press.
Medina, José. 2013. *The Epistemology of Resistance: Gender and Racial Oppression, Epistemic Injustice, and Resistant Imaginations*. New York: Oxford University Press.
Midgley, Mary. 1984. *Wickedness: A Philosophical Essay*. London: Routledge & Kegan Paul.
Miller, Jon, ed. 2013. *The Reception of Aristotle's Ethics*. Cambridge: Cambridge University Press.
Mills, Charles W. 2007. "White Ignorance." In *Race and Epistemologies of Ignorance*, edited by Shannon Sullivan and Nancy Tuana, 11–38. Albany: State University of New York Press.
Mills, Charles W. 2017. *Black Rights/White Wrongs: The Critique of Racial Liberalism*. New York: Oxford University Press.
Mishra, Pankaj. 2017. *Age of Anger: A History of the Present*. New York: Farrar, Straus and Giroux.
Molière. 2008. *The Misanthrope, Tartuffe, and Other Plays*. Translated by Maya Slater. London: Penguin.

Moore, Kathrine Jebsen. 2019. "A Witch-Hunt on Instagram." *Quillette*, February 17, 2019.
Moran, Richard. 2001. *Authority and Estrangement: An Essay on Self-Knowledge*. Princeton: Princeton University Press.
Morris, Herbert. 1971. "Guilt and Suffering." *Philosophy East and West* 21 (4): 419–34.
Morrison, Toni. 1970. *The Bluest Eye*. London: Penguin.
Msimang, Sisonke. 2014. "Limpho Hani, Clive Derby-Lewis, and the Power of Refusing to Forgive." *Daily Maverick*, June 11, 2014.
———. 2016. "You may Free Apartheid Killers But You Can't Force Their Victims to Forgive." *The Guardian*, March 11, 2016.
Msimang, Sisonke. 2017. *Always Another Country*. Cape Town: Jonathan Ball.
Mudde, Cas. 2005. "Racist Extremism in Central and Eastern Europe." *East European Politics and Societies* 19 (2): 161–84.
Müller, Jean M. 2021. "The Spontaneity of Emotion." *European Journal of Philosophy*, 1–19. DOI: https://doi.org/10.1111/ejop.12625.
Müller, Jozef. 2019. "Aristotle on Virtue of Character and the Authority of Reason." *Phronesis* 64: 10–56.
Murphy, Jeffrie. 1988. "Hatred: A Qualified Defense." In *Forgiveness and Mercy*, edited by Jean Hampton and Jeffrie Murphy, 88–110. Cambridge: Cambridge University Press.
Murphy, Jeffrie, and Jean Hampton. 1988. *Forgiveness and Mercy*. Cambridge: Cambridge University Press.
Naess, Arne. 1973. "The Shallow and the Deep, Long-range Ecology Movement." *Inquiry* 16: 95–100.
Ñāṇamoli, Bhikkhu and Bhikkhu Bodhi, trans. and eds. 1995. *The Middle Length Discourses of the Buddha: A New Translation of the Majjhima Nikāya*. Boston: Wisdom Publications.
Nash, Roderick. 1982. *Wilderness and the American Mind*. New Haven: Yale University Press.
Noor, Masi, Nurit Shnabel, Samer Halabi, and Arie Nadler. 2012. "When Suffering Begets Suffering: The Psychology of Competitive Victimhood Between Adversarial Groups in Violent Conflicts." *Personality and Social Psychology Review* 16: 351–74.
Nunberg, Geoff. 2017. "The Social Life of Slurs." In *New Work on Speech Acts*, edited by Daniel Fogal, Daniel Harris, and Matt Moss, 238–295. Oxford: Oxford University Press.
Nussbaum, Martha C. 2001. *Upheavals of Thought*. Cambridge: Cambridge University Press.
———. 2016. *Anger and Forgiveness: Resentment, Generosity, Justice*. Oxford: Oxford University Press.
Oatley, Keith, and Jennifer M. Jenkins. 1996. *Understanding Emotions*. Malden: Blackwell.
O'Gorman, Edmundo. 2017 [1960]. "Art or Monstrosity." In *Mexican Philosophy in the 20th Century: Essential Readings*, edited by Carlos Alberto Sánchez and Robert Eli Sanchez, Jr., 196–205. New York: Oxford University Press.
Opotow, Susan, and Sara I. McClelland. 2007. "The Intensification of Hating: A Theory." *Social Justice Research* 20 (1): 68–97.

Ortony, Andrew, Gerald L. Clore, and Allan Collins. 1988. *The Cognitive Structure of Emotions*. Cambridge: Cambridge University Press.

Orwell, George. 2000 [1968]. "Looking Back on the Spanish War." In *The Collected Essays, Journalism and Letters, II: My Country Right or Left, 1940–1943*, 249–67. Boston: David R. Godine.

Pacherie, Elisabeth. 2002. "The Role of Emotions in the Explanation of Action." *European Review of Philosophy* 5: 53–92.

Pagden, Anthony. 1982. *The Fall of Natural Man: The American Indian and the Origins of Comparative Ethnology*. Cambridge: Cambridge University Press.

Palmer, Craig T., David N. DiBari, and Scott A. Wright. 1999. "Is It Sex Yet?: Theoretical and Practical Implications of the Debate Over Rapists' Motives." *Jurimetrics* 39 (3): 271–82.

Park, Peter K. J. 2013. *Africa, Asia, and the History of Philosophy: Racism in the Formation of the Philosophical Canon, 1780–1830*. Albany: State University of New York Press.

Pearson, Giles. 2012. *Aristotle on Desire*. Cambridge: Cambridge University Press.

Pennock, Caroline Dodds. 2008. *Bonds of Blood: Gender, Lifecycle and Sacrifice in Aztec Culture*. Basingstoke: Palgrave Macmillan.

Perry, Barbara. 2003. "Where Do We Go from Here? Researching Hate Crime." *Internet Journal of Criminology* 3: 45–47.

Petersen, Roger D. 2002. *Understanding Ethnic Violence: Fear, Hatred, and Resentment in Twentieth-Century Eastern Europe*. Cambridge: Cambridge University Press.

Pettigrew, Thomas F., and Linda R. Tropp. 2006. "A Meta-Analytic Test of Intergroup Contact Theory." *Journal of Personality and Social Psychology* 90 (5): 751–83.

Pluckrose, Helen, and James Lindsay. 2020. *Cynical Theories: How Activist Scholarship Made Everything About Race, Gender, and Identity—and Why This Harms Everybody*. London: Swift Press.

Pohlhaus, Jr., Gaile. 2012. "Relational Knowing and Epistemic Injustice: Toward a Theory of 'Willful Hermeneutical Ignorance.'" *Hypatia* 27 (4): 715–35.

Porat, Roni, Eran Halperin, Ittay Mannheim, and Maya Tamir. 2016. "Together We Cry: Social Motives and Preferences for Group-Based Sadness." *Cognition and Emotion* 30 (1): 66–79.

Portilla, Jorge. 2020 [1952]. "The Spiritual Crisis of the United States." In *The Disintegration of Community: On Jorge Portilla's Social and Political Philosophy*, edited by Carlos Sanchez and Francisco Gallegos, 175–90. Albany: State University of New York Press.

Power, Mick, and Tim Dalgleish. 1997. *Cognition and Emotion: From Order to Disorder*. Hove: Psychology Press.

Purcell, L. Sebastian. 2017. "Eudaimonia and Neltiliztli: Aristotle and the Aztecs on the Good Life." *APA Newsletter on Hispanic/Latino Issues in Philosophy* 16 (2): 10–21.

Ramirez, Mark D. and David A. M. Peterson. 2020. *Ignored Racism: White Animus Towards Latinos*. New York: Cambridge University Press.

Rapp, Christof. 2002. *Aristoteles: Rhetorik*. Translation and Commentary. 2 Vols. Berlin: Akademie Verlag.
Redfern, Katrin, and Richard Whatmore. 2020. "History Tells Us that Ideological 'Purity Spirals' Rarely end Well." *The Conversation,* July 1, 2020.
Reeve, C. D. C. 2004. *Plato: Republic*. Indianapolis: Hackett.
Regan, Tom. 1983. *The Case for Animal Rights*. Los Angeles: University of California Press.
Reifen Tagar, Michal, Christopher M. Federico, and Eran Halperin. 2011. "The Positive Effect of Negative Emotions in Protracted Conflict: The Case of Anger." *Journal of Experimental Social Psychology* 47 (1): 157–64.
Rempel, John K., and Christopher T. Burris. 2005. "Let Me Count the Ways: An Integrative Theory of Love and Hate." *Personal Relationships* 12 (2): 297–313.
Repetti, Rick, ed. 2017. *Buddhist Perspectives on Free Will: Agentless Agency?* London: Routledge.
Richardson Lear, Gabriel. 2004. *Happy Lives and the Highest Good: An Essay on Aristotle's Nicomachean Ethics*. Princeton: Princeton University Press.
Rimé, Bernard. 2009. "Emotion Elicits the Social Sharing of Emotion: Theory and Empirical Review." *Emotion Review* 1: 60–85.
Roberts, Robert. 2003. *Emotions: An Essay in Aid of Moral Psychology*. Cambridge: Cambridge University Press.
Rorty, Richard. 1989. *Contingency, Irony, and Solidarity*. New York: Cambridge University Press.
Roseman, Ira J. 1984. "Cognitive Determinants of Emotion: A Structural Theory." *Review of Personality and Social Psychology* 5: 11–36.
Roseman, Ira J., Cynthia Wiest, and Tamara S. Swartz. 1994. "Phenomenology, Behaviors, and Goals Differentiate Discrete Emotions." *Journal of Personality and Social Psychology* 67 (2): 206–21.
Ross, Alex. 2018. "The Hitler Vortex: How American Racism Influenced Nazi Thought." *The New Yorker*, April 30, 2018, 66–73.
Ross, Lee. 1977. "The Intuitive Psychologist and His Shortcoming: Distortions in the Attribution Process." In *Advances in Experimental Social Psychology*, edited by Leonard Berkowitz, 174–214. New York: Academic Press.
Rousseau, Jean-Jacques. 1969. *Emile, ou de l' education*. Edited by Bernard Gagnebin and Marcel Raymond. Paris: Gallimard.
Royzman, Edward B., Clark McCauley, and Paul Rozin. 2005. "From Plato to Putnam: Four Ways to Think about Hate." In *The Psychology of Hate*, edited by Robert J. Sternberg, 3–35. Washington, DC: American Psychological Association.
Rozin, Paul. 1999. "The Process of Moralization." *Psychological Science* 10 (3): 218–21.
Rorty, Amélie O. 1988. "The Historicity of Psychological Attitudes: Love Is Not Love Which Alters Not When It Alteration Finds." In *Mind in Action: Essays in the Philosophy of Mind*, edited by Amélie O. Rorty. Boston: Beacon Press, 121–34. First published in *Midwest Studies in Philosophy* X (1986): 399–412.

Ruiz, Neil G., Khadijah Edwards, and Mark Hugo Lopez. 2021. "One-Third of Asian Americans Fear Threats, Physical Attacks, and Most Say Violence against Them is Rising." *Pew Research Center*, April 21, 2021. https://www.pewresearch.org/fact-tank/2021/04/21/one-third-of-asian-americans-fear-threats-physical-attacks-and-most-say-violence-against-them-is-rising/. Accessed June 27, 2021.

Russell, Pascale Sophie, and Roger Giner-Sorolla. 2011. "Moral Anger is More Flexible than Moral Disgust." *Social Psychological and Personality Science* 2 (4): 360–64.

Ryan, Barbara. 2013. *Feminism and the Women's Movement*. Abingdon: Routledge.

Sagahún, Bernardino de. 1950–1982. *Florentine Codex*. 13 Vols. Translated by Arthur J. O. Anderson and Charles E. Dibble. Santa Fe: School of American Research.

Salmela, Mikko, and Christian von Scheve. 2017. "Emotional Roots of Right-Wing Political Populism." *Social Science Information* 4: 567–95.

Salwén, Håkan. 2014. "The Land Ethic and the Significance of the Fascist Objection." *Ethics, Policy & Environment* 17 (2): 192–207.

Santana, Alejandro. 2019. "'The Indian Problem': Conquest and the Valladolid Debate." In *Latin American and Latinx Philosophy: A Collaborative Introduction*, edited by Robert Eli Sanchez, Jr., 36–57. New York: Routledge.

Śāntideva. 1995. *Śāntideva: The Bodhicaryāvatāra*. Translated by Kate Crosby and Andrew Skilton. Oxford: Oxford University Press.

Sartre, J. P. 1976. *Anti-Semite and Jew*. Translated by George J. Becker. New York: Schocken Books.

Scanlon, T. M. 1998. *What We Owe to Each Other*. Cambridge, MA: Harvard University Press.

Scheffler, Samuel. 1992. *Human Morality*. New York: Oxford University Press.

Scherer, Klaus R. 2005. "What are Emotions? And How Can They be Measured?" *Social Science Information* 44 (4): 695–729.

Schoenewolf, Gerald. 1996. "The Couple Who Fell in Hate: Eclectic Psychodynamic Therapy with an Angry Couple." *Journal of Contemporary Psychotherapy* 26 (1): 65–71.

Schopenhauer, Arthur. 1969. *The World as Will and Representation*. 2 Vols. Translated by E. F. J. Payne. New York: Dover.

———. 1994 [1851]. *Parerga and Paralipomena*. 2 Vols. Translated by E. F. J. Payne. Oxford: Clarendon Press.

———. 2010 [1841]. *The Two Fundamental Problems of Ethics*. Translated by David E. Cartwright and Edward E. Eerdman. Oxford: Oxford University Press.

Schulman, Sarah. 2019. *Conflict is Not Abuse*. Vancouver: Arsenal Pulp Press.

Schutte, Ofelia. 1993. *Cultural Identity and Social Liberation in Latin American Thought*. Albany: State University of New York Press.

Seip, Elise C. 2016. "Desire for Vengeance: An Emotion-Based Approach to Revenge." Unpublished doctoral thesis. University of Amsterdam, Amsterdam, The Netherlands.

Seip, Elise C., Mark Rotteveel, Lotte F. van Dillen, and Wilco W. van Dijk, W. W. 2014. "Schadenfreude and the Desire for Vengeance." In *Schadenfreude:*

Understanding Pleasure at the Misfortune of Others, edited by Wilco W. van Dijk and Jaap W. Ouwerkerk, 227–41. Cambridge: Cambridge University Press.

Sellars, John, ed. 2016. *The Routledge Handbook of the Stoic Tradition.* London: Routledge.

Seneca. 2010. *Anger, Mercy, Revenge.* Translated by Robert A. Kaster and Martha C. Nussbaum. Chicago: University of Chicago Press.

Shaaban, Eslam. 2015. *Controlling the Other Edge of Social Media, Hate Speech and Terrorism Propaganda.* https://papers.ssrn.com/sol3/papers.cfm?abstract_id =2589254.

Shanmugasundaram, Swathi. 2018. "Hate Crimes, Explained." *Southern Poverty Law Center.* https://www.splcenter.org/20180415/hate-crimes-explained. Accessed June 27, 2021.

Shklar, Judith. 1984. *Ordinary Vices.* Harvard: Harvard University Press.

Showalter, Elaine. 1987. *The Female Malady: Women, Madness, and English Culture, 1830–1980.* London: Virago.

Siderits, Mark. 2007. *Buddhism as Philosophy: An Introduction.* Indianapolis: Hackett Publishing Company.

Silva, Grant J. 2019. "Racism as Self-Love." *Radical Philosophy Review* 22 (1): 85–112.

———. 2021. "On 'Ur-Contempt' and the Maintenance of Racial Injustice: A Response to Monahan's 'Racism and "Self-Love": The Case of White Nationalism'." *Critical Philosophies of Race* 9 (1): 16–26.

———. 2022. "A Tradition Grounded in Hate: Racist Hatred and Anti-Immigrant Fervor." In *The Moral Psychology of Hate*, edited by Noell Birondo. Lanham: Rowman & Littlefield

Simon, Bernd, and Amélie Mummendey. 1990. "Perceptions of Relative Group Size and Group Homogeneity: We Are the Majority and They Are All the Same." *European Journal of Social Psychology* 20 (4): 351–56.

Smith, Blake 2019. "In Praise of Hate." *Tablet Magazine*, August 18, 2019. https://www.tabletmag.com/jewish-arts-and-culture/289639/in-praise-of-hate.

Solomon, Robert C. 1977. "The Rationality of the Emotions." *The Southwestern Journal of Philosophy* 8 (2): 105–14.

Spelman, Elizabeth V. 1978. "On Treating Persons as Persons." *Ethics* 88 (2): 150–61.

Stangl, Rebecca. 2020. *Neither Heroes nor Saints: Ordinary Virtue, Extraordinary Virtue, and Self-Cultivation.* New York: Oxford University Press.

Staub, Ervin. 1989. *The Roots of Evil: The Origins of Genocide and Other Group Violence.* New York: Cambridge University Press.

———. 2005. "The Origins and Evolution of Hate, with Notes on Prevention." In *The Psychology of Hate*, edited by R. J. Sternberg, 51–66. Washington, DC: American Psychological Association.

Sternberg, Robert J. 2003. "A Duplex Theory of Hate: Development and Application to Terrorism, Massacres, and Genocide." *Review of General Psychology* 7 (3): 299–328.

———. 2005. "Understanding and Combating Hate." In *The Psychology of Hate*, edited by Robert J. Sternberg, 37–49. Washington, DC: American Psychological Association.

Sternberg, Robert J. and Karin Sternberg. 2008. *The Nature of Hate*. Cambridge: Cambridge University Press.
Stikkers, Kenneth W. 2014. "'...But I'm not Racist': Towards a Pragmatist Conception of 'Racism'." *The Pluralist* 9 (3): 1–17.
Stouffer, Samuel A. 1955. *Communism, Conformity, and Civil Liberties: A Cross-section of the Nation Speaks its Mind*. Livingstone: Transaction.
Strawson, P. F. 1974. "Freedom and Resentment." In *Freedom and Resentment*, editor by Sonia Orwell, Ian Angus, 1 -25. London: Methuen.
Succession, Seasons One and Two. 2018– . Showrunner: Jesse Armstrong. HBO, June 3, 2018.
Sullivan, Alison C., Aaron C. H. Ong, Stephen T. La Macchia, and Winnifred R. Louis. 2016. "The Impact of Unpunished Hate Crimes: When Derogating the Victim Extends into Derogating the Group." *Social Justice Research* 29: 310–30.
Sun, Key. 2006. "The Legal Definition of Hate Crime and the Hate Offender's Distorted Cognition." *Issues in Mental Health Nursing* 27 (6): 597–604.
Swift, Jonathan. 1843. *The Works of Jonathan Swift, Containing Interesting and Valuable Papers, Not Hitherto Published, in Two Volumes*. London: Henry G. Bohn.
Szanto, Thomas. 2020. "In Hate We Trust: The Collectivization and Habitualization of Hatred." *Phenomenology and the Cognitive Sciences* 19: 453–80.
Tarantino, Quentin, dir. 2009. *Inglourious Basterds*. Los Angeles: Universal Pictures.
———. 2012. *Django Unchained*. Los Angeles: Columbia Pictures.
———. 2019. *Once Upon a Time in Hollywood*. Los Angeles: Columbia Pictures.
Tausch, Nicole, Julia C. Becker, Russell Spears, Oliver Christ, Rim Saab, Purnima Singh, and Roomana N. Siddiqui. 2011. "Explaining Radical Group Behavior: Developing Emotion and Efficacy Routes to Normative and Non-normative Collective Action." *Journal of Personality and Social Psychology* 101 (1): 129–48.
Taylor, Charles. 1992. *Sources of the Self: The Making of the Modern Identity*. Cambridge: Cambridge University Press.
———. 2002. "Understanding the Other: A Gadamerian View on Conceptual Schemes." In *Gadamer's Century: Essays in Honor of Hans-Georg Gadamer*, edited by Jeff Malpas, Ulrich Arnswald, and Jens Kertscher, 279–98. Cambridge: MIT Press.
Taylor, Gabriele. 2006. *Deadly Vices*. Oxford: Oxford University Press.
Taylor, Paul. 1992. "The Ethics of Respect for Nature." In *The Animal Rights/ Environmental Debate: The Environmental Perspective*, edited by Eugene C. Hargrove, 95–121. New York: State University of New York Press, 1992.
Tessman, Lisa. 2005. *Burdened Virtues: Virtue Ethics for Liberatory Struggles*. New York: Oxford University Press.
Thurman, Robert A. F. 2005. *Anger: The Seven Deadly Sins*. New York: Oxford University Press.
Tosi, Justin, and Brandon Warmke. 2016. "Moral Grandstanding." *Philosophy & Public Affairs* 44 (3): 197–217.
Tov-Ruach, Leila [Amélie Oksenberg Rorty]. 1980. "Jealousy, Attention and Loss." In *Explaining Emotions*, edited by Amélie Oksenberg Rorty, 465–88. Berkeley: University of California Press.

Trimble, Stephen, ed. 1995. *Words from the Land: Encounters with Natural History Writing*. Expanded edition. Reno and Las Vegas: University of Nevada Press.

Trullinger, Joseph. 2015. "Kant's Neglected Account of the Virtuous Solitary." *International Philosophical Quarterly* 55 (1): 67–83.

Tuwim, Julian. 1944. "We Polish Jews." http://www.polish-jewish-heritage.org/Eng/RYTM_Tuwim_Eng.htm.

Van Bavel, J. J., J. L. Ray, Y. Granot, and W. A. Cunningham. 2018. "The Psychology of Hate: Moral Concerns Differentiate Hate from Dislike." Unpublished manuscript.

Van Dam, Nicholas T., et al. 2017. "Mind the Hype: A Critical Evaluation and Prescriptive Agenda for Research on Mindfulness and Meditation." *Perspectives on Psychological Science* 13 (1): 36–61.

Van Dijk, Wilco W., and Jaap W. Ouwerkerk, eds. 2014. *Schadenfreude: Understanding Pleasure at the Misfortune of Others*. Cambridge: Cambridge University Press.

Van Norden, Bryan W., and Jay L. Garfield. 2017. *Taking Back Philosophy: A Multicultural Manifesto*. New York: Columbia University Press.

Velleman, J. David. 1996. "The Possibility of Practical Reason." *Ethics* 106 (4): 694–726.

———. 1999. "A Rational Superego." *The Philosophical Review* 108 (4): 529–58.

VicHealth. *Violence Against Women in Australia. An Overview of Research and Approaches to Primary Prevention*. Melbourne: Victorian Health Promotion Foundation.

Victoria, Brian Daizen. 2006. *Zen at War*. 2nd ed. Lanham, MD: Rowman & Littlefield.

———. 2010. "A Buddhological Critique of 'Soldier-Zen' in Wartime Japan." In *Buddhist Warfare*, edited by Michael K. Jerryson and Mark Juergensmeyer, 105–30. Oxford: Oxford University Press.

Volkan, Vamik. 1997. *Bloodlines: From Ethnic Pride to Ethnic Terrorism*. New York: Farrar, Straus and Giroux.

Vollhardt, Johanna Ray 2012. "Collective Victimization." In *Oxford Handbook of Intergroup Conflict*, edited by Linda R. Tropp, 136–57. New York: Oxford University Press.

von Vacano, Diego A. 2012. *The Color of Citizenship: Race, Modernity, and Latin American/Hispanic Political Thought*. New York: Oxford University Press.

Walker-Barnes, Chanequa. 2020. "Prayer of a Weary Black Woman." In *A Rhythm of Prayer*, edited by Sarah Bessey, 69–72. New York: Convergent.

Wallace, B. Alan. 2010. *The Four Immeasurable: Practices to Open the Heart*. 3rd ed. Ithaca, NY: Snow Lion Publications.

Waller, James. 2002. "Perpetrators of Genocide: An Explanatory Model of Extraordinary Human Evil." *Journal of Hate Studies* 1 (1): 5–22.

Walton, Matthew J. and Susan Hayward. 2014. *Contrasting Buddhist Narratives: Democratization, Nationalism, and Communal Violence in Myanmar*. Honolulu: East-West Center.

Webster, Kim. 2016. *A Preventable Burden: Measuring and Addressing the Prevalence and Health Impacts of Intimate Partner Violence in Australian Women.* Sydney: ANROWS.

Weng, Helen Y. et al. 2013. "Compassion Training Alters Altruism and Neural Responses to Suffering." *Psychological Science* 24: 1171–80.

White, Robert S. 1996. "Psychoanalytic Process and Interactive Phenomena." *Journal of the American Psychoanalytic Association* 44 (3): 699–722.

Williams, Bernard. 1972. *Morality: An Introduction to Ethics.* Cambridge: Cambridge University Press.

———. 1985. "Resisting the Avalanche." *London Review of Books* 7 (10) (6 June): 6.

———. 1993. *Shame and Necessity.* Berkeley: University of California Press.

———. 2014. "*After Virtue: A Study in Moral Theory*, by Alasdair MacIntyre, *Sunday Times* (1981)." In *Essays and Reviews: 1959–2002.* Princeton: Princeton University Press.

Wilson, Catherine. 2014. "Kant on Civilization, Culture, and Moralisation." In *Kant's Lectures on Anthropology*, edited by Alix Cohen, 191–210. Cambridge: Cambridge University Press.

Wittgenstein, Ludwig. 1998. *Culture and Value.* Edited by George Henrik von Wright in collaboration with Heikki Nyman. Revised by Alois Pichler. Translated by Peter Winch. Oxford: Blackwell.

Wolfendale, Jessica. 2005. "The Hardened Heart: The Moral Dangers of Not Forgiving." *Journal of Social Philosophy* 36 (3): 344–63.

Wonderly, Monique. 2017. "Love and Attachment." *American Philosophical Quarterly* 54 (3): 235–50.

Wood, Ann Douglas. 1973. "'The Fashionable Diseases': Women's Complaints and Their Treatment in Nineteenth-Century America." *Journal of Interdisciplinary History* 4 (1): 25–52.

World Health Organization. 2013. *Global and Regional Estimates of Violence Against Women: Prevalence and Health Effects of Intimate Partner Violence and Non-Partner Sexual Violence.* Geneva: World Health Organization.

Wright, Dale S. 2009. *The Six Perfections: Buddhism and the Cultivation of Character.* New York: Oxford University Press.

Yancy, George. 2008. "Elevators, Social Spaces and Racism: A Philosophical Analysis." *Philosophy and Social Criticism* 34 (8): 843–76.

Yang, Wesley. 2018. *The Souls of Yellow Folk.* W. W. Norton & Company.

Young, Iris Marion. 1990. "Five Faces of Oppression." In *Justice and the Politics of Difference*, 39–65. Princeton: Princeton University Press.

Yzerbyt, Vincent, Muriel Dumont, Daniel Wigboldus, and Ernestine Gordijn. 2003. "I Feel For Us: The Impact of Categorization and Identification on Emotions and Action Tendencies." *The British Journal of Social Psychology* 42 (4): 533–49.

Zea, Leopoldo. 1992 [1957]. *The Role of the Americas in History.* Edited and with an Introduction by Amy A. Oliver. Translated by Sonja Karsen. Savage: Rowman & Littlefield.

Zea, Leopoldo and David R. Maciel. 1985. "An Interview with Leopoldo Zea." *The Hispanic American Historical Review* 65 (1) 1–20.

Index

Abbey, Edward, 91–93
affliction (*kilesa/kleśa*), 24
African Americans, xxiii, 55, 66–69, 72n14, 104–7, 149–50, 225–26, 229
African National Congress (ANC), 240
African slave trade, xxii
After Virtue (MacIntyre), xxiv
agential reasons. *See* motivating reasons
aggregates (*khandhas/skandhas*), 33–35
aggression, 54, 64, 126
Ahmed, Sarah, 100, 103–4, 109, 112, 196
Albanian Kosovars, 146
Alcoff, Linda Martín, 258–61
Allport, Gordon W., 149
Always Another Country (Msimang), 185
American war, xi–xv, xx–xxii, xxivn1, 42
Ameriks, Karl, 259n7, 260n20
ANC. *See* African National Congress (ANC)
anger (*kohda/krodha*), 8–13, 24–26, 30, 32–37, 41–44, 45n12, 53, 60, 63–64, 113, 127, 138–41, 146–47, 150, 153–54, 187, 191, 196, 208, 215–16, 221, 235–36, 240–41
Anglo-American philosophy, 257, 261n21

Another Country (Baldwin), 55
anti-apartheid struggle, 239
antidiscrimination laws, 100
antifa movement, 239
antihate speech laws, 150
anti-hierarchy, 211–13
anti-immigrant sentiment, 99–101, 109–14
anti-patriotism, xxii
anti-Semitism, xi, xii, xxiii, 125; Polish, 237
anxiety, 34, 41, 56, 63–64, 100, 108
appetite (*epithumia*), 12, 20n16
Aquinas, 24
Arahant, 27, 29, 38
Arendt, Hannah, xii
Aristotelian ethics, 251–52
Aristotle, 3–20, 25, 147, 177, 236, 241, 251–52, 254, 257, 259n6, 260n13
asylum-seekers, 101, 114n3
Atkinson, Ti-Grace, 120
attachment, 26, 31, 38, 44, 61, 111–12
Attenborough, David, 88
attention, 62, 64–68, 90
attitude(s), 4, 11, 17, 35–36, 40, 53, 56, 60–63, 79, 91, 102, 171, 180, 201; affective, 187, 189–90, 194, 196; anti-humanist, 93; emotional, 172, 176–77; engaged/hot, 176; negative,

287

6, 12, 15, 18, 145; objective, 36; possessive, 26, 44; psychological, 166–69, 182; stoic/cool, 176
Aumer, Katherine, 144
authority, problem of, 54–61
aversions, 23–24, 26, 38, 40–41, 44, 122
Awakening Mind (*bodhicitta*), 32
Aztecs, 251, 254, 255, 259n9; as alien others, 252–53

Baldwin, James, 55, 70n2
Bari, Judi, 93
Barrett, Lisa Feldman, 109
Bar-Tal, Daniel, 140
Bartholomeusz, Tessa, 43, 46n43
Beauvoir, Simone de, 168–70, 172, 179–81
behavior patterns, 173
Beiser, Frederick, 83
Beltrán, Cristina, 108, 113–14
Bendik-Keymer, Jeremy, 88
Ben-Ze'ev, Aaron, 166
Bernasconi, Robert, 261n20
Beuchot, Mauricio, 254, 259–60
Bhikkhu Bodhi, 28
bhikkhus/bhikṣus, 28
Biko, Steve, 240
biocentrism, 93
biospheric egalitarianism, 88, 91
blackness, 68–69, 225–26
black South Africans, xxiii, 240–41, 245–46
blame, 13–14, 35, 104–5
The Bluest Eye (Morrison), 67–68
The Bodhicaryāvatāra (*The Guide to Bodhisattva Practice*, Śāntideva), 32
Bodhisattva, 31–35, 38, 40
Bolsonaro, Jair, 173
Bonhoeffer, Dietrich, xxi–xxii
Bookchin, Murray, 92
Bowlby, John, 61
breastfeeding, 223–24, 231n29
Brecht, Bertolt, 247
Brennan, Geoffrey, 210
Brogaard, Berit, 70n6, 106

Brontë, Charlotte, 131
The Buddha, 25–29, 33–34, 38–39, 43
Buddhaghosa, 25, 28–31, 34–36, 39, 45n21
Buddhist nationalist movements, 43–44
Buddhist teaching, 23–24, 30, 37, 40–44
Buddhist thought and practice, 23–26, 29–31, 38–42
Bulger, Jamie, 244–45
burdened virtues, 236–37, 252; complex hatreds of Tuwim, 237–39; Hani refusal to forgive, 239–41; hard-heartedness, 242–48; vicious and virtuous hatred, 241–42, 248n5
Burke, Edmund, xi
Burma. *See* Myanmar
Burnyeat, Myles, 19n5
bystander ideology, xi–xv

Callicot, J. Baird, 89
calm misanthrope, 77
canceling, 207, 228
Canetti, Daphna, 169
Carlsson, Ulrika, 60
Cassirer, Ernst, 81
Charles V (Holy Roman Empire), 252
Chauvin, Derek, 115n6
Chesler, Phyllis, 127, 212, 217–18
China, 35, 42, 105
Chiune Sugihara, xiv
Christianity, 107, 252–53, 255
Christian radicalism, xxi
Christian theology, 86
citizenship, 104, 113–14
Civilization and Its Discontents (Freud), 70n1
civil rights struggle, 214
clinging. *See* attachment
cognitive abilities, 39
cognitive closure, 14, 16
cognitive dissonance, 113
cognitive distortions, 103
collective victimhood, 148
Collins, Randall, 221
colonialism, xxivn2, 42, 219

colored South Africans, xxiii, 240–41, 245–46
compassion (*karuṇā*), 29–35, 37–44, 247
conceptual misanthropy, 88, 94
Cone, James H., 104
Conflict of the Faculties (Kant), 81
Congress to Unite Women, 212
conscience, 53–56, 70n6
conscious belief, 122
contempt, 10, 59, 68, 75–78, 80, 82, 90, 93, 99–102, 106–9, 112–14, 131–32, 135, 138–41, 147, 154, 169, 208, 214
Cooper, David E., 83
Council of the Indies, 252–53
Covid-19, 105
craving (*taṇhā/tṛṣṇā*), 26
Critique of the Power of Judgement (Kant), 86
Cruelty as Citizenship: How Migrant Suffering Sustains White Democracy (Beltrán), 113
Crusius, Patrick, 113–14
cultural alienation, 100, 108
cultural values, 151
Curzer, Howard, 238
Cynical Theories (Lindsay), 219
cynicism, 90

Dalai Lama, 32–33, 35, 37, 42, 45n27
Daly, Mary, 208
deep ecology, 88–91
definitional credibility, 58, 60, 62
Deigh, John, 64
dell'Olio, Anselma, 212
delusion (*moha*), 27–29, 38
dependent origination, 32
Derby-Lewis, Clive, 239–41
desires, 4, 7, 12, 14–15, 23–24, 26, 38
destruction, 27, 64, 88–89, 107, 170, 236
Dhammapada, 28
Diotima, 18n2
discrimination: racial, 110; sex, 213

disgust (*duscherainein*), 3, 4, 68, 76–77, 88–89, 138–41, 154, 169
divine abidings, 29, 31, 40
Dixley, Allison, 224
Django Unchained (Tarantino), 181
Down Girl: The Logic of Misogyny (Manne), 123
Dreyfus, Georges, 40
Dussel, Enrique, 261n21
Dworkin, Andrea, 119–20, 125, 132, 135, 209, 213

Eagleton, Terry, 244
Earth First! (political movement), 91–94
eco-fascism, 89
eco-misanthropes, 88–91, 93–94
eco-misanthropy, 88, 90, 92–94
eco-terrorism, 89
ego, 56–57
Eichmann, Adolf, xiv
Eightfold Path, 23, 27, 29, 31, 38–40
Emile (Rousseau), 81
emotion (*pathos*), 7–9, 16, 25, 56–57, 60, 101, 108, 110, 137–38, 148–50, 153–54, 166, 167, 176, 186, 198–99, 221; abuse, 175–76; considerations, 189, 191–93, 195, 198–99, 201; episodic, 187; focus of, 111, 191–92, 194–95, 197, 200–202; formal object of, 110–11, 189–92, 194–98, 200–202, 203n10; framework for, 188–93; intentional content, 189, 190, 201; moral, 168, 177–82, 221; negative, 9, 40, 138–40, 144–48, 152, 154, 208, 227; response, 58, 191; and sentiments, 142–43; sociality of, 109; target of, 110, 191, 192
emotivational goals, 140–41, 146, 154, 169–70, 186
emptiness, 23, 31–33, 36, 39
enemies, 85–88
enjoy (*chairein*), 3, 4
enlightenment, 23–24, 28, 30, 31, 36, 38, 39, 44

enmity (*ekhthra*), 8, 10
environmental activism, 91
environmental doctrines, 89–90, 94
environmentalism, 89
envy, 31, 82, 107, 223–24
epistemic condition, 172
epistemic credibility, 58–59, 62
epistemic injustice, 231n27, 252, 256–58, 259n6; hermeneutical, 231n24; structural, 113; testimonial, 231n24
equanimity (*upekkhā/upekṣā*), 29–30, 40
Eriksson, Lina, 210
eroticization of dominance, 120–21, 130, 132
eroticization of subordination, 120–22, 130, 132
erotic love (*erōs*), 18n2
ethics: dialogical, 252; environmental, 88–89; Western, 252, 256–58, 259n7
ethnic cleansing, 146
eudaimonia. See happiness (*eudaimonia*)
Eudemian Ethics (Aristotle), 4, 14–16, 19n10
Eurocentrism, 252, 259n5
European barbarism, 257
evaluative credibility, 58, 60, 62
evaluative significance, 58
evangelization, 256
evil, xxi, xxii, 5–6, 10, 16, 18, 101, 112, 113, 151, 172, 178, 181, 244–45; dehumanizing, 243; radical, 86
expressive actions, 202
An Eye for an Eye (Beauvoir), 181

Fanon, Franz, 99, 109, 111
Fascism, 237–38
fear, 11, 64, 108, 114, 143, 150, 153
feminine socialization, 225–26
femininity, 225–28
feminism, 208–13, 217–19, 221, 223, 227–28, 229n16
feminist activism, 218, 222, 224, 227, 231n29
feminist movement, 208–18, 226–27
feminists, 119, 120, 123–27, 132, 135, 207, 212–15, 220, 222–24, 226–28, 228–29n7
Feminist Theory (hooks), 226
Fergus, Denise, 244–46
Fields, Barbara J., 103
Fields, Karen E., 103
Filipovic, Jill, 211, 219
financial security, 190, 192
"the fine" (*philokalos*), 3–6, 15
"Fire Sermon," 27, 38
Firestone, Shulamith, 120
Fischer, Agneta H., 107, 142, 146, 149, 169, 170, 186, 194, 196, 199
Fitness, Julie, 139
Fletcher, Garth J. O., 139
Floyd, George, 115n6
Folger, Abigail, 181
forbearance (*kṣānti*), 31–33, 38, 40
Foreman, Dave, 91
forgiveness, 152, 155, 185, 199, 235, 236, 238–46; conditional, 243; unconditional, 243
Four Noble Truths, 25, 26, 29
Fowler, David, 115n6
Fox, Warwick, 93
Frankfurt, Harry, 61
"Freedom and Resentment" (Strawson), 243
Freeman, Jo, 207–9, 212, 214, 216, 225–28, 229n17
Freud, Sigmund, 54–57, 60, 69n1
Fricker, Miranda, 236, 259n6, 261n21
Frierson, Patrick, 80, 86
Frye, Marilyn, 123, 131
Frykowski, Wojciech, 181
fugitives, 85–88
full personhood, 123

Gadamer, Hans-Georg, 260n17
Gandhi, 238, 248n6
gaslighting, 209, 231n27
gender critical feminism, 216, 230n18, 231n31
genders, 120–35

generalization, 11–15, 17
generosity, 27, 31, 36, 39, 40
genocide, xii, xxi, 151, 152
gentle misanthropy, 80
Gerber, Lisa, 88, 90
Germans Fascists, 237
Germany, 150
Gibson, Andrew, 79, 88
gladness (*muditā*), 29, 30, 40
good hate, 165–82. *See also* hate (*misein*)/hating
Goodin, Robert, 210
greed (*lobha*), 24, 26–29, 34, 38–39
Green Rage (Manes), 92
Grenberg, Jeanine, 86
grief, 61, 64, 172
The Guardian, 211
guilt, 53–58, 60–63, 66
Gutiérrez, Gustavo, 255–56, 259–60
Gyn/Ecology (Daly), 208

habituation, 4, 19nn5, 6
Hacker-Wright, John, 248n1
Halperin, Eran, 137, 142–43, 146, 169
Hampton, Jean, 57, 186, 187
Haney López, Ian, 105–6
Hani, Chris, 239
Hani, Limpho, 239–44, 246–47
happiness (*eudaimonia*), 4, 6, 14–18, 18–19n4, 26, 30, 40–41
hard-heartedness, 242–48
Hartsock, Nancy, 212
Harvard University, 215
hateful actions, 186–88, 193, 194, 202; implications for, 198–201
hateful misanthropy, 77–79, 84, 87–88
hate (*misein*)/hating, xxii, 3–6, 27, 30, 111, 137, 188; act of, 107–9, 111–12; appropriate, 169–74; characteristics, 138–41, 148; crimes, xxiii, 100–104, 106, 115n7, 138, 147, 149–51; in Eastern and Western philosophical traditions, xxiii; enduring, 166; and happiness, 14–17; intergroup, 145–48, 152–54; interpersonal, 144–45, 147, 148, 154, 196; malicious, 186, 187; messages, 150; messiness of, 194–98; moral, 187; as moral emotion, 177–82; nature of, 7–14; out-group, 142, 145; in politics and society, 151–54; role in flourishing life, 174–77; speech, 137, 138, 149–51; spreading, 147–49; target, 143, 154–55, 186, 194–98, 200–202. *See also individual entries*
hateworthiness, 166–70, 173, 180–81, 187, 194–97, 199–202
hatred, 99, 109–12, 142, 208; affective-intentional structure, 100, 102, 110, 195; anti-Semite, 241–42; concept of, 113, 137; in conflict zones, 138; contempt-based, 113; doctrines of, 75, 78; group-directed, 99–108, 111–12, 114n4, 146–47, 198; identity-preserving, 236, 244, 247, 248n5; and misanthropy, 76–80; personal, 165, 169–73, 177–78, 180, 185; political, 235; racialized, 252; social-identity-based, 99–106; and tradition, 100, 102, 108–9, 112, 114. *See also* burdened virtues
hatred (*dosa/dveṣa*) in Buddhism, 23–44; The Buddha, 25–28; Buddhaghosa, 28–31; challenge from philosophy, 33–37; challenge from politics, 42–44; challenge from psychology, 37–42; Śāntideva, 31–33
Haynes, Gavin, 221–22
Hayward, Susan, 43
Hebrew Bible, 24
Heim, Maria, 29, 30
Helm, Bennett, 192, 203n10
Hemon, Aleksandar, 239
Heraclitus, 82
heterosexual feminists, 210–11, 220, 229n9
heterosexualism, 120
Hilberg, Raul, xii
"The Historicity of Psychological Attitudes: Love Is Not Love Which

Alters Not When It Alteration Finds" (Rorty), 165
Hitler, Adolph, xxi, xxii, 170–71, 180
Hoagland, Sarah, 119–20, 126
Hochschild, Arlie, 105–6
Holocaust, xi–xiv
homelessness, 217
Homer, 257
homophobia, 94
hooks, bell, 210, 226
hostility, 53–57, 59–61, 63–65, 68, 71n11, 94, 119, 126–29, 166, 177–78, 180–81
human existence, 75, 77, 80, 84, 87
humanitas, 80, 86, 94
humanity, 60, 75, 77–80, 82–84, 86, 88–91, 93–95, 123, 238, 242; biological, 123
human nature, 23, 251–52
human relationships, 35
human rights, 36–37
human sacrifice, 251–55
humiliation, 139–41, 144, 154, 170–71
Hurka, Thomas, 177, 178
Ibn Rushd (Averroës, 1126–1198 CE), 108

ideal state of being, 23
identify-preserving, 235
identity, 26, 34, 58, 62–69, 71n10, 101, 108, 221, 235–36; based movements, 211; feminist, 220; formation, 103, 114; group, 42, 154; in-group, 145, 211; national, 43, 44; Polish, 239; political, 44; religious, 44; social, 149
ignorance, epistemology of, xxii, 252, 256–58, 259n5
illegality, 99, 101
ill will (*vyāpāda*), 24, 30, 59, 85
immeasurable deliverances of mind. *See* divine abidings
immigrants, xxiii, 101, 114
imperialism, cultural, 217; European, xxiv; intercultural, 252; Western, 251–52, 257

indigenous people, 251, 253
individual misanthropy, 79
industrial-technocratic societies, 93
Inglourious Basterds (Tarantino), 181
injustice, 11, 33–34, 37, 172. *See also* epistemic injustice
insight meditation (*vipassanā-bhāvanā*), 40
Instagram knitting community, 218
intentional action, 188–90
internalization, 56–59, 66–69, 79
Internet, 150
interpersonal love, 57, 61
interpersonal moral violations, 221
ISIS, 152
Israeli-Palestinian conflict, 138
Israelson, 86

Jane Eyre (Brontë), 131
Japanese militarism, 42
Jasini, Alba, 142, 146, 149, 169
Jefferson, Thomas, xxi
Jesus Christ, 255
Jewish Israelis, 146, 149, 153
Jews, xii, xiii
Jones, David H., 56
Jones, Karen, 188
justice, 6, 36, 103, 150, 168, 169, 177, 179, 180, 182; epistemic, 256–58; social, 219, 228
just world belief, 150

"Kālāma Sutta" (Bhikkhu Bodhi), 28
Kant, Immanuel, 56, 80–87, 90, 92, 94
Kantian approach, 55
Kantian judgment, 172
Kantian tradition, 242–44
karma, 26, 32, 34–36, 38, 46n34
Kauppinen, Antti, 187
Kershaw, Ian, xi
Kezar, Ron, 91
King, Martin Luther, Jr., 112, 238
KKK. *See* Ku Klux Klan (KKK)
knowledge, 7, 13–15, 17–18, 18n2, 26, 40, 172–73, 255

Koehler, Bart, 91
Kolnai, Aurel, 196
Konstan, David, 8
Kosovo War (1998–1999), 146
Kotef, Hagar, 108
Ku Klux Klan (KKK), 104
Kuran, Timur, 222

La Caze, Marguerite, 179
lack of ambition, 58
Las Casas, Bartolomé de, xxi–xxii, xxiv, 252–57, 259–60
Latin American philosophy, 261n21
Law and Justice Party, 239
Lawrence, Gavin, 18n1
leadership qualities, 212
Lectures on Anthropology (Kant), 81
Lectures on Ethics (Kant), 80–81, 85, 86
Legislating the Holocaust (Lösener), xiii
Le misanthrope (Molière), 75–76
lesbianism, 127
lesbian separatist feminists, 210, 211, 220
Levin, Jack, 102, 149, 150
liberal democracies, xxiii
liberation, 214, 217, 221, 226
Liberation Paradigm, 25–26
life, 6, 7, 15, 16, 26; good, 4–7, 14, 16–18; human, 23, 38, 80–82, 87, 90, 137; moral, 81
Lindsay, James, 219
Lorde, Audre, 214–16, 225–27
Lösener, Bernhard, xiii
love (*stergein*), 3, 4, 6, 7, 9–10, 15, 16, 18, 19n6, 33, 55, 60–69, 119–21, 132, 144, 166, 238; in-group, 142
loving-kindness (*mettā/mairtī*), 27–31, 34–38, 40–44
Lowrey, Kathleen, 207, 228n3
Loy, David, 44
lust (*rāga*), 24, 26–28, 34, 38
lynching, 104, 110

MaBaTha (Organization for the Protection of Race and Religion), 43

MacIntyre, Alasdair, xxiv, 260n17
MacKinnon, Catharine, 120–21, 130
Mahāvaṃsa, 43, 46n43
Mahāyāna Buddhism, 23, 31–32, 34, 39–40
Mailer, Norman, 119
Malcolm X, 215, 238
Malcolm X Weekend, 215
male dominance, 122–24, 129–30, 213
male-dominant society, 119–21, 219
Mandela, Nelson, 238, 245–46, 248n6
Mandela, Winnie, 238
Manes, Christopher, 92
Manne, Kate, 119, 123–29, 132
"Man: The Planetary Disease" (McHarg), 89
Martin, George R. R., 257
Marxian idea of ideology, 122
Marxist feminists, 220
Mason Family, 181
mass killings, 151–52
McCarthy, Joseph, 6
McDevitt, Jack, 102, 149–50
McHarg, Ian, 89
meditation, 27–30, 39–42
meditative awareness, 34
meditative practices, 27, 40–41
Meiji Restoration, 42
Memoirs of an Ex-Prom Queen (Shulman), 126
mental states (*jhānas/dhyānas*), 40
mestizaje ("admixture"), 256–58
Mignolo, Walter, 260n20
Mills, Charles W., 100, 260n20
mindfulness meditation. *See* nonjudgmental mental attention
misanthropic stances, 85–87, 90, 94
misanthropy, 13, 75–95; enemies, 85–88; fugitives, 85–88; hatred, violence and, 76–80; humanity, nature and, 88–90; Kant, Immanuel, 80–85; Schopenhauer, Arthur, 80–85; "unmaking of civilization", 91–94
misogyny, 123–29, 132–33, 213–15, 228

misologia (hate of arguments), 13
"mission-driven" hate crimes, 102, 150
Mister Rogers' Neighborhood (TV series), 6
mokṣa, 26–29
Molière, 75
The Monkey Wrench Gang (Abbey), 93
moral crimes, xii, xv
moral depravity, 101
moral dispositions, 27, 34
moral duty, 56, 64
moralism: overzealous, 220–22; performative, 222–23
morality, xiv, 26, 31, 39–42, 168, 177, 221
moral law, 56, 64
moral philosophy, 76, 81, 256–58
moral-political philosophy, 251
moral reform, 81
moral values, 67, 153, 166, 180
moral work, 179–81
Moran, Richard, 70n2
Morris, Herbert, 61, 63, 65
Morrison, Toni, 67
motivating reasons, 188–91
mournful misanthropy, 82
Mourning and Melancholia (Freud), 70n1
Ms. (magazine), 207–8
Msimang, Sisonke, 185, 194, 199, 201
Müller, Jean Moritz, 190–91
Murphy, Jeffrie, 58–59, 66
Muslims, 43
Mussolini, 170
Myanmar, 43
"My Żydzi Polscy" ("We Polish Jews," Tuwim), 237–39

Naess, Arne, 90–91
Nālandā, 32
Nash, Roderick, 90
National Independence Day, 239
nationalism, 42–43
National Organization of Women (NOW), 230n24

national psyche, 112
natural light of reason, 254–56
nature, 88–91, 92, 94
negative dialectics, 111
negative misanthrope, 85
Nhat Hanh, Thich, 37, 42
Nicomachean Ethics (Aristotle), 3–18, 19n10, 256–58
nirvana. *See mokṣa*
nīvaraṇa, 24
non-European people, xxivn2
nonjudgmental mental attention, 41
normative reasons, 188–91, 203n6
no-self teaching, 29–31, 35–36, 39, 41
NOW. *See* National Organization of Women (NOW)
Nuremberg race laws, xiii
Nussbaum, Martha, 61, 235, 248n6

Oeconomica (Aristotle), 11
Once Upon a Time in Hollywood (Tarantino), 181
online propaganda, 152
oppression, 25, 33, 42, 120–21, 135, 214–19, 226, 235–37
Ordinary Vices (Shklar), 77–78
Orwell, George, 237–38, 247
out-group behavior, 147–48, 211
out-group exclusionism, 147
out-group harm, 146–47
own being (*svabhāva*), 31

Pagden, Anthony, 259nn5, 9
pain, 8, 10, 19n6, 34, 53, 61–65, 179
Palestinians, 149, 153
Pāli Canon, 25, 28–30
Parerga and Paralipomena (Schopenhauer), 84
participant reactive attitudes, 35, 36
Passionate Politics (Collins), 221
A Passion for Friends (Raymond), 209
patriarchal social order, 124, 127, 129
patriotism, xxii
person of color, xxiii
pessimism, 80–83

pessimistic misanthropy, 81
Phaedo (Plato), 13–14, 77
"phenomenology of hatred," 29
philanthropic spirit, 85–86
philia (love/friendly feeling), 8
philosophical anthropology, 86
Plato, 6, 13
"Please Call Me by My True Names" (Nhat Hanh), 37
Polish Fascism, 239
Polish Fascists, 239, 242, 244, 247
political intolerance, 153
A Politically Correct Feminist (Chesler), 217
Politics (Aristotle), 10
Portilla, Jorge, 112
positive misanthrope, 85
possessive orientation, 31, 34, 38
"Prayer of a Weary Black Woman" (Walker-Barnes), 107
psychological connections, 24–25
Ptolemaism, 228n3
puke-ins, 91
punishment, 150, 179
purity policing, 221
purity spirals, 221–22, 228

Quietist misanthrope, 87

race, xiii–xiv, 100–103, 217–18
racecraft, 103, 108
racial difference, 101, 112
racialized minorities, xxiii, 100–101, 106
racism, 94, 100–103, 107, 112–13, 172, 219
racist hatred, xxi, xxii, 99–101
radical feminists, 120, 220
radicalism, xxi, 94
radical resistance movements, 247
Rainbow Nation, 240, 245
ramping up, 230n25, 231n30
rational agency, 187–94, 201–2
Raymond, Janice, 209
reasoning (*logismos*), 10–11

rebirth, 26, 30–32, 34–35, 38
receptivity, 53, 57
recognition, 35, 60, 61, 72n14, 93, 175, 219, 224, 238
redescription, 120, 130, 135
The Redstockings, 211–12
refugees, 99, 101, 152
Regan, Tom, 88
re-habituation, 39
Religion within the Boundaries of Mere Reason (Kant), 80–82
resentment, 29, 30, 35, 58, 60, 83, 99, 105, 144, 166, 187, 236; justified, 223–25
ressentiment, 152, 171
retaliatory attacks, 102, 150
revenge, 8, 10, 93, 139–41, 143, 146, 150, 154
Rhetoric (Aristotle), 3–20, 25, 236, 241
Rhodes, Cecil, 180, 241
"Rhodes Must Fall" movement, 241
right effort, 27, 40
Rimé, Bernard, 148
Rogers, Fred, 6
romantic love, 119–20
Rorty, Amélie (Leila Tov-Ruach), 62–63, 165–66
Rorty, Richard, 120, 132
Roselle, Mike, 91
Roseman, Ira J., 140, 169
Rousseau, Jean-Jacques, 81, 86, 90
Royzman, Edward B., 137
ruling class, 122
Rwandan Genocide, 240
Ryan, Barbara, 220, 227

Śāntideva, 25, 31–36, 40–41
SARS-CoV-2 virus, 105
Sartre, Jean-Paul, 241, 242
Schopenhauer, Arthur, 80–85
Sebring, Jay, 181
Second Amendment, U.S. Constitution, 114
second wave feminism, 209–12, 219–20
Section 249, Title 18, U.S. Code, 103

security threats, 152
self, 24–26, 30–31, 34, 54, 65, 100, 103; inner, 16; relational, 61–63; sense of, 62, 126
self-conceptions, 62, 68, 69, 71n10
self-condemnatory tendency, 79
self-cultivation philosophy, 23, 44
self-defense, 102, 147, 150, 154, 167
self-hatred, xxiii, 53–69, 70n2, 214; authority and vulnerability, 54–61; love, remorse and, 63–69; love and relational self, 61–63; of women, 70n6
self-love, 80
self-respect, 59, 61, 173
sense of loss, 100, 105, 108
Sepúlveda, Juan Ginés de, 251, 252
serenity meditation (*samatha-bhāvanā*), 40
sex, 120–21
sexual abuse, 121–23, 130, 131, 217, 248n1
sexual desire, 121, 127
sexuality, 120
sexual relations, 121, 130–33
Shakespeare, 77
shame, 53, 58, 66, 152
Shiva, Vandana, 93
Shklar, Judith, 77–80, 87, 92, 95, 95n2
Showalter, Elaine, 127
Shulman, Alix Kates, 126
simple hate, 187
Singh, Bhagat, 238
sisterhood, 207–9, 226–27
Six Perfections (*pāramitās*), 23, 31, 38, 40
Smith, Blake, 168
socialist feminists, 220
social media, 150, 219, 221, 225, 231n31
social movements, 87, 220, 221
social relations, 108
Socrates, 77
solidarity, 153, 221
sorrow, 64, 67, 86

sorrowful misanthropy, 86
soul, 7, 14–16, 18
South Africa, 239, 240, 241
Southwood, Nicholas, 210
Spanish Civil War, 237, 238
Sparta, 9
Spelman, Elizabeth, 71n10
spinsterhood, 127
spirit (*thumos*), 11, 12, 20n20
"The Spiritual Crisis of the United States" (Portilla), 112
Sri Lankan civil war (1983–2009), 43
Staub, Ervin, 151, 152
stoic contempt, 176–77
Stoics, 25
Strangers in Their Own Land: Anger and Mourning on the American Right (Hochschild), 105–6
Strawson, P. F., 35–36, 58–60, 66, 243
striking miners massacre (2012), 240
Succession (TV series, 2018–), 169, 174–77
suffering (*dukkha/duḥkha*), 23–29, 31–36, 38, 40–44, 53, 55, 61, 63–65, 154, 170–72, 179–80
Sugimoto Gorō, 42
Sun, Key, 103–4
superego, 54–56, 60
Swift, Jonathan, 79
symbolic actions, 202
Szanto, Thomas, 102, 107, 109–11, 187, 190, 194–98, 201

tall poppy syndrome, 212
Tarantino, Quentin, 181
Tate, Sharon, 181
Taylor, Paul, 90
Templer, Karen, 218–19
terrorist attacks, 150, 152
Tessman, Lisa, 236, 247, 259n6
Theravāda Buddhism, 23, 28–31
three poisons (*triviṣa*), 27
thrill-seeking behavior, 102, 150
Tibet, 33, 42
Tibetan Buddhism, 32, 45n21

Topics (Aristotle), 254
"Tragedy and Resentment" (Carlsson), 60
transubstantiation, 255
transwomen, 223
trashing, 207–11, 214–28
"Trashing: The Dark Side of Sisterhood" (Freeman), 207–8
trauma, 216–17
TRC. *See* Truth and Reconciliation Commission (TRC)
tree-sitting, 91
tribalism, 209–11, 223
Trullinger, Joseph, 85
Trump, Donald, 173
trumping up, 230n25, 231n30
Truth and Reconciliation Commission (TRC), 239–41, 248n6
Tusken, Maria, 219
Tuwim, Julian, 237–39, 241–44, 246, 247
The Two Fundamental Problems of Ethics (Schopenhauer), 83, 84

unconscious belief, 122–23, 130
undeserving, 106
United States, 99–101, 104–5, 110–14, 149, 150
universal responsibility, 37
unwholesome (*akusala/akuśala*), 24–29
upstander ideology, xii–xiii, xxi, xxii

Velleman, David, 56, 57, 60
vengeance, 12, 168, 178–81
vices, 77–79, 81–84, 87, 91, 94–95, 107
Victoria, Brian Daizen, 42
Vietnam, 42
violence, 76–80, 85, 90, 94, 108, 236; anti-Asian, xxiii, 101, 115n7; antiblack, 100; male intimate partner, 216, 230n20; racial, 100–101, 106, 110–13; sexual, 216–17, 248n1
violent misanthrope, 77
virtue, 3, 6, 16, 18, 18n2, 23, 31, 34, 36, 38–40, 45n17, 191, 192, 202, 252. *See also* burdened virtues

virtue ethics, 78, 177, 251–52, 259n6
virtuous actions, 4, 19n6
Visuddhimagga (*Path of Perfection*, Buddhaghosa), 28–31, 36
vulnerability, problem of, 57–60

Walker-Barnes, Chanequa, 107
Wallace, B. Alan, 31
Waller, James, 151
Walton, Matthew J., 43
Waluś, Janusz, 239–42
Weinberg, Rivka, xxi, xxii
Western traditions, 24–25, 260n17
white supremacy, 100, 104, 109–14
willful historical ignorance, xxii, 256–58
Williams, Bernard, xxiv, 59–60, 66, 67, 79, 87, 95
Wilson, Catherine, 86
Wirathu, U, 43
wisdom (*paññā/prajñā*), 27, 32, 39–42
Wittgenstein, Ludwig, 80
Wolfendale, Jessica, 242–46
Wolke, Howie, 91
woman-hating, 119–35; departure from womanhood norms, 127–29; Marxian idea of ideology, 122–23; men's oppression of women, 120–21, 135; misogyny, 123–27; sexual relations and abuse, 121–22; in vocabulary, 130–35
Woman-Hating (Dworkin), 213
womanhood, 124–30, 226
women: Australian, 216–17; leaders, 225
women hating women, 207–28; anti-hierarchy, 211–13; feminine socialization and social roles, 225–26; feminism, 217–18; justified resentment, 223–25; misdirected rage, 215–16; misogyny, 213–15; overzealous moralism, 220–22; performative moralism, 222–23; sisterhood, 226–27; status hierarchies/power grabs, 218–20; trauma, 216–17; tribalism, 209–11
Wonderly, Monique, 61

Wood, Ann, 127
The World as Will and Representation (Schopenhauer), 84
World Health Organization, 216
World War II, xi–xv, xx–xxii, xxivn1, 42, 145, 170
Wuhan Institute of Virology, 105

xenophobic attacks, 241

Yancy, George, 72n14
Yang, Wesley, 71n12
Yeats, W. B., 242
"The Yellow Wallpaper" (Gilman), 134

Zea, Leopoldo, 251, 258n1, 261n1
Zen at War (Victoria), 42
Zen Buddhists, 42
Zionism, 237

Notes on Contributors

Noell Birondo is professor of philosophy at the University of Texas at El Paso, USA. He works primarily in moral philosophy and the history of ethics. His previous book is *Virtue's Reasons: New Essays on Virtue, Character, and Reasons* (Routledge, 2017), which he coedited with S. Stewart Braun. Winner of the American Philosophical Association's 2019 Essay Prize in Latin American thought, he is currently writing a book on the influence of Western imperialism on our conceptions of the moral virtues.

Daphna Canetti is professor of political psychology and the dean of the Herta and Paul Amir Faculty of Social Sciences at the University of Haifa, Israel. Her research focuses on the micro-foundations and psychological mechanisms of political conflicts. She is particularly interested in the impact of civilian exposure to terrorism—conventional and cyber—on political behavior. Methodologically, she uses controlled randomized lab and field experiments, spatial analysis, survey experiments, biopolitical, and physiological-political research techniques.

Mary Carman is a lecturer in the Department of Philosophy at the University of the Witwatersrand, South Africa. She previously held a postdoctoral position at the Swiss Centre for Affective Sciences in Geneva, Switzerland. Her research interests lie broadly in examining the roles that emotions play in our lives, with a specific focus on the intersection of emotions and conceptions of rational action.

Damian Cox teaches philosophy at Bond University, Australia. He is coauthor of *Integrity and the Fragile Self* (Ashgate, 2003), *Politics Most Unusual*

(Palgrave Macmillan, 2009), and *Thinking through Film* (Blackwell, 2011). He publishes in ethics, moral psychology, and philosophy and film.

Agneta Fischer is professor of emotions and affective processes in the Psychology Department at the University of Amsterdam, the Netherlands, and currently dean of the Faculty of Social and Behavioral Sciences. She is the author of several edited volumes and many papers on the topic of emotional mimicry, gender differences in emotion, emotion recognition, empathy, emotions in intergroup relations, and specific emotions, such as contempt and hate. She has been president of the International Society for Research on Emotion (ISRE), coeditor of *Cognition and Emotion*, and consulting editor of *Emotion* and *Personality and Social Psychology Science*.

Christopher W. Gowans is professor of philosophy at Fordham University in New York City, USA. He works in moral philosophy, Buddhist philosophy, and other Asian philosophical traditions. He is the author of *Innocence Lost: An Examination of Inescapable Moral Wrongdoing* (Oxford), *Philosophy of the Buddha* (Routledge), and *Self-Cultivation Philosophies in Ancient India, Greece, and China* (Oxford).

Eran Halperin is professor of psychology at the Hebrew University of Jerusalem, Israel. His work develops new approaches for modifying the psychological roots of intolerance, exclusion, and intergroup violence. Halperin is author of more than 200 peer-reviewed papers in journals such as *Science*, *Proceedings of the National Academy of Science*, and *Psychological Science*. He completed his PhD at Haifa University and was a postdoctoral researcher at Stanford University on a Fulbright Scholarship.

Richard Paul Hamilton is senior lecturer in philosophy in the School of Philosophy and Theology, University of Notre Dame Australia. He completed his PhD in 2004 from Birkbeck College, University of London and has worked for NDA since then. He works in the area of virtue ethics with interests in moral and political philosophy, philosophy of biology, and philosophy of social science. He is currently completing a monograph, *Natural Citizens: Ethical Formation as Biological Development*, which is under contract with Lexington Books and due out in early 2022. He is a committed trades unionist and political activist.

Alba Jasini is a social and cultural psychologist. She is currently a postdoctoral researcher at the Center for Social and Cultural Psychology, the University of Leuven, Belgium. In her research, she aims to understand the role of culture and social context in shaping the meaning and experience of emotions. Specifically, her research interests lie in the topics of emotion, culture, emotional acculturation, and intergroup relations.

Ian James Kidd is a lecturer in philosophy at the University of Nottingham, UK. His research interests include ethics, philosophical anthropology, and themes in the Indian and Chinese philosophical traditions. Recent publications include *Vice Epistemology* (Routledge, 2020) coedited with Heather Battaly and Quassim Cassam, and he is currently writing a book on misanthropy.

Holly Lawford-Smith is an associate professor in political philosophy at the University of Melbourne, Australia. Her current research is focused on radical and gender critical feminism. Her next book, *Gender-Critical Feminism*, is coming out with Oxford University Press, expected some time in 2022.

Michael P. Levine is emeritus professor at the University of Western Australia. He has taught at the University of Pennsylvania, Swarthmore College, the University of Virginia, and in Moscow as a Fulbright Fellow. His publications include *Pantheism: A Non-Theistic Concept of Deity*, *Racism in Mind* (edited with Tamas Pataki), *Thinking through Film* (with Damian Cox), *Politics Most Unusual* (with Damian Cox and Saul Newman), and *Integrity and the Fragile Self* (with Damian Cox and Marguerite La Caze).

Jozef Müller is associate professor of philosophy at the University of California, Riverside, USA. He was previously assistant professor of Philosophy at the University of Florida. He completed his PhD from Princeton University and is author of several articles on Aristotle's moral psychology. He is currently completing a book titled *Aristotle's Characters*, a study of the four paradigmatic states of character in Aristotle's ethics.

Kate M. Phelan is a lecturer in the School of Global, Urban, and Social Studies at RMIT University, Melbourne, Australia. She works primarily in feminist theory. Her publications have appeared, among other places, in the *Journal of Political Philosophy* and *Social Epistemology*.

Grant J. Silva is associate professor of philosophy at Marquette University, USA. He has published widely on the philosophy of race and racism, immigration ethics, and liberation philosophy. He is currently working on a monograph entitled *Racism as Self-Love*, which explores the egoist motivations at the core of racist activity.

Rivka Weinberg is professor of philosophy at Scripps College, Claremont, California, USA. She is the author of *The Risk of A Lifetime: How, When, and Why Procreation May Be Permissible* (Oxford, 2015). She specializes in ethical and metaphysical issues regarding birth, death, and meaning, and is currently working on a book about death, time, and meaning.

Vida Yao is assistant professor of Philosophy at Rice University, USA. Her main areas of research are ethics, moral theory, and moral psychology. Her publications have appeared, among other places, in *Philosophy and Phenomenological Research*, Philosophers' Imprint, and *Oxford Studies in Agency and Responsibility*. Her current research focuses on the relationships between the emotions and the self, and on the value of grace and gracious love.

www.ingramcontent.com/pod-product-compliance
Lightning Source LLC
Chambersburg PA
CBHW021847300426
44115CB00005B/39